Theory of Computation

P. Balamurugan

V. Sharmila

Published by

Theory of Computation

ISBN 978-93-86176-24-0

Authors

P. Balamurugan

V. Sharmila

Bonfring

309, 2nd Floor, 5th Street Extension, Gandhipuram,

Coimbatore-641 012.

Tamilnadu, India.

E-mail: info@bonfring.org

Website: www.bonfring.org

Phone: 0422 4213231

Preface

Theory of computation book has been designed for students of computer science and information technology. This book deals with fundamental concepts of theory of computation starting from basic building structure to deep knowledge in a simple language for understanding of the students. It includes vast number of examples problems, more material on writing proofs, more figures and pictures with adequate explanation to convey ideas.

This book covers the curricula for BE (CSE), B.Tech (IT), MSc (Computer Science) and MCA at Anna University, and various Universities and gives a strong foundation for studying in the field.

The principle topics in the subject are:

- Finite automata and regular languages.
- Context free grammar and language.
- Pushdown automata.
- Turing machine.
- Decidability of problems.
- Tractability of problems.

<table>
<tr><th>Chapter</th><th>Contents</th><th>Page No</th></tr>
</table>

CHAPTER 1

BASIC CONCEPTS

1.1. Mathematical Notations and Preliminaries

1.1.1. Set

A set is a group of items, every item in the group presented inside the { }. E.g., {12, 24, 5} is a set with three items. A set with no items is an empty set denoted by { } or φ .

Set Operations

Union: Given two sets A and B, A∪B is the set obtained by combining all elements of A and B in a single set. Example, A = {1, 2, 4}, B = {2, 5}

$$A∪B = \{1, 2, 4, 5\}$$

Intersection: A ∩ B is the set of common items of A and B, in the above example, A∩B = {2}

Complement: Complement of a set A is represented as A'. A' is a set of every element that is not in A.

Set difference: The set difference of two sets A&B is represented as A-B. It is the set of those elements of A which are not in B.

1.1.2. Function

If f is a function, which gives an output b when input is a, we write f (a) = b. For a particular function f, the set of all possible input is called f's domain, the outputs of a function come from a set called f's range.

1.1.3. Graph

A graph is a set of points with lines connecting some of the points & points are called vertices, lines are called edges. The number of edges at a particular vertex is the degree of the vertex.

A graph can be described by telling what its vertices are, and what its edges are, formally, a graph G can be written as G =(V, E), where V is the set of vertices, and E is the set of edges.

A path is a sequence of vertices connected by edges If every two nodes have a path between them, the graph is connected. A cycle is a path that starts and ends at the same vertex. A tree is a connected graph with no cycles.

Directed Graph

If lines are replaced by arrows, the graph becomes directed. The number of arrows pointing into a vertex is called in-degree of the vertex. The number of arrows pointing from a vertex is called out-degree of the vertex. A directed path is a path from one vertex to the other vertex, following the direction of the "arrows".

Preliminaries

1.1.4. Alphabet

An alphabet is a finite set of symbols. These are the basic building blocks of a formal language. E.g., the English Alphabet = {A, B, C... Z}.

1.1.5. String

A string is a sequence of characters over an alphabet. The list of strings is called a formal language.

A string over an alphabet A is a finite ordered sequence of symbols from A, note that repetitions are allowed.

The length of a string w, denoted by $|w|$, is the number of characters in w. The empty string is a string of length 0. The length of a string is the number of symbols in the string, with repetitions counted. (e.g., $|aabbcc| = 6$).

1.1.6. Language

A set of strings of all which are chosen from some Σ^*, where Σ is a particular alphabet is called a language.

If Σ is an alphabet and $L \subseteq \Sigma^*$ then L is a language over Σ.

1.2. Introduction to Formal Proofs

The truth of statements is solved by a detailed sequence of steps and reasons. Computer scientist can give, proof of the correctness of the program with writing of program itself. Testing programs are very essential because it cannot try the program an every input. More complex programs are solved by recursion or iteration.

1.2.1. Deductive Proof

It consists of sequence of statement whose truth leads us from some initial statement called hypothesis on the given statement to a conclusion statement.

Hypothesis may be true or false typically depends on values of its parameter.

Example: Theorem If $x \geq 4$ then $2^x \geq x^2$

If H then C$\rightarrow$ format,

H is true for x=6 and false x=2

C is false for x=3 and true x=4

Proof

$2^x \geq x^2$ will be true whenever $x \geq 4$

L.H.S

2^x doubles each time x increases by 1 as $x \geq 4$

Ex: $2^5 = 32$, $26 = 64$

R.H.S

X^2 grows by the relation $(x+1/x)^2$

ie.., $1,4,9,16,25\ldots\ldots x^2,(x+1)^2$

If x=4, then $(x+1/x) = (5/4) = 1.25$

$(x+1/x)^2 = (1.25)^2 = 1.5625$

If x=4, then $(x+1/x)$ cannot be greater than 1.25

$(x+1/x)^2$ cannot be bigger than 1.5625

Conclusion

Since $1.5625 < 2$ each time x increases above 4 when the left side 2^x grows more than the right side x^2

Theorem: If x is the sum of the square of four positive integers than $2^x \geq x^2$

Proof

Statement	Justification
1. $x = a^2 + b^2 + c^2 + d^2$	given
2. $a \geq 1, b \geq 1, c \geq 1, d \geq 1$	given
3. $a^2 \geq 1, b^2 \geq 1, c^2 \geq 1, d^2 \geq 1$	properties of arithmetic
4. $x \geq 4$	
5. $2^x \geq x^2$	

1.2.2. Deduction and Definitions

If you are not sure how to start a proof convert all terms in the hypothesis to their definition.

1. A set S is finite if there exist an integer, such that S has exactly n element where we write $||s||=n$ where $||s||$ is used to denote the number of elements in a set S.

   If a set is not finite we say S is infinite. An infinite is a set that contains more than any integer number of elements.

2. If S and Tare both subsets of some set U, then T is the complements of S (with respect to U) that means S and T subset of U. that means S and T subset of U.

   $S\&T\subseteq U.$ If S UT=U and S$\cap$T=NULL (ϕ)

   That is each element of U is exactly one of S and T; put another way, T consists of exactly those elements of U, which are not in S.

1.2.3. Other Theorem Proofs

The "if-then" form of theorem is most common in typical areas of mathematics. There are some other forms of statements proved as theorem also.

1. Way of Saying "If-then"

"If H then C" may appear as

1. H implies C (H→C)
2. H only if C
3. C if H
4. Whenever H holds, C follows or if H holds, then C follows.

Example

The statement of theorem1 would appear in these four forms as

1. $x\geq 4$ implies $2^x \geq x^2$
2. $x\geq 4$ only if $2x\geq x^2$
3. $2^x \geq x^2$ if $x\geq 4$
4. Whenever $x\geq 4$ holds $2^x \geq x^2$ follows

2. If and only if Statements

There is a statement of the form "A if and only if B" .The other form is "A iff B". The other forms of "if and only if "statements are as follows:

1. A if and only if B
2. A if B

3. A is equivalent to B

4. A exactly when B

Additional Forms of Proof

Other than formal proofs, there are some additional proofs,

1. proof about sets

RU (S∩T) = (RUS) ∩(RUT)

Let x=RU (S∩T)

A= (RUS)∩ (RUT)

1. x is in RU(S∩T)	given
2. x is in R or x is in (S∩T)	definition(1)&union
3. x is in R or x is in both S and T.	definition (2) and definition of union
4. x is in RUS	definition of union
5. x is in RUT	definition of union
6. x is in (RUS)∩(RUT)	definition of intersection &definition of4&5

Contra Positive

The contra positive of the statement if H then C, is if not C then not H and it is represented as,

$$H→C <→1C→1H$$

To prove that "If H then C" and "if not C, then not H" are logically equivalent, there are four cases to consider

1. H and C both true

2. H true and C false

3. H false and C true

4. H and C both false

1.2.4. Inductive Proofs

This is a special kind of proof called inductive .ie., essential when dealing with recursively defined objects like trees, expressions of various sorts etc.,

Induction on Integers

Statement: S (n) about an integer n, To prove: it has two approaches

1. The **basis,** where we show S (i) for a particular integer i. Usually i=0 (or)i=1,but there are examples where we want to start at some higher i, **Perhaps** because the statement S is false, for a few small integer.

2. **Inductive** step where we assume n≥i, where i is the basis integer and we show that " **if** S (n) then S (n+1) ".

Eg:

for all n≥0, $\sum_{i=1}^{n} i^2 = \frac{n(n+1)(2n+1)}{6}$

Basis: Let n=0

$$L.H.S = i^2 = 0 \qquad (1)$$

$$R.H.S = \frac{0(0+1)(2(0)+1)}{6} = 0 \qquad (2)$$

∴L.H.S=R.H.S (1)=(2)

Induction:

Assume n≥0, by induction, Let n=n+1;

L.H.S=> $\sum_{i=1}^{n+1} i^2 = \sum_{i=1}^{n} i^2 + (n+1)^2$

$$= \frac{n(n+1)(2n+1)}{6} + (n+1)^2$$

$$= \frac{n(n+1)(2n+1)}{6} + n^2 + 1 + 2n$$

$$= \frac{2n^3 + n^2 + 2n^2 + n + 6n^2 + 6 + 12n}{6}$$

$$= \frac{2n^3 + 9n^2 + 13n + 6}{6} \qquad (3)$$

R.H.S = $\frac{(n+1)(2n+1)}{6}$

$$= \frac{(n+1)(2n+1)(2(n+1)+1)}{6}$$

$$= \frac{(n^2 + 2n + n + 2)(2n+2+1)}{6}$$

$$= \frac{(n^3 + 3n + 2)(2n+3)}{6}$$

$$= \frac{2n^3 + 3n^2 + 6n^2 + 9n + 4n + 6}{6}$$

$$= \frac{2n^3 + 9n^3 + 13n + 6}{6} \qquad (4)$$

So L.H.S=R.H.S (3) = (4)

The theorem is proved.

1.2.5. Structural Induction

This is applicable for proving recursively defined structures. This is similar to inductions where it has a basis and inductive cases.

Eg., the recursive definition of a tree.

Basis:

A single node is a tree and that node is the root of the tree.

Eg.,

Induction step:

If T1, T2,...Tk are trees, then we can form a new tree.

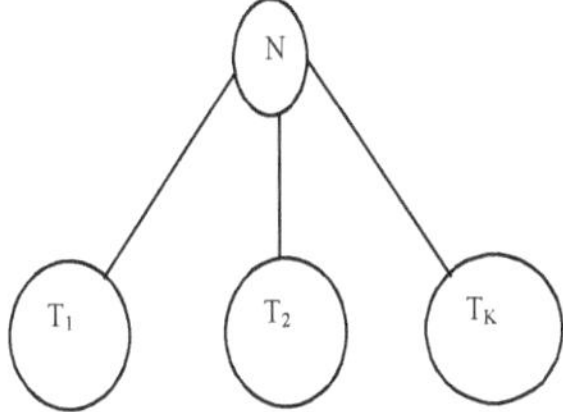

1.2.6. Mutual Induction

Instead of proving a single statement by induction it is necessary to prove a group of statements S1 (n), S2(n),.....Sk(n) together by induction on n. This type of proof is called proofs by mutual induction.

1.3. Introduction

1.3.1. Automata Theory

Automata Theory (AT) is study of Abstract Computing Device (ACD) or Abstract Machine. In 1930, Turing studied about ACD that had all capabilities of today's computer.

- In the 1940-1950's, number of researcher's were studying about the finite automata.
- In 1950's, Linquist N.Chomsky, who studied the grammar (Language Generator).
- In 1969's, S.Cook who extended the study of the abstract computing device.
- At present number of scientists use this theory for developing software.

1.3.2. Why Automata Theory?

- Finite Automata (FA) is a useful mathematical model for many important kinds of hardware and software (subsystem).
- This is the simplest model for a computing device.

1.3.3. Finite Automata

FA has a set of states and its control moves from state to state in response to external inputs. Whether the control is deterministic meant that automaton cannot be in more than one state as any one time, non deterministic meant that it may in several states at once.

1.3.4. Applications

- Used for pattern matching in text editor.
- Used in software for design and checking the behavior of digital circuits.
- Verifying all types of communication protocol.
- Design of digital circuits.
- String matching.
- Communication protocols for information exchange.
- Lexical analyzer of typical compiler.

Simple Example to FA

The simple model is a finite automaton modeling an on/off switch.

In figure 1, the states represented by circles. It has named as states "on" and "off". Arcs between states are labeled by input "push" when the "push" input is received by any state it goes to other state.

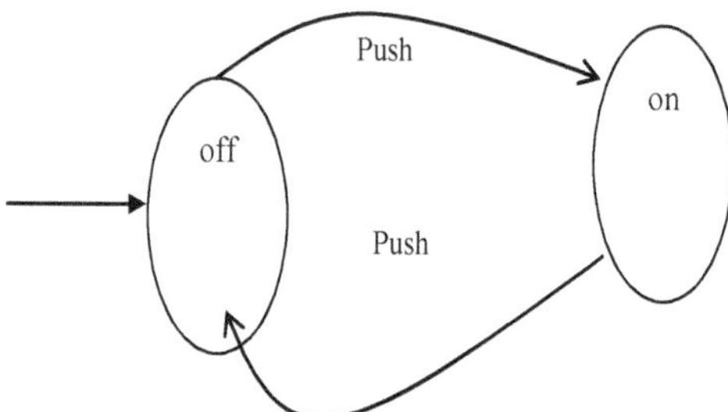

Figure 1

1.4. Concepts of Automata Theory

It introduces the most important definitions of terms that the theory of automata. These concepts include the alphabets, string and languages.

1. Alphabets (A-Z)

An alphabet is a finite, non empty set of symbols. We use the symbol Σ for an alphabet.

Eg.,
1. $\Sigma=\{0,1\}$,the binary alphabet
2. $\Sigma=\{a,b,c....z\}$,set of all lower case letters.
3. A set of all ASCII characters or the set of printable ASCII characters.

2. Strings

A string is a finite sequence of symbols over an alphabet Σ.

Eg., 0101, abcd.

i. Empty String

An empty string is a string with a zero occurrences of symbols. It is represented by ε (epsilon).

ii. Length of String

The length of a string is a number of symbols in the string.

It is represented by $|\omega|$.

Eg., $\omega=0011$

$|\omega|=4, |1100|=5$

$|\varepsilon|=0$

iii. Concatenation of strings

Let x and y be the string, x=aa,y=bb, The concatenation of x&y is, xy=aabb and

x=01,y=11

xy=0111

yx=1101

iv. Power of an alphabet

If Σ is an alphabet, the power of an alphabet Σ^k is the set of all strings of a certain length k from that alphabet by using an exponential notation.

Eg.,$\Sigma=\{0,1\}$

$\Sigma^0=\{\varepsilon\}$

$\Sigma^1=\{0, 1\}$

$\Sigma^2=\{00, 01, 10, 11\}$

$\Sigma^3=\{000,001,010,011,100,101,110,111\}$

Kleen Closure (or) Star Closure (Σ^*)

A set of all strings over an alphabet Σ is given by Σ^*, which consists of all strings including empty string. It is represented by $\Sigma^*=\bigcup_{i=0}^{n} L^i$, $\Sigma^*=\Sigma^0 U\Sigma^1 U\Sigma^2 U\Sigma^3......\Sigma^K$

Positive Closure (Σ^+)

The set of non empty strings from alphabet Σ is denoted by Σ^+, which consists of all strings expect empty string.

$\Sigma^+=\{0,1,00,01,10,11,000,001\}$

It is represented by $\Sigma^+=\bigcup_{i=1}^{n}L^i$, $\Sigma^+=\Sigma^1 U\Sigma^2 U\Sigma3.........U\Sigma^K$

$\Sigma^*=\Sigma^+ U \{\varepsilon\}$

3. *Language*

A set of strings of all which are chosen from some Σ^*, where Σ is a particular alphabet is called a language.

If Σ is an alphabet and L$\subseteq \Sigma^*$ then L is a language over Σ.

Eg.,

1. The languages of all strings consisting of n 0's followed by n 1's for some n$\geq$0
    Eg.,$\{\varepsilon,0,01,001,010,011...\}$
2. The set of the strings of 0's and 1's with the equal number of each
    Eg.,$\{\varepsilon,01,10,0011,1010\}$
3. The set of binary numbers whose value is prime.
    Eg.,$\{01,11,101,111\}$
4. Σ^* is a language for any alphabet Σ.
5. ϕ, the empty language, is a language over any alphabet.
6. $\{\varepsilon\}$, the language consisting of only the empty string, is also a language over any alphabet.

CHAPTER 2

AUTOMATA

2.1. Finite Automaton

An automaton model is an abstract model of a digital computer. It performs some functions without direct involvement of human being. A finite automaton is also called a finite state machine. There are two classes of finite automata namely, Deterministic finite automata (DFA) and Non-Deterministic finite automata (NFA).

2.1.1. Finite State Machine

It is a mathematical model for actual physical process. By considering the possible inputs on which these machines can work, we can analyze their strengths and weaknesses.

A finite automaton has a set of states and its control moves from state to state in response to external inputs.

2.1.2. DFA or FA or Automaton

The word "deterministic" refers to the fact that the transition is deterministic. There is only one state to which an automaton can transit from current state on each input. The word "finite" implies that number of states is finite.

2.1.2.1. Definition of DFA

DFA consists of a 5 tuples (Q, Σ, δ, q0, F)

Q$\rightarrow$a finite set of states.

$\Sigma$$\rightarrow$a finite set of symbols or alphabets (inputs)

$\delta$$\rightarrow$A transition function or a function defined for going to next state, Q: QXΣ

$q_0$$\rightarrow$The initial or start state ($q_0 \in$Q)

F$\rightarrow$The set of finite or accepting states (F$\subseteq$ Q).

Language of DFA

The language of DFA M={ Q,Σ,δ,q0,F} is denoted by L(M) and it is defined as,

$$L(M) = \{(w/ \delta (q0,w) \text{is in F)}\}$$

That is the language of M is the set of strings 'w' that starts with state q0 to reach one of the accepting state. If L is L (M) for some DFA M, then L is a Regular Language.

2.1.2.2. Representation for DFA's

There are two representations for transition function

1. **Transition table:** Transition table is a conventional table representation of a function like δ that takes two arguments (state, input) and returns a value (output). The row of the table corresponds to the states, the column of the table corresponds to the inputs.
2. **Transition graph/diagram:** FA is associated with the directed graph called a transition diagram/graph. The vertex of the graph corresponds to the states. The edges are transitions which denoted by "arrow"($\rightarrow$).

    There is an arrow into the start state q0, labeled "start". This arrow does not originate at any node and "final" (or) accepting states are marked by a double circle and the rest of the nodes usually marked by a single circle.

2.1.2.3. Example Problems

1. Let the machine M be the deterministic finite automata $M=\{Q,\Sigma,\delta,q_0,F\}$where $Q=\{q_0,q_1\},\Sigma=(0,1),q_0=$starting state, $F=\{q_1\}$ and δ is the transition as given below

    $\delta(q_0,0)=q_0$

    $\delta(q_0,0)=q_1$

    $\delta(q_1,0)=q_1$

    $\delta(q_1,1)=q_0$

    i.   Show transition table.
    ii. Show transition diagram.

    i).Transition table

State/input	0	1
$\rightarrow q_0$	q_0	q_1
$*q_1$	q_1	q_0

    ii).Transition Diagram

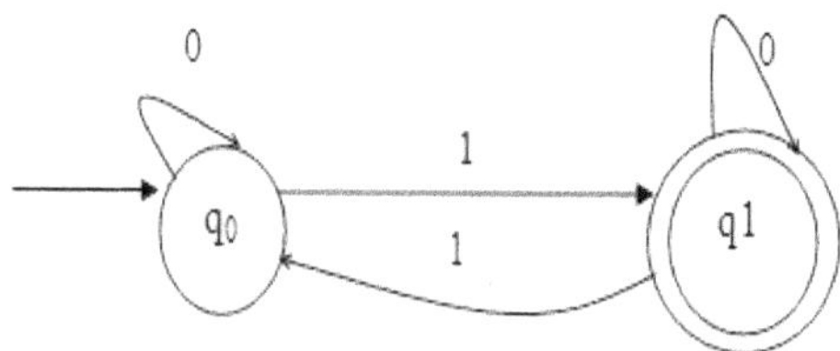

2. Design DFA language of string 0 and 1 that ending with 01, 001, 0001

   i).end with 01

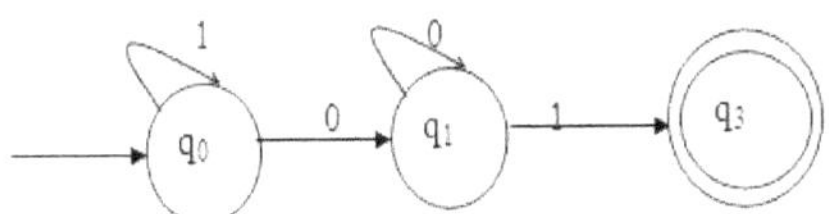

   ii).end with 0011

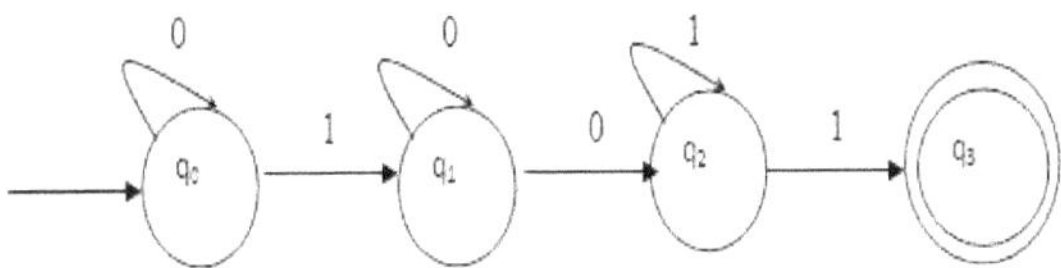

   iii).end with 0001

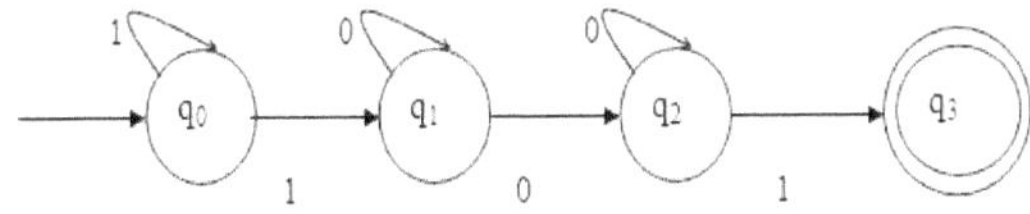

3. Draw DFA for the following language over {a,b}

   a. All string stating with abb

   b. All string with abb as substring ie., abb anywhere in the string

   c. All string ending in abb.

   a. starting with abb

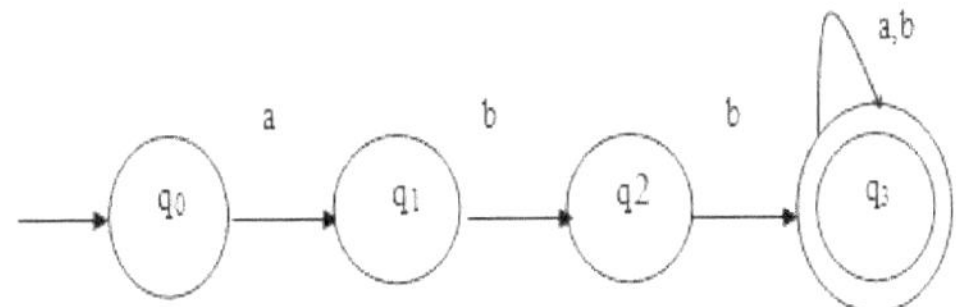

   b.abb as substring:

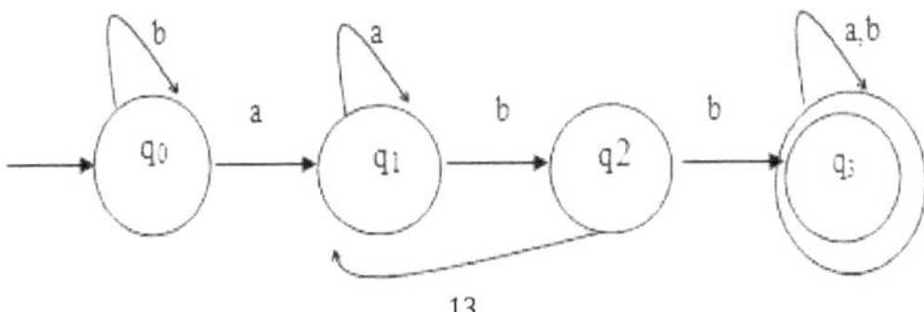

c. ending with abb

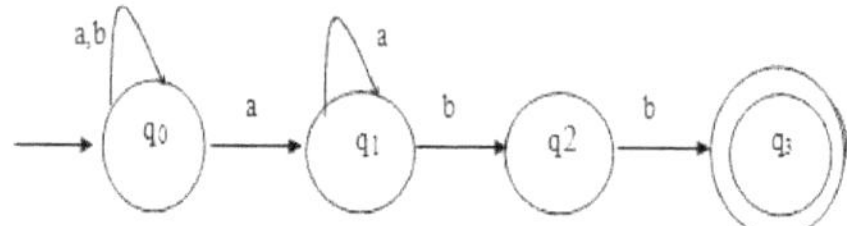

4. Give DFA's accepting the following strings over the alphabet {0, 1}.

   a) The set of all strings such that the number of 1's is even and the number of 0's is a multiple of 3

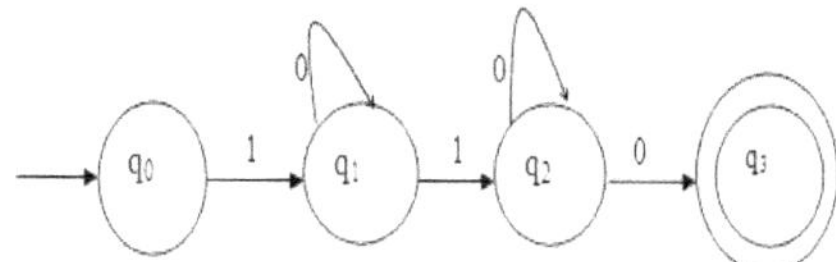

   b) The set of all strings not containing 110.

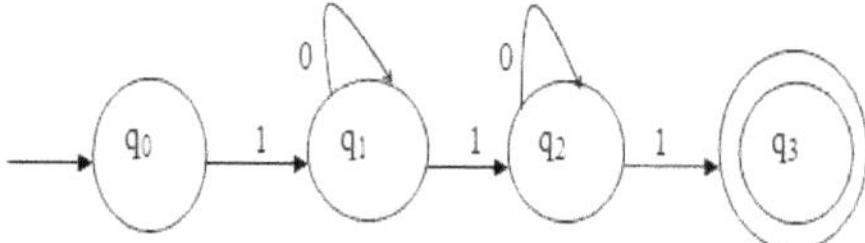

   c) The set of all strings that begins with 01 and end with 11.

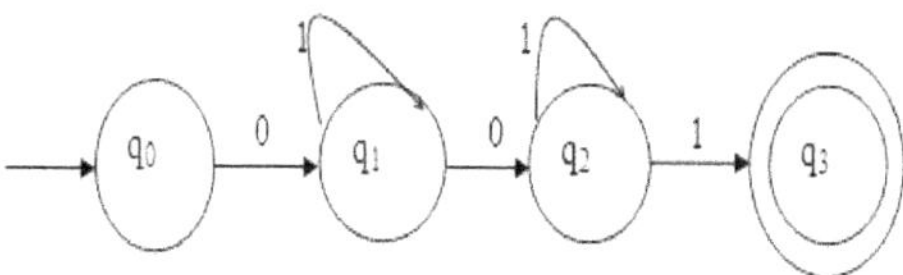

   d) The set of all strings which when interpreted as a binary integer is a multiple of 3.

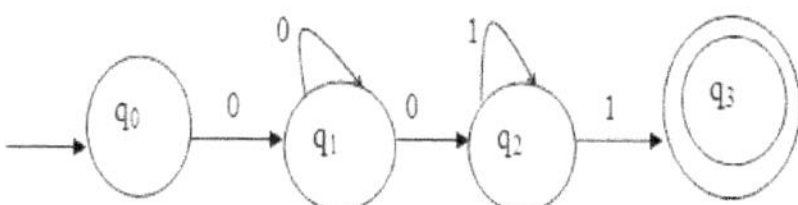

5. Draw state diagram for FA over {a,b} containing aabb.

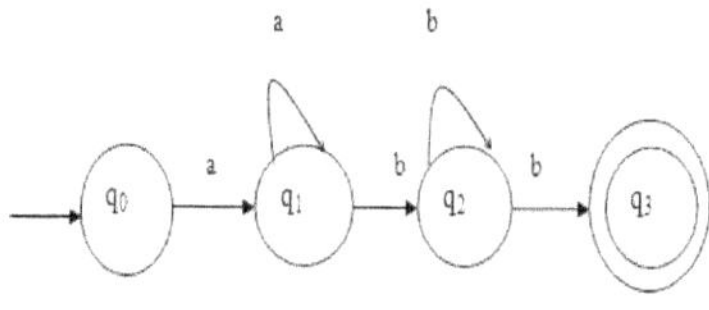

6. Construct a DFA that accept all the string on {0,1}except those containing the substring 101.

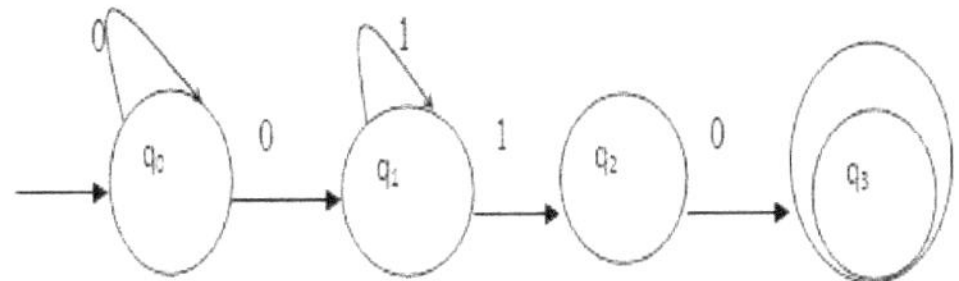

7. Give DFA accepting the following languages over the alphabet {0,1}

a)No. of 1's is even and no. of 0's is even.

b) Number of 1's is odd and the no. of 0's is odd.

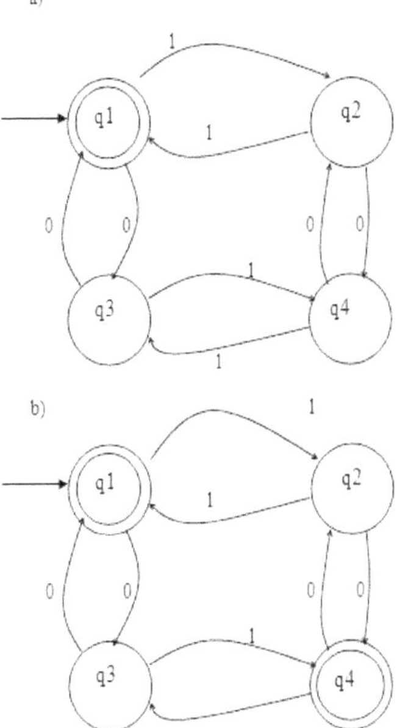

8. For the finite state machine M, given in the following table, test whether the string101101, 11111 are accepted by M.

State \input	0	1
q_0	q_0	q_1
q_1	q_3	q_0
q_2	q_0	q_3
q_3	q_1	q_2

Solution:

a)101101

$\delta(q_0,1)= q_1=01101$

$\delta(q_1,0)= q_3=1101$

$\delta(q_2,0)= q_2=101$

$\delta(q_2,1)= q_3=01$

$\delta(q_3,0)= q_1=1$

$\delta(q_0,1)= q_0=\phi$

The string 101101 is accepted by the machine M.

b) 11111

$\delta(q_0,1)= q_1=1111$

$\delta(q_1,1)= q_0=111$

$\delta(q_0,1)= q_1=11$

$\delta(q_1,1)= q_0=1$

$\delta(q_0,1)= q_1=\phi$

This string is not accepted by M.

9. Design a DFA, the language recognized by automata n being L=$\{a^nb, n\geq0\}$.

Solution:

L= {b,ab,aab...}

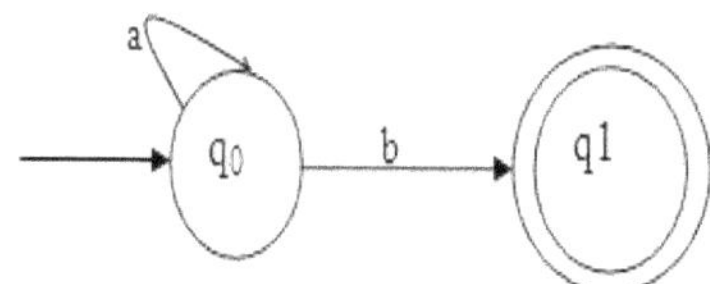

10. Construct a finite automata for the language $|0^n|n \bmod 3=2; n\geq0$.

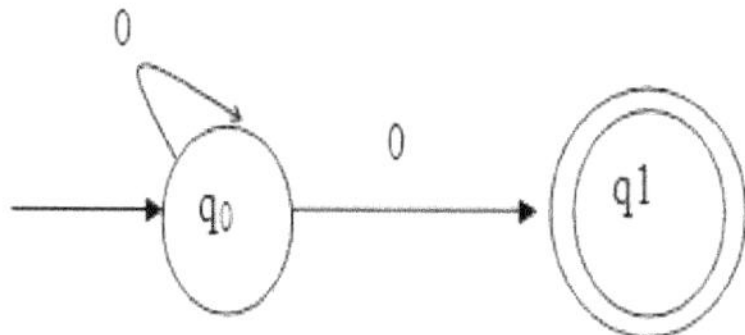

11. Construct a DFA that will accept strings on {a,b} where the number of b's are divisible by 3.

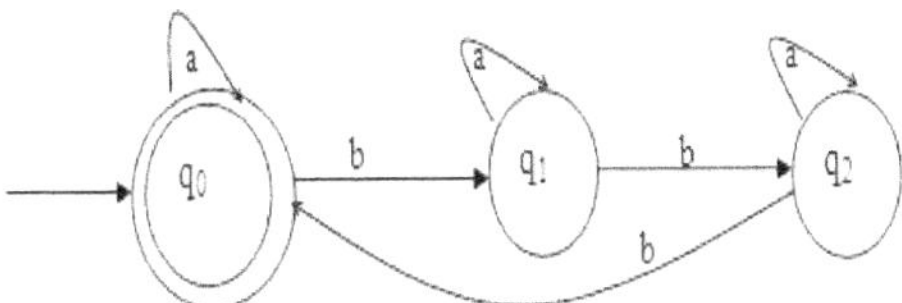

2.1.3. *Non Deterministic Finite Automata (NFA)*

NFA is same as DFA but differs from its transition function ,after receiving or reading the input symbol it can move zero, one or more states .

Definition of NFA

NFA consists of a 5 tuples$(Q, \Sigma, \delta, q0, F)$

Where,

Q→A finite set of states.

Σ→A finite set of symbols or alphabets (inputs)

δ→A transition function $\delta: Q X \Sigma \rightarrow 2^Q$ is the transition function.

Q_0→The initial or start state $(q_0 \epsilon Q)$

F→The set of finite or accepting states $(F \subseteq Q)$.

2.1.3.1. Example Problems

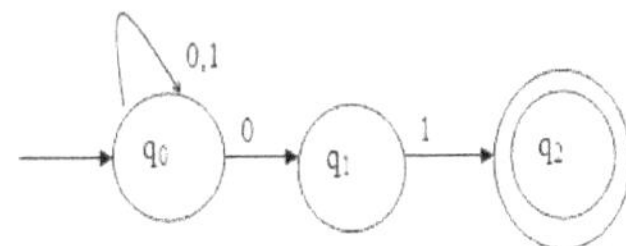

Transition table:

DFA:

State \input	0	1
→ q_0	q_0	ϕ
q_1	ϕ	q_2
*q_2	ϕ	ϕ

NFA:

State \input	0	1
→ q_0	$\{q_0, q_1\}$	Φ
q_1	Φ	q_2
*q_2	Φ	Φ

1. Design NFA accessing all string that end in 01.

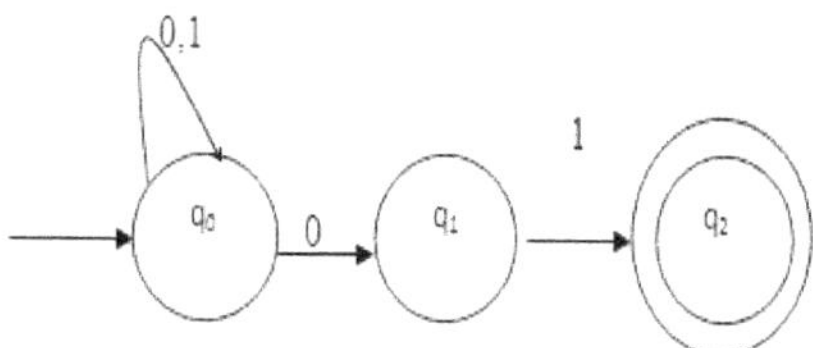

Transition table:

State \input	0	1
→ q_0	$\{q_0, q_1\}$	q_0
q_1	Φ	q_2
*q_2	Φ	Φ

2. Design NFA for a binary number where the first and last digits are same.

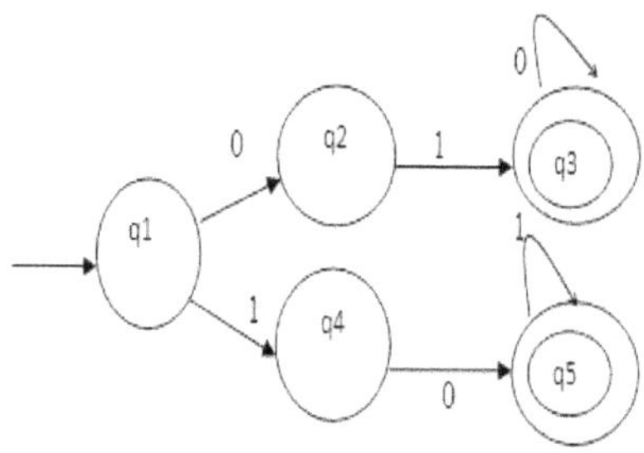

3. Design NFA for a given transition table.

Transition table:

State \input	0	1
→ q_0	q_1	Φ
q_1	$\{q_1, q_2\}$	q_1
*q_2	Φ	Φ

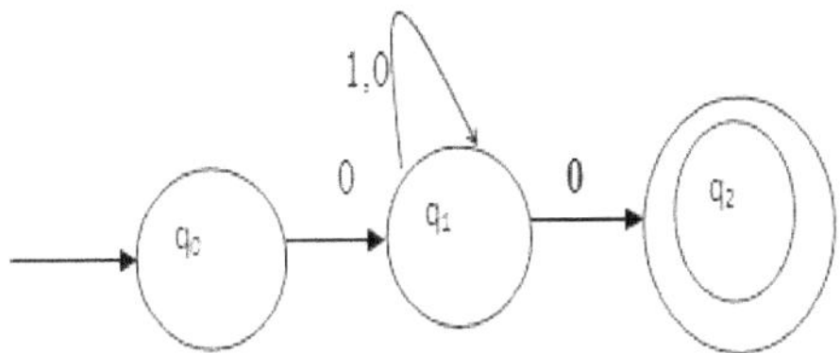

4. Design NFA for the set of strings on the alphabet {0,1}that start with 01 and end with 1

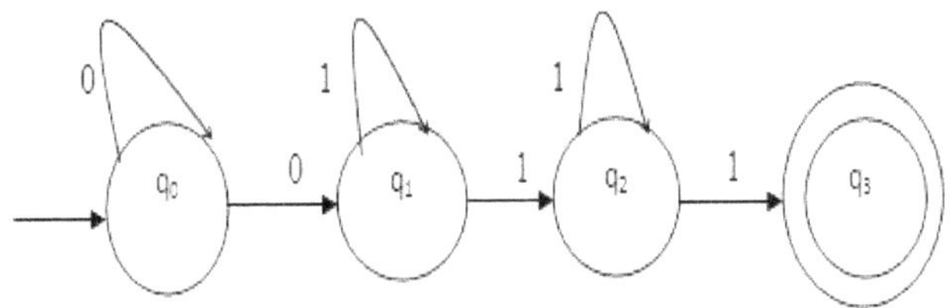

5. Design NFA accepting the language L={a* U b*} that start with 01 and end with 10.

    L= {a* U b*}

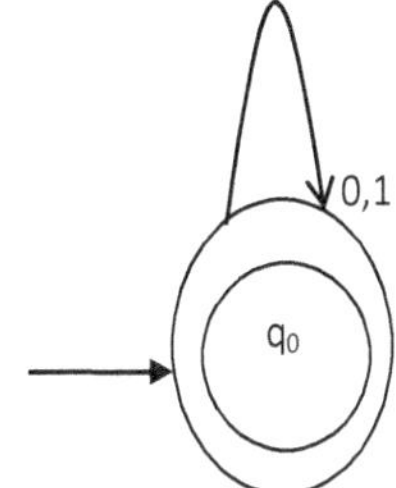

6. Determine the NFA accept the language

    1. (0+1)*01

    2. 00+11

    3. (0+1)*(00+11)

    4. a+b

    1. (0+1)*01

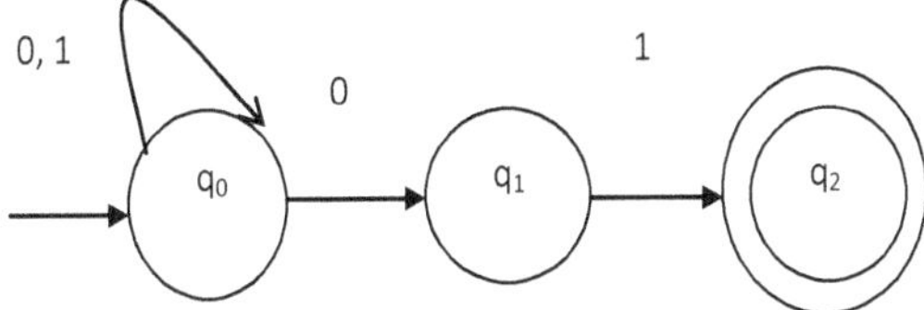

2. 00+11

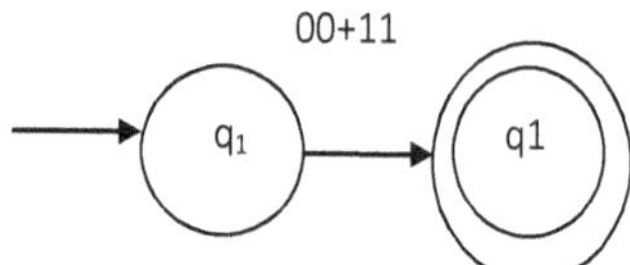

3. (0+1)*(00+11)

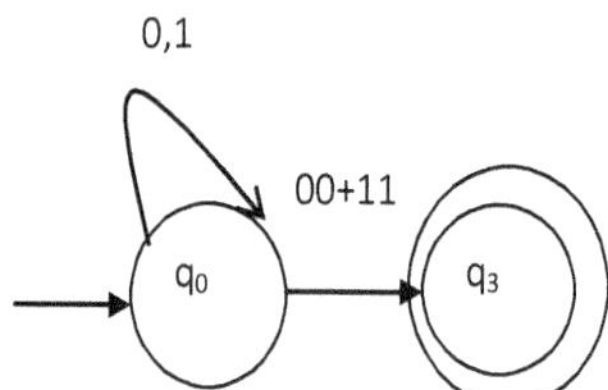

4. a+b

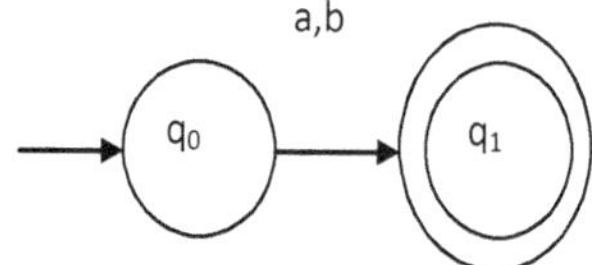

2.1.4. Differentiate DFA and NFA

DFA	NFA
1. All transition is Deterministic.	1. Some transition is not Deterministic.
2.Accepts input if the last state is in F.	2. Accepts input if one of the state is in F.
3. Sometimes harder to construct because of the number of states.	3. Generally easier than DFA to construct.
4. Practical implementation is feasible.	4. Practical implementation has to be deterministic. (convert to DFA)
5. Backtracking is allowed, and it requires more space than NFA.	5. Backtracking is not always allowed.
6.More number of states	6. Less number of states.
7.More powerful	7. Less powerful compare to DFA.
8. It does not allow ε- moves	8. It allows ε- moves

2.2. Equivalence of DFA and NFA (NFA to DFA Conversion)

2.2.1. Theorem

A Language L is accepted by some NFA if and only if it is accepted by some DFA.

(OR)

For every NFA, there exists an equivalent DFA.

(OR)

Let L be a set, accepted by NFA, and then there exists a DFA that accepts L.

Proof

This is implemented by subset construction method because it involves constructing all subsets of the set of states of the NFA

Let $N=\{Q_N, \Sigma, \delta_N, q_0, F_N\}$

$D=\{Q_D, \Sigma, \delta_D, q_0, F_D\}$

The states of D are all the subsets of the set of states of N i.e $Q_D = 2^{Q_N}$

An element of Q_D will be denoted by $[q_1, q_2, \dots q_i]$ where $q_1, q_2, \dots q_i$ in Q.

Define, $\delta_D([q_1, q_2, \dots q_i], a) = [p_1, p_2, \dots p_j]$

If and only if $\delta_N([q_1, q_2, \dots q_i]), a) = [p_1, p_2, \dots p_i]$

δ_D is computed by applying δ_N to each state of Q_D represented by $[q_1, q_2, \dots q_i]$.

On applying to each of $q_1, q_2, \dots q_i$ and taking the union.

We get, $[p_1, p_2, \dots p_i]$ in Q_D.

To show $\delta_D(\{q_0\}, x) = [q_0, q_1, \dots q_i]$ if and only if $\delta_N(\{q_0\}, x) = [q_0, q_1, \dots q_i]$

This is proved by the method of induction

F_D is the set of subsets of S of Q_N such that $S_n \cap F_n \neq \varphi$.

2.2.2. Procedure for Finding Whether the Given String is Accepted by NFA

1. Tracing the various paths followed by the machine for the given string.
2. Finding the set of sets reached from the starting state by applying the symbols of the string.
3. If the number of states obtained in step2 contains a final state, a given string is accepted by NFA .Otherwise not accepted.

NFA to DFA Conversion based on Subset Construction Algorithm

The NFA to DFA conversion is based on subset construction.

Eg: Set={a,b,c}

Subset constructions are {},{a},{b},{c},{a,b},{a,c},{b,c},{a,b,c}.

2.2.3. Example Problems

Example 1: Convert the DFA from NFA for the given diagram.

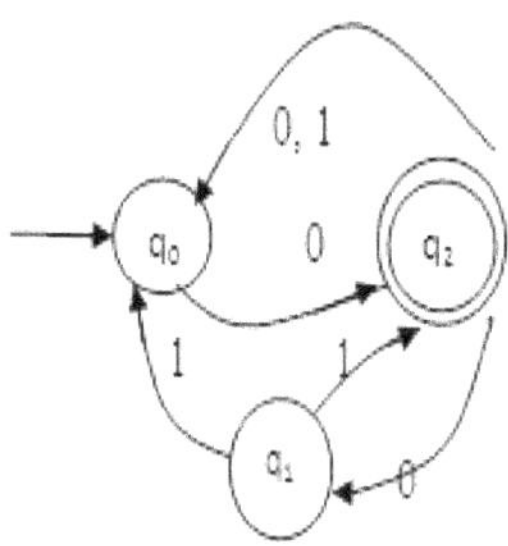

Solution

NFA => Q= {q_0, q1, q2}   (set of states given in the diagram)

Transition diagram

State\Input	0	1
q_0	q_2	Φ
q_1	q_2	q_0
q_2	q_0	{ q_0, q_1}

Step 1: Initial state q_0 is considered as first subset.

Step 2: find the transition for first subset q_0

0 - successor of q_0 is δ (q_0, 0) = q_2

1 - Successor of q_0 is δ (q_0, 1) = φ

State\Input	0	1
q_0	q_2	Φ

Here, new subset $q_2$is generated.

Step 3: Find the transition for new subset q_2.

0 - successor of q_2 is δ (q_2, 0) = q_0

1 - Successor of q_2 is δ (q_2, 1) = {q_0, q1}

State\Input	0	1
q_0	q_2	Φ
q_2	q_0	$\{q_0, q_1\}$

Here, new subset $\{q_0, q_1\}$ is generated.

Step 4: Find the transition for new subset $\{q_0, q_1\}$.

0 - successor of $\{q_0, q_1\}$ is δ ($\{q_0, q_1\}$, 0)

$$= \delta\ (q_0, 0)\ U\ \delta\ (q_1, 0)$$

$$= q_2\ U\ q_2$$

$$= q_2$$

1 - Successor of $\{q_0, q_1\}$ is δ (q_0, 1) U δ (q_1, 1)

$$= \varphi\ U\ q_0$$

$$= q_0$$

Since a new subset is not generated, the process of subset generation stops.

Step 5: Construct transition table for all the subsets

The q2 is the final state, every subset containing q2 should be taken as final state.

State\Input	0	1
$\rightarrow q_0$	q_2	Φ
$*q_2$	q_0	$\{q_0, q_1\}$
$\{q0,q1\}$	$q2$	$q0$

Step 6: The equivalent DFA diagram.

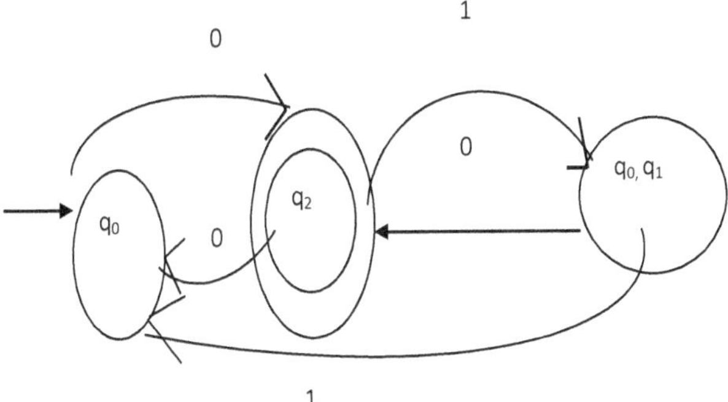

2. Convert from NFA to DFA.

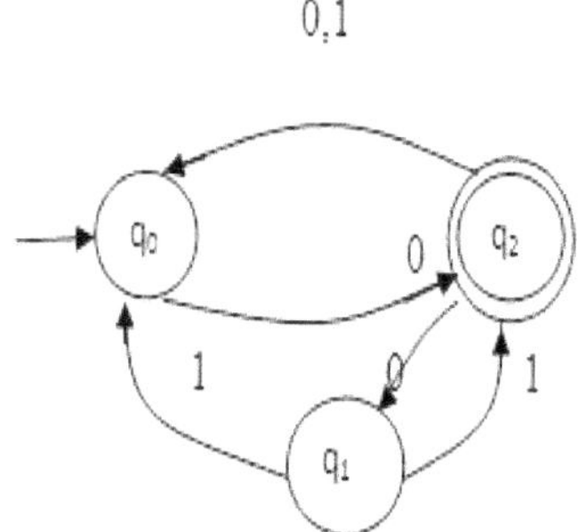

NFA =>Q = {q0, q1, q2}

state\Input	0	1
q_0	q_2	Φ
q_1	Φ	$\{q_0, q_2\}$
q_2	$\{q_0, q_1\}$	q_0

Step 1: Initial state q_0 is considered as first subset.

Step 2: Find the transition for first subset q0

0 - successor of q_0 is δ $(q_0, 0) = q_2$

1 - Successor of q_0 is δ $(q_0, 1) = φ$

State\Input	0	1
q_0	q_2	Φ

Here, new subset q_2 is generated.

Step 3: Find the transition for new subset q_2

successor of the subset $\{q_2\}$ are generated.

0 - successor of q_2 is δ$(q_2,0)= \{q_0,q_1\}$

1 - successor of q_2 is δ$(q_2,1)= q_0$

State\Input	0	1
q_0	q_2	Φ
q_2	$\{q_0, q_1\}$	q_0

Here new subset $\{q0, q_1\}$is generated.

Step 4: Find the transition for new subset $\{q0, q_1\}$

successor of the subset $\{q_0, q_1\}$ are generated.

0 - successor of $\{q_0, q1\}$ is $\delta(\{q_0, q1\}, 0)$

$$= \delta(q_0, 0)\ U\ \delta(q_1, 0)$$

$$= q_2\ U\ \varphi$$

$$= q_2$$

1 - Successor of $\{q_0, q1\}$ is $\delta(q_0, 1)\ U\ \delta(q_1, 1)$

$$= \varphi\ U\ \{q_0, q2\}$$

$$= \{q_0, q2\}$$

State\Input	0	1
$\{q_0,q_1\}$	q_2	$\{q_0,q_2\}$

Here new subset $\{q0, q_2\}$ is generated.

Step 5: Find the transition for new subset $\{q0, q_2\}$

successor of the subset $\{q_0, q_2\}$ are generated.

0 - successor of $\{q_0, q_2\}$ is $\delta(\{q_0, q_2\}, 0)$

$$= \delta(q_0, 0)\ U\ \delta(q_2, 0)$$

$$= q_2\ U\ \{q_0, q_1\}$$

$$= \{q_0, q_1, q_2\}$$

1 - successor of $\{q_0, q_2\}$ is $\delta(q_0, 1)\ U\ \delta(q_2, 1)$

$$= \varphi\ U\ \{q_0\}$$

Here, new subset $\{q_0, q1, q2\}$ is generated.

Step 6: Find the transition for new subset $\{q_0, q1, q2\}$

Successor of the subset $\{q_0, q1, q2\}$ are generated.

0 - successor of $\{q_0, q1, q2\}$ is $\delta(\{q_0, q1, q2\}, 0)$

$$= \delta(q_0, 0)\ U\ \delta(q_1, 0)\ U\ \delta(q_2, 0)$$

$$= q_2\ U\ \varphi\ U\ \{q_0, q1, q2\}$$

$$= \{q_0, q1, q2\}$$

1 - Successor of $\{q_0, q1, q2\}$ is δ ($\{q_0, q1, q2\}$, 1)

$$= \varphi \cup \{q_0, q2\} \cup \{q_0\}$$

$$= \{q_0, q_2\}$$

Since a new subset is not generated, the process of subset generation stops.

Step 7: The q_2 is the final state; every subset containing q_2 should be taken as a final state.

State\Input	0	1
→ $\{q_0\}$	q_2	φ
*$\{q_2\}$	$\{q_0, q_1\}$	q_0
$\{q_0,q_1\}$	q_2	$\{q_0,q_2\}$
*$\{q_0, q_2\}$	$\{q_0,q_1,q_2\}$	q_0
*$\{q_0,q_1,q_2\}$	$\{q_0,q_1,q_2\}$	$\{q_0, q_2\}$

Step 8: The equivalent DFA diagram:

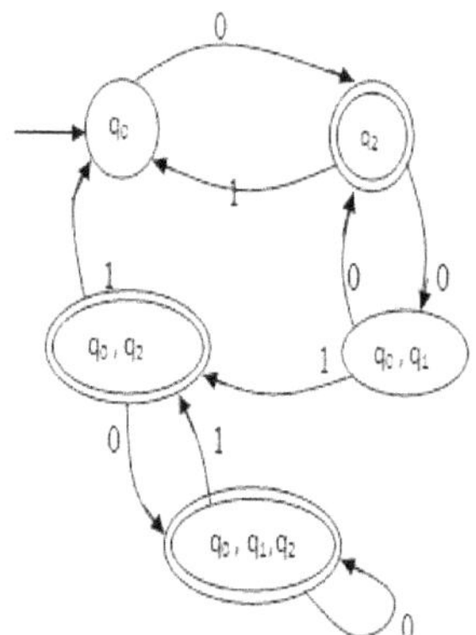

3. Convert DFA to NFA.

State\Input	0	1
->$\{p\}$	$\{q,s\}$	$\{q\}$
*q	$\{r\}$	$\{q,r\}$
r	$\{s\}$	$\{p\}$
*s	$\{\varphi\}$	$\{p\}$

Step 1: Initial state $\{p\}$ is taken as the first subset

Find the transition for new subset $\{p\}$

0-successor of p δ (p, 0) = $\{q, s\}$

1-successor of p δ (p, 1) = $\{q\}$

State\Input	0	1
{p}	{q,s}	{q}

Here, two new subsets {q, s} and {q} are generated.

Step 2: Find the transition for new subset {q, s} and {q}

Successors of {q,s} and {q} are generated.

0-successor of q δ (q, 0) = {r}

1-successor of q δ (q, 1) = {q, r}

0-successor of (q,s) => δ({q,s},0)

$$=δ(q,0) \cup (s,0)$$

$$=r \cup φ$$

$$=\{r\}$$

1-successor of (q,s) => δ({q,s},1)

$$=δ(q,1) \cup (s,1)$$

$$=δ(q,1) \cup δ (s,1)$$

$$=\{q,r\} \cup \{p\}$$

$$=\{p,q,r\}$$

	0	1
{p}	{q,s}	{q}
{q,s}	{r}	{p,q,r}
{q}	{r}	{q,r}

Here, three new subsets {r},{p, q, r} and {q, r} are generated.

Step 3: Find the transition for new subset { r},{p, q, r} and {q, r}.

Their successors are generated.

0-successor of (q,r)=> δ({q,r},0)

$$=δ(q,0) \cup (r,0)$$

$$=(r) \cup (s)$$

$$=\{r,s\}$$

1-successor of (q,r)=> δ({q,r},1)

$$=δ(q,1) \cup δ(r,1)$$

$$=\{q,r\} \cup \{p\}$$

$$=\{p,q,r\}$$

Here, three new subsets {s},{r,s} and {q,r,s} are generated.

Step 4:Find the transition for new subset {s},{r,s} and {q,r,s}

Successors of {s},{r,s} and {q,r,s}} are generated

0-successor of (r,s)=> δ({r,s},0)

$$=δ(r,0) \cup (s,0)$$

$$=(s) \cup φ$$

$$=\{s\}$$

1-successor of (r,s) => δ({r,s},1)

$$=δ(r,1) \cup δ(s,1)$$

$$=p \cup p$$

$$=\{p\}$$

0-successor of (q,r,s)=> δ({q,r,s},0)

$$=δ(q,0) \cup δ(r,0) \cup δ(s,0)$$

$$=(r) \cup (s) \cup (φ)$$

$$=\{r,s\}$$

1-successor of (q,r,s)= δ({q,r,s},1)

$$=δ(q,1) \cup δ(r,1) \cup δ(s,1)$$

$$=\{p,q,r\}$$

0-successor of (s)   => δ(s,0)

$$=φ$$

1-successor of (S)   => δ(s,1)

$$= p$$

Since a new subset is not generated, the process of subset generation stops.

Step 5: The q and s are the final states; every subset containing q and s should be taken as final states.

Step 6: The transition table:

	0	1
→ p	q,s	q
* q	r	q,s
r	s	p
* s	φ	φ
* q,s	r	q,r
* q,r	r,s	p,q,r
* r,s	s	p
*p,q,r	q,r,s	p,q,r
* q,r,s	r,s	p,q,r

Step 7: The equivalents DFA diagram:

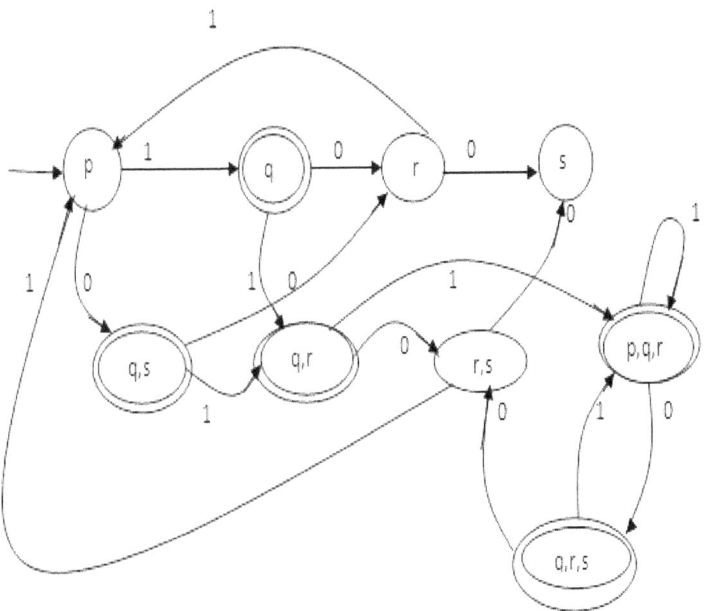

4. Convert the DFA from NFA.

States/ip	0	1
→ q_0	q_0, q_1	Φ
q_1	Φ	q_2
* q_2	Φ	q_2

Step 1: Initial state q_0 is taken as the first subset

Find the transition for new subset q_0.

Successors of q0 are generated

0-successor of $q_0 \delta(q_0,0)=q_0,q_1$

1-successor of $q_0 \delta(q_0,1)=\varphi$

Here, new subset {q_0, q1} is generated.

Step 2: Find the transition for new subset {q_0, q1}.

Successors of {q_0, q1 are generated

0-successor of $(q_0,q_1)=> \delta(q_0,q_1),0)$

$$=\delta(q_0,0) \text{ U } \delta(q_1,0)$$

$$= q_0,q_1 \text{ U } \varphi$$

$$=\{ q_0,q_1\}$$

1-successor of $(q_0,q_1)= \delta[\{q_0,q_1\},1]$

$$=\delta(q_0,1) \text{ U } \delta(q_1,1)$$

$$=\varphi \text{ U } \{q_2\} = \{q_2\}$$

Here, new subset {q_2} is generated.

Step 3: Find the transition for new subset { q_2}.

Successors of {q2} are generated

0-successor of $(q_2,0) = \delta(\{q_2\},0)$

$$=\varphi$$

1-successor of $(q_2,1)= \delta(\{q_2\},1)$

$$= \delta (q_2,1)$$

$$= \{q_2\}$$

Since a new subset is not generated, the process of subset generation stops.

Step 4: The q2 is the final state, every subset containing q2 should be taken as final state.

Step 5: The transition table:

States/Input	0	1
→ q_0	q_0,q_1	φ
q_0,q_1	q_0,q_1	q_2
* q_2	Φ	q_2

Step 6: The equivalent DFA diagram:

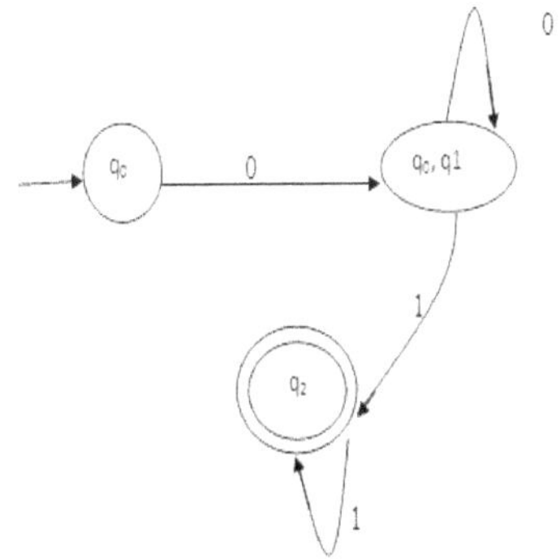

2.3.   Finite Automata with ε-transition:(NFA with ε Transitions)

The ε transition allows transition on ε symbol (no i/p) or the empty string.

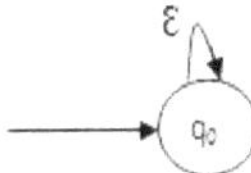

This implies that a machine can make a transition without any input.

Advantages

When finding the string described by a path containing arc (→) with label ε symbol, the ε are discarded. E.g.

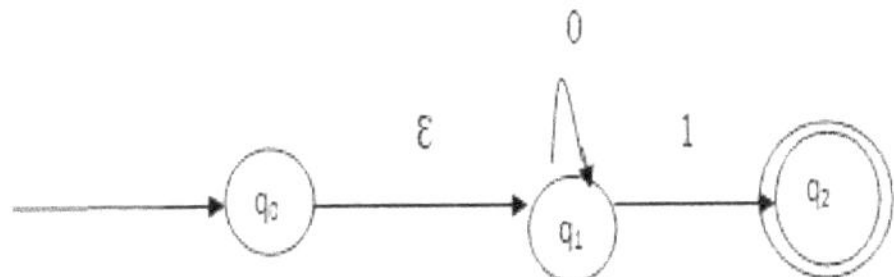

The use of ε transition may simplify a transition graph by reducing the no. of label arcs.

2.3.1. *A Formal Notation for Ɛ-NFA*

A NFA M with Ɛ transition is given by, where M={Q, Ɛ,δ,q₀,F}

Q→finite set of states

Ɛ→finite set of symbols

δ→is a transition function from {∑ U {ε}} to the power set of Q is 2^Q

Q₀→initial state(q₀ƐQ)

F→accepting state or final state$(F \subseteq Q)$

Eg:

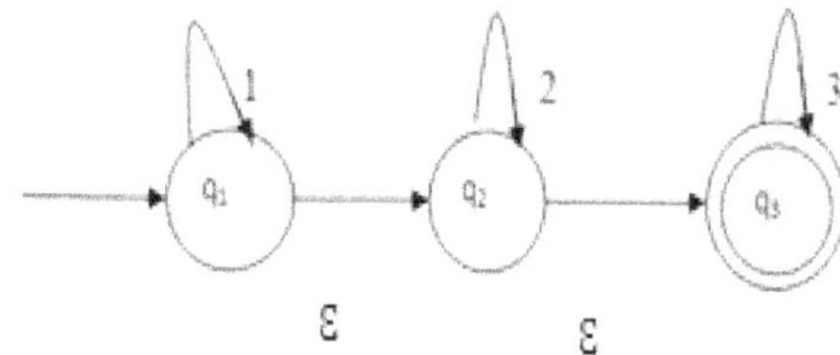

state\ip	ε	1	2	3
→q₁	q₂	q₁	φ	φ
q₂	q₃	φ	q₂	φ
q₃	φ	φ	φ	q₃

Q={q₁,q₂,q₃}

M=({q₁,q₂,q₃} , {1,2,3},δ,q₁,q₃)

2.3.2. *Definition of ε- closure*

ε- closure of a state q_i is the set of states including q_i. Where, qi can reach any number of ε moves of the given NFA.

ε- closure of q_i:

- ε- closure of a state q_i, includes q_i
- set of the states reachable from q_i on ε move

1. Find the ε closure of the states 1, 2 and 3 in the following transition diagram.

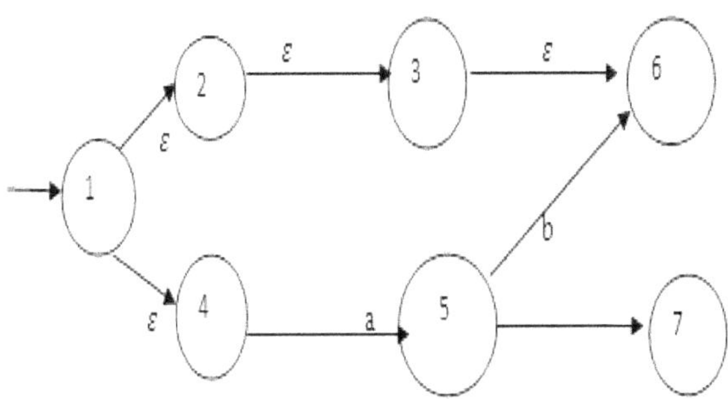

States	ε-closure
1	{1, 2,3,4,6}
2	{2, 3,6}
3	{3,6}

2. Obtain ε-closure of each state in the following NFA with ε moves.

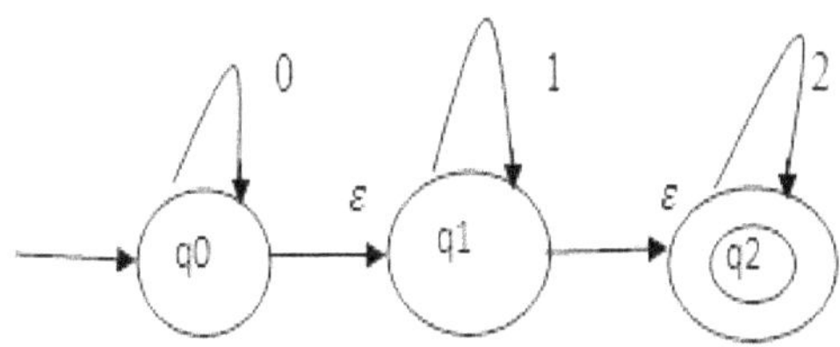

States	ε-closure
q₀	{q0,q1,q2}
q₁	{q1, q2}
q₂	{q2}

3. Compute ε-closure

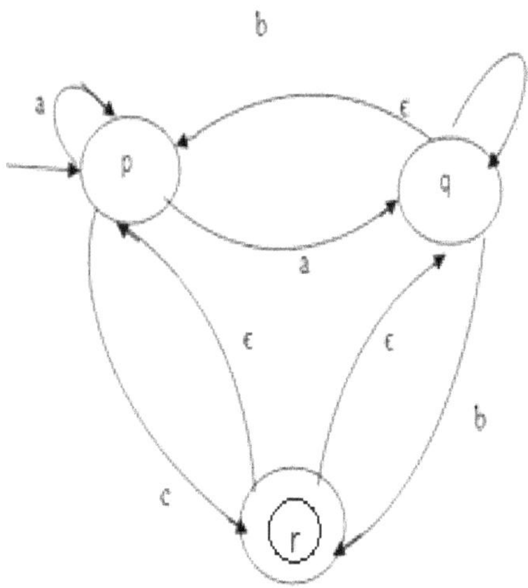

States	ε-closure
→P	{p}
q	{q,p}
*r	{r,p,q}

2.3.3. *Equivalence of NFA with ε Transition and NFA Without εTransition*

A language L is accepted by some ε-NFA if and only if L is accepted by NFA without ε transition

(Or)

A language L is accepted by some NFA with ε transition if and only if L is accepted by some DFA

$$E=(Q_E, \Sigma, \delta_E, q_0, F_E)$$

$$D=(Q_D, \Sigma, \delta_D, q_D, F_D)$$

We need to show that L(D)=L(E), and we do so by showing that the extended transition function of E and D are the same. Formally, we show $\delta_E(q_0,w)= \delta_D(q_D,w)$ by induction on the length of w.

Basis

If $|w| = 0$, then $w = \varepsilon$ we know $\delta_E(q_0,\varepsilon) = \varepsilon\text{-closure}(q_0)$, We also know that $q_D = \varepsilon\text{-closure}(q_0)$, because that is how the start of D is defined.

Finally for a DFA, we know that $\delta(p,\varepsilon) = p$ for any start p, so in particular, $\delta_D(q_D,\varepsilon) = \varepsilon\text{-closure}(q_0)$. we have thus proved that $\delta_E(q_0,\varepsilon) = \delta_D(q_D,\varepsilon)$.

Induction

Suppose $w = xa$, where a is the final symbol of w, and assume that the state holds for x. That is $\delta_E(q_0,x) = \delta_D(q_D,x)$. Let both these sets of states be $\{p_1,p_2,....,p_k\}$.

By the definition of for δ for ε-NFA's we compute $\delta_E(q_0,w)$ by:

1. Let $\{r_1, r_2,.....,r_m\}$ be $\bigcup^k_{i=1}\delta_E(p_i,a)$.
2. Then $\delta E(q_0,w) = \bigcup^m_{j=1}\varepsilon\text{-closure}(r_j)$

If we examine the construction of DFA, D in the modified subset construction above, we see that $\delta_D(\{p_1,p_2,....,p_k\},a)$ is constructed by the same two steps (1) and (2) above. Thus, $\delta_D(q_D,w)$, which is $\delta_D(\{p_1,p_2,....,p_k\},a)$ is the same set as $\delta_E(q_0,w)$, we have how proved that $\delta_E(q_0,w) = \delta_D(q_D,w)$ and completed the inductive part.

1. Consider the following ϵ-NFA

	ϵ	a	b	c
$\rightarrow p$	$\{q,r\}$	ϕ	$\{q\}$	$\{r\}$
q	ϕ	$\{p\}$	$\{r\}$	$\{p,q\}$
$* r$	ϕ	ϕ	ϕ	ϕ

a) Compute ϵ-closure of each state.

b) Convert the automaton of a DFA

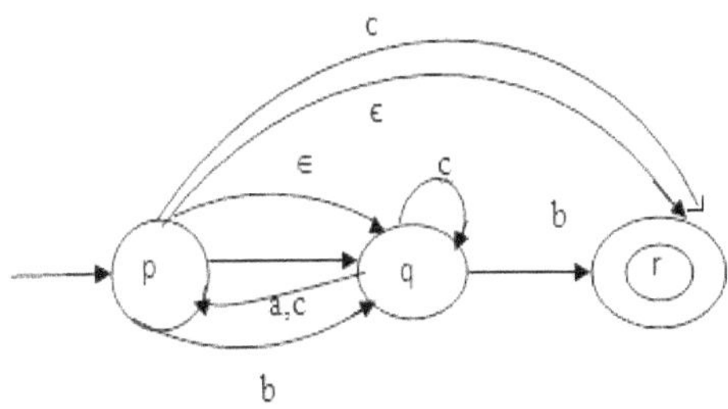

a) ε-closure of states.

States	ε-closure
→p	{p,q,r}
q	{q}
*r	{r}

b) Conversion of NFA to DFA.

Step 1: ε-closure of the initial state p is taken as first subset.

ε-closure (p)={p,q,r}

Successor of {p,q,r} are calculated as:

a-successor of{p,q,r}=ε-closure (p,q,r)

$$=\text{ε-closure } \delta(\{p,q,r\},a)$$

$$= \text{ε-closure } (\delta \ (p,a)\cup\delta(q,a)\cup \delta(r,a))$$

$$= \text{ε-closure } (\phi\cup p\cup\phi)$$

$$= \text{ε-closure } (p)$$

$$=(p,q,r)$$

b-successor of (p,q,r)= ε-closure(p,q,r)

$$= \text{ε-closure } \delta(\{p,q,r\},b)$$

$$= \text{ε-closure } (\delta(p,b)\cup\delta(q,b)\cup\delta(r,b))$$

$$=\text{ε-closure } (q\cup r\cup\phi)$$

$$=\text{ε-closure}(q) \cup \text{ε-closure } (r)$$

$$=q\cup r$$

$$=\{q,r\}$$

C-successor of (p,q,r) = ε-closure(p,q,r)

$$=\text{ε-closure } \delta((p,q,r),c)$$

$$=\text{ε-closure } (\delta(p,c)\cup\delta(q,c)\cup\delta(r,c))$$

$$=\text{ε-closure } (\{r\}\cup\{p,q\}\cup\{\phi\})$$

$$=\text{ε-closure } \{r\} \cup \text{ε-closure}\{p,q\}$$

$$= r \cup \epsilon\text{-closure (p)} \cup \epsilon\text{-closure (q)}$$

$$= r \cup \{p,q,r\} \cup q$$

$$= \{p,q,r\}$$

Here, a new subset {q,r} is generated.

Step 2: Find the transition for new subset {q,r}

a- successor of (q,r) $= \epsilon\text{-closure (q,r)}$

$$= \epsilon\text{-closure } \delta((q,r),a)$$

$$= \epsilon\text{-closure } (\delta(q,a) \cup \delta((r,a))$$

$$= \epsilon\text{-closure } (p \cup \phi)$$

$$= \{p,q,r\}$$

b- successor of (q,r) $= \epsilon\text{-closure (q,r)}$

$$= \epsilon\text{-closure } \delta((q,r),b)$$

$$= \epsilon\text{-closure } (\delta(q,b) \cup \delta((r,b))$$

$$= \epsilon\text{-closure } (r \cup \phi)$$

$$= \{r\}$$

c- successor of (q,r) $= \epsilon\text{-closure (q,r)}$

$$= \epsilon\text{-closure } \delta((q,r),c)$$

$$= \epsilon\text{-closure } (\delta(q,c) \cup \delta((r,c))$$

$$= \epsilon\text{-closure } (\{p,q\} \cup \phi)$$

$$= \epsilon\text{-closure of (p)} \cup \epsilon\text{-closure of (q)}$$

$$= \{p,q,r\} \cup \{q\}$$

$$= \{p,q,r\}$$

Here, a new subset {r} is founded.

Step 3: Find the transition for new subset{r}

$$\epsilon\text{-closure of } \delta(r,a) = \phi$$

$$\epsilon\text{-closure of } \delta(r,b) = \phi$$

$$\epsilon\text{-closure of } \delta(r,c) = \phi$$

Since a new subset is not generated, the process of subset generation stops.

Step 4: Transition table

Every subset containing r is taken as a final state.

state /input	a	b	c
→ * {p,q,r}	{p,q,r}	{q,r}	{p,q,r}
* {q,r}	{p,q,r}	{r}	{p,q,r}
* {r}	φ	φ	φ
φ	φ	φ	φ

Step 5: The equivalent DFA

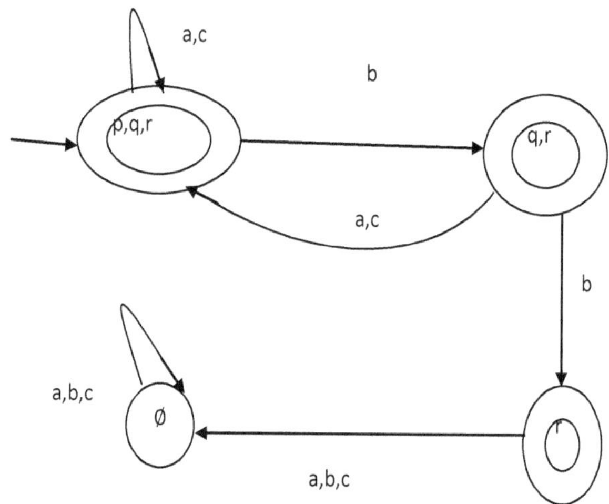

2. Consider the following ε-NFA. Compute the ε-closure of each state and find the equivalent DFA.

	ε	a	b	c
→p	{q}	{p}	φ	φ
q	{r}	φ	{q}	φ
*r	φ	φ	φ	{r}

a) ε-closure of states:

states	ε-closure
p	{p,q,r}
q	{q,r}
r	{r}

b) Conversion of NFA to DFA

Step 1: ε-closure of the initial states p is taken as first subset

ε-closure (p)={p,q,r}

Successor of (p,q,r) are calculated as

a-Successor of (p,q,r) =ε-closure (p,q,r)

$\quad\quad$ =ε-closure δ({p,q,r},a)

$\quad\quad$ =ε-closure(δ (p,a)$\cup\delta$(q,a))$\cup\delta$(r,a)

$\quad\quad$ =ε-closure (p$\cup\phi\cup\phi$)

$\quad\quad$ =ε-closure (p)

$\quad\quad$ ={p,q,r}

b-Successor of (p,q,r) =ε-closure (p,q,r)

$\quad\quad$ =ε-closure δ({p,q,r},b)

$\quad\quad$ =ε-closure(δ (p,b)$\cup\delta$(q,b))$\cup\delta$(r,b))

$\quad\quad$ =ε-closure ($\phi\cup$q$\cup\phi$)

$\quad\quad$ ={q,r}

c-Successor of (p,q,r) =ε-closure (p,q,r)

$\quad\quad$ =ε-closure δ({p,q,r},c)

$\quad\quad$ =ε-closure(δ (p,c)$\cup\delta$(q,c))$\cup\delta$(r,c))

$\quad\quad$ =ε-closure ($\phi\cup\phi\cup$r)

$\quad\quad$ ={r}

Here, two new subsets {q,r},{r} are generated.

Step 2: Find the transition for new subsets {q,r}&{r}

(i) {q,r}

a-Successor of (q,r) $=\epsilon$-closure (q,r)

$=\epsilon$-closure $\delta(\{q,r\},a)$

$=\epsilon$-closure$(\delta(q,a)\cup\delta(r,a))$

$=\epsilon$-closure $(\phi\cup\phi)$

$=\{\phi\}$

b-Successor of (q,r) $=\epsilon$-closure (q,r)

$=\epsilon$-closure $\delta(\{q,r\},b)$

$=\epsilon$-closure$(\delta(q,b)\cup\delta(r,b))$

$=\epsilon$-closure $(q\cup\phi)$

$=\{q,r\}$

c-Successor of (q,r) $=\epsilon$-closure (q,r)

$=\epsilon$-closure $\delta(\{q,r\},c)$

$=\epsilon$-closure$(\delta(q,c))\cup\delta(r,c))$

$=\epsilon$-closure $(\phi\cup\{r\})$

$=\{r\}$

(ii) {r}

a- Successor of (r) $=\epsilon$-closure (r)

$=\epsilon$-closure $(\delta\{r,a\})$

ϕ

b-Successor of (r) $=\epsilon$-closure (r)

$=\epsilon$-closure$(\delta\{r,b\})$

ϕ

c-Successor of (r) $=\epsilon$-closure (r)

$=\epsilon$-closure$(\delta\{r,c\})$

$=\{r\}$

Since a new subset is not generated, the process of subset generation stops.

Step 3: Transition table

Every subset containing r is taken as a final state.

state/input	a	b	c
→*{p,q,r}	{p,q,r}	{q,r}	{r}
*{q,r}	φ	{q,r}	{r}
*{r}	φ	φ	{r}

Step 4: The equivalent DFA

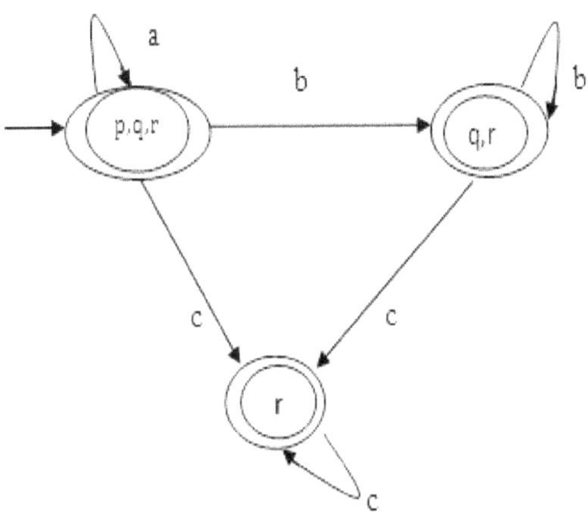

3. Consider the following ε-NFA. Compute the ε-closure of each state and find the equivalent DFA.

	ε	a	b	c
→p	{q,r}	φ	{q}	{r}
q	φ	{r}	{r}	{p,q}
*r	φ	φ	Φ	{r}

a) ε-closure of states:

states	ε-closure
→ p	{p,q,r}
q	{q}
* r	{r}

b) Conversion of NFA to DFA.

Step 1: ε-closure of the initial state p is taken as first subset.

ε-closure (p) ={p,q,r}

successor of {p,q,r} are calculated as

a- Successor of (p,q,r) =ε-closure (p,q,r)

$$=\text{ε-closure } \delta(\{p,q,r\},a)$$

$$=\text{ε-closure}(\delta (p,a)\cup\delta(q,a) \cup\delta(r,a)$$

$$=\text{ε-closure } (\phi\cup r\cup\phi)$$

$$=\{r\}$$

b-Successor of (p,q,r) =ε-closure (p,q,r)

$$=\text{ε-closure } \delta(\{p,q,r\},b)$$

$$=\text{ε-closure}(\delta (p,b)\cup\delta(q,b)\cup\delta(r,b)$$

$$=\text{ε-closure } (q\cup r\cup\phi)$$

$$=\{q,r\}$$

c-Successor of (p,q,r) =ε-closure (p,q,r)

$$=\text{ε-closure } \delta(\{p,q,r\},c)$$

$$=\text{ε-closure}(\delta (p,c)\cup\delta(q,c)\cup\delta(r,c))$$

$$=\text{ε-closure } (\{r\} \cup \{p\cup q\} \cup \{r\})$$

$$=\{p,q,r\}$$

Here, two new subsets {q,r} & {r} are generated.

Step 2: Find the transition for two new subsets.

(i) {q,r}

a- Successor of (q,r) =ε-closure (q,r)

$$=\epsilon\text{-closure }\delta(\{q,r\},a)$$

$$=\epsilon\text{-closure}(\delta(q,a)\cup\delta(r,a))$$

$$=\epsilon\text{-closure }(r\cup\phi)$$

$$=\{r\}$$

b-Successor of (q,r) =ε-closure (q,r)

$$=\epsilon\text{-closure }\delta(q,r\},b)$$

$$=\epsilon\text{-closure}(\delta\,(q,b)\cup\delta(r,b))$$

$$=\epsilon\text{-closure }(r\cup\phi)$$

$$=\{r\}$$

c-Successor of (q,r) =ε-closure (q,r)

$$=\epsilon\text{-closure }\delta(\{q,r\},c)$$

$$=\epsilon\text{-closure}(\delta(q,c)\cup\delta(r,c))$$

$$=\epsilon\text{-closure }((p,q)\cup(r))$$

$$=\{p,q,r\}$$

(ii) new subset {r}

$$a\text{- successor of } r\ \delta(r,a)=\phi$$

$$b\text{- successor of } r\ \delta(r,b)=\phi$$

$$c\text{- successor of } r\ \delta(r,c)=r$$

Since a new subset is not generated, the process of subset generation stops.

Step 3: Transition table

Every subset containing r is taken as a final state.

State/input	a	b	c
→ {p,q,r}	{r}	{q,r}	{p,q,r}
*{q,r}	{r}	{r}	{p,q,r}
*{r}	φ	φ	{r}

Step 4: The equivalent DFA

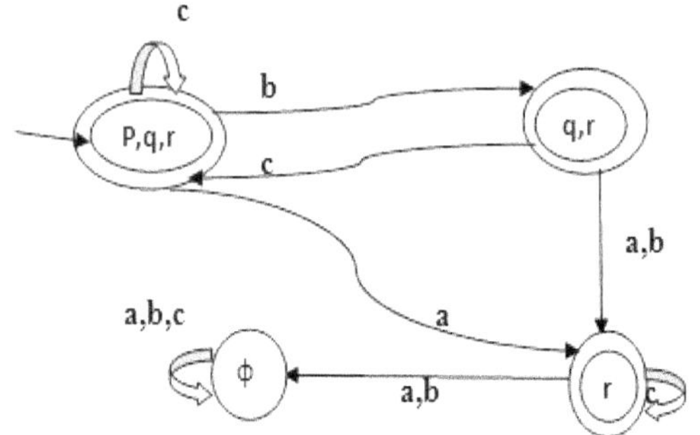

4. Consider the following ε-NFA.

i)

	ε	a	b	c
→p	φ	{p}	{q}	{r}
q	{p}	{q}	{r}	Φ
*r	{q}	{r}	φ	{p}

(i) Compute ε-closure of each state

(ii) Convert the automata to a DFA

    a)ε- closure of state

state	ε- closure
→ P	{p}
q	{p,q}
*r	{p,q,r}

    b) Conversion of NFA to DFA

Step 1: ε- closure of the initial state p is taken as first subset

ε- closure   (p)   ={p}

successor of {p} is calculated as:

a-successor of {p}   = ε- closure (p)

                = ε- closure δ({p},a)

          ={p}

b-successor of {p} $= \varepsilon$- closure(p)

$= \varepsilon$- closure $\delta(\{p\},b)$

$= \varepsilon$- closure(q)

$=\{q,p\}$.

c-successor of {p} $= \varepsilon$- closure(p)

$= \varepsilon$- closure $\delta(\{p\},c)$

$= \varepsilon$- closure(r)

$= \{p,q,r\}$.

Here, two new subsets {p,q} and {p,q,r} are generated.

Step 2: Find the transition for two new subsets.

(i) {p,q}

a-successor of {p,q} $= \varepsilon$- closure (p,q)

$= \varepsilon$- closure $\delta(\{p,q\},a)$

$= \varepsilon$- closure $\delta((p,a) \cup \delta(q,a))$

$= \varepsilon$- closure(p$\cup$ q)

$= \varepsilon$- closure(p) $\cup \varepsilon$- closure (q)

$= \{p\} \cup \{q,p\}$

$=\{p,q\}$

b-successor of {p,q} $= \varepsilon$- closure(p,q)

$= \varepsilon$- closure $\delta(\{p,q\},b)$

$= \varepsilon$- closure $\delta((p,b) \cup \delta(q,b))$

$= \varepsilon$- closure(q$\cup$ r)

$= \varepsilon$- closure(q) $\cup \varepsilon$- closure (r)

$= \{q,p\} \cup \{p,q,r\}$

$=\{p,q,r\}$.

c-successor of {p,q} $= \varepsilon$- closure(p,q)

$= \varepsilon$- closure $\delta(\{p,q\},c)$

$= \varepsilon$- closure $\delta((p,c) \cup \delta(q,c))$

$= \varepsilon\text{- closure}(r \cup \phi)$

$= \varepsilon\text{- closure}(r)$

$= \{p,q,r\}.$

(ii)$\{p,q,r\}$

a-successor of $\{p,q,r\}$ = $\varepsilon\text{- closure}(p,q,r)$

$= \varepsilon\text{- closure } \delta(\{p,q,r\},a)$

$= \varepsilon\text{- closure } \delta((p,a) \cup \delta(q,a) \cup \delta(r,a))$

$= \varepsilon\text{- closure } (p \cup q \cup r)$

$= \varepsilon\text{- closure } (p) \cup \varepsilon\text{- closure } (q) \cup \varepsilon\text{- closure}(r)$

$= \{p\} \cup \{p,q\} \cup \{p,q,r\} = \{p,q,r\}.$

b-successor of $\{p,q,r\}$ = $\varepsilon\text{- closure}(p,q,r)$

$= \varepsilon\text{- closure } \delta(\{p,q,r\},b)$

$= \varepsilon\text{- closure } \delta((p,b) \cup \delta(q,b) \cup \delta(r,b))$

$= \varepsilon\text{- closure}(q \cup r \cup \phi)$

$= \varepsilon\text{- closure}(q) \cup \varepsilon\text{- closure } (r)$

$= \{p,q\} \cup \{p,q,r\}$

$= \{p,q,r\}.$

c-successor of $\{p,q,r\}$ = $\varepsilon\text{- closure}(p,q,r)$

$= \varepsilon\text{- closure } \delta(\{p,q,r\},c)$

$= \varepsilon\text{- closure } \delta((p,c) \cup \delta(q,c) \cup \delta(r,c))$

$= \varepsilon\text{- closure}(r \cup \phi \cup p)$

$= \varepsilon\text{- closure}(r) \cup \varepsilon\text{- closure}(p)$

$= \{p,q,r\} \cup \{p\}$

$= \{p,q,r\}$

No new subsets are generated, Each subset containing r is taken as final state

Step 3: Transition Table:

State/input	a	b	c
→ {p}	{p}	{p,q}	{p,q,r}
{p,q}	{p,q}	{p,q,r}	{p,q,r}
*{p,q,r}	{p,q,r}	{p,q,r}	{p,q,r}

Step 4: The equivalent DFA

(i)

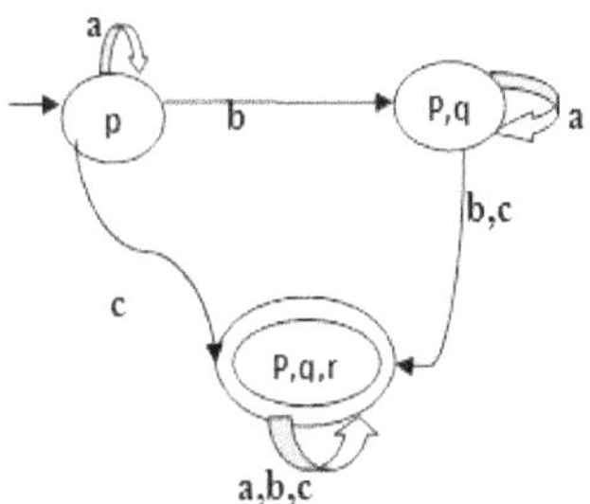

(ii)

	ε	a	b	c
→ p	{q,r}	Φ	{q}	{r}
q	Φ	{p}	{r}	{p,q}
r*	Φ	φ	Φ	Φ

(i) Compute ε-closure of each state

(ii) Convert the automata to a DFA

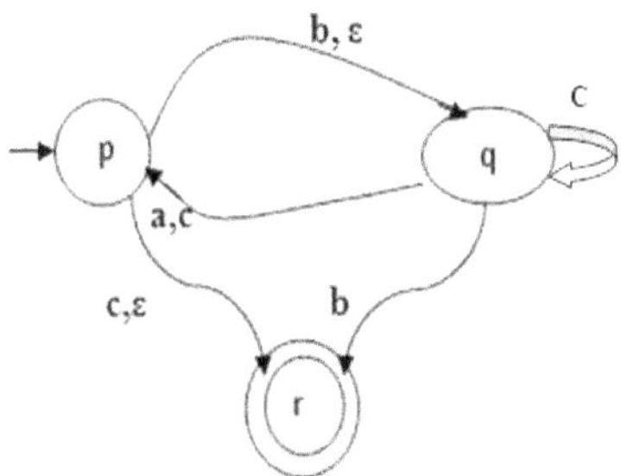

a)ε- closure of state

state	ε- closure
→ p	{p.q.r}
q	{q}
*r	{r}

Step 1: ε-closure of the initial state p is taken as first subset.

ε- closure(p) ={p,q,r}

successor of {p,q,r} is calculated as:

a-successor of {p,q,r} = ε- closure (p,q,r)

$\qquad$ = ε- closure δ({p,q,r},a)

$\qquad$ = ε- closure δ((p,a) ∪ δ(q,a) ∪ δ(r,a))

$\qquad$ = ε- closure (φ ∪ p ∪φ)

$\qquad$ = ε- closure{p}

$\qquad$ =ε-closure{p}

$\qquad$ ={p,q,r}

b-successor of {p,q,r} = ε- closure(p,q,r)

$\qquad$ = ε- closure δ({p,q,r},b)

$\qquad$ = ε- closure δ((p,b) ∪ δ(q,b) ∪ δ(r,b))

$\qquad$ = ε- closure(q∪ r ∪ φ)

$\qquad$ = ε- closure{q, r}

$\qquad$ =ε-closure{q}∪ε-closure{r}

$\qquad$ = {q} ∪{r}

$\qquad$ = {q,r}

c-successor of {p,q,r} = ε- closure (p,q,r)

$\qquad$ = ε- closure δ({p,q,r},c)

$$= \varepsilon\text{-}closure\ \delta((p,c) \cup \delta(q,c) \cup \delta(r,c))$$

$$= \varepsilon\text{-}closure(r \cup \{p, q\} \cup \phi)$$

$$= \varepsilon\text{-}closure\ \{p,q,r\}$$

$$= \varepsilon\text{-}closure\ \{p\} \cup \varepsilon\text{-}closure\ \{q\} \cup \varepsilon\text{-}closure\{r\}$$

$$= \{p,\ q,\ r\}$$

Step 2: A new state {q,r} is generated and it is successor are generated.

successor of {q,r} is calculated as:

a-successor of {q,r} $= \varepsilon\text{-}closure((q,r),a)$

$$= \varepsilon\text{-}closure\ \delta(q,a) \cup \delta(r,a)$$

$$= \varepsilon\text{-}closure(\ p \cup \phi\ )$$

$$= \varepsilon\text{-}closure\{p\}$$

$$= \{p,q,r\}$$

b-successor of {q,r} $= \varepsilon\text{-}closure((q,r),b)$

$$= \varepsilon\text{-}closure\ \delta(q,b) \cup \delta(r,b)$$

$$= \varepsilon\text{-}closure(\ r \cup \phi\ )$$

$$= \{r\}$$

c-successor of {q,r} $= \varepsilon\text{-}closure((q,r),c)$

$$= \varepsilon\text{-}closure\ \delta(q,c) \cup \delta(r,c)$$

$$= \varepsilon\text{-}closure\{p,q\} \cup \phi\ )$$

$$= \varepsilon\text{-}closure\{p\} \cup \varepsilon\text{-}closure\{q\}$$

$$= \{p,r\} \cup \{q\}$$

$$= \{p,q,r\}$$

Step 3: A new subset {r} is generated and it is successor are calculated.

a-successor of r $= \varepsilon\text{-}closure\ (r)$

$$= \varepsilon\text{-}closure\ \delta(r,a)$$

$$= \varepsilon\text{-}closure\ (\ \phi\ )$$

$$= \phi$$

b-successor of r   = ε- closure (r,b)

$$= \phi$$

c-successor of r   = ε- closure (r,c)

$$= \phi$$

Step 4: Transition table

Every subset containing r is taken as a final state

State/input	a	b	c
*{r}	φ	Φ	Φ
*{q,r}	{p,q,r}	{r}	{p,q,r}
→*{p,q,r}	{p,q,r}	{q,r}	{p,q,r}

Step 5: The equivalent DFA

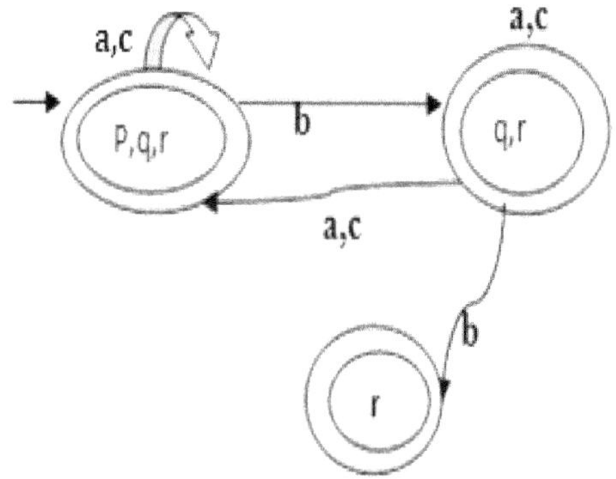

CHAPTER 3

REGULAR EXPRESSIONS AND REGULAR LANGUAGES

3.1. Regular Language

The set of strings which are accepted by finite automata called as Regular language.

Regular expression: An expression written using the set of operators and describing a regular language that is regular expression is a language defining notation. The operators are:

1. Union ($\cup$)
2. Concatenation (.)
3. Closure(*)

The regular expressions serve as an input language for many systems that process strings like 'grep' command in UNIX.

3.1.1. The Operators of Regular Expression

There are three operators which are used to represent the regular expressions.

1. Union ($\cup$)
2. Concatenation (.)
3. Closure(*)

Union

The union of two languages L&M denoted L$\cup$M, ie the set of strings that are in either L or M or both.

Let L= {001, 10,111} M= {$\in$, 001}

L$\cup$M= {$\in$, 10, 001, 111}

Concatenation

The concatenation of two languages L1 and L2 is L1.L2, which is formed by taking any string in L1 and concatenating it with any string in L2.

Closure (Star or kleene) (L*): Let L= {0,11} ,The kleene closure of language L is denoted by L*, which represents set of strings that can be formed by taking any number of string from L, possibly with repetitions [that is same string may be selected more than once.

$$L^* = \{00, 011, 11110, \in \}$$

Building Regular Expression

Basics

It consist of three parts

1. The constants $\in$ and $\emptyset$ are regular expressions, denoting the languages $\{\in\}$ and $\emptyset$
   i.e., L $(\in)$ = $\{\in\}$, L $(\emptyset)$ =$\emptyset$.
2. If **a** is any symbol, then **a** is a regular expression, denoting the language $\{a\}$
   i.e., L (a) = $\{a\}$
3. A variable (L) is a variable that is denoted by capitalized and Italic such as L.

Induction

It has four parts.

1. UNION: If E and F are regular expressions, then E+F is a regular expression denoting the union of L (E) and L (F).
   i.e., L (E+F) = L (E) $\cup$ L (F)
2. CONCATENATION: If E and F are regular expressions, then EF is a regular expression denoting the concatenation of L (E) and L (F).
   i.e., L (E.F) = L (E).L (F).
3. CLOSURE: If E is a regular expression, then E* is a regular expression
   i.e., L (E*) = (L (E))*
4. If E is a regular expression, then a parenthesis (E) is also a regular expression
   i.e., L ((E)) =L (E).

Regular Expression for Some Basic Automata are given below

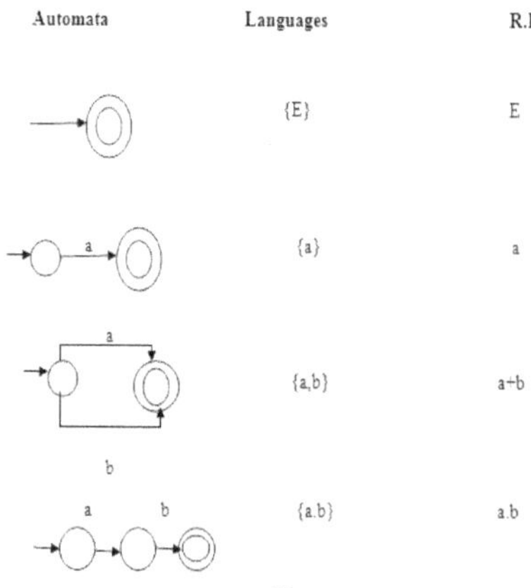

1. Write regular expression for the language accepting the strings which are starting with 1 and ending with 0 over the set $\Sigma = \{0,1\}$

   RE=1(0+1)*0

2. Write the regular expression for the following languages,

   a. The set {∈, 10, 01} =∈+10+01

   b. The set {∈, 0, 00, 000...}=0*

   c. The set {0, 00, 000...}=0+

3. The set of strings over alphabet {0,1} starting with 0.

   RE=0(0+1)*

4. Represent the following sets by RE

   (i) The set of all strings over {0,1}, which has at most two 0's.

   RE=1*001*

   (ii) The set of all strings over {a,b} beginning and ending with a.

   RE=a(a+b)*a

5. Write the regular expression for the language accepting the strings which ending with aba over the set $\Sigma = \{a, b\}$

   RE=(a+b)* aba

6. Write the regular expression for the language accepting the strings with any number of 0's followed by any number of b's followed by any number of c's over the set $\Sigma = \{a, b, c\}$

   RE= a*b*c*

7. Represent the following sets by RE

   (i).The set of {0,1} not containing 101 as substring

   RE=0*(0+1)*110*

   (ii). The set of strings of 0's and 1's with at most one pair of 3 consecutive 1's

   RE=(0+1)*111(0+1)*

3.2. Equivalence of Finite Automaton and Regular Expressions

There are three popular approaches for constructing a RE from finite automata (FA)

1) Basic method
2) State/loop elimination method
3) Arden's theorem

Finite Automata and Regular Expressions

In this section we discuss the equivalence of four different notations for regular expression.

1. NFA
2. DFA
3. E-NFA
4. RE

3.2.1. DFA to Regular Expression (Basic Method)

If L=L(A) for some DFA A, then there is a regular expression R such that L=L(R)

Proof

Let us prove the theorem by basis and $R_{ij}{}^k$ method.

i.   Basis method

(1) if k=0 there will be no intermediate node between i and j

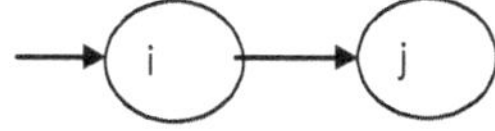

An arc from i to j

(2) an arc to that node itself

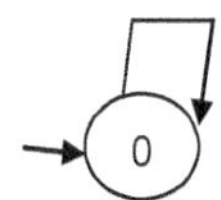

The transition may be

1. If no symbol, $R_{ij}{}^k=\emptyset$
2. If any symbol, $R_{ij}{}^k=a$
3. If many transitions, , $R_{ij}{}^k=a_1+a_2+...a_n$

Considering two nodes as i and j,

1. if i=j then $R_{ij}{}^k=\epsilon$
2. ifi≠j then $R_{ij}{}^k=\emptyset$

ii.   Induction

Suppose there is path from state i to state j that goes through no state greater than k. There are two possible cases to consider.

i) The path does not go through state k at all, then the path will be

$$R_{ij}{}^k= R_{ij}{}^{k-1} \quad (1)$$

ii) The path goes through state k atleast once, then break the path into several pieces as follows.

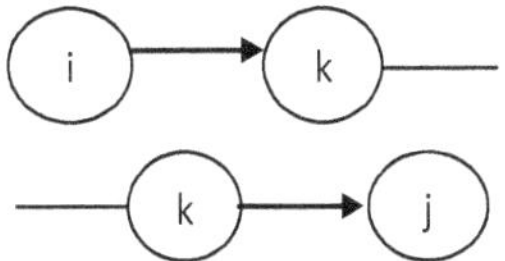

Path from i to j

$$R_{ij}^{k} \quad (1)$$

The first piece goes from state i to state k without passing through k.

The second piece goes from k to j without passing through k

The last piece goes from k to j.

The set of pieces for all paths is represented by the

$$RE = R_{ik}^{k-1}(R_{kk}^{k-1})*R_{kj}^{k-1} \quad (2)$$

When we combine the expressions for the paths of the two types above, we finally get the expression

$$R_{ij}^{k} = R_{ij}^{k-1} + R_{ik}^{k-1}(R_{kk}^{k-1})*R_{kj}^{k-1}$$

where   i-initial state

j-final state

k-number of states

we can starts with k=0 and work towards k=n ,if '1' is start state and 'n' is final state then R_{1n}^{n} gives the set of strings which are accepted by the Finite Automata.

3.2.2. Basic Formula on R.E

1. $1^*(\epsilon+1) = 1^*$
2. $(\epsilon+1) + 1^* = 1^*$
3. $0 + 1^*1 = 1^*1$
4. $0 + 01^* = 01^*$
5. $\epsilon + 00^* = 0^*$
6. $(1+0)^* = (1^*0^*)^*$
7. $\emptyset 0 = \emptyset ; \emptyset + 0 = 0$
8. $\epsilon 0 = 0, \; \epsilon^* = \epsilon$

9. $r^*(\epsilon+r)=(\epsilon+r)^*=r^*$

10. $R+\epsilon=R$

11. $rr^*=r^*r=r^*$

12. $\emptyset.\emptyset=\emptyset$

13. $\epsilon^*=\epsilon$

14. $(01)^*0=0(10)^*$

15. $(0^*1)^*0^*=(0+1)^*$

16. $\emptyset\,\epsilon=\emptyset$

17. $\emptyset+\emptyset=\emptyset$

18. $\epsilon.\epsilon=\epsilon$

19. $\epsilon.0=0$

20. $r^*r+r=r^*r$

21. $(r+\epsilon)^*=r^*$

22. $\epsilon+r^*=r^*$

23. $\emptyset.R=R.\,\emptyset=\emptyset$

24. $\emptyset.0=\emptyset$

25. $\epsilon+\epsilon=\epsilon$

26. $\emptyset+R=R$

27. $\emptyset+\epsilon=\epsilon$

28. $0+0=0$

29. $\epsilon.R=R$

30. $(R+S)+T=R+(S+T)$

31. $R+R=R$

32. $R+\varphi=\varphi+R=R$

33. $R+S=S+R$

34. $R\,\varphi=\varphi\,R=\varphi$

35. $R.\epsilon=\epsilon.R=R$

36. $(RS)T=R(ST)$

37. $R(S+T)=RS+RT$

38. $(S+T)R=SR+TR$

39. $\varphi^*=\epsilon^*=\epsilon$

40. $R^*.R^*=R^*=(R^*)^*$

41. $R.R^*=R^*R=R^*=\epsilon+RR^*$

42. $(R+S)^*=(R^*S^*)^*=(R^*+S^*)^*$

43. $(RS)^* = (R^*S^*)^* = (R^*+S^*)^*$

44. $(\epsilon + R)(\epsilon + R)^* = R^*$

45. $(\epsilon + R)R^* = R^*$

46. $0 + 01^* = 01^*$

47. $(\epsilon + 1)^* = 1^*$

48. $\epsilon + 00^* = 0^*$

49. $(01)^*0 = 0(10)^*$

50. $\epsilon . R = R$

51. $\epsilon . 0 = 0$

52. $\varphi + (\epsilon + 1) = \epsilon + 1$

1. Construct the RE for the finite automata given below

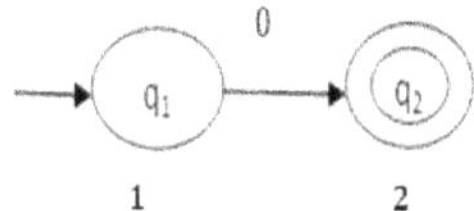

The regular expression for the given DFA is given by

Here

$$R_{ij}{}^k = R_{ij}{}^{k-1} + R_{ik}{}^{k-1}(R_{kk}{}^{k-1})^* R_{kj}{}^{k-1}$$

i-initial state, j-final state, k-> no of states

i=1,j=2,k=2

we know that, we will get the answer in $R_{12}{}^2 = R_{12}{}^1 + (R_{12}{}^1)(R_{22}{}^1)^*(R_{22}{}^1)$

Compute when k=0

$R_{11}{}^0 = \emptyset + \epsilon$

$R_{12}{}^0 = 0$

$R_{21}{}^0 = \emptyset$

$R_{22}{}^0 = \emptyset + \epsilon$

When k=1

$R_{11}{}^1 = R_{11}{}^0 + R_{11}{}^0 (R_{11}{}^0)^* (R_{11}{}^0)$

$\quad = \emptyset + \epsilon + \emptyset + \epsilon (\emptyset + \epsilon)^* (\emptyset + \epsilon)$

$\quad = \emptyset$

$R_{12}{}^1 = R_{12}{}^0 + R_{11}{}^0 (R_{11}{}^0)^* (R_{12}{}^0)$

$= 0 + \emptyset + \in (\emptyset + \in)^* 0$

$= 0 + \emptyset$

$= 0$

Regular expression is 0.

2. Convert the given DFA to regular expression

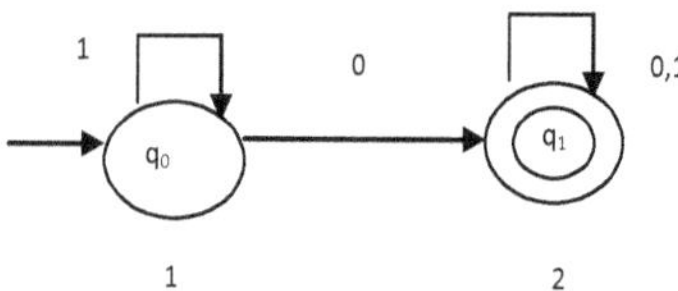

The regular expression for the given DFA is given by K=2,i=1,j=2,we will get the answer in,

$R_{12}{}^2 = R_{12}{}^1 + R_{12}{}^1 (R_{22}{}^1)^* R_{22}{}^1$

Compute when K=0

$R_{11}{}^0 = \in + 1$

$R_{12}{}^0 = 0$

$R_{21}{}^0 = \emptyset$

$R_{22}{}^0 = \in + (0+1)$

When K=1

$R_{12}{}^1 = R_{12}{}^0 + R_{11}{}^0 (R_{11}{}^0)^* (R_{12}{}^0)$

$= 0 + \in + 1 (\in + 1)^* (0)$

$= 0 + (\in + 1) \, 1^* (0)$

$= 0 + 1^* . 0$

$= 0 1^*$

$R_{22}{}^1 = R_{22}{}^0 + R_{21}{}^0 (R_{11}{}^0)^* (R_{12}{}^0)$

$= (0 + 1) + \emptyset . (\in + 1)^* . 0 + \in$

$= (0 + 1) + \emptyset . 0 + \in$

$= 0 + 1 + \in$

$= \in + 0 + 1$

Solution

$$R_{12}{}^2 = R_{12}{}^1 + R_{12}{}^1 (R_{12}{}^1)^* (R_{22}{}^1)$$

$$= 01^* + 01^*(\epsilon + 0 + 1)^* (\epsilon + 0 + 1)$$

$$= 01^* + 01^*(0 + 1)^* (\epsilon + 0 + 1)$$

$$= 01^* + 01^*(0 + 1)^*$$

$$= 01^*(0 + 1)^*$$

3. Convert the given DFA to regular expression

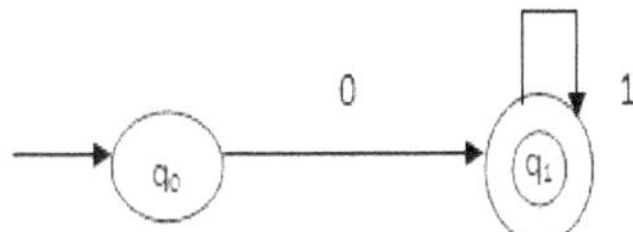

K=2,j=2,i=1

We will get the answer in,

$$R_{12}{}^2 = R_{12}{}^1 + R_{12}{}^1 (R_{22}{}^1)^* R_{22}{}^1$$

Compute when k=0

$$R_{11}{}^0 = \emptyset + \epsilon$$

$$R_{12}{}^0 = 0$$

$$R_{21}{}^0 = \emptyset$$

$$R_{22}{}^0 = \epsilon + 1$$

K=1:

$$R_{11}{}^1 = R_{11}{}^0 + R_{11}{}^0 (R_{11}{}^0)^* (R_{11}{}^0)$$

$$= \epsilon + \epsilon\, (\epsilon)^* (\epsilon)$$

$$= \epsilon + \epsilon.\epsilon.\,\epsilon$$

$$= \epsilon.\,\epsilon$$

$$= \epsilon + \epsilon$$

$$= \epsilon$$

When k=1

$$R_{12}{}^1 = R_{12}{}^0 + R_{11}{}^0 (R_{11}{}^0)^* (R_{12}{}^0)$$

$$=0+\epsilon\,(\epsilon)^*\,(0)$$

$$=0+\epsilon.\,\epsilon\,.0$$

$$=0+\epsilon\,.0$$

$$=0+0$$

$$=0$$

$$R_{21}{}^1= R_{21}{}^0 +R_{21}{}^0\,(R_{11}{}^0)^*\,(R_{11}{}^0)$$

$$=\emptyset + \emptyset\,(\epsilon)^*\epsilon$$

$$=\emptyset + \emptyset.\epsilon.\epsilon$$

$$=\emptyset + \emptyset.\epsilon$$

$$=\emptyset+\emptyset$$

$$=\emptyset$$

$$R_{22}{}^1= R_{22}{}^0 +R_{21}{}^0\,(R_{11}{}^0)^*\,(R_{12}{}^0)$$

$$=(\epsilon +1) + \emptyset(\epsilon)^*\,(0)$$

$$=(\epsilon +1) + \emptyset.\epsilon.\,\emptyset$$

$$=(\epsilon +1)\emptyset.0$$

$$=(\epsilon +1)\emptyset$$

$$=\epsilon+1$$

Solution

$$R_{12}{}^2=0+0(\epsilon+1)^*\,(\epsilon+1)$$

$$=0+(0)(1)^*\,(\epsilon+1)$$

$$=0+0.1^*$$

$$=01^*$$

4. Convert the given DFA to regular expression

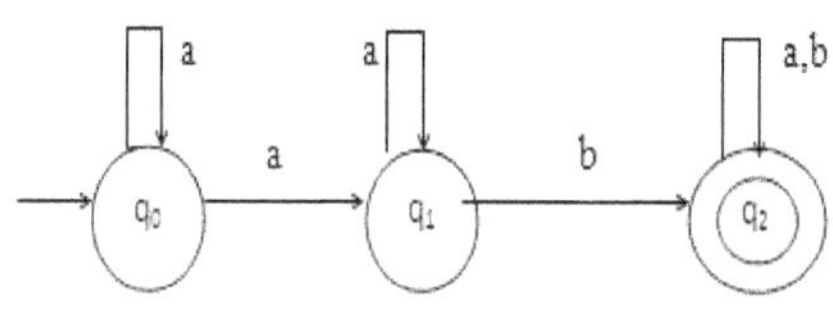

k=3,i=1,j=3

$R_{13}{}^2 = R_{13}{}^2 + R_{13}{}^2 (R_{33}{}^2)^* R_{33}{}^2$

Compute when K=0:

$R_{11}{}^0 = \epsilon + a$ $\qquad R_{12}{}^0 = \emptyset$ $\qquad R_{13}{}^0 = \emptyset$

$R_{21}{}^0 = \emptyset$ $\qquad R_{22}{}^0 = \epsilon + a$ $\qquad R_{23}{}^0 = \emptyset$

$R_{31}{}^0 = \emptyset$ $\qquad R_{32}{}^0 = b$ $\qquad R_{33}{}^0 = \epsilon + (a+b)$

K=1:

$R_{11}{}^1 = R_{11}{}^0 + R_{11}{}^0 (R_{11}{}^0)^* R_{11}{}^0$

$\qquad = (\epsilon + a) + (\epsilon + a)(\epsilon + a)^*(\epsilon + a)$

$\qquad = (\epsilon + a) + (\epsilon + a)a^*(\epsilon + a)$

$\qquad = (\epsilon + a) + (\epsilon + a)a^*$

$\qquad = (\epsilon + a) + a^*$

$\qquad = a^*$

$R_{12}{}^1 = R_{12}{}^0 + R_{11}{}^0 (R_{11}{}^0)^* R_{12}{}^0$

$\qquad = a + (\epsilon + a)(\epsilon + a)^*.a$

$\qquad = a + (\epsilon + a)a^*.a$

$\qquad = a + a^*.a$

$\qquad = a^*a$

$R_{13}{}^1 = R_{13}{}^0 + R_{11}{}^0 (R_{11}{}^0)^* R_{13}{}^0$

$\qquad = \emptyset + (\epsilon + a)(\epsilon + a)^* \emptyset$

$\qquad = \emptyset + (\epsilon + a)a^* . \emptyset$

$\qquad = \emptyset + a^* . \emptyset$

$\qquad = \emptyset + \emptyset$

$\qquad = \emptyset$

$R_{21}{}^1 = R_{21}{}^0 + R_{21}{}^0 (R_{11}{}^0)^* R_{12}{}^0$

$\qquad = \emptyset + \emptyset(\epsilon + a)^*(a + \epsilon)$

$\qquad = \emptyset + \emptyset.a^*(a + \epsilon)$

$\qquad = \emptyset + a^*.\emptyset$

$$=\emptyset+\emptyset$$

$$=\emptyset$$

$$R_{22}{}^1 = R_{22}{}^0 + R_{21}{}^0(R_{11}{}^0)^* R_{12}{}^0$$

$$=(a+\epsilon)+\emptyset(\,a+\epsilon)^*a$$

$$=(a+\epsilon)+\emptyset.a^*.a$$

$$=(a+\epsilon)+\emptyset.a$$

$$=(a+\epsilon)+\emptyset$$

$$=(a+\epsilon)$$

$$R_{23}{}^1 = R_{23}{}^0 + R_{21}{}^0(R_{11}{}^0)^* R_{13}{}^0$$

$$=b+\emptyset(\,a+\epsilon)^*.\emptyset$$

$$= b+\emptyset.\,a^*.\emptyset$$

$$= b+\emptyset.\,\emptyset$$

$$=b+\phi$$

$$=b$$

$$R_{31}{}^1 = R_{31}{}^0 + R_{31}{}^0(R_{11}{}^0)^*.R_{11}{}^0$$

$$=\phi+\phi(a+\epsilon)^*.(a+\epsilon)$$

$$=\phi+\phi.a^*(a+\epsilon)$$

$$=\phi+\phi.a^*$$

$$=\phi+\phi$$

$$=\phi$$

$$R_{32}{}^1 = R_{32}{}^0 + R_{31}{}^0(R_{11}{}^0)^*.R_{12}{}^0$$

$$=\phi+\phi(a+\epsilon)^*.a$$

$$=\phi+\phi.a^*a$$

$$=\phi+\phi.a$$

$$=\phi+\phi$$

$$=\phi$$

$$R_{33}{}^1 = R_{33}{}^0 + R_{31}{}^0(R_{11}{}^0)^*.R_{13}$$

$$=\epsilon+(a+b)+\phi(a+\epsilon)^*.\phi$$

$$=\epsilon+(a+b)+\phi.a^*\phi$$

$$=\epsilon+(a+b)+\phi.\phi$$

$$=\epsilon+(a+b)+\phi$$

$$=\epsilon+(a+b)$$

$$=a+b$$

Compute when K=2

$$R_{11}^2=R_{11}^1+R_{12}^1(R_{22}^1)^*.(R_{21}^1)$$

$$=a^*+a^*.a(a+\epsilon)^*(\phi)$$

$$=a^*+a^*.a.a^*\phi$$

$$=a^*+a^*.a.\phi$$

$$=a^*+a^*.\phi$$

$$=a^*+\phi=a^*$$

$$R_{12}^2=R_{12}^1+R_{12}^1(R_{22}^1)^*.(R_{22}^1)$$

$$=a^*a+a^*a(\epsilon+a)^*(\epsilon+a)$$

$$=a^*a+a^*a\ .a^*(\epsilon+a)$$

$$=a^*a+a^*a.a^*$$

$$R_{13}^2=R_{13}^1+R_{12}^1(R_{22}^1)^*.(R_{23}^1)$$

$$=\phi+a^*a(\epsilon+a)^*(b)$$

$$=\phi+a^*.a\ a^*b$$

$$=a^*a\ a^*b$$

$$R_{21}^2=R_{21}^1+R_{22}^1(R_{22}^1)^*.(R_{21}^1)$$

$$=\phi+(\epsilon+a)(\epsilon+a)^*(\phi)$$

$$=\phi+(\epsilon+a)(a^*)\phi$$

$$=\phi+a^*.\phi$$

$$=\phi+\phi$$

$$=\phi$$

$R_{22}{}^2 = R_{22}{}^1 + R_{22}{}^1 (R_{22}{}^1)^* . (R_{22}{}^1)$

$\quad = (\epsilon + a) + (\epsilon + a)(\epsilon + a)^* (\epsilon + a)$

$\quad = (\epsilon + a) + (\epsilon + a) a^* (\epsilon + a)$

$\quad = (\epsilon + a) + a^* (\epsilon + a)$

$\quad = (\epsilon + a) + a^*$

$\quad = a + a^*$

$R_{23}{}^2 = R_{23}{}^1 + R_{22}{}^1 (R_{22}{}^1)^* . (R_{23}{}^1)$

$\quad = b + (\epsilon + a)(\epsilon + a)^* b$

$\quad = b + (\epsilon + a) a^* . b$

$\quad = b + a^* b$

$R_{31}{}^2 = R_{31}{}^1 + R_{32}{}^1 (R_{22}{}^1)^* . (R_{21}{}^1)$

$\quad = \phi + \phi (\epsilon + a)^* \phi$

$\quad = \phi + \phi . a^* . \phi$

$\quad = \phi + \phi . \phi$

$\quad = \phi + \phi$

$\quad = \phi$

$R_{32}{}^2 = R_{32}{}^1 + R_{32}{}^1 (R_{22}{}^1)^* . (R_{22}{}^1)$

$\quad = \phi + \phi (\epsilon + a)^* (\epsilon + a)$

$\quad = \phi + \phi . a^* . (\epsilon + a)$

$\quad = \phi + \phi . a^*$

$\quad = \phi + \phi$

$\quad = \phi$

$R_{33}{}^2 = R_{33}{}^1 + R_{32}{}^1 (R_{22}{}^1)^* . (R_{23}{}^1)$

$\quad = (a + b) + \phi (\epsilon + a)^* (b)$

$\quad = (a + b) + \phi . a^* . b$

$\quad = (a + b) + \phi . b$

$\quad = (a + b) + \phi$

$$=(a+b)$$

$$R_{13}{}^3=R_{13}{}^2+R_{13}{}^2(R_{33}{}^2)^*.(R_{33}{}^2)$$

$$=a^*a\ a^*b+a^*a\ a^*b(a+b)^*(a+b)$$

$$=a^*a\ a^*b\ +a^*a\ a^*b(a+b)^*\quad[R+RR''=RR'']$$

$$=a^*a\ a^*b(a+b)^*$$

5. Convert the given DFA to regular expression

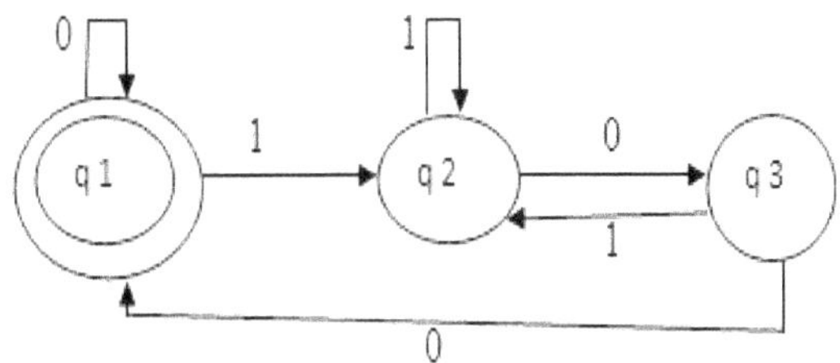

K=3,i=1,j=1

The regular expression for the given DFA is given by

$$R_{11}{}^3\qquad=R_{11}{}^2+R_{13}{}^2(R_{33}{}^2)^*.(R_{31}{}^2)$$

Compute when K=0

$$R_{11}{}^1=\epsilon+0\quad R_{21}{}^0=\phi\qquad\qquad R_{31}{}^0=0$$

$$R_{12}{}^0=1\quad\ R_{22}{}^0=\epsilon+1\qquad R_{32}{}^0=1$$

$$R_{13}{}^0=\phi\quad\ R_{23}{}^0=0\qquad\qquad R_{33}{}^0=\epsilon$$

When   k=1

$$R_{11}{}^1=R_{11}{}^0+R_{11}{}^0(R_{11}{}^0)^*.(R_{11}{}^0)$$

$$=(\epsilon+0)+\ (\epsilon+0)\ (\epsilon+0)^*\ (\epsilon+0)$$

$$=(\epsilon+0)+(\epsilon+0)0^*(\epsilon+0)$$

$$=(\epsilon+0)+\ (\epsilon+0)0^*$$

$$=(\epsilon+0)+0^*$$

$$R_{12}{}^1=R_{12}{}^0+R_{11}{}^0(R_{11}{}^0)^*.(R_{12}{}^0)$$

$$=1+(\epsilon+0)\ (\epsilon+0)^*1$$

$$=1+(\epsilon+0)0^*1$$

$$=1+0^*.1$$

$$=0^*1$$

$$R_{13}{}^1=R_{13}{}^0+R_{11}{}^0(R_{11}{}^0)^*.(R_{13}{}^0)$$

$$=\phi+(\epsilon+0)(\epsilon+0)^*\phi$$

$$=\phi+(\epsilon+0)0^*.\phi$$

$$=\phi+0^*.\phi$$

$$=\phi+\phi$$

$$=\phi$$

$$R_{21}{}^1=R_{21}{}^0+R_{21}{}^0(R_{11}{}^0)^*.(R_{11}{}^0)$$

$$=\phi+\phi(\epsilon+0)^*(\epsilon+0)$$

$$=\phi+\phi\ 0^*(\epsilon+0)$$

$$=\phi+\phi\ 0^*$$

$$=\phi+\phi$$

$$=\phi$$

$$R_{22}{}^1=R_{22}{}^0+R_{21}{}^0(R_{11}{}^0)^*.(R_{12}{}^0)$$

$$=(\epsilon+1)+\phi(\epsilon+0)^*1$$

$$=(\epsilon+1)+\phi.0^*1$$

$$=(\epsilon+1)+\phi.1$$

$$=(\epsilon+1)+\phi$$

$$=(\epsilon+1)$$

$$R_{23}{}^1=R_{23}{}^0+R_{21}{}^0(R_{11}{}^0)^*.(R_{13}{}^0)$$

$$=0+\phi(\epsilon+0)^*\phi$$

$$=0+\phi.0^*.\phi$$

$$=0+\phi.\phi$$

$$=0+\phi$$

$$=0$$

$R_{31}{}^1 = R_{31}{}^0 + R_{31}{}^0 (R_{11}{}^0)^* . (R_{11}{}^0)$

$\qquad = 0 + 0(\epsilon+0)^*(\epsilon+0)$

$\qquad = 0 + 0(0^*)(\epsilon+0)$

$\qquad = 0 + 0.0^*$

$\qquad = 0.0^*$

$\qquad = 0$

$R_{32}{}^1 = R_{32}{}^0 + R_{31}{}^0 (R_{11}{}^0)^* . (R_{12}{}^0)$

$\qquad = 1 + 0(\epsilon+0)^* 1$

$\qquad = 1 + 0\ 0^* . 1$

$R_{33}{}^1 = R_{33}{}^0 + R_{31}{}^0 (R_{11}{}^0)^* . (R_{13}{}^0)$

$\qquad = \epsilon + 0(\epsilon+0)^* \phi$

$\qquad = \epsilon + 0.0^* . \phi$

$\qquad = \epsilon + 0.\phi$

$\qquad = \epsilon + \phi$

$\qquad = \epsilon$

When k=2

$\qquad R_{11}{}^2 = R_{11}{}^1 + R_{12}{}^1 (R_{22}{}^1)^* . (R_{21}{}^1)$

$\qquad\qquad = 0^* + 0^* . 1(\epsilon+1)^* \phi$

$\qquad\qquad = 0^* + 0^* . 1 . 1^* . \phi$

$\qquad\qquad = 0^* + 0^* 1 . \phi$

$\qquad\qquad = 0^* + 0^* . \phi$

$\qquad\qquad = 0^* + \phi$

$\qquad\qquad = 0^*$

$\qquad R_{12}{}^2 = R_{12}{}^1 + R_{12}{}^1 (R_{22}{}^1)^* . (R_{22}{}^1)$

$\qquad\qquad = 0^* . 1 + 0^* . 1(\epsilon+1)^*(\epsilon+1)$

$\qquad\qquad = 0^* . 1 + 0\ ^* . 1.\ 1^*(\epsilon+1)$

$\qquad\qquad = 0^* . 1 + 0^* 1.1^*$

$R_{13}{}^2 = R_{13}{}^1 + R_{12}{}^1 (R_{22}{}^1)^* . (R_{23}{}^1)$

$\quad = \phi + 0^* . 1 (\epsilon + 1)^* 0$

$\quad = \phi + 0^* . 1\ 1^* 0$

$\quad = 0^* . 1\ . 1^* . 0$

$R_{21}{}^2 = R_{21}{}^1 + R_{22}{}^1 (R_{22}{}^1)^* . (R_{21}{}^1)$

$\quad = \phi + (\epsilon + 1)(\epsilon + 1)^* \phi$

$\quad = \phi + (\epsilon + 1) . 1^* . \phi$

$\quad = \phi + 1^* . \phi$

$\quad = \phi + \phi$

$\quad = \phi$

$R_{22}{}^2 = R_{22}{}^1 + R_{22}{}^1 (R_{22}{}^1)^* . (R_{22}{}^1)$

$\quad = (\epsilon + 1) + (\epsilon + 1)(\epsilon + 1)^* (\epsilon + 1)$

$\quad = (\epsilon + 1) + (\epsilon + 1) 1^* (\epsilon + 1)$

$\quad = (\epsilon + 1) + (\epsilon + 1) 1^*$

$\quad = (\epsilon + 1) + 1^*$

$\quad = 1^*$

$R_{23}{}^2 = R_{23}{}^1 + R_{22}{}^1 (R_{22}{}^1)^* . (R_{23}{}^1)$

$\quad = 0 + (\epsilon + 1)(\epsilon + 1)^* 0$

$\quad = 0 + (\epsilon + 1) 1^* 0$

$\quad = 0 + 1^* . 0$

$\quad = 0 1^*$

$R_{31}{}^2 = R_{31}{}^1 + R_{32}{}^1 (R_{22}{}^1)^* . (R_{22}{}^1)$

$\quad = 0 . 0^* + 1 + 00^* 1 (\epsilon + 1)^* \phi$

$\quad = 00^* + (1 + 00^* 1) . 1^* . \phi$

$\quad = 00^* + (1 + 00^* 1) . \phi$

$\quad = 00^* + \phi = 00^*$

$R_{32}{}^2 = R_{32}{}^1 + R_{32}{}^1 (R_{22}{}^1)^*.(R_{22}{}^1)$

$\qquad = (1+00^*1)+(1+00^*1)(1+\varepsilon)^*(\varepsilon+1)$

$\qquad = (1+00^*1)+(1+00^*1)1^*.(\varepsilon+1)$

$\qquad = (1+00^*1)+(1+00^*1).1^*$

$R_{33}{}^2 = R_{33}{}^1 + R_{32}{}^1 (R_{22}{}^1)^*.(R_{23}{}^1)$

$\qquad = \varepsilon+(1+00^*1)(\varepsilon+1)^*(0)$

$\qquad = \varepsilon+(1+00^*1)1^*.0$

$\qquad = (1+00^*1)1^*.0$

$R_{11}{}^3 = R_{11}{}^2 + R_{13}{}^2 (R_{33}{}^2)^*.(R_{31}{}^2)$

$\qquad = 0^*+0^*11^*.0((1+00^*1).1^*0)^*(00^*)$

Dead State

All the non-final states which transit to itself for all input symbols in Σ.

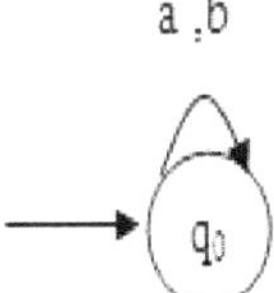

3.2.3. Regular Expression using State Elimination

1. It is used to avoid number of intermediate or looping states.
2. Eliminate the states except start and accept state.

Ex:

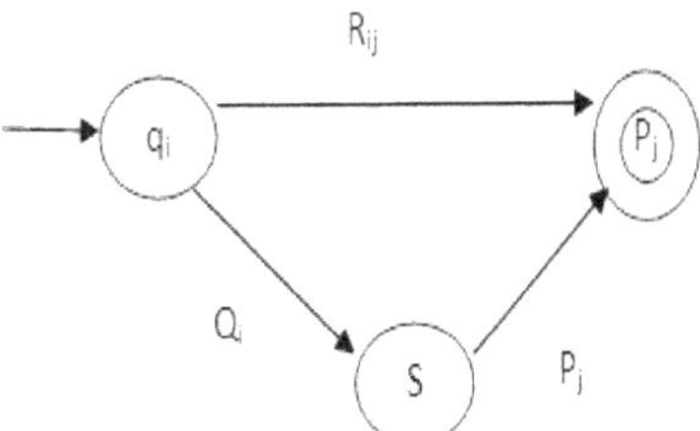

Consider the above diagram in which the state is to be eliminated. Let us take the RE as $R_{ij}+Q_i S^* P_j$ which is to be labelled to arc Q_i to P_j.

3.2.3.1. Steps for Constructing a RE from a Finite Automaton

1. For each accepting state q, eliminate all states except q and start state q_0 by applying the induction process to produce an equivalent automaton with RE labels on the arcs.

2. If $q \neq q_0$, i.e accepting state and start state are distinct, then we have a two state automaton as given diagram.

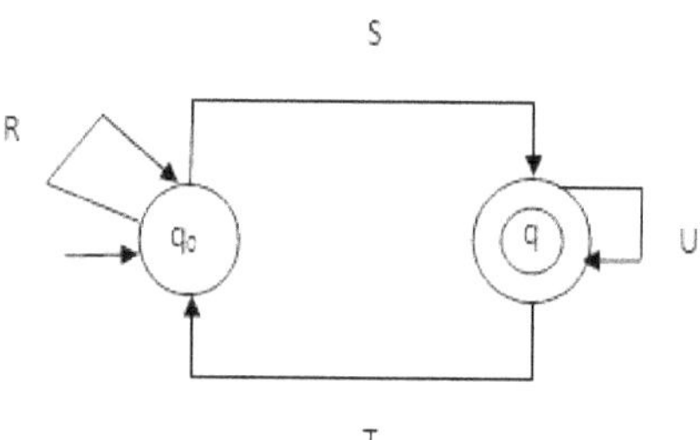

Two state automaton

RE=(R+SU*T)*SU*

3. If the start state and the accept state are same, then we are left with one state automaton as given diagram.

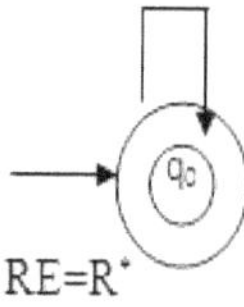

RE=R*

4. The required regular expression is the sum of all expression from the reduced automaton for each accepting state

Ex 1: Reduce the given automata

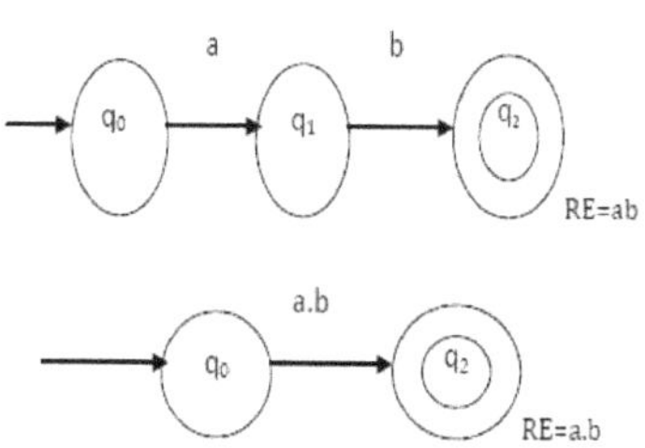

Ex 2:

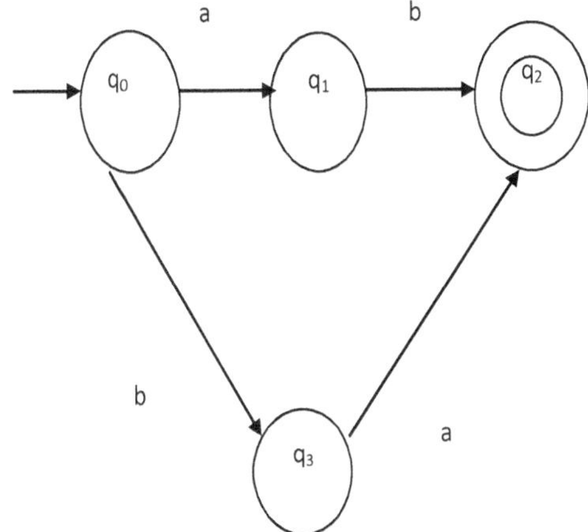

Eliminate q₁:

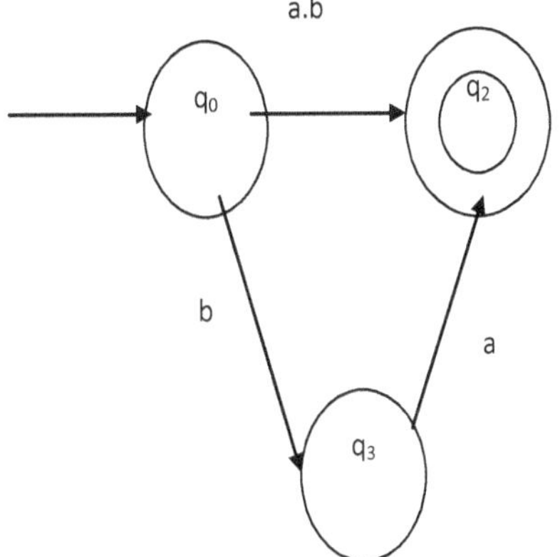

Eliminate q₃:

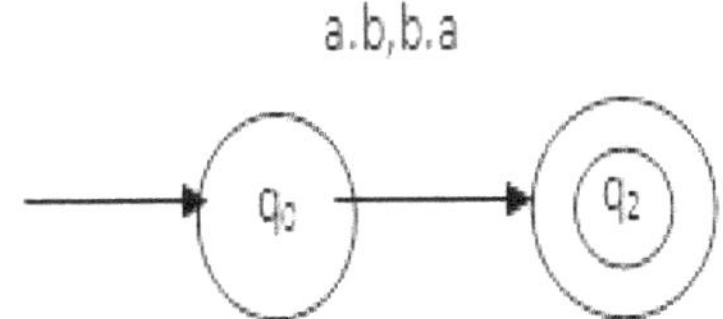

1. Construct the transition diagram and RE for the given DFA using state elimination method

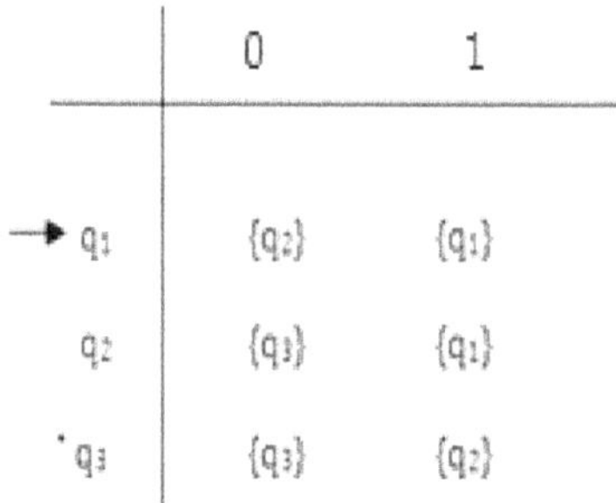

First eliminate state q_2 and find the RE by using the formula

$$R_{ij}+q_iS^*P_j$$

Where $R_{ij}=\emptyset$ [there is no direct link between start and final state]

For q_1 to q_3, $q_i=0$

S=∈ [transition is processed through q_2 but there is no self transition]

$P_j=0$

Then

$RE_1=\emptyset+0.∈^*.0$

=$\emptyset+0.∈.0$

=$\emptyset+0.0$

=00

For q_3 to q_1:

$R_{ij}=\emptyset$

$q_i=1$

S=∈

$P_j=1$

$RE_2=R_2=\emptyset+1.∈^*.1$

=$\emptyset+1.1$

=11

Considering two paths q1-q2-q1 and q3-q2-q3 we get,

q1-q2-q1=1+01

q3-q2-q3=0+10

The reduced automata is

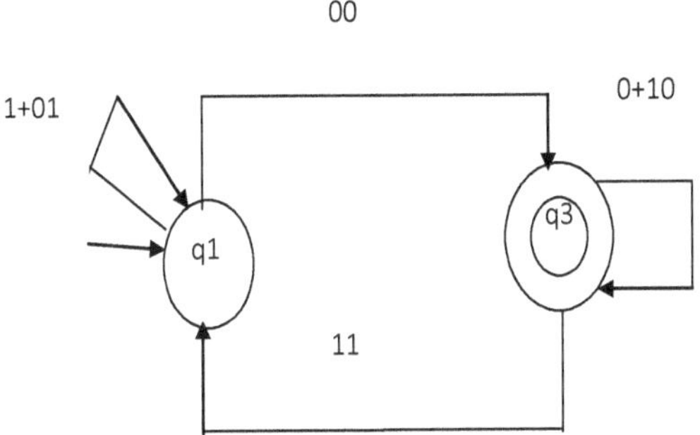

It is again like a two state automaton where the RE is given by

RE=(R+SU*T)*SU*

R=1+0.1,S=00,U=(0+10)*,T=11

The required RE is

RE=((1+01)+00(0+10)*11)* 00(0+10)*

2. Convert the following NFA into a RE

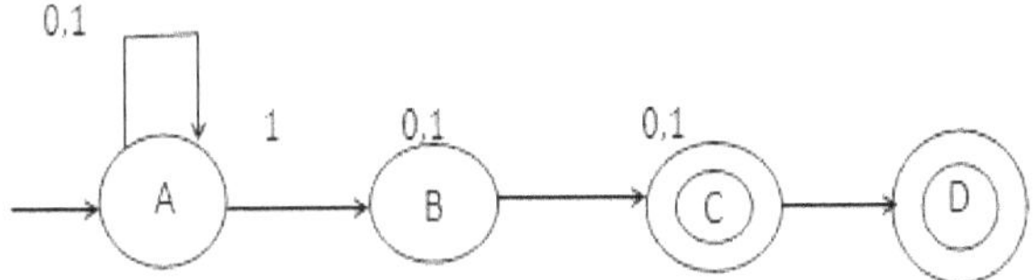

Step 1: B is the intermediate state. It should be eliminated

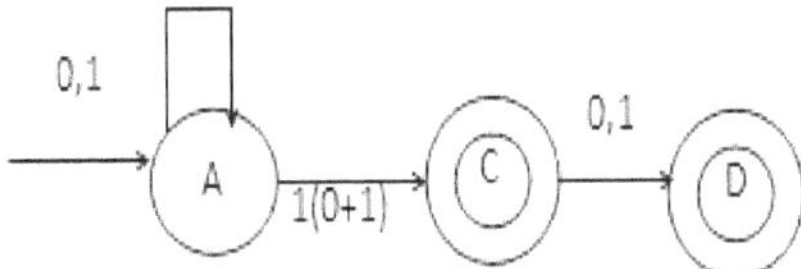

Step 2: C is the intermediate state, it should be eliminated

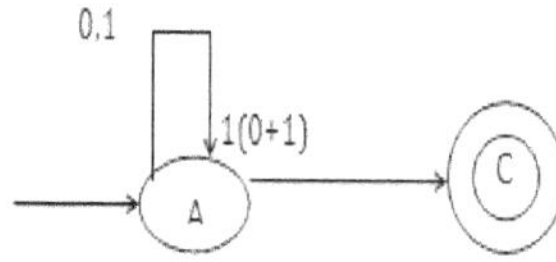

RE1=(0+1)*1(0+1)(0+1)

Consider D is to be eliminated

RE2=(0+1)*1(0+1)

RE=RE1+RE2

RE=(0+1)*1(0+1)(0+1)+ (0+1)*1(0+1)

3.2.4. Arden's Theorem

Use of Theorem:

1. For checking the equivalence of two regular expression
2. Conversion of DFA to regular expression

Theorem

Let   P   and Q be two regular expression over the input set Σ. The Regular expression R is given as R=Q+R.P which is equivalent to R=QP*

1. Find out the Regular expression from the given DFA using Arden's Theorem:

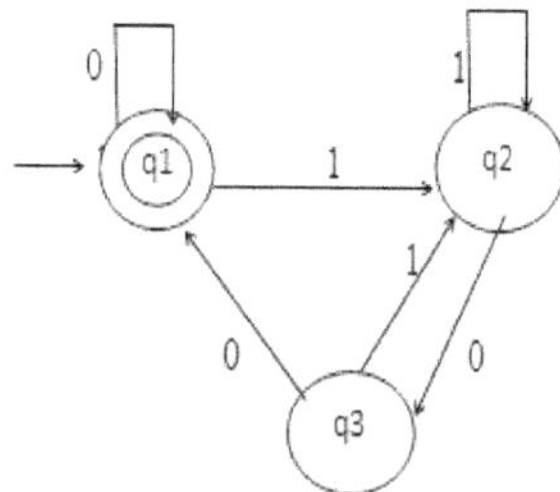

Let us solve DFA by writing the regular expression for each state (ϵ should be added only in initial state)

q 1=q1.0+q3.0+ε

q2=q1.1+q2.1+q3.1

q3=q2.0

For getting the RE, we have to solve final state q1, before that solve q3

q2=q1.1+q2.1+q2 0.1

q2=q1+q2(1+01)

Compare to ARDEN'S Theorem [R=RP+Q]

R=q2,Q=q1 1,P=(1+01)

Which is equal to R=QP*

q2=q1 1(1+01)*

Substitute this value to q1

q1=q1.0+q3.0+ε

q1=q1.0+q2.00+ε

q1=q1.0+q1.1(1+01)*00+ε

q1=q1(0+1(1+01)*00)+ε

Compare ARDEN'S theorem

R=q1 Q=ε P=(0+1(1+01)*00)

R=QP*

q1=ε.(0+1(1+01)*00)*

q1=(0+1(1+01)*00)*

The required RE is (0+1(1+01)*00)

2. Construct the regular expression for the given DFA

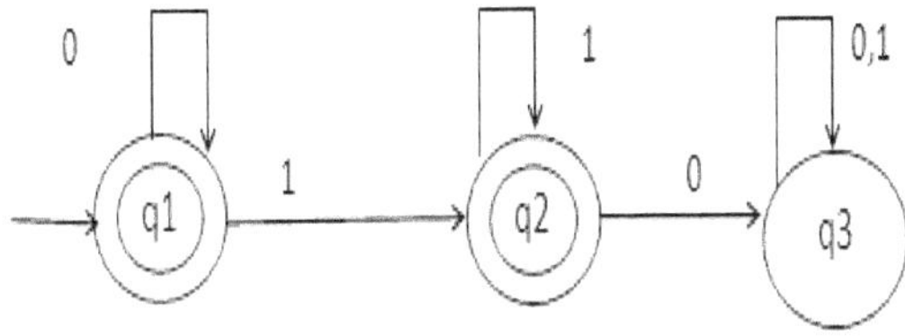

Let us built RE for each state,

q 1=q1.0+ε

q2=q1.1+q2.1

q3=q2.0+q3(0+1)

Here the final states are q1&q2.So we need to solve q1&q2

Let to solve q1: q1=q1.0+ε

compare to Arden's theorem

R=q1 ,Q=ε ,p=0

q 1=ε.0*

q1=0*

Let to solve q2:q2=q1.1+q2.1

q2=0*1+q2.1

Compare to Arden's theorem

R=q2, Q=0*1   P=1

q 2=0*1(1*)

The final result is given:

RE=q1+q2

=0*+0*11*

=0*+0*11*

The Required RE is 0* +0*11*

3. Construct the regular expression for the given DFA

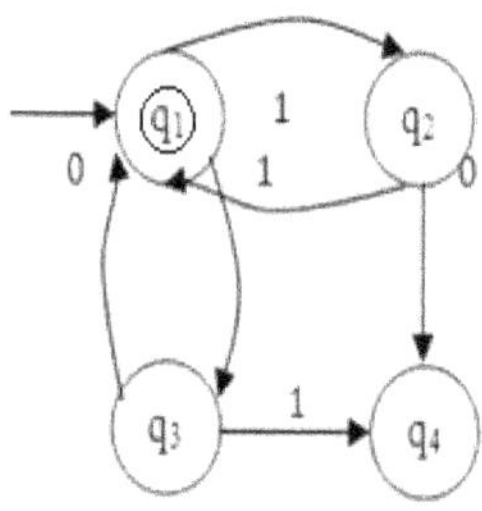

Let us solve DFA by writing the RE for each state.

$q_1 = q_2.1 + q_3.0 + \varepsilon$

$q_2 = q_1.0$

$q_3 = q_1.1$

$q_4 = q_2.0 + q_3.1 + q_4(0+1)$

$q_1 = (q_1 1)0 + (q_1 0)1 + \varepsilon$

$q_1 = q_1 10 + q_1 01 + \varepsilon$

$q_1 = q_1(10 + 01) + \varepsilon$

$R = Q + RP$

$R = q, Q = \varepsilon, P = (10+01)$

$R = QP^*$

$q_1 = \varepsilon(10+01)^*$

$q_1 = (10+01)^*$

4. Construct the regular expression for the given DFA

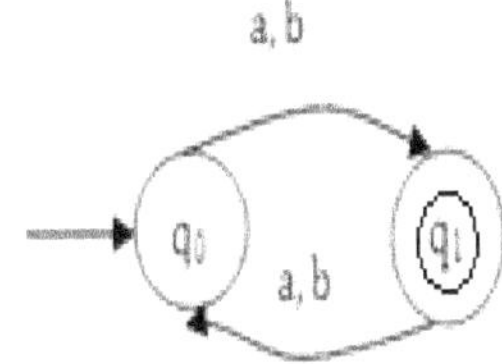

Let us solve DFA by writing the RE for each state.

$q_0 = q_1(a+b) + \varepsilon$

$q_0 = (a+b)^*$

$q_1 = q_0(a+b)$

$q_1 = q_0(a+b)$

Substitute q_0

$= ((a+b)(a+b))^*$

3.3.   Finite Automata and Regular Expression

3.3.1. *Conversion of RE to Finite Automata*

Every language defined by a regular expression is also defined by finite automation.

Proof

Suppose L= L(R) for a regular expression R. We show that L = L(E) for some ε -NFA E with

1. Exactly one accepting state
2. No arcs into the initial state.
3. No arcs out of the accepting state.

Basis

There are three parts, in part (i) only path form 1st start state to an accepting state is labeled ε.

	FA	Language	R.E
1.	ε	$\{\varepsilon\}$	ε
2.		ϕ	ϕ
3.	a	$\{a\}$	a

In part (ii) there is no path form start state to accepting state, the language of this automaton is ϕ

Induction: in part (iii) It consist of single input symbol.

1. **Union (+)**

The union of two R.E R_1 and R_2 is $R_1 + R_2$.

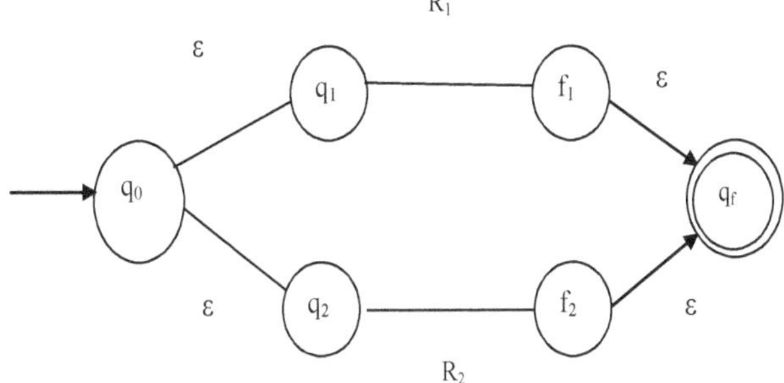

The above diagram shows that, any path of N from q_0 to q_f must begin by either going to q_1 or q_2 on ϵ.

- If a path goes to q_1, then follow any path in R_1 to f_1 and then goes to q_f on ϵ.
- If a path goes to q_2, the follow any path in R_2 to f_2 and then goes to q_f on ϵ.

$$\text{Thus, } L(R) = L(R_1) \cup L(R_2)$$

2. Concatenation (.)

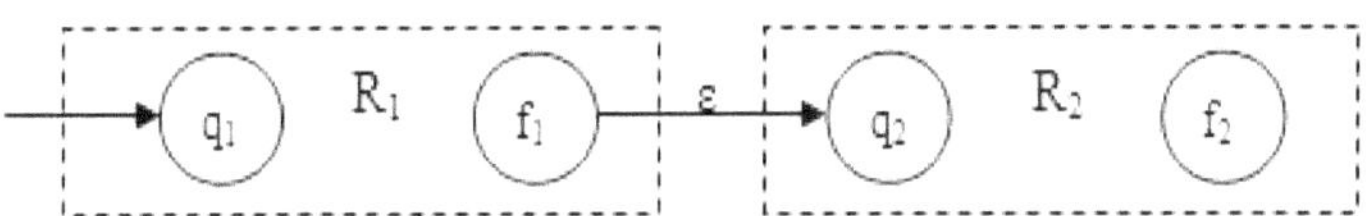

The concatenation of two RE R_1 and R_2 is $R_1.R_2$.

- The above diagram shows that, any path of R, from q_1 to f_2 must begin by going from q_1 to f_1 for some string w_1, followed by f_1 to q_2 on ϵ, followed by any path from q_2 to f_2 for some string w_2.

$$\text{Thus, } L(R) = L(R_1).L(R_2).$$

3. Closure (*)

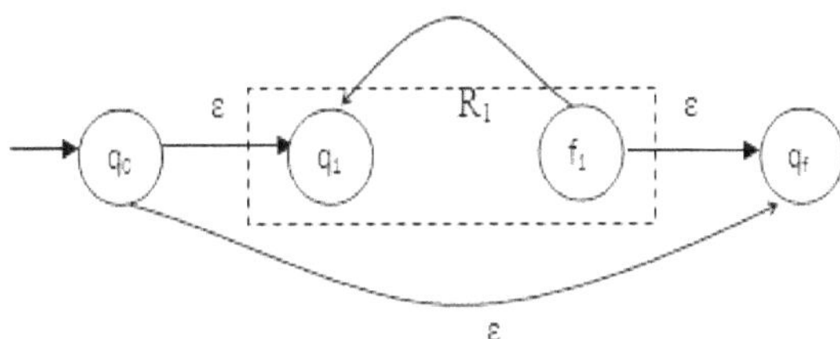

The above diagram shows that, any path from q_0 to q_f consists either the path from q_0 to q_f on ϵ or a path from q_0 to q_1 on ϵ, followed some string of paths from q_1 to f_1, then back to q_1 on ϵ followed by a path from q_1 to f_1, then to q_f on ϵ.

$$\text{Thus, } L(R) = L (R_1)^*$$

1. Construct Finite Automata From The Regular Expression $(0+1)^*$

$R = (0+1)^*$

$R = (R_1+R_2)^*$

$R_1 = 0$

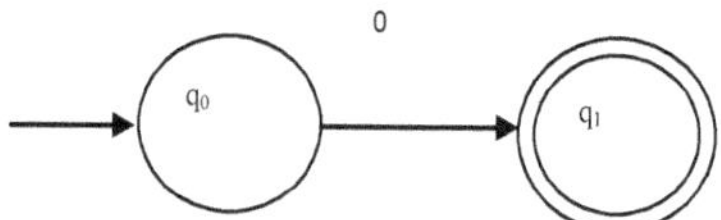

$R_2 = 1$

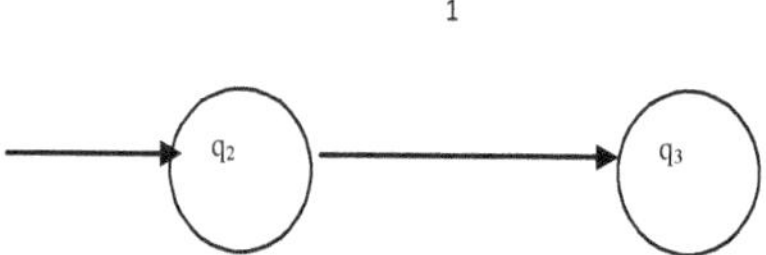

$R = R_1+R_2$

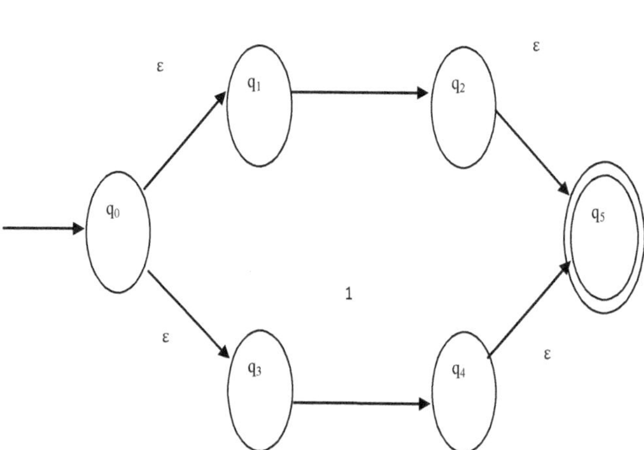

R=(R1+R2)*

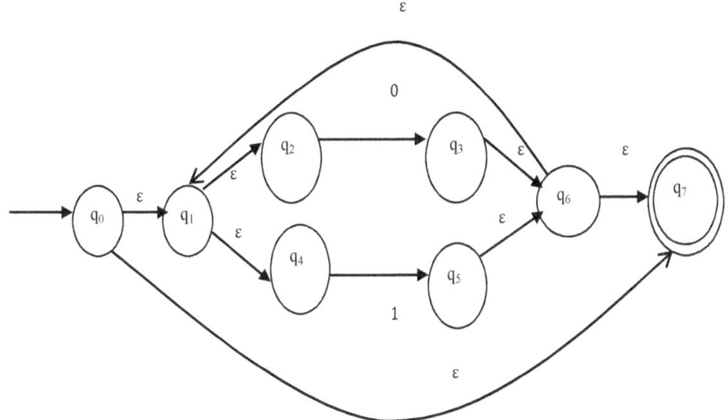

2. Construct finite automata for the given below

R = (01+10)⁺

R = (R₁+R₂)⁺

R₁ = 01

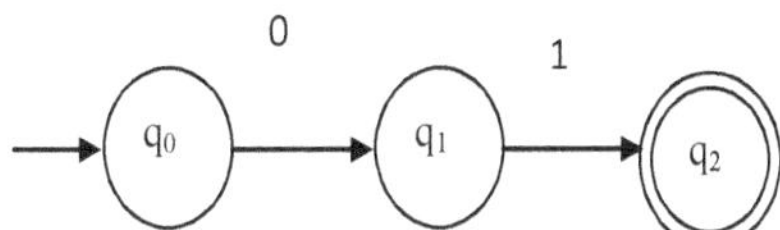

R₂ = 10

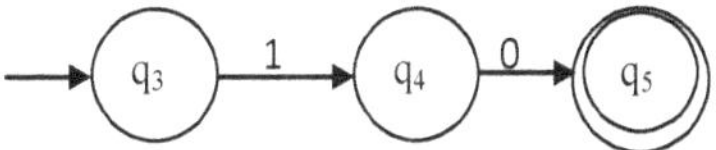

R = R₁ + R₂

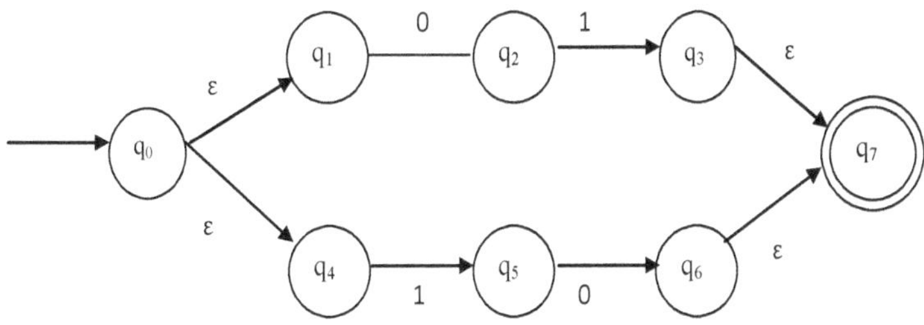

$R = (R_1 + R_2)^+$

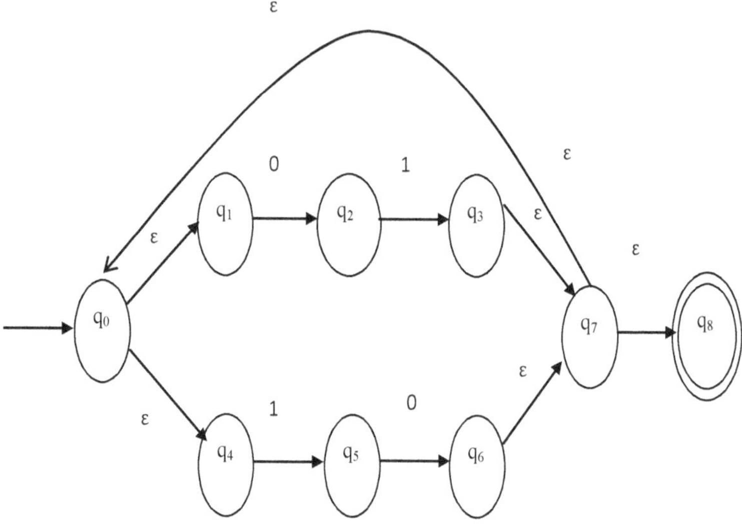

3. Convert finite automata for the regular expression (ab+c*)*b

$R_1 = ab$

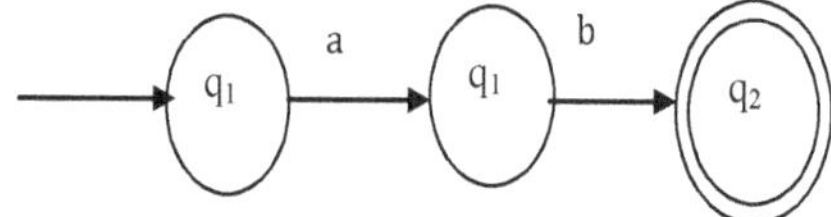

$R2 = c^*$

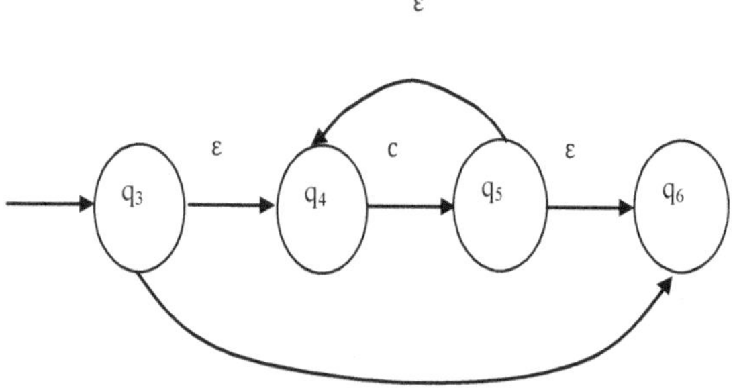

R3 = R$_1$ + R$_2$

   = (ab+c*)

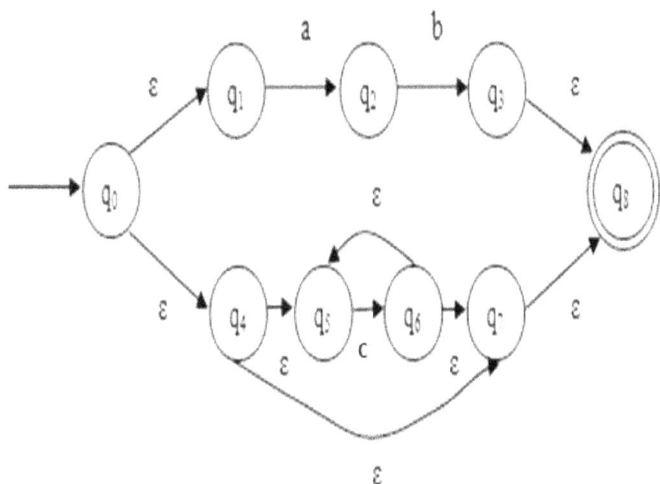

R4 =(R3)* = (ab+c*)*

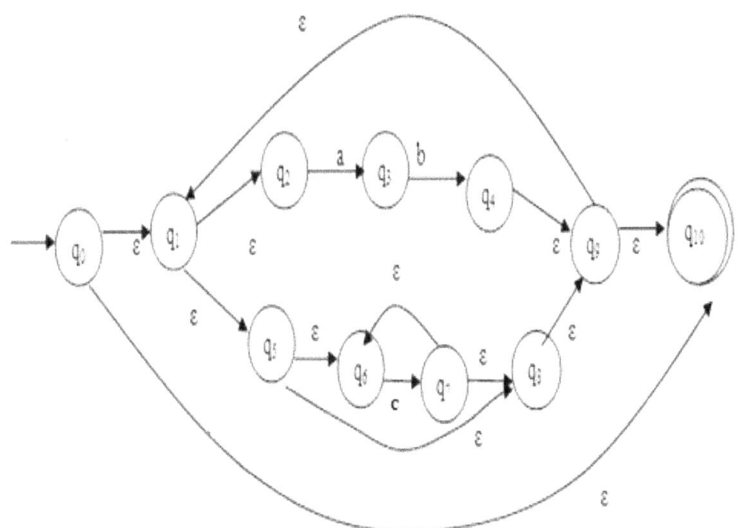

R5= (R4)*b

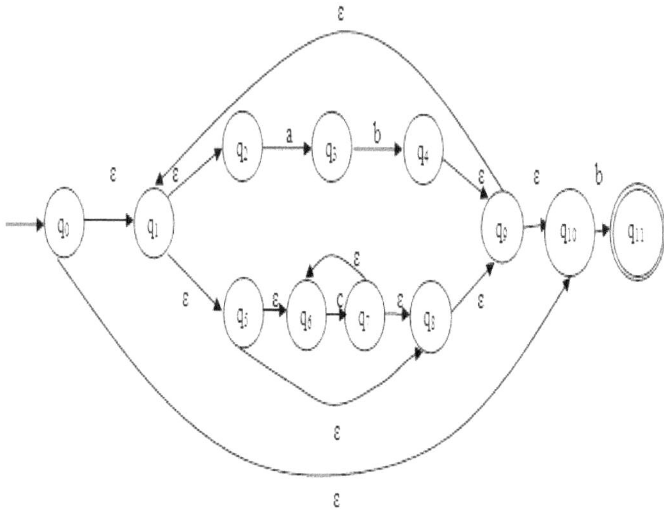

4. **Convert finite automata from the regular expression ((10)+(0+1)*)01**

   R = (R$_1$ + R$_2$) 01

   R$_1$ = 10

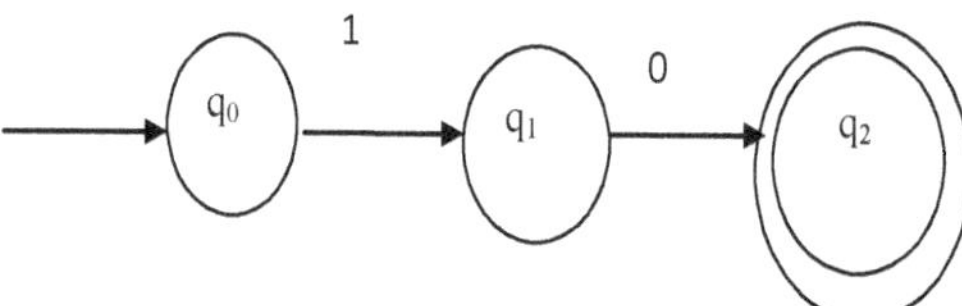

R$_2$ = 0+1

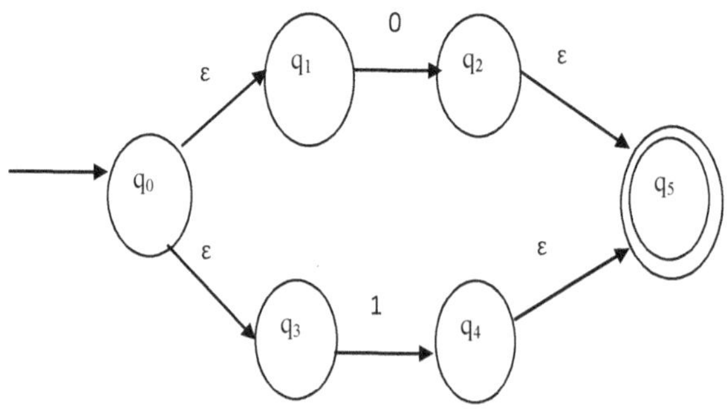

$R_2 = (0 + 1)^*$

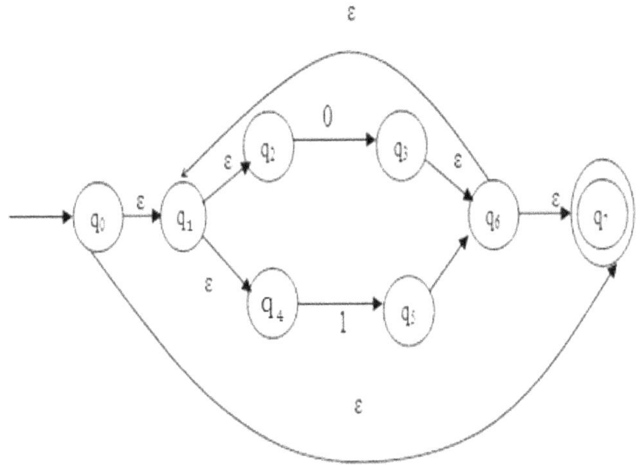

RE= $R_1 + R_2$

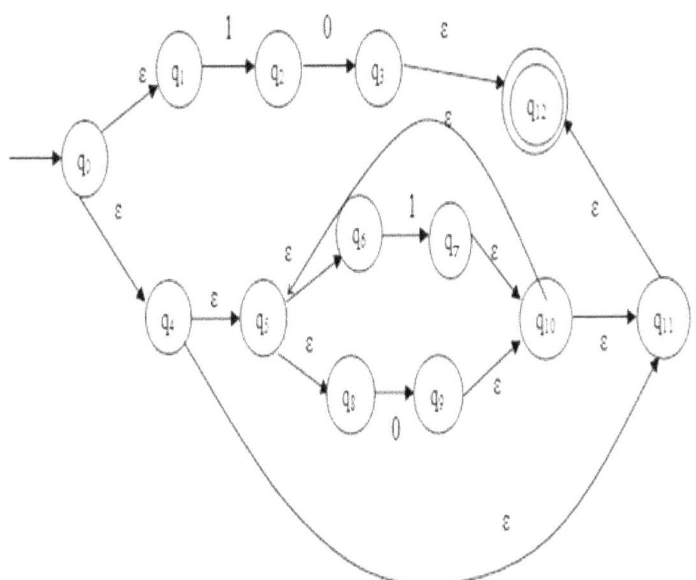

RE= ((10)+(0+1)*)01

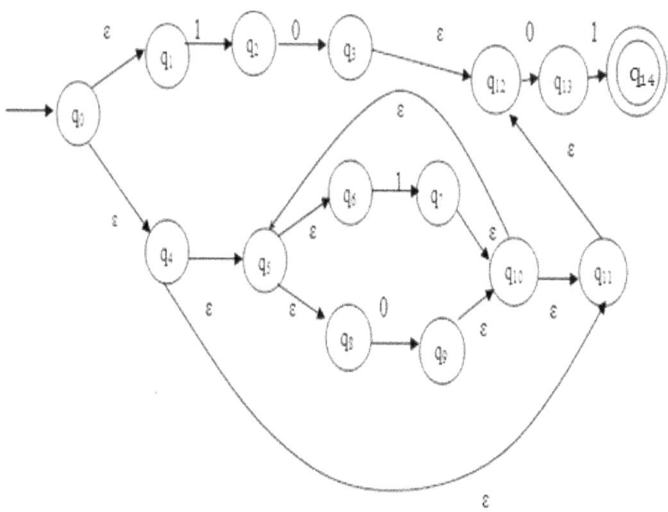

5. **Convert finite automata from the regular expression 1*0 + 0**

R = (1*0 + 0)

R = R₁ + R₂

1*

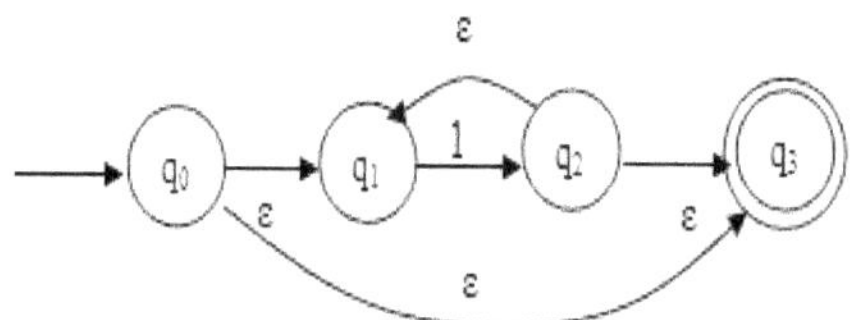

1*0

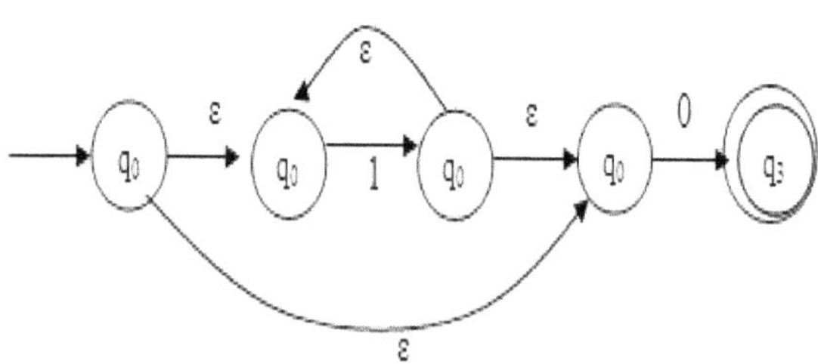

R=1*0 + 0

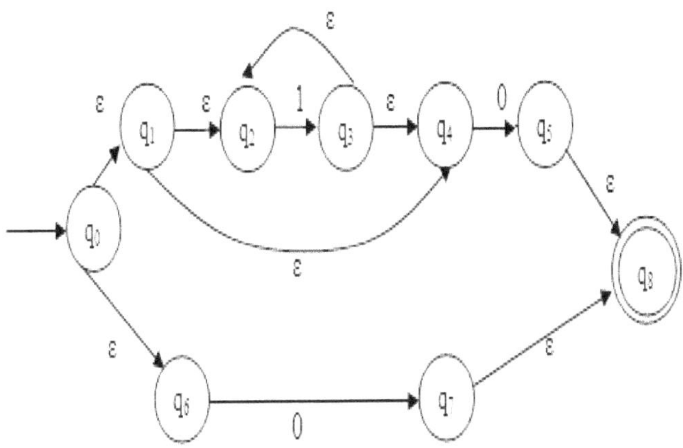

3.4.   Equivalence and Minimization of DFA

The two regular languages are said to be equivalent, if they define or accept the same language. It can be checked by minimization of DFA. That is, any DFA D, and we can find an equivalent DFA D's with minimum number of states.

3.4.1. Equivalent States

Consider states r and s are equivalent states then,

$$\Delta(r,w)= T$$

$\Delta(s,w)=T$ The states are equivalent if " for all input strings w, $\Delta(r,w)$ is an accepting state if and only if $\Delta(s,w)$ is also an accepting state.

3.4.2. Distinguishable States

If two states are not equivalent, then we say that both states are distinguishable states. That is, the state r is distinguishable from state s if there is at least one string w such that one of $\Delta(r,w)$ is accepting and it reaches final state $\Delta(s,w)$ reaches non-accepting states.

3.4.3. Table Filling Algorithm

To find the states are equivalent, we try to find the pairs of states that are distinguishable. *In table filling algorithm, if the two states are distinguishable, then the two states are equivalent.*

Basics

If the state r is an accepting state and s is non-accepting state, then the pair {r,s} is said to be distinguishable states.

Induction

Consider r and s be the states for some input symbol a , if

$^\delta(r,a)=t,\quad ^\delta(s,a)=t,$

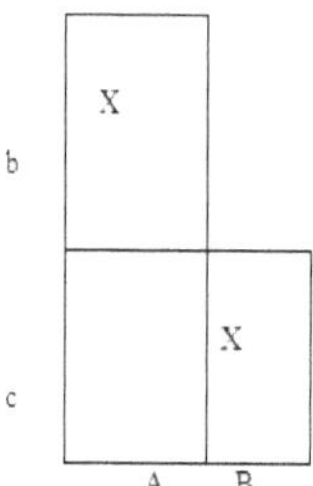

Then the states r and s are distinguishable states.

3.5. Minimization of DFA

Minimization is a task of transforming a given DFA into an equivalent DFA , which has the minimum number of states but both are accepting the same language L.

Algorithm for Minimizing a DFA:

1. Find equivalent and non-equivalent states of a given DFA by using table filling algorithm.
2. The start or initial state of a minimized DFA is a start state of a given DFA.
3. The accepting states of a minimized DFA are accepting states of a given DFA.

1. Find the equivalence and minimization of finite automata for following FA.

Input States	0	1
→ A	B	F
B	G	C
*C	A	C
D	C	G
E	H	F
F	C	G
G	G	E
H	G	C

Step 1: The states are A, B, C, D, E, F, G, H. .

Initial state A, Final state C

Step 2: Find the pairs for all states except final state

A: (A,B),(A,D),(A,E),(A,F),(A,G),(A,H)

B:(B,D),(B,E),(B,F),(B,G),(B,H)

D:(D,E),(D,F),(D,G),(D,H)

E:(E,F),(E,G),(E,H)

F:(F,G),(F,H)

G:(G,H)

Step 3: Find the transition for all pairs

Input Symbols States	0	1
A.B	B.G	F.C
A.D	B.C	F.G
A.E	B.H	F.F
A.F	B.C	F.G
A.G	B.G	F.E
A.H	B.G	F.C
B.D	G.C	C.G
B.E	G.H	C.F
B.F	G.C	C.G
B.G	G.G	C.E
B.H	G.G	C.C
D.E	C.H	G.F
D.F	C.C	G.G
D.G	C.G	G.E
D.H	C.G	G.C
E.F	H.C	F.G
E.G	H.G	F.E
E.H	H.G	F.C
F.G	C.G	G.E
F.H	C.G	G.C
G.H	G.G	E.C

Equivalent states: (A, E),(A,G), (B,H),(D,F),(E,G)

Non Equivalent states: C,G

In the above table take the pair (A,B) to check whether A and B are equivalent states

$\delta(A,0) =B, \delta(A,1) =F$

$\delta(B,0) =G, \delta(B,1) =C$, so A ,B are not equivalent .

In the above table take the pair (A,E) to check whether A and E are equivalent states

$\delta(A,0) =B, \delta(A,1) =F$

δ(E,0) =H, δ(E,1) =F so A,E are equivalent .

Table filling algorithm:

B							
C							
D							
E	✓						
F				✓			
G	✓				✓		
H							
	A	B	C	D	E	F	G

Step 4: Find the transition for all equivalent and non-equivalent pairs, check with input string 01 and 10.

State \ input symbol pair	01	10
A,E	(A,01)=C (E,01)=C	(A,10)=C (E,10)=C
A,G	(A,01)=C (G,01)=E	(A,10)=C (G,10)=H
B,H	(B,01)=E (H,01)=E	(B,10)=A (H,10)=A
D,F	(D,01)=C (F,01)=C	(D,10)=G (F,10)=G
E,G	(E,01)=C (G,01)=E	(E,10)=C (G,10)=H

In the above table take the pair (A,E) to check whether A and E are equivalent states.

δ(A,01) =C, δ(A,10) =C

δ(E,01) =C, δ(E,10) =C   so A,E are equivalent.

Take the pair (A,G) to check whether A and G are equivalent states.

δ(A,01) =C, δ(A,10) =C

δ(G,01) =E, δ(G,10) =H   so A,E are non-equivalent states.

The equivalent states are (A=E),(B=H),(D=F)

The non-equivalent states C, G

Table filling algorithm:

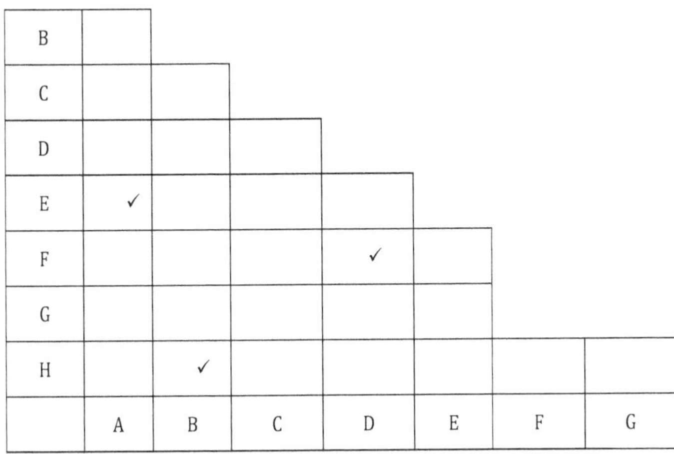

	A	B	C	D	E	F	G
B							
C							
D							
E	✓						
F				✓			
G							
H		✓					

Step 5: Find the transition function for all equivalent and non-equivalent states

State/Pair input symbol	0	1
→ A,E	A,0=B E,0=H	A,1=D E,1=F
B,H	B,0=G H,0=G	B,1=G H,1=G
D,F	D,0=C F,1=C	D,1=G F,1=G
*C	A	C
G	G	E

Step 6: Construct the minimized DFA from the above transition table

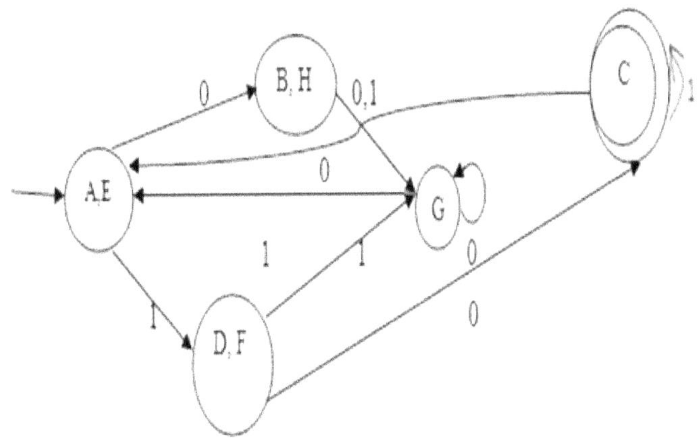

2. Find the equivalence and minimization of finite automata for following FA.

Input States	0	1
→ A	B	E
B	C	F
*C	D	H
D	E	H
E	F	I
*F	G	B
G	H	B
H	I	C
*I	A	E

Step 1: The states are A, B, C, D, E, F, G, H, I. Here Initial state A, Final states C,F,I.

Step 2: Comparing the equivalence of all the states, we can't compare the accepting state to non-accepting states.

A:(A,B),(A,D),(A,E),(A,G),(A,H)

B:(B,D),(B,E),(B,G),(B,H)

D:(D,E),(D,G),(D,H)

E:(E,G),(E,H)

G:(G,H)

STEP 3: Find the transition for all pairs

B								
C								
D	✓							
E		✓						
F								
G	✓			✓				
H		✓			✓			
I								
	A	B	C	D	E	F	G	H

	0	1
State input		
A,B	(A.0)=B (B,0)=C	(A,1)=E (B,1)=F
A,D	B,E	E,H
A,E	B,F	E,I
A,G	B,H	E,B
A,H	B,I	E,C
B,D	C,E	F,H
B,E	C,F	F,I
B,G	C,H	F,B
B,H	C,I	F,C
D,E	E,F	H,I
D,G	E,H	H,B
D,H	E,I	H,C
E,G	F,H	H,B
E,H	F,I	I,C
G,H	H,I	B,C

The equivalent states are: (A,D),(A,G),(B,E),(B,H),(D,G),(E,H)

The non-equivalent states are: C,F,I

In the above table take the pair (A,B) to check whether A and B are equivalent states

δ(A,0) =B, δ(A,1) =E

δ(B,0) =C, δ(B,1) =F   so A,B are non-equivalent.

Take the pair (A,G) to check whether A and G are equivalent states.

δ(A,0) =B, δ(A,1) =E

δ(G,0) =H, δ(G,1) =B   so A,G are equivalent states.

The equivalent states are: (A=D),(A=G),(B=E),(B=H),(D=G),(E=H)

The non-equivalent states are: C, F, I

Table filling algorithm:

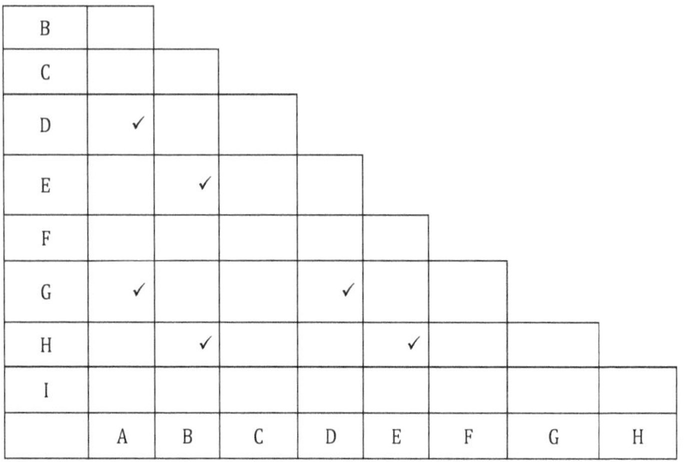

Step 4: Find the transition for all equivalent and non-equivalent pairs, check with input string 01 and 10.

State/ input symbol	01	10
A,D	(A,01)=F (D,01)=I	(A,10)=F (D,10)=I
A,G	F,C	F,C
B,E	H,B	G,A
B,H	H,A	G,D
D,G	I,C	I,C
E,H	B,A	A,D

In the above table take the pair (A,D) to check whether A and D are equivalent states.

$\delta(A,01)$ =F, $\delta(A,10)$ =F

$\delta(E,01)$ =I, $\delta(E,10)$ =I   so A,E are equivalent.

Take the pair (A,G) to check whether A and G are equivalent states.

$\delta(A,01)$ =F, $\delta(A,10)$ =F

$\delta(G,01)$ =C, $\delta(G,10)$ =C   so A,E are equivalent states.

The equivalent states are (A=D),(A=G),(B=E),(B=H),(D,G),(E,H)

Here we can written as,

(A=D=G),(B=E=H)

The non-equivalent states (C,F,I)

Table filling algorithm:

B							
C							
D	✓						
E		✓					
F							
G	✓			✓			
H		✓			✓		
I							
	A	B	C	D	E	F	G	H

Step 5: Find the transition function for all equivalent and non-equivalent states

State input symbol	0	1
→ (A,D,G)	(A,0)=B (D,0)=E (G,0)=H	(A,1)=E (D,1)=H (G,1)=B
(B,E,H)	(C,F,I)	(F,I,C)
*(C,F,I)	(D,G,A)	(H,B,E)

Step 6: Construct the minimized DFA from the above transition table

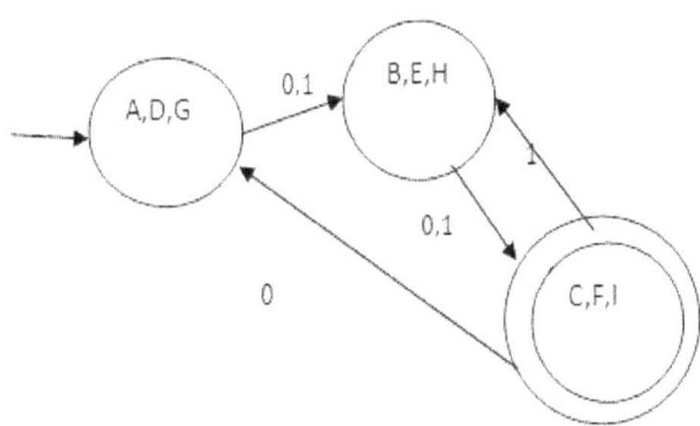

3. Find the minimized DFA for a given DFA.

i/p States	a	b
→ q0	q1	q3
q1	q2	q4
q2	q1	q4
q3	q2	q4
*q4	q4	q4

Step 1: The states are q0,q1,q2,q3,q4. Initial state q0, Final state q4

Step 2: Comparing the equivalence of all the states, we can't compare the accepting state to non-accepting states.

q0 : (q0,q1),(q0,q2),(q0,q3)

q1:(q1,q2),(q1,q3)

q2:(q2,q3)

Step 3 :Find the transition for all pairs

Input Symbols States	a	b
q0,q1	q1,q2	q3,q4
q0,q2	q1,q1	q3,q4
q0,q3	q1,q2	q3,q4
q1,q2	q2,q1	q4,q4
q1,q3	q2,q2	q4,q4
q2,q3	q1,q2	q4,q4

Equivalent states are: (q1,q2),(q1,q3),(q2,q3)

Non Equivalent states are: (q0,q1),(q0,q2),(q0,q3)

In the above table take the pair (q1,q2) to check whether q1 and q2 are equivalent states

δ(q1,a) =q2, δ(q1,b) =q4

δ(q2,a) =q1, δ(q2,b) =q4 , so q1 ,q2 are equivalent .

In the above table take the pair (q0,q1) to check whether q0 and q1 are equivalent states

δ(q0,a) =q1, δ(q0,b) =q3

δ(q1,a) =q2, δ(q1,b) =q4   so q0,q1 are not equivalent .

Table filling algorithm:

q1			
q2		✓	
q3		✓	✓
q4				
	q0	q1	q2	q3

Step 4: Find the transition for all equivalent and non-equivalent pairs.

State/ input symbol pair	ab	ba
q1,q2	(q1,ab)=q4 (q2,ab)=q4	(q1,ba)=q4 (q2,ba)=q4
q1,q3	(q1,ab)=q4 (q3,ab)=q4	(q1,ba)=q4 (q3,ba)=q4
q2,q3	(q2,ab)=q4 (q3,ab)=q4	(q2,ba)=q4 (q3,ba)=q4

In the above table take the pair (q1,q2) to check whether q1 and q2 are equivalent states.

$^{\delta}$(q1,ab) =q4, $^{\delta}$(q1,ba) =q4

$^{\delta}$(q2,ab) =q4, $^{\delta}$(q2,ba) =q4   so q2,q4 are equivalent.

The equivalent states are :(q1=q2),(q1=q3),(q2=q3)

We can written as,

(q1=q2=q3)

The non-equivalent states are: q0, q4

Table filling algorithm:

q1				
q2		✓		
q3		✓	✓	
q4				
	q0	q1	q2	q3

Step 5: Find the transition function for all equivalent and non-equivalent states

State/ pair input symbol	a	b
→ q0	q1	q3
(q1=q2=q3)	(q2,q1,q2)	(q4,q4,q4)
*q4	q4	q4

Step 6: Construct the minimized DFA from the above transition table

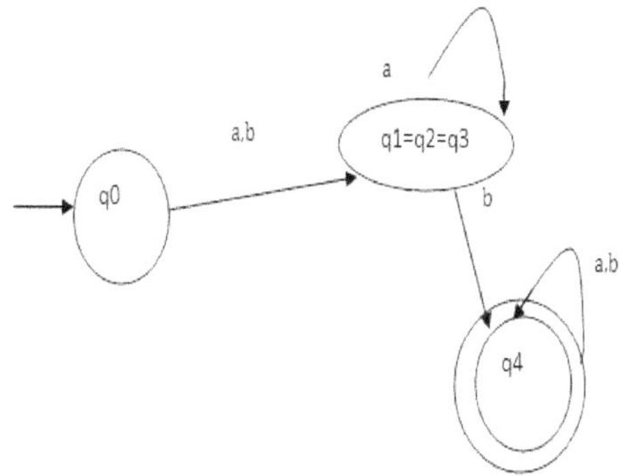

3.6. Pumping Lemma for Regular Sets

Some languages are regular. There are other languages which are not regular. One can neither express a non-regular language using regular expression nor design finite automata for it.

- Pumping lemma gives a necessary condition for an input string to belong to a regular set.
- Pumping lemma does not give sufficient condition for a language to be regular.
- Pumping lemma should not be used to establish that a given language is regular.

- Pumping lemma should be used to establish that a given language is not regular.
- The pumping lemma uses the pigeonhole principle which states that if n pigeons are placed into less than n holes, some hole have more than one pigeon in it. Similarly, a string of length >= n when recognized by a FA with n states will see some states repeating.

3.6.1. Definition of Pumping Lemma

Let L be a regular language and $M=(Q,\Sigma,\delta,q_0,F)$ be a finite automata with n-states. Language L is accepted by m. let $\omega \in L$ and $|\omega|>=n$, then ω can be written as xyz, where

1. $|y|>0$
2. $|xy|<=n$
3. $xy^iz \in L$ for all i>=0 here y^i denotes that y is repeated or pumped i times.

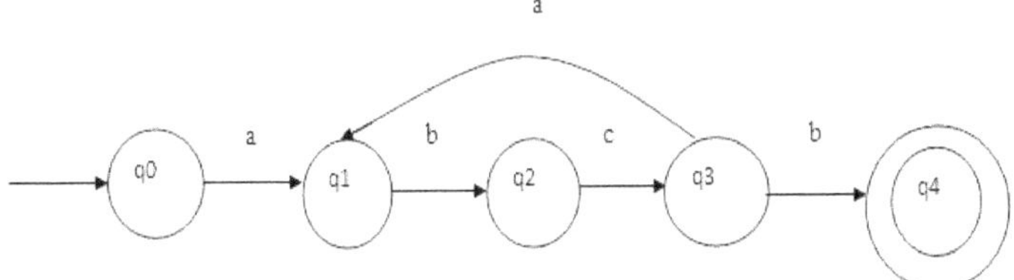

Let us consider the FA

No. of states = $5(q_0$ to $q_4)$

Let us take a string ω with $|\omega|$ >=5, recognized by the FA.

ω = abcabcb

Ti recognizes the string ω = abcabcb, machine will transit through various states.

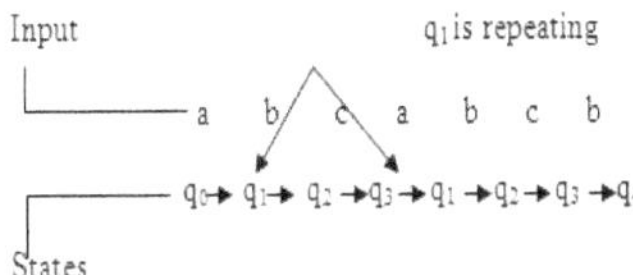

As the input abcabcb takes the machine through the loop $q_1 \rightarrow q_2 \rightarrow q_3 \rightarrow q_1$, this loop can repeat any number of times. In terms of abcabcb, we can say that if abcabcb is accepted by FA then every string in a(bca)*bcb will be accepted by the FA. The portion bca is input during the loop.

$$q_1 \rightarrow q_2 \rightarrow q_3 \rightarrow q_4.$$

Thus, if abcabcb is accepted by the FA then abcabcb can be written as xyz, with

X=a

Y=bca

Z=bcb

- Length of abcabcb is >=n
- Xy^1z for every i>=0 or a $(bca)^1bcb$ for every i>=0 will be accepted by the FA.

3.6.2. *Theorem for Pumping Lemma for Regular Languages*

1. Suppose L is a regular language.
2. Suppose M be a DFA with n states, such that DFA accept the given regular language L.

   i.e. L=L(M), Language of M is same as the given regular language.
3. Let us consider a string $\omega \in L|\omega| \geq n$.

   String ω can be written as

   $a_1\,a_2\,a_3 \dots a_m$ with m>=n.
4. Let us assume that states of M are given by $q_0 \quad q_1 \quad q_2 \dots q_{n-1}$ with q_0 as a starting state and q_{n-1} as final state.
5. Let us assume that after feeding the first i character of the word $\omega = a_1\,a_2 \dots a_m$, machine will be in a state r_i.

   $\delta^*(q_0,a_1,a_2, \dots a_i) = r_i$
6. As the word ω is fed through the machine M, the machine will go through the various states as:

   $q_0 \qquad r_1 \qquad r_2 \qquad \dots r_{m-1} \qquad\qquad q_{n-1} \qquad$ state

   $\qquad\quad a_1 \qquad a_2 \quad \dots a_{m-1} \qquad a_m \qquad\quad$ input

   Since the length of $\omega, |\omega| \geq n$ it is not possible for the machine to move through distinct states.
7. Let us assume that r_i and r_j are same. There is a loop from r_i to r_j.
8. The string ω can be divided into three parts.

   x=position before loop=$a_1\,a_2 \dots a_i$

   y=position of loop=$a_{i+1}\,a_{i+2} \dots a_j$

   z=position of loop=$a_{j+1}\,a_{j+2} \dots a_m$
9. Since y is a portion relating to loop, it can repeat any number of times.

   x=$a_1\,a_2 \dots a_i$

   y=$a_{i+1}\,a_{i+2} \dots a_j$

$$z = a_{j+1}\, a_{j+2} \ldots a_m$$

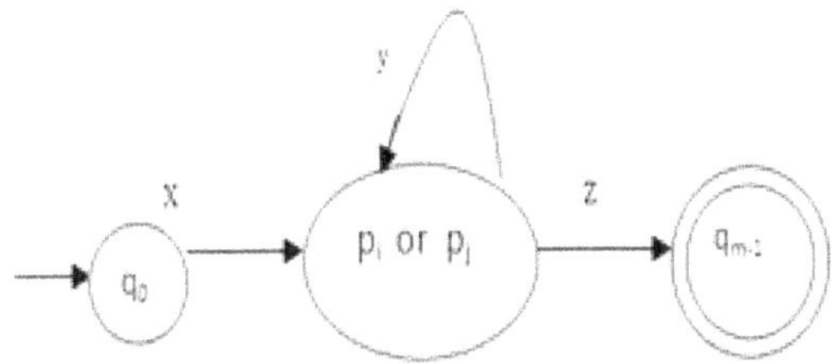

10. If $xyz \in L$ then xy^iz will also the accepted by the machine for every $i>=0$.

3.6.3. Problems Related to Pumping Lemma

1. Prove that the language $L=\{a^n b^n\}$ is not regular

Solution

Step 1: Let us assume that L is regular and L is accepted by a FA with n states.

Step 2: Let us choose a string

$$\omega = a^n b^n$$

$$|\omega| = 2n>=n$$

Let us write w as xyz, with

$$|y|>0$$

And $|xy|<=n$

$$|w|=2n>=n$$

Let us write w as xyz, with

$$|y|>0$$

and $|xy|<=n$

Since $|xy|<=n$, y must be of the form $a^r | r>0$

Since $|xy|<=n$, x must be the form a^s.

Now, $a^n b^n$ can be written as

$$a^s \quad a^r \quad a^{n-s-r} \quad b^n$$

$$x \quad y \quad z$$

step 3: Let us check whether xy^iz for i=2 belongs to L.

$$xy^2z=a^s(a^r)^2a^{n-s-r}b^n$$

$$=a^sa^{2r}a^{n-s-r}b^n$$

$$= a^{s+2r+n-s-r}b^n$$

$$= a^{n+r}b^n$$

Since r>0, number of a's in $a^{n+r}b^n$ is greater than number of b's. Therefore, $xy^2z \in L$. Hence by contradiction we can say that the given language is not regular.

2. ***Using pumping lemma for regular sets prove that the language,L={$0^n1^n0^{m+n}$ |m>=1 and n>=1} is not regular***

Solution

Step 1: Let us assume that L is regular and Lis accepted by a FA with n states.

Step 2: Let us choose a string.

$$\omega = 0^n1^m0^{m+n}$$

$$|\omega|=2(m+n)>=n$$

Let us write ω as xyz with

$$|y|>0$$

And $|xy|<=n$.

Since $|xy|<=n$, y must be of the form $0^r|r>0$

Since $|xy|<=n$, x must be of the form 0^s

Now,

$$\omega = 0^s \quad 0^r \quad 0^{n-r-s} \; 1^m \; 0^{m+n}$$

$$\qquad x \quad y \qquad z$$

Step 3: Let check whether xy^iz for i=2 belongs to L.

$$xy^2z=0^s \; 0^{2r} \; 0^{n-r-s} \; 1^m \; 0^{m+n}$$

$$=0^{n+r} \; 1^m \; 0^{m+n}$$

Since r>0, $0^{n+r} \; 1^m \; 0^{m+n}$ is not of the form

$$0^i \; 1^j \; 0^{i+j}$$

Therefore, $xy^2z \notin L$. hence by contradiction, we can say that given language is not regular.

3. Using pumping lemma for regular sets, prove that the language $L=\{\omega\omega^R \mid \omega \in \{0,1\}^*\}$ is not regular

Solution

Step 1: Let us assume that L is regular and L is accepted by a FA with n states.

Step 2: Let us choose a string

$$\omega = a^n b \ b a^n$$

$$\omega \quad \omega^R$$

$$|\omega|=2n+2>=n$$

Let us write w as xyz with

$$|y|>0$$

$$\text{And} \quad |xy|<=n$$

Since $|xy|<=n$, x must be of the form a^s.

Since $|xy|<=n$, y must be of the form $a^r \mid r>0$.

Now,

$$\omega = a^n b b a^n = a^s \ a^r \ a^{n-s-r} b b a^n$$

$$x \quad y \quad z$$

step 3: Let us check whether $xy^i z$ for i=2 belongs to L.

$$xy^2 z = a^s \ a^{2r} \ a^{n-s-r} b b a^n = a^{n+r} b b a^n.$$

Since r>0, $a^{n+r}bba^n$ is not of the form $\omega\omega^R$ as the strings starts with (n+r) a's but ends in (n) a's. therefore, $xy^2z \notin L$. Hence by contradiction, we can say that the given language is not regular.

4. Using pumping lemma for regular sets, prove that the language, $L=\{a^p \mid p \text{ is a prime}\}$ is not regular

Solution

Step 1: Let us assume that L is regular and L is accepted by a FA with n states.

Step 2: Let us choose a string

$$\omega = a^p (p=n)$$

$$|\omega| = 2n>=n$$

Let us write w as xyz, with

|y|>0,

And |xy|<=n

|w|=2n>=n

Let us write w as xyz, with |y|>0

and |xy|<=n ,Since |xy|<=n, y must be of the form $a^r|r>0$

Since |xy|<=n, x must be the form a^s.

Now, a^n can be written as

a^s a^r a^{n-s-r}

x   y   z

step 3: Let us check whether xy^iz for i=2 belongs to L.

$xy^2z = a^s(a^r)^2a^{n-s-r}$

$= a^sa^{2r}a^{n-s-r}$

$= a^{s+2r+n-s-r}$

$= a^{n+r}(n=p)$

Since r>0, a^{n+r} is not equal to a^p Therefore, $xy^2z \in L$. hence by contradiction, we can say that given language is not regular.

5. ***Using pumping lemma for regular sets, prove that the language, $L=\{a^{i2} \,|i>=1\}$ is not regular.***

Solution

Step 1: Let us assume that L is regular and L is accepted by a FA with n states.

Step 2: Let us choose a string

$\omega = a^{i2}(i2=n)$

$|\omega| = 2n>=n$

Let us write w as xyz, with

|y|>0,

And |xy|<=n

|w|=2n>=n

Let us write w as xyz, with |y|>0

and |xy|<=n ,Since |xy|<=n, y must be of the form $a^r | r>0$

Since |xy|<=n, x must be the form a^s.

Now, a^n can be written as

a^s a^r a^{n-s-r}

x   y   z

step 3: Let us check whether xy^iz for i=2 belongs to L.

$xy^2z=a^s(a^r)^2a^{n-s-r}$

$=a^sa^{2r}a^{n-s-r}$

$= a^{s+2r+n-s-r}$

$= a^{n+r}(n=i2)$

Since r>0, a^{n+r} (n=i2) is not equal to a^n(n=i2) Therefore, $xy^2z \in L$. hence by contradiction, we can say that given language is not regular.

3.7.   Closure Properties of Regular Languages

The closure properties of the regular languages are used to prove languages as regular languages. The closure properties is used to prove the theorem of the form "If   certain languages are regular, and language L is formed from them by certain operations then L is also regular". These theorems are called as **closure properties** of the regular languages since they show that the class of regular languages is closed under the operations. When one language is regular, then the related language is also regular.

The principal closure properties of regular languages are:

- Union of two regular languages are regular.
- Intersections of two regular languages are regular.
- Complements of two regular languages are regular.
- Reversal of regular language is regular.
- Closures of regular language are regular.

- Concatenation of two regular languages are regular.

- Homomorphism (Substitution of strings for symbols) of a regular language is regular.

i.   *Union*

Theorem: If L and M are regular languages, then L∪M is also the regular language.

Proof: Since L and M are regular languages, then they have regular expressions say the language L = L(R) and M = L(S). Then L∪M = L(R+S).

ii.   *Concatenation*

Theorem: If L and M are regular languages, then LM is also the regular language.

Proof: Since L and M are regular languages, then they have regular expressions of the form, L = L(R) and M = L(S) such that L(M) = L(R).L(S)

$$L(M) = L(RS)$$

iii.   *Closure Operation*

Theorem: If L is a regular language, then L* is also a regular language.

Proof: Since L is a regular language, then it has a regular expression of the form of language L = L(R) such that **L* = (L(R))***

iv.   *Complementation*

The complementation of the regular language 'L" is denoted as L'.

The complementation is denoted as,

$$L' = \epsilon^* - L$$

The complementation of the regular language 'L" is the set of strings ϵ^* that are not in L.

If ϵ^* = { ϵ, a, b, aa, ab, aab, ...} and L = { a,b, ab }

Then L' = { ϵ, aa, aab,.........}

The steps for finding a regular expression for its complement are as follows,

1. Convert the regular expressions to NFA - ϵ

2. Convert the regular NFA-ϵ to DFA by the subset construction

3. Complement the accepting states of that DFA

Example to Find the Regular Expression for its Complement

*Find the complement of the regular expression R = (0+1)*01.*

v.   *Intersection*

Once we have obtained the union and the complementation of the regular language, then we can obtain the intersection of the regular languages L and M by the following.

Generally the intersection of two sets is the set of element that are not in the complement of either set.

$$L \cap M = \overline{L} \cup \overline{M}$$

Theorem

If L and M are regular language, then the intersection of the language L and M is $L \cap M$ is also regular.

Proof

Let L and M be the language of automata

$$A_L = (Q_L, \in, \delta L, q_L, F_L)$$
$$A_M = (Q_M, \in, \delta M, q_M, F_M)$$

Here we are assuming that the alphabets of both the automata are the same. Σ is the union of the alphabets of L and M, if those alphabets are different. Now we have to construct the intersection of L and M, L∩M that simulates both A_L and A_M. Here we assume that both A_L and A_M are DFA and construct 'A'. The states of A are pairs of states, the first form A_L and the second form A_M.

To design the transitions of A, suppose A is the state (p, q) where p is the state of A_L and q is the state of A_M. If 'a' is the input symbol, then the transitions of A_L and A_M are as follows,

$$\delta (p, a) = s$$
$$\delta (q, a) = t$$

A → DFA →$A_L \cap A_M$.

So the next state of A will be(s,t). So now A has simulated the effect of both A_L and A_M. This is shown in below figure. The automata simulating two other automata and accepting if and only if both accept is shown below.

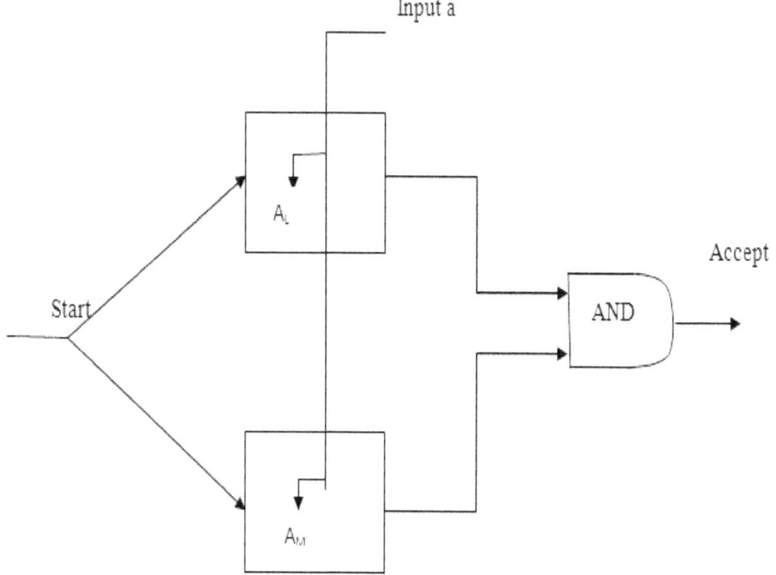

Closure Under Intersection

The start of A is the pair of start states of A_L and A_M. Since we want to accept if and only if both the automata accept. So we select those pairs (p, q) such that q is the accepting state of A_L and q is the accepting state of A_M. So we can formally defined A as,

$$A = (Q_L \times Q_M, \in, \delta, (q_L q_M), F_L \times F_M)$$

Where

$$\delta((p,q), a) = (\delta L(p, a), \delta M(q,a))$$

So string 'w' is accepted by A if and only if both A_L and A_M accepts the string w.

$$\delta`((q_L, q_M)), a) = (\delta'L(q_L, w), \delta'M(q_M, w)).$$

But A accepts the string w if and only if $\delta'((q_L, q_M), w)$ is a pair of accepting states such that,

$$\delta'L(q_L, w) = F_L$$

$$\delta' M(q_L, w) = F_M$$

Thus A accepts the intersection of L and M.

Example Problem

Construct A∩ B where A and B are DFA and it is given below.

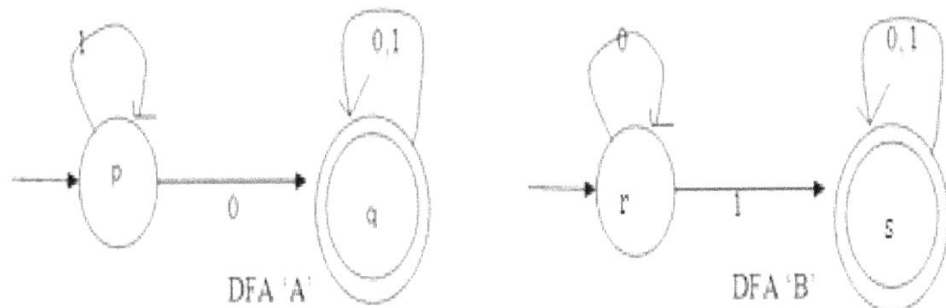

Solution

The definition for the DFA 'A' is A = (Q_A, ∈, δA, p,q)

The definition for the 'B' is B = (Q_B, ∈, δB,r,s)

Now we have to construct A ∩ B and the definition

$$A∩B = ((Q_A X Q_B), ∈, \delta\ AX\ \delta\ B,(p,r),\ (r,s))$$

So the DFA for A ∩B is,

$$Q_A X Q_B = \{\ p,q\}X\{r,s\} = \{\ (p,r)\ (p,s)(q,r)(q,s)\ \}$$

Find the transition

$\delta\ ((p,r),0)=\{q,r\}$

$\delta\ ((p,r),1)=\{p,s\}$

$\delta\ ((p,s),0)=\{q,s\}$

$\delta\ ((p,s),1)=\{p,s\}$

$\delta\ ((q,r),0)=\{q,r\}$

$\delta\ ((q,r),1)=\{q,s\}$

$\delta\ ((q,s),0)=\{q,s\}$

$\delta\ ((p,r),1)=\{q,s\}$

Initial state=$\{p,r\}$

Final state=$\{q,s\}$

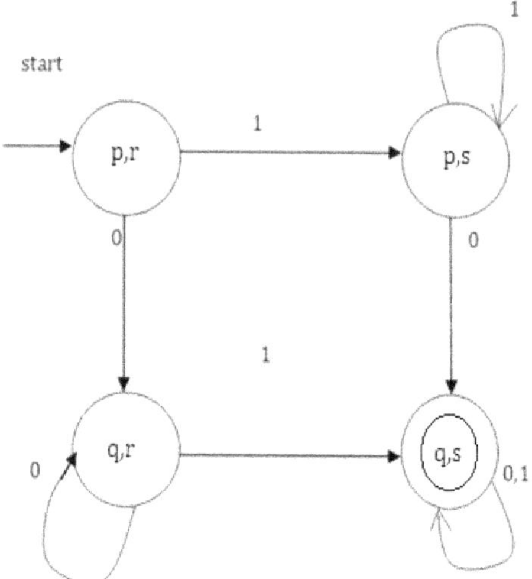

vi.   *Difference*

The difference of the regular language L and M is denoted by L-M. The difference L-M is the set of strings that are in language L but not in the language M.

Theorem: If L and M are regular languages, then the difference L-M is also regular language.

Proof

The difference of the regular language L-M is denoted as, L-M = L∩$\overline{\text{M}}$

By the previously proved theorems, we know that M is regular, L∩M is also regular.

vii.   *Reversal*

The reverse of the string W is w^R. If the string 'w' is given as ,

$$W = a_1a_2,a_3,\ldots\ldots\ldots\ldots a_n$$

Then $W^R = a_n,a_{n-1}\ldots\ldots\ldots\ldots\ldots a_3a_2a_1$

Example: if l = {001, 1011, 1111} then

$$L^R = \{100, 1101, 1111\}$$

If the language is reversed from regular language L, then the reversed language is also regular language.

Proof Based on the Regular Expression

Theorem: if a language L is a regular, then its reverse is also regular language, so is L^R.

Proof

Assume that the language defined by the regular expression E is denoted by L(E). Here we show that there is another regular expression E^R which is the reverse of the regular expression E such that

$$L(E^R) = (L(E^R))$$

Where $L(E^R)$ is the language of the regular expression E^R.

Basis

- If $E = \phi$ then $\phi R = \phi$
- If $E = a$ then $a^R = a$

Introduction

There are three cases for the regular expression E involving the three operations of the regular expressions such as union, concatenation, closure.

Case 1

$E = E_1 + E_2 \rightarrow E^R = E_1{}^R + E_2{}^R$

The reversal of the union of two languages is obtained by computing the reversals of the two languages and talking the union of those languages.

Case 2

If $E = E_1 E_2 \rightarrow$ then $E^R = E_2{}^R E_1{}^R$

While finding the reverse of the concatenation, we reverse the order of the two languages as well as reversing the language themselves.

$L(E_1) = \{01, 111\}$

$L(E_2) = \{00, 10\}$

Then $L(E_1 E_2) = \{0100, 0110, 11100, 11110\}$

The reversal of the language $L(E_1 E_2)$ is $L(E_1 E_2)^R$

$L(E_1 E_2)^R = \{0010, 0110, 00111, 01111\}$

Now we concatenate the reversal of $L(E_1)$ and $L(E_2)$

$L(E_1{}^R) = \{10,111\}$

$L(E_2{}^R) = \{00,01\}$

$L(E_2{}^R\, E_1{}^R) = \{00,01\}\, \{10,111\} = \{0010, 0110, 00111, 01111\}$

So in general if a word w in L(E) is the concatenation of w_1 form $L(E_1)$ and w_2 from $L(E_2)$, then

$w^R = w_2{}^R w_1{}^R$

Case 3

$E = E1^*$ then $E^R = (E^R)^*$

If there, is a string w is in L(E), then w^R is the reverse of the string w.

$w = w_1 w_2 {\ldots\ldots} w$

$w^R = w_n w_{n-1} {\ldots\ldots} w_2 w_1$

Then the string w^R is in the language $L\ (E_1{}^R)^*$ since w^R is in L(E) if and only if its reversal is in $(L(E_1{}^R)^*)$

viii.   *Homomorphism*

Homomorphism is a function on strings that works by substituting a particular string for each symbol. The homomorphism of the language 'L' is denoted as h(L). for example if the function is defined by,

$h(0) = ab$

$h(1) = \epsilon$

By the above function of homomorphism, given any string of 0's and 1's, it replaces all 0's by the string ab, since h(0) =ab. It replaces all the occurrence of the string 1's by, since $h(1) = \epsilon$

For example if the string w= 0011, then

$h(w) = h(0)h(0)h(1)h(1) = (ab)(ab)(\epsilon)(\epsilon)$

h(w) = abab

So by the above example, if 'h' is a homomorphism on the alphabet h and $w = a_1 a_2 \ldots a_n$ is a string of symbols in ϵ then $h(w) = h(a_1)h(a_2)\ldots\ldots h(a_n)$

So we have to apply homomorphism function 'h' to each symbol of string w and concatenate the results in order. Thus if L is a language over alphabet ϵ and h is a homomorphism on ϵ, then

$$h(L) = \{h(w)/w \text{ is in L}\}$$

Theorem: if L is a regular language over an alphabet h and h is a homomorphism on h, then h(L) ia also regular language.

Proof

Let L=L® for some regular expression R. if E is the regular expression with symbols in ϵ, let h(E) is the expression that is obtained by replacing each symbol a in ϵ that is present in E by h(a). We have to prove that h(R) defines the language h(L), such that,

L(h(E)) = h(L(E))

Basis

1. If E is ϵ or ϕ, then h(E) is same as E then,

    h(ϵ) = E

    h(ϕ) = E

    E = a$\rightarrow$h(a)=E

2. If E is ϕ or ϵ, then L(E) contains strings. Thus ,

    h(L(E)) = L(E)

    thus we can conclude.

    L(h(E)) = L(E)=h(L(E))

    So ,**L(h(E)) = L(E)=h(L(E))**

if E=a for some symbol a in ϵ, such that L(E)=a

    h(a)=E

and h(L(E))=h(a)

and L(h(E)) is also h(a). so we can conclude

    L(h(E))=h(L(E)

Induction

There are three cases in the induction part.

Case 1: E=F+G where E,F,G are the regular expressions denoting the language L(E), L(F) and L(G) respectively.

By applying homomorphism to the regular expressions as,

    h(E)=h(F+G)=h(F)+h(G)

    we know that L(E)=L(F) $\cup$ L(G)

so

L(h(E))=h(L(F) ∪L(G))

h(L(E))=h(L(F)) ∪h(L(G))

Case 2: E=FG where E is a regular expression formed by the concatenation of the regular expression F and G. By applying homomorphism, we get

h(E)=h(FG)

L(F)=L(F).L(G)

SO,   L(h(E))=L(h(F).h(G))

=L(h(F)).L(h(G))

Case 3: and $E=E_1^*$ by applying a homomorphism

$h(E) =h(E_1)^*$

we know that $L(E)=(L(E))^*$

so $L(h(E))=L(h(E))^*$

$h(L(E))=h(L(E))^*$

thus by applying homomrphism h to the regular expression for the language L results in a regular expression that defines the language h(L)

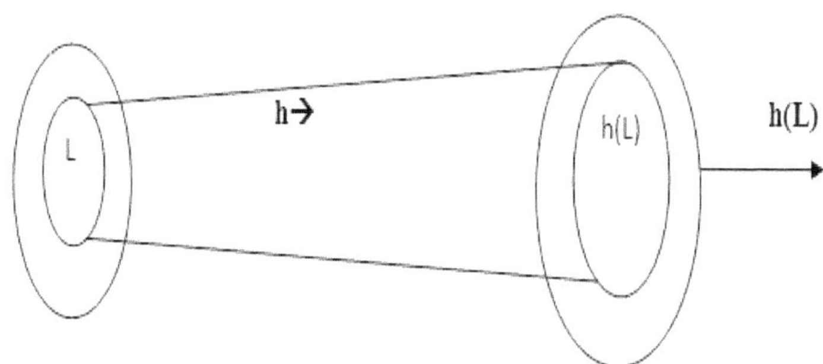

Applying the Homomorphism to the Language L

ix.   *Inverse Homomorphism*

Let L be the language over alphabet T. Then $h^{-1}(L)$ is read as "h inverse of L" is the set of string w in ϵ^* such that h(w) is in L.

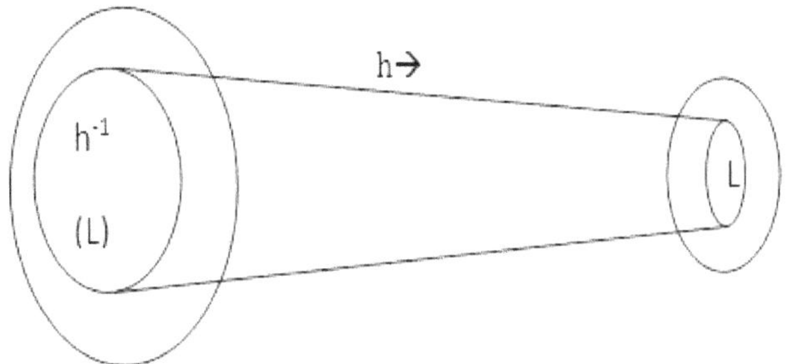

Inverse Homomorphism of Language 'L'

Theorem: if h is a homomorphism from alphabet ∈ to alphabet T, and L is a regular language over T, then h⁻¹(L) the inverse homomorphism of the language L is also a regular language

Proof

Let us assume a DFA 'A' for L. Let us construct a DFA for h⁻¹(L) from DFA 'A' and h as shown below,

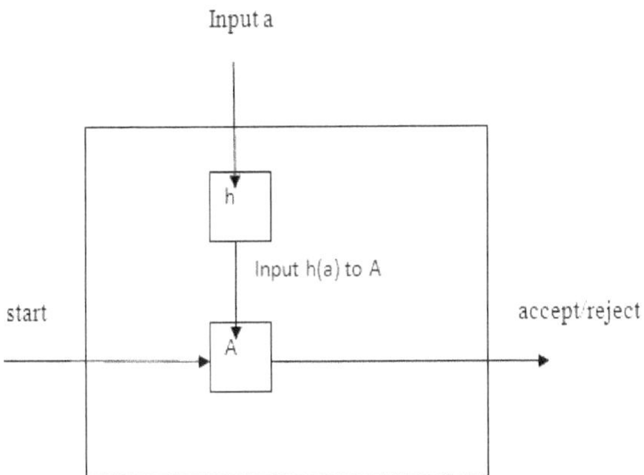

Inverse Homomorphism of Language 'L'

The above figure represents "DFA for h⁻¹(L) applies h to its input and then simulates DFA L". This above DFA uses the states of A but translates the input symbol according to "h" before deciding on the next state. Let L be (A) where DFA A=(Q,T, δ,q₀,F). Define a DFA B as B=(Q, ∈, δ ,q₀,F) where δ is the transition function constructed by the rule,

$$\delta\,(q,a) = \delta\,(q,h(a))$$

That is the transition B makes on input a is the result of the sequence of transions that A makes on the string of symbols h(a). thus

$$\delta\ (q_0,w) = \delta\ (q_0,h(w))$$

Since, the accepting states of A and B are the same, B accepts w if and only if A accepts h(w). B accepts exactly those strings w that are in $h^{-1}(L)$. Thus the language $h^{-1}(L)$ is regular language, if there exists a regular language 'L'.

CHAPTER 4

CONTEXT-FREE GRAMMARS AND LANGUAGES

4.1. Introduction: Grammar

Grammar is a set of rules that is used to define the language.

Types of Grammar

1. Type 0 Grammar
2. Type 1 Grammar
3. Type 2 Grammar
4. Type 3 Grammar

1. Type 0 Grammar

The grammar with no restriction on the production is called type 0 grammar. A language which is generated by type 0 grammar is called type 0 language. The production in the type 0 grammar in the form of a→b in which there is no restriction for the length of a and b. Here a and b can contain either any number of terminals and non-terminals. It is also called as recursive grammar.

Eg. ABc→ CabcDE

2. Type 1 Grammar

This grammar contains the restriction that, the production of the a and b ,the length of b is larger than or equal to the length of a.

That is a→b, (|a|<=|b|)

A language which is generated by type 1 grammar is called as type 1 language .The production in the type 1 grammar is in the form of a→b where a is non-terminal and b is terminal. Here b should contain a terminal followed by any number of non-terminals .It is also called as context sensitive grammar.

Eg.,

S→Abc

A→aBcd

AC→bA

3. *Type 2 Grammar*

In this grammar, the production in the form of a→b, (|a|<=|b|) here left side of the production should contain only one non-terminal but no restriction on the right side of the production. The language which is generated by type 2 grammar is called as context free grammar.

Eg.,

    S→Aa

    A→aBs

4. *Type 3 Grammar*

Type 3 grammar is also called as regular grammar. In this grammar, production in the form of a→b,(|a|<|b|) and a contain only one non-terminal and b can contain only a terminal or terminal followed by a single non-terminal. The language which is generated by type 3 grammar is called as type 3 language or regular language.

Eg.,

    S→a

    A→cBa

4.2. Context Free Grammar and Language (CFG)

A context free grammar is a type 2 grammar, in this the production in the form of a→b, the left side of the production should contain only one non-terminal but no restriction on the right side of the production.

Applications

- Used in defining programming languages
- Formalizing the notion of parsing
- Simplifying translation of programming languages
- String processing applications

CFG: Most widely used in the study of human languages

Definition: A Context Free Grammar G= (V, T, P, S),

Where, V -Set of variables or non-terminals

    T - Terminals

    P - set of productions or rules

S - Start symbols or variable (S≤ V)

T-Terminals are denoted by lower case letters, these are the basic symbols from which strings are formed.

E.g: identifier, operators and keywords

+,*, (,), digits (0 to 9), and lower case letters (a-z)

V- Non-terminals or Variables which represents a language.

E.g: upper case letters(A-Z)

P- Set of rules which produces the production

e.g., A→ Ba

A →a

S- Start symbol

e.g., A→ Ba here A is a starting symbol.

4.2.1. CFG for Simple Expression

1. Construct the CFG for a given Expression (a+b)

This regular expression does not use directly in the grammar.

So it uses the set of productions that say essentially the same thing as this regular expression.

Possible strings for (a + b): {a, b, ab, ba}

Productions are:

E → (E)
E → E+E
E → a
E → b

Here,

V => {E}

T => {+, (,), a, b}

P => { E → E+E, E → (E), E → a, E → b }

S => {E}

2. **Construct a CFG for the Given Expression (a+b)(a+b+0+1)***

Possible strings: {a, b, aa*,ab*, a0*, a1*, ba*, bb*, b0*, b1*}

Productions are:

E⟶E+E

E

E⟶E*E

E⟶(E)

E⟶a

E⟶b

E⟶Ea

E⟶Eb

E⟶E0

E⟶E1

Here,

V => {E}

T => {a, b, 0, 1, +, *, (,) }

P => {E⟶E+E/(E)/E*E/a/b/Ea/Eb/E0/E1}

S => {E}

3. **Construct the CFG Consists of Any Number of a's over the Set Σ= {a}**

Regular expression = a*

Productions are:

S⟶ε

S⟶aS

Here,

V = {S}

T = {a}

P⟶{S ⟶ε / aS}

S⟶{S}

4. **Construct the CFG for the Language L={a^n | n is odd }**

Productions are:

S⟶aS

S⟶aaS

S⟶ε

Here,

$V = \{S\}$

$T = \{a\}$

$P \rightarrow \{S \rightarrow aS \: / \: aaS \: / \: \varepsilon \}$

$S \rightarrow \{S\}$

4.3. Derivations and Languages

- While inferring the given input string belongs to the given CFG. There are two approaches

Recursive inference: Using the rules from body to head

Derivation: Using the rules from head to body that is derivation derives the input string from start symbol S.

Recursive inference

- Here we take strings from each variable and concatenate them in proper order, and infer that resulting strings is in the language of variable in the head.

Derivation

- Here we use the productions from head to body i.e., from start symbol expanding till reaches the given string.
    - The sequence of substitutions used to obtain a string called derivation.
    - Derivation produces a new string from a given strings.
    - If the string obtained as a result of the derivation, contains only terminal symbols, then no further derivations are possible.

Example: For language, L= {wcw^R / wΣ (0+1)*} check whether the string 01c10 belongs the language L or not.

Production: For the language L the following productions are generated.

i) $E \rightarrow c$

ii) $E \rightarrow 0E0$

iii) $E \rightarrow 1E1$

Regular Inference:

	String Interval	For Language	Production used	String used
1.	c	E	(i)	--
2.	0E0	E	(ii)	--
3.	01E10	E	(iii)	(2)
4.	01c10	E	(i)	(1)(3)

1. Derivations:

$E \rightarrow 0E0$ $[E \rightarrow 0E0]$

$E \rightarrow 01E10$ $[E \rightarrow 1E1]$

$E \rightarrow 01c10$ $[E \rightarrow c]$

The given string 01c10 belongs to the language L = {wcw^R / w$\sum$(0+1)*}

Relation

There are two relations between the strings,

1. Single Relation => $E \rightarrow id$
2. Multiple Relation => $E \xrightarrow{*} id * id$

4.3.1. Left Most and Right Most Derivation

If at each step in a derivation a production is applied to the left most variable.(that is in each step left most variable is replaced).

The derivation in which right most variable is replaced at each step is called right most derivation.

e.g., Let G= (V, T, P, S), V = {E}, T = {+, *, id}, S= E where P is given by

$E \rightarrow E+E$

$E \rightarrow E*E$

$E \rightarrow id$

a. Construct the left Most Derivation for id+id*id

$E \xrightarrow{LM} E+E$ $[E \rightarrow id]$

$\xrightarrow{LM} id+ E$ $[E \rightarrow E*E]$

$\xrightarrow{LM} id+ E*E$ $[E \rightarrow id]$

$\xrightarrow{LM} id+ id*E$ $[E \rightarrow id]$

$\xrightarrow{LM} id+ id*id$

b. Right Most Derivation

$E \xrightarrow{RM} E+E$ $[E \rightarrow E*E]$

$\xrightarrow{RM} E+ E *E$ $[E \rightarrow id]$

$\xrightarrow{RM} E+ E*id$ $[E \rightarrow id]$

$\xrightarrow{RM} E+ id*id$ $[E \rightarrow id]$

$\xrightarrow{RM} id+ id*id$

1. Derive the string 1000111 for left most and right most derivation using CFG, G = (V, T, P, S), V = {0,1}, T = {S⟶T00T, T⟶0T / 1T / ε }

Left Most Derivation for 1000111

S $\xrightarrow{LM}$ T00T   [T⟶T00T]

$\xrightarrow{LM}$ 1T00T   [T⟶1T]

$\xrightarrow{LM}$ 10T00T   [T⟶0T]

$\xrightarrow{LM}$ 1000T   [T⟶ε]

$\xrightarrow{LM}$ 1000T   [T⟶1T]

$\xrightarrow{LM}$ 10001T   [T⟶1T]

$\xrightarrow{LM}$ 100011T   [T⟶1T]

$\xrightarrow{LM}$ 1000111T   [T⟶ε]

$\xrightarrow{LM}$ 1000111

$\xrightarrow{LM}$ 1000111

Right Most Derivation for 1000111

S $\xrightarrow{RM}$ T00T   [T⟶T00T]

$\xrightarrow{RM}$ T001T   [T⟶1T]

$\xrightarrow{RM}$ T0011T   [T⟶1T]

$\xrightarrow{RM}$ T00111T   [T⟶1T]

$\xrightarrow{RM}$ T00111   [T⟶ε]

$\xrightarrow{RM}$ 1T00111   [T⟶1T]

$\xrightarrow{RM}$ 10T00111   [T⟶0T]

$\xrightarrow{RM}$ 10T00111   [T⟶ε]

$\xrightarrow{RM}$ 1000111

4.3.2. Sentential Form

A string which consists of terminals and non-terminals. The strings are produced/ Derived from the start symbol is known as sentential form.

Let G = (V, T, P, S) is a CFG then a in (VU (Union) T)* such that

i) $S \xrightarrow{*}_{=>} \alpha$, then α is a sentential form

ii) $S \xrightarrow[LM]{*}_{=>} \alpha$, then α is a left most sentential form

iii) $S \xrightarrow[RM]{*}_{=>} \alpha$, then α is a right most sentential form

1. Derive the string "aabbabba" for the left most and right most derivation using CFG given by S⟶aB / bA, A⟶a / aS/bAA, B⟶b / bS/ aBB

Left Most Derivation for aabbabba

$S\overrightarrow{LM}$ aB

$\overrightarrow{LM}$ aaBB   [B→aBB]

$\overrightarrow{LM}$ aabSB   [B→bS]

$\overrightarrow{LM}$ aabbAB   [S→bA]

$\overrightarrow{LM}$ aabbaB   [A→a]

$\overrightarrow{LM}$ aabbabS   [B→bS]

$\overrightarrow{LM}$ aabbabbA [S→bA]

$\overrightarrow{LM}$ aabbabba [A→a]

Right Most Derivation for aabbabba

$S\ \overrightarrow{RM}$ aB

$\overrightarrow{RM}$ aaBB   [B→aBB]

$\overrightarrow{RM}$ aaBbS   [B→bS]

$\overrightarrow{RM}$ aaBbaB [S→aB]

$\overrightarrow{RM}$ aaBbabS [B→bS]

$\overrightarrow{RM}$ aaBbabbA[S→bA]

$\overrightarrow{RM}$ aaBbabba [A→a]

$\overrightarrow{RM}$ aabbabba [B→b]

4.4. Parse Tree/Derivation Tree

A graphical (or) pictorial representation of a derivation is called as parse tree.

The derivations can be represented by trees using parse tree.

Rules for Constructing Parse Tree

1. A root node is always a node indicating start symbol.

2. The leaf nodes are always terminal node.

3. The interior nodes (non-leaf) always be non-terminal node.

4. The derivation is read from left to right.

1. Construct a parse tree from the grammar S→bSb / a / b

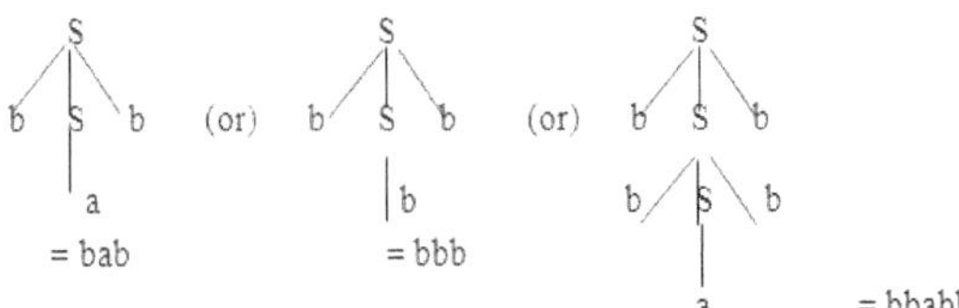

    = bab   = bbb   = bbabb

2. Construct a parse tree for the grammar E→E*E, E→id

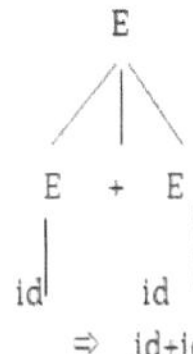

$$\Rightarrow \quad id+id$$

Yield of a Parse Tree

The string obtained by concatenating the leaves of parse tree from left to right is called yield of a parse tree.

1. For a given G defined by the production S →A1B, A →0A / ε , B → 0B / 1B / ε. Find the parse tree for the yields i) 1001, ii) 00101, iii) 00011

i)   W= 1001

→S

→A1B

→1B   [A→ε]

→10B   [B→0B]

→100B [B→0B]

→1001B [B→1B]

→1001   [A→ε]

S= > 1001

=>1001

ii) 00101

→A1B

→0A1B   [A →0A]

→00A1B   [A→0A]

→001B   [A→ε]

→0010B   [B→0B]

→00101B   [B→1B]

→00101   [B→ε]

S* = > 00101

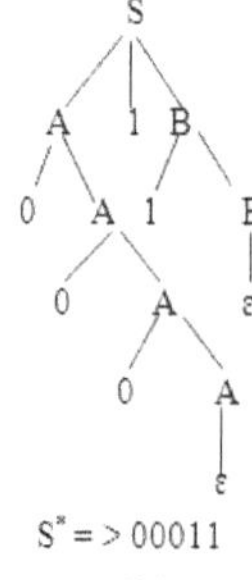

S* = > 00101

iii) 00011

→S

→A1B

→0A1B   [A →0A]

→00A1B   [A→0A]

→000A1B   [A→0A]

→0001B   [A→ε]

→00011B   [B→1B]

→00011   [B→ε]

S* = > 00011

S* = > 00011

iv) Construct the parse tree for the string aabbabba from CFG given by S ⟶ aB / bA, A ⟶ a / aS / bAA, B ⟶ b / bS / aBB.

S ⟶ aB

S ⟶ aaBB [B ⟶ aBB]

S ⟶ aabSB [B ⟶ bS]

S ⟶ aabbAB [S ⟶ bA]

S ⟶ aabbaB [A ⟶ a]

S ⟶ aabbabS [B ⟶ Bs]

S ⟶ aabbabbA [S ⟶ bA]

S ⟶ aabbabba [A ⟶ a]

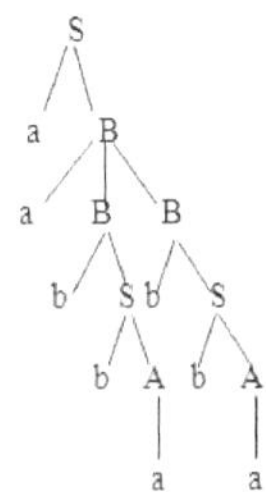

Applications of CFG

1. Parser
2. YACC parser – Generator (Yet Another Compiler Compiler)
3. Markup languages
4. XML – DTD(Extendible Markup Language-Document Type Definition)

4.5. Ambiguity in Grammar and Languages

4.5.1. *Ambiguous Grammar*

A CFG = (V, T, P, S) is ambiguous if there is at least one string w in T* is having two different parse trees [either two left most or two right most parse tree] each with same root S and same yield w.

1. Show that the grammar defined by the productions E ⟶ E+E / E*E / a is ambiguous.

Let w = a+a*a

LMD1:

E ⟶ E+E [E ⟶ a]

 ⟶ a+E [E ⟶ E*E]

→a+E*E [E →a]

→a+a*E [E→a]

→a+a*a

E→a+a*a

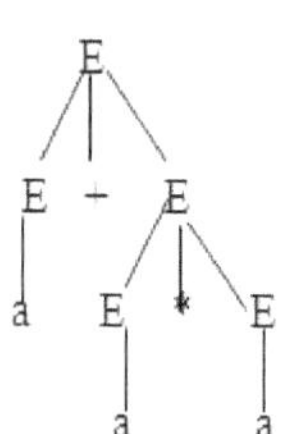

LMD 2:

E→E*E   [E→ E+E]

→E+E*E   [E→a]

→a+E*E   [E→a]

→a+a*E   [E→a]

E→a+a*a

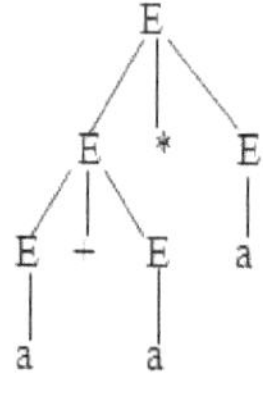

LMD1=LMD2

Therefore, Grammar G is ambiguous.

2. If G is a grammar S→aS / aSbS / ε , Show that G is ambiguous for the string 'aab'.

LMD1:

S→aS   [S→aSbS]

→aaSbS   [S→ε]

→aabS   [S→ε]

→aabS

S→ aab

128

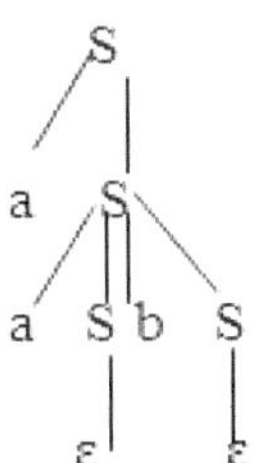

LMD2:

    S → aSbS   [S → aS]

    → aaSbS   [S → ε]

    → aabS   [S → ε]

    → aab

    S → aab

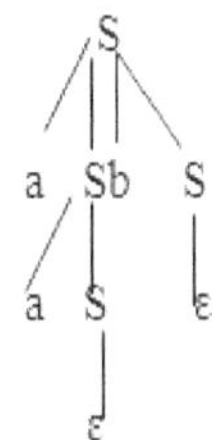

MD1=LMD2 and LMPT1=LMPT2

Therefore, G is ambiguous

3.   Show that the grammar is ambiguous.

S→a / abSb/ aAb , A→ bS/aAAb ,w=abab

LMD1:

S→abSb [S→a]

  →abab

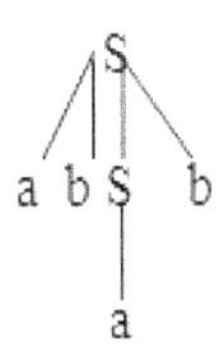

LMD2:

S→aAb [A→bS]

→abSb [S→a]

→abab

LMD1=LMD2, A given grammar is ambiguous.

4.5.2. *Inherently Ambiguity*

A CFG L is said to be inherently ambiguous if all its grammar are ambiguous. If even one grammar for L is unambiguous, then L is unambiguous language.

1.   A grammar for an inherently ambiguous language S→ aAS / a, A→ SbA / ba.
Let w = aabbaa
LMD1

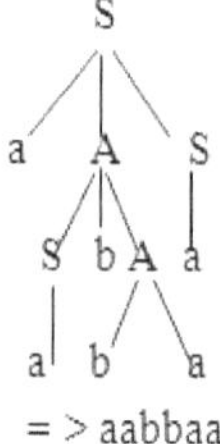

LMD 2

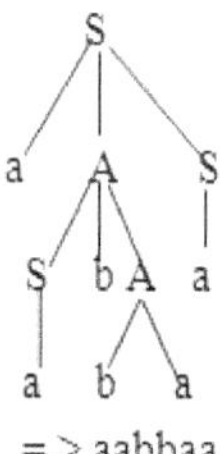

Therefore, G is ambiguous

2. Consider the grammar S⟶SbS / a. This grammar is ambiguous. Show in particular that the string abababa has to,

   a) Left most derivation

   b) Right most derivation

   c) Parse tree

Left most:

S⟶SbS	[S⟶SbS]
⟶ SbSbS	[S⟶SbS]
⟶ SbSbSbS	[S⟶a]
⟶ abSbSbS	[S⟶a]
⟶ ababSbS	[S⟶a]
⟶ abababS	[S⟶a]
⟶ abababa	[S⟶a]

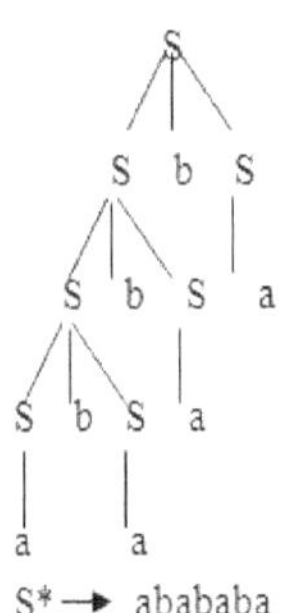

S* ⟶ abababa

Right most:

S⟶SbS	[S⟶SbS]
⟶SbSbS	[S⟶SbS]
⟶SbSbSbS	[S⟶a]
⟶SbSbSba	[S⟶a]
⟶SbSbaba	[S⟶a]
⟶Sbababa	[S⟶a]
⟶abababa	

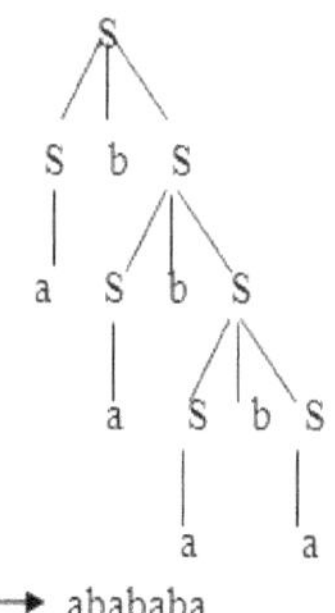

S* ⟶ abababa

4.5.3. Solved Problems

1. Show that the grammar S⟶ a / Sa / bSS / SSb / SbS is ambiguous.

2. Let G = ({S, C}, {a, b}, P, S) where P consists of S⟶aCa , C⟶aCa / b find L(G)

3. Find L(G), where G = ({S}, {0,1}, {S⟶ 0S1, S⟶ ε }, S)

4. Find the CFL S → aSb / aAb, A → bAa, A → ba productions for the language L = {ab, aabb, ... $a^n b^n$}

5. Construct the CFG for generating the language L = { $a^n b^n$ / n≥ 1}

6. Let the productions of a grammar be S ⟶ 0B / 1A, A ⟶0 / 0S / 1AA, B ⟶1 / 1S / 0BB for the string 0110. Find the right most derivation.

7. Find the derivation tree of a*b+a*b given that a*b+a*b is in L(G) where G is given by S S+S / S*S, S⟶ a / b.

8. Construct G whose productions are S⟶ aAS/a, A⟶ SbA / SS/ ba. Show that S $\overset{*}{\Rightarrow}$ aabbaa and construct a derivation tree whose yield is aabbaa.

Answer

1. w = aabaa

LMD 1:

S→Sa   [S→SbS]

 →SbSa   [S→Sa]

 →SabSa [S→a]

 →aabSa [S→a]

 →aabaa

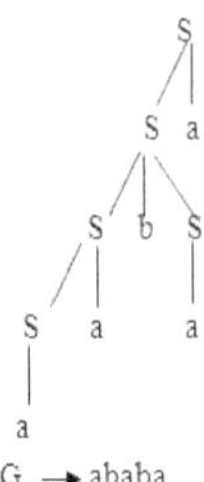

G → ababa

LMD2:

S→SbS   [S→Sa]

→SabS   [S→a]

→aabS   [S→Sa]

→aabSa   [S→a]

→aabaa

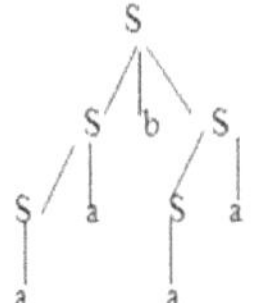

w →aabaa ,Therefore the given grammar is ambiguous.

2.   Let $G = (\{S, C\}, \{a, b\}, P, S)$

$V = \{S, C\}$, $T = \{a, b\}$

Productions are S →aCa, C→aCa / b

S→aaCaa   [C→aCa]

S→aabaa   [C→b]

So L(G) = aabaa

$L(G) = \{ a^n b^n a^n, n \geq 1 \}$

3.   S→0S1 $L = \{0,1\}$

S→00S11 $L = \{0011\}$

S→000S111 $L = \{000111\}$

$L = \{0^n 1^n \mid n \geq 0\}$

4.   S$\rightarrow$aSb / aAb

A$\rightarrow$bAa/ba

$\rightarrow$aSb

$\rightarrow$aaAbb

$\rightarrow$aabAabb

$\rightarrow$aabbaabb

So L(G)= $\{a^n b^m a^n b^m / n, m >= 1\}$

5.   L = $\{ab, aabb, \ldots, a^n b^n\}$

Productions are:

S$\rightarrow$ aSb

S$\rightarrow\varepsilon$/ a/b

6.   S$\rightarrow$0B / 1A

A$\rightarrow$0 / 0S / 1AA

B$\rightarrow$1 / 1S / 0BB

w$\rightarrow$ 0110

Right most derivation:

$\rightarrow$0B

$\rightarrow$01S   [B$\rightarrow$1S]

$\rightarrow$011A   [S$\rightarrow$1A]

$\rightarrow$0110   [A$\rightarrow$0]

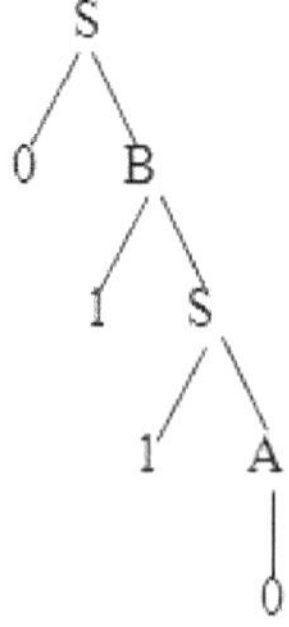

7.   Given productions: S→S+S / S*S, S→a / b

Input string = a*b+a*b

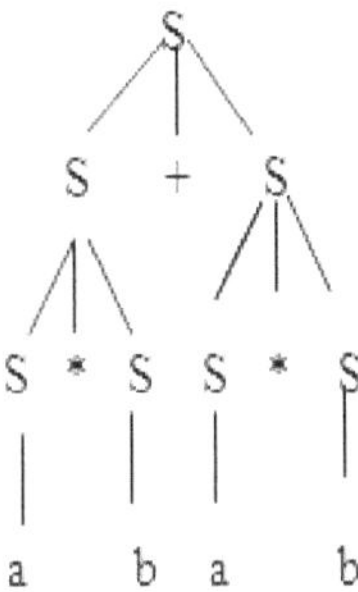

= > a*b+a*b

8.   Given productions: S→aAS/a,

A→SbA / SS/ ba

Input string = aabbaa

→aAS

→aSbAS   [A→SbA]

→aabAS   [S→a]

→aabbaS   [A→ba]

→aabbaa   [S→a]

S* = > aabbaa

Derivation tree:

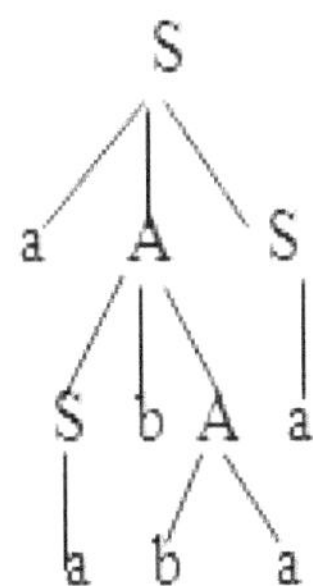

4.5.4. Derivation: Examples

1. For the grammar given below

S→ A1B, A→ 0A/ϵ, B→ 0B/1B/ϵ give left most and right most derivation of the string 1001.

Solution

Right most derivation for 1001.

    S→A1B   [B→0B]

    →A10B   [B→0B]

    →A100B   [B→1B]

    →A1001B [B→ ϵ]

    →A1001   [A→ ϵ]

    →1001

Left most derivation for 1001.

S   →A1B   [A→ ϵ]

    →1B   [B→0B]

    →10B   [B→0B]

    →100B   [B→1B]

    →1001B [B→ ϵ]

    →1001

2. Consider G= {{S,A}, {a,b}, P, S}, where P is, S→ aAS/a, A→SbA/SS/ba, find the LMD & RMD derivation for aabbaa.

Solution

LMD:

    S→ aAS [A→ SbA]

    → aSbAS [S→a]

    → aabAS [A→ba]

    →aabbaS [S→a]

RMD:

    S→ AaS [S→a]

    → aAa   [A→SbA]

    →aSbAa [A→ba]

    →aSbbaa [S→a]

    →aabbaa

3. The following grammar generates the grammar of the language consisting of all strings of even length, S→AS/ε, A→aa/ab/ba/bb. Give LMD & RMD for the following strings

   i.   aabbba
   ii.   baabab

Solution

1) aabbba

LMD:

    S→AS   [A→ aa]

    →aaS   [S→AS]

    →aaAS   [A→bb]

    →aabbS [A→AS]

    →aabbAS [A→ba]

    → aabbba [S→ε]

    → aabbba

RMD:

    S→AS   [S→AS]

    →AAS   [S→AS]

    →AASAS [S→ε]

    →AASAa [A→ba]

    →AASba [S→ε]

    →AAba   [A→bb]

    →Abbba [A→aa]

→aabbba.

2) baabab

LMD:

S→AS   [A→ba]

→baS   [S→AS]

→baAS   [A→ab]

→baabS   [S→AS]

→baabAS   [A→ab]

→baababS [S→Ɛ]

→baabab.

RMD:

S→AS   [S→AS]

→AAS   [S→AS]

→AAAS   [S→ Ɛ]

→AAA   [A→ab]

→AAab   [A→ab]

→Aabab   [A→ba]

→baabab

4.5.5. *Sentential Form*

1. Let G={ V,T,P,S},Where p is Sentential form S→AB , A→aaA/Ɛ , B→Bb/Ɛ. Generate the left & Right Sentential form.

Left Sentential form:

S→AB   [A→aaA]

→aaAB   [A→Ɛ]

→aaB   [B→Bb]

→aaBb   [B→Ɛ]

→aab

Right Sentential form:

S→AB   [B→Bb]

   →ABb   [B→Ɛ]

   →Ab   [A→aaA]

   →aaAb   [A→Ɛ]

   →aab

2. Let G= {V, T, P, S}, Where P is sentential form S→A1B, A→0A/Ɛ, B→0B/1B/Ɛ. Generate the leftmost & right most sentential form for 1001.

Left Sentential Form:

S→A1B   [A→Ɛ]

   → 1B   [B→0B]

   → 10B   [B→0B]

   → 100B   [B→1B]

   → 1001B   [B→Ɛ]

   → 1001

Right Sentential Form:

S→A1B   [B→0B]

   → A10B   [B→0B]

   → A100B   [B→1B]

   → A1001B   [b→Ɛ]

   → A1001   [A→ϵ]

   →1001

3. A Grammar for an inherently ambiguous language

S→AB/C

A→aAb/ab,

B→CBd/cd,

C→aCd/aDd,

d→bDc/bc,

W=aabbccdd.

Solution

LMD 1:

    S→AB   [A→aAb]

     →aAbB   [A→ab]

     →aabbB   [B→cBd]

     →aabbcBd   [B→cd]

     →aabbccdd

LMD 2:

    S→C   [C→aCd]

     →aCd   [C→aDd]

     →aaDdd   [D→bDc]

     →aabDcdd [D→bc]

     →aabbccdd

This grammar is inherently ambiguous. Because the string aabbccdd has the two left most derivations

LMD 1:

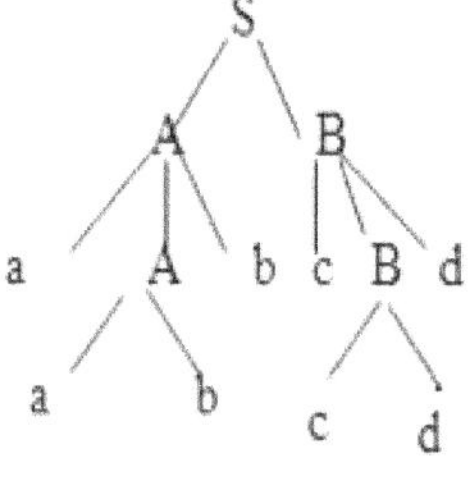

LMD 2:

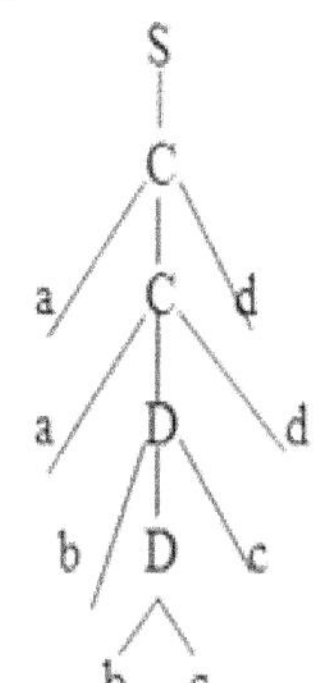

CHAPTER 5

PROPERTIES OF CONTEXT-FREE LANGUAGE

5.1. Simplification of CFG

5.1.1. ε – production

Steps for Eliminating the ε – production

1) Find nullable variables

2) Addition of productions with nullable variables removed

3) Remove ε-production

Eg 1. Consider the given productions

$S{\rightarrow}aS, S{\rightarrow}\varepsilon$.

S is nullable as $S{\rightarrow}\varepsilon$

Nullable ={S}

$S{\rightarrow}aS$

$S{\rightarrow}a\varepsilon$ [$S{\rightarrow} \varepsilon$]

Finally, we can write as

$S{\rightarrow}aS/a$

Eg 2. Consider the given productions

$S {\rightarrow}ACB|CbB|Ba$

$A{\rightarrow}da|BC$

$B{\rightarrow}gC|\varepsilon$

$C{\rightarrow}ha|\varepsilon$.

It is clear that

$B{\rightarrow}\in, C{\rightarrow}\varepsilon$ so B and C are ε productions

Consider, $A{\rightarrow}BC$

$A{\rightarrow}B\varepsilon$ [$C{\rightarrow}\varepsilon$]

$A{\rightarrow}\varepsilon$ [$B{\rightarrow}\varepsilon$]

Consider, S→ACB

    →ACε [B→ε]

    →Aε   [C→ε]

    S→ε [A→ε]

The nullable variables = {B, C, A, S}

    S→ACB|CbB|Ba

    →AC|CB|BA|A|B|C|Bb|cb|a   [after substitute each nullable variable in S]

    A→da|BC   [Original production]

    →da|C|B   [after substitute each nullable variable in A]

    B→gC

    →g   [after substitute each nullable variable in B]

Finally, we can write it as

    S →ACB|CbB|Ba| AC|CB|BA|A|B|C|Bb|cb|a

    A→da|BC | da|C|B

    B→gc|g

    C→ha

5.1.2. *Eliminate Unit Production*

Steps

- Any production of the form A→B, whose RHS consist of a single variable is called the unit production. All other productions including A→a|ε are non unit production. *Substitute non-unit productions into unit productions.*

  - A production of the form A→B, where A and B are both non terminals is called a unit production

Eg., 1. Consider the grammar

    S →AB, A→a

    C→D, D→E, E→a.

Here unit productions are

    C→D

    D→E

Non unit productions are

    S →AB

    A→a, E→a

Substitute non unit productions in unit productions

    C→D

    C→E   [D→E]

    C→a   [E→a]

Set of productions are

    S →AB

    A→a

    C→a

    D→a

    E→a

Now clear that there is no unit production.

Eg. 2. for the grammar

    A→B

    B→aa|C

    C→b.

Unit productions are

    A→B

    B→C

Non unit productions are

    B→aa

    C→b

Substitute non-unit production in unit production

    A→aa

    B→aa|b

    C→b.

Now clear that there is no unit production.

5.1.3. Useless Symbols

It consists of non-generating and non reachable symbols. First we find non-generating symbols and then only find the non-reachable variables.

Steps: Non-generating symbols

A symbol X $\in$ V [set of variables] is generating symbol if $x \ast \underset{G}{\Rightarrow} w$, Where w$\in$ T* that is every variable must generate a string of terminals.

Example 1: Identify the useless symbols in G= {V, T, P, S}, Given V={S, A, B}, T= {a} and P is S→a|AB and A→a.

Finding a non-generating symbols

S→a|AB

A→a

S and A are deriving the terminal strings that is

S→a

A→a

But B does not derive any terminal string that is S→AB, so B is non-generating symbol.

Find Non-reachable Symbol

A symbol A is reachable if it can be reached from the start symbols S that is if $S \underset{G}{\Rightarrow} \gamma$ and γ contains a variable A then A is reachable

S→a|AB

A→a

A, B are reachable from the start symbol S. so there is no non-reachable symbol

Eg:1 consider the Grammar

S→aAa

A→bBB

B→ab

C→aB, find the useless symbols.

Non-generating Symbol

All are generating symbols because every variable are forming the terminal symbols

Non-reachable Symbols

C is non-reachable symbol because S→A→B← C

5.2. Normal Form

When the production is CFG are made to satisfy certain restriction, the CFG is set to be in Normal form.

There are two types of Normal forms:
1. Chomsky Normal form (CNF)
2. Greibash Normal form (GNF)

5.2.1. Chomsky Normal Form (CNF)

A CFG without ε production is said to be in CNF if every production in the form of

1. A→BC where A, B, C $\in$ V
2. A→a where A $\in$ V and a $\in$ T.

Every CFG without ε productions can be converted into any equivalent CNF form.

Algorithm for CFG to CNF (or) Theorem

Step1: Eliminate unit production,ε-production, useless symbols from the grammar.

Step2: Every variable deriving the string of length two (or) more should consist only of variable ie. Every production of the form A→α with $|\alpha|{\geq}2$, α should consist only of variable.

Eg: consider a production A→V1V2aV3bV4

Terminal symbols a and b can be removed by overwriting the production

A→ V1V2aV3bV4 as

A→V1V2CaV3CbV4 and adding two productions

Ca→a

Cb→b

Step 3: Every production deriving three or more variable (A→α with $|\alpha|{>=}3$) can be broken down into a cascade of production with each deriving a string of two variables.

Eg: consider a production A→X1, X2....Xn.

Where n>=3 and as Xi's are variable

The production A→X1.X2...Xn should be broken down as given below

A→X1C1

C1→X2C2

C2→X3C3

:

Cn-2=Xn-1X n, each with two variables on right.

1. Find the CNF equivalent to S→aAbB,A→aA/a,B→bB/b.

Step 1: Simplification

The grammar is already in a simplified form without $\varepsilon-$ production, unit production and useless symbols

Step 2: Every symbol in α is the production of the form A → α where |α|>=2 should be a variable. This can be done by adding two productions

Ca→a

Cb→b

The set of productions after replacing the terminal symbols a and b

S→CaACbB

A→CaA/Ca

B→CbB/Cb

Step 3: Convert to CNF as the per rules given by the algorithm

$$S→C_1C_2$$
$$C1→CaA$$
$$C2→CbB$$

corresponding to S->CaACbB

A→CaA

A→Ca

B→CbB

B→Cb

Ca→a

Cb→b

Step 4: Finally the set of production are,

$$S→C_1C_2$$

C1→ CaA, C2→ CbB

A→CaA/Ca

B→CbB/Cb

Ca→a

Cb→b

2. Find a grammar in CNF equivalent to S →aAD, A→aB/bAB, B→b,D→d

Step 1: Simplification

The grammar is already in a simplified form without ε production, unit productions and the useless symbols.

Step 2: Every symbol in α in a production of the form A→α where |α|>=2 should be a variable

This can be done by adding two productions,

Ca→a

Cb→b

The set of production after replacing the terminal symbols a and b.

S→CaAD

A→CaB/CbAB

B→Cb

D→d

Step 3: Convert to CNF as per the rules given in the algorithm

S→CaC1 | corresponding to S→aAD
C1→AD

A→CaB
A→CbC2 | corresponding to A→aB/bAB
C2→AB

B→Cb | corresponding to B→b

Step 4: Finally the set of production are,

S→CaC1

C1→AD

A→CaB/CbC2

C2→AB

B→Cb

B→d

Ca→a

Cb→b

3. Convert the grammar S→AB/aB,A→aab/ε,B→bbA into CNF.

Step 1: Simplification

Eliminate ε production

Here the nullable variable is {A}

After eliminating the ε production

The set of production are

    S→AB/aB/B

    A→aab

    B→bbA/bb

Eliminate unit production

     S→B

After eliminating the unit production

The productions are

    S→AB/aB/bbA/bb

    A→aab

    B→bbA/bb

There are no useless symbols in the above production.

Step 2: Every symbol in α in production of the form A→α where |α|>=2 should be a variable

This can be done by adding two productions,

    Ca→a

    Cb→b

The set of production after replacing the terminal symbol a and b.

    S→AB/CaB/CbCbA/CbCb.

    A→CaCaCb.

    B→CbCbA/CbCb.

Step 3: Convert to CNF as per the rules given in the algorithm.

    S→AB/CaB/DbA/CbCb

    Db→CbCb

    A→DaCb.

    Da→CaCa.

    B→DbA/Db.

Step 4: Finally the productions are

    S→AB/CaB/DbA/CbCb

    Db→CbCb

    A→DaCb

    Da→CaCa

    B→DbA/CbCb

4. **Check whether the given grammar is in CNF**

    S→bA| aB

    A→bAA |aS|a

    B→aBB|bS|b   if it is not in CNF find the equivalent CNF.

Step 1: Simplification:

The given grammar is not in CNF. The following productions are not allowed in CNF

    S→bA| aB

    A→bAA |aS

    B→aBB|bS

Step 2: Finding the equivalent CNF

1. The grammar is already in simplified form.

Every symbol in α in production of the form A→α where $|\alpha|\geq2$ should be a variable.

This can be done by adding two productions

    Ca→a

    Cb→b

The set of productions after replacing the terminal symbols a and b

    S→CbA|CaB

    A→CbAA |CaS

    B→CaBB|CbS

Step 3: Convert to CNF as per the rules given in the algorithm

    S→C1A|C aB

    A→CbC$_1$

    C$_1$→AA   corresponding to A→CbAA

$A \rightarrow CaS$

$B \rightarrow CaC_2$

$C_2 \rightarrow BB \quad \Big| \; \text{corresponding to } B \rightarrow CaBB$

$B \rightarrow CbS$

$Ca \rightarrow a$

$Cb \rightarrow b$

Step 4: Finally the productions are,

$S \rightarrow CbA | C \, aB$

$A \rightarrow CbC_1 | CaS$

$B \rightarrow CaC_2 | CbS$

5. **Convert the grammar into CNF**

$S \rightarrow aSaA | A$

$A \rightarrow abA | b.$

Step 1: Simplification

There is no epsilon production

Eliminate unit production

$S \rightarrow A$

$S \rightarrow aSaA | abA | b$

$A \rightarrow abA | b$

There is no useless symbol

Step 2: Convert to CNF

This can be done by adding two new productions,

$Ca \rightarrow a$

$Cb \rightarrow b$

The set of production after replacing the terminal symbol a and b

$S \rightarrow CaSCaA | CaCbA | b$

$A \rightarrow CaCbA | b$

Step 3: Convert to CNF as per the rules given in the algorithm,

$S \rightarrow D_1D_2$

$D_1 \rightarrow CaS$

$D_2 \rightarrow CaA$

$S \rightarrow CaCbA$

$D_3 \rightarrow CbA$

$S \rightarrow CaD_3$

$A \rightarrow CaCbA$

$D_3 \rightarrow CbA$

$A \rightarrow CaD_3$

Step 4: The productions are,

$S \rightarrow D_1D_2 | CaD_3 | b$

$A \rightarrow CaD_3 | b$

5.2.2. *Greiback Normal Form (GNF)*

A context free grammar G={V,T,P,S} is said to be in GNF if every production is of the form $A \rightarrow a\alpha$, Where aϵt is a terminal and α is a string of zero or more variables.

Algorithm for Conversion from CFG to GNF

1. Eliminate ϵ-production, unit production and useless symbols from the grammar
2. In the production of the form, $A \rightarrow X1, X2,....Xi...Xn$, other than X1,

    Every other symbol should be a variable.

    X1 could be a terminal.

    Ex: all the productions must be of the form

    a) $A \rightarrow \alpha$ b) $A \rightarrow a$ c) $A \rightarrow a\alpha$
3. Rename variable as

    A1, A2, A3....An to create A production.

    Ex: $A \rightarrow aAB/B$

    A and B can be renamed as A1, A2 respectively.

    $A1 \rightarrow aA1A2/A2$
4. Modify the production to ensure that if there is a production

    $Ai \rightarrow Aj\gamma$ then i should be i<=j

If there is a production Ai→Ajα with i>j then we must generate production substituting for Aj.

5. Repeat step 5 until get production Ai→Ajα i<=j
6. Remove left recursion from every production of the form Ak→Akα

   B production should be added to remove left recursion
7. Modify Ai productions to the form Ai→aα where a is a terminal and α is a string of non terminal
8. Modify Bi productions to the form Bi→aα, where a is a terminal and α is a string of non terminal.

1. Construct a grammar in GNF which is equivalent to the grammar

S→AA/a

A→SS/b

Step 1: Simplification: The grammar is already in simple form without ε production, unit production useless symbols,

Step 2: No production is in the form A→aα   hence there is no second step

1) Variables S and A are renamed as A1 and A2

   A1→A2A2/a

   A2→A1A1/b

2) Every production of the form Ai→Ajα with i>j must be modified to make i<=j

   A2→A1A1.....substitute A1in A2

   $$A2 \rightarrow A1A1 => \begin{cases} A2 \rightarrow A2A2A1 \\ A2 \rightarrow aA1 \end{cases}$$

   The resultant production is

   A2→A2A2A1/aA1/b

   As per algorithm remove left regression

3) A2→A2A2A1/aA1/b   contains left recursion, so it can be removed through introduction of B2 production

   A2→aA1B2/aA1 $A_i \rightarrow A_i\gamma|\beta$

                             $A_i \rightarrow \beta B_i$

                             $B_i \rightarrow \gamma|\gamma\beta_i$

   A2→bB2/b

   Consider,

   A2→aA1B2/aA1/bB2/b

   B2→A2A1B2/A2A1

Step 3: The resultant productions are

A1→A2A2/a

A2→aA1B2/aA1/bB2/b

B2→A2A1B2/A2A1

A2 productions are in GNF

A1 and B2 productions can be converted to GNF with the help of A2 production

A1→A2A2/a   apply A_2 in A_1

A1→aA1B2A2/aA1A2/bB2A2/bA2/a

For B2

B2→A2A1B2

B2→aA1B2A1B2/aA1A1B2/bB2A1B2/bA1A2

B2→A2A1

B2→aA1B2A1/aA1A1/bB2A1/bA1

Step 4: The final sets of productions are

A1→aA1B2A2/aA1A2/bB2A2/bA2/a

B2→aA1B2A1B2/aA1A1B2/bB2A1B2/bA1A2/aA1B2A1/aA1A1/bB2A1/bA1

A2→aA1B2/aA1/bB2/b

Variables = {A1, A2, B2}

Terminals= {a,b}

Start symbol= {A1}

2.   Give the GNF for the following CFG, S→AB, A→BS/b,B→SA/a

Step 1: Simplification

There is no Ɛ production, unit production and useless symbols in given grammar

Step 2:

No production is in the form of A→aα

Step 3:

1) Variables S, A, B are renamed as A1, A2, and A3

A1➔A2A3

A2➔A3A1/b

A3➔A1A2/a

2) Every production of the form Ai➔Ajα with i>j must be modified to make i<=j

i<=j is not satisfied with A3.so substitute A1 in A3

A3➔A2A3A2/a

Again i<=j is not satisfied with A3 so substitute A2 in A3

A3➔A3A1A3A2/bA3A2/a

As per algorithm remove left recursion,A3 contains left recursion, left recursion from A3 production can be removed through introduction of B2 production

A➔βB/β

B➔αB/α

A3➔bA3A2B3/bA3A2

A3➔aB2/a

B3➔A1A3A2B3/A1A3A2

Step 4: The resultant productions are

A1➔A2A3

A2➔A3A1/b

A3➔bA3A2B3/bA3A2/aB2/a

B3➔A1A3A2B3/A1A3A2

A1, A2 and B3 production can be converted to GNF with the help of A3 production.

A1➔A2A3

A2➔A3A1/b

A2➔bA3A2B3A1/bA3A2A1/aB2A1/aA1/b

A1➔bA3A2B3A1A3/bA3A2A1A3/aB2A1A3/aA1A3/bA3

B3➔bA3A2B3A1A3A3A2B3/bA3A2A1A3A3A2B3/aB2A1A3A3A2B3/aA1A3A3A2B3/bA3A3
A2B3/bA3A2B3A1A3A3A2/bA3A2A1A3A3A2/aB2A1A3A3A2/aA1A3A3A2/bA3A3A2.

3. Give the GNF for the following CNF

S→ABAb|ab

B→ABA|a

A→a|b

Simplification: There is no epsilon production, unit production and useless symbols.

Consider the production S→ABAb|ab

Terminal symbol b should be removed by rewriting the production because every symbol should be variable expect first symbol.

S→ABAb/ab, S→ABACb/aCb adding one production Cb→b

S→ABACb/aCb

B→ABA/a

A→a/b

Cb→b

A is already in GNF so simply substitute A in S and B

S→aBACb/aCb/bBACb

B→aBA/bBA/a

A→a/b

Cb→b,

Hence all the productions are in GNF.

4. Give the GNF for the following CFG

S→AB

A→aA/bB/b

B→b.

A and B are already in GNF so simply substitute A in S

S→aAB/bBB/bB

A→aA/bB/b

B→b

Hence all the productions are in GNF.

5. Find the GNF equivalent to CFG

   $S \rightarrow BS$

   $S \rightarrow Aa$ $A \rightarrow bc$, $B \rightarrow Ac$

The productions are already in simplified form

   $S \rightarrow BS$, $A \rightarrow bc$

Consider the production $S \rightarrow Aa$ and $B \rightarrow Ac$

Terminal symbols a and c should be removed by rewriting the production because every symbol should be variable expect first symbol

   $S \rightarrow ACa$

   $B \rightarrow ACc$ and adding two productions

   $Ca \rightarrow a$

   $Cc \rightarrow c$

   $S \rightarrow BS$

   $S \rightarrow ACa$

   $A \rightarrow Bc$

   $B \rightarrow ACc$

Rename the variables S, A, B, Ca, and Cc as A_1, A2, A3, A4 and A_5

   $A1 \rightarrow A_3A_1 / A_2A_4$

   $A2 \rightarrow bA_5$

   $A3 \rightarrow A_2A_5$

   $A4 \rightarrow a$

   $A5 \rightarrow c$

Productions A_2, A_4, A_5 are already in GNF. So substitute A_2 in A_1 and A_3

   $A1 \rightarrow bA_5A_4$

   $A3 \rightarrow bA_5A_5$

Substitute A_3 in $A1 \rightarrow A_3A_1$

   $A1 \rightarrow bA_5A_5A_1$

The final sets of productions are,

$A1 \rightarrow bA_5A_5A_1$

$A1 \rightarrow bA_5A_4$

$A2 \rightarrow bA_5$

$A3 \rightarrow bA_5A_5$

$A4 \rightarrow a$

$A5 \rightarrow c$

5.3.   Closure Properties of Context-Free Languages

Closure Properties

A Context free language is closed under following operations:

a. Union
b. Concatenation
c. Kleene star
d. Context free languages are not closed under intersection.
e. The CFL is not closed under complementation.
f. The CFL is closed under reversal.

(i) CFL is Closed Under Union

Theorem

If L1 and L2 are Context free languages, then L1 ∪ L2 is a context free languages.

Proof

Let L1 be a CFL. It is generated by a context free grammar $G1 = (V_1, T_1, P_1, S_1)$.

Similarly, L2 is another CFL generated by a context-free grammar $G2 = (V_2, T_2, P_2, S_2)$.

We can combine the two grammars G1 and G2 into one grammar G that will generate the union of the two languages.

- A new start symbol S is added to G.
- Two new productions are added to G.
  $S \rightarrow S_1$
  $S \rightarrow S_2$

The grammar G can be written as:

$$G = (V_1 \cup V2 \cup \{S\},\ T_1 \cup T_2,\ P_1 \cup P_2 \cup \{S \rightarrow S_1 \mid S_2\}, S)$$

S can generate a string of terminals either by selecting start symbol S_1 of G_1 or start symbol S_2 of G_2. Thus S can generate a string from L_1 or from L_2.

Therefore, $L(G) = L_1 \cup L_2$.

(ii) CFL is closed under Concatenation

Theorem

If L1 and L2 are context free languages, then $L_1 L_2$ is a context free language.

Proof

Let L_1 be a CFL with the grammar $G_1 = (V_1,\ T_1,\ P_1,\ S_1)$.

Let L_2 be a CFL with the grammar $G_2 = (V_2,\ T_2,\ P_2,\ S_2)$.

A new language L is constructed by combining the two grammars G1 and G2 into one grammar G that will generate the concatenation of two languages.

- A new start symbol S is added to G.
- A new production is added to G.

   S→S₁S2

   The start symbol S will generate a string w of the form:

   $$W = w_1 w_2,\ \text{where } w_1 \in L_1 \text{ and } w_2 \in L_2.$$

   The grammar G can be written as:

   $$G = (V_1 \cup V2 \cup \{S\},\ T_1 \cup T_2,\ P_1 \cup P_2 \cup \{S \rightarrow S_1 S_2\}, S)$$

(iii) CFL is Closed under Kleene Star

Theorem

If L is a context-free language, then L^* is a context-free language.

Proof

Let L_1 be a CFL with the grammar $G_1 = (V_1,\ T_1,\ P_1, S_1)$.

A new language L is constructed from L_1, which is L_1^*.

$$\text{i.e. } L = L_1^*$$

- A new start symbol S is added to the grammar G of L.
- Two new productions are added to G.

   $S \rightarrow SS_1$

$$S \rightarrow \in$$

The production $S \rightarrow SS_1 \mid \in$ will **generate** a string w^* where $w \in L_1$.

The grammar G can be written as:

$$G = (V_1, T_1, P_1 \cup \{ S \rightarrow SS_1 \mid \in \}, S)$$

(iv) CFL is not Closed under Intersection

Theorem

Context-free languages are not closed under intersection.

Proof

Let us consider two context-free languages L_1 and L_2.

Where,

$$L_1 = \{ a^n b^n c^m \mid n, m >= 0\}$$

$$L_2 = \{ a^m b^n c^n \mid n, m >= 0\}$$

The language L_1 is a CFL with set of productions given below:

$$S \rightarrow AB$$

$$A \rightarrow aAb \mid \in$$

$$B \rightarrow cB \mid \in$$

The language L_2 is a CFL with set of productions given below:

$$S \rightarrow AB$$

$$A \rightarrow aA \mid \in$$

$$B \rightarrow bBc \mid \in$$

- A String $w1 \in L_1$ contains equal number of a's and b's.
- A String $w2 \in L_2$ contains equal number of b's and c's.
- A String $w \in L_1 \cap L_2$ will contain equal number of a's and b's and equal number of b's and c's.

  Thus, $L_1 \cap L_2 = \{ a^n b^n c^n \mid n >= 0\}$.

  From pumping lemma for CFL, a string of the form $a^n b^n c^n$ cannot be generated by a CFG.

  Therefore, the class of context-free languages is not closed under intersection.

(v) CFL is not Closed Under Complementation

Theorem

Context-free languages are not closed under intersection.

Proof

This theorem can be provided through contradiction.

Let us assume that CFL is closed under complementation..

If L_1 is context-free then L_1' is also context- free.

If L_2 is context-free then L_2' is also context- free.

Now, $L_1 \cup L_2$ can be written as $(L_1' \cup L_2')'$, which should also be a context-free.

Since, $L_1 \cup L_2$ is not guaranted to be context-free, our assumption that CFL is closed under complementation is wrong.

(vi) Intersection of CFL and RL

Theorem

If L is a CFL and R is a regular language, then $R \cap L$ is a CFL.

Proof

Let us assume that L is accepted by a PDA

$$M_1 = (Q, \in 1, \ \Gamma, \delta_1, q_1, z_1, F_1)$$

And R is accepted by a FA

$$M_2 = (Q_2, \in 1, \delta_2, q_2, F_2)$$

We can combine M_1 and M_2 into a single PDA $M = (Q, \Sigma, \ \Gamma, \delta, q, z, F)$. The PDA M will accept a string w if it accepted by the PDA M_1 and FA M_2 both executing in parallel.

The construction of M is given below:

$Q = Q_1 * Q_2$, the Cartesian product of states of M_1 and M_2

$$\Sigma = \Sigma_1 \cup \Sigma_2$$

$$\Gamma = \Gamma_1$$

$$q = (q_1, q_2)$$

$$z = z_1$$

$$F = F_1 * F_2$$

The transition function δ is defined as:

$$\delta\,((q_1,q_2),u,\beta\,) = ((p_1,\ p_2),y) \qquad \text{[transaction for M]}$$

If and only if

$$\delta_1(q_1,\,u,\,\beta) = (p_1,y) \qquad \text{[transaction for } M_1]$$

And

$$(q_2,u)\xrightarrow[M_2]{*}(p_2,\in)$$

- When M passes from state $(q_1,\ q_2)$ to state $(p_1,\ p_2)$, M_1 passes from state q_1 to p_1.
- Since, M_2 will read one symbol at a times, it requires $|u|$ steps to reach the state p_2 from q_2.

  Thus M is a PDA for intersection of $L(M_1)\cap L(M_2)$

(vii) CFL is closed under Reversal

Theorem

If L is a context-free language, then so is L^R.

Proof

Let us assume that $L = L(G)$ for some context-free grammar $G = (V,T,P,S)$

A grammar generating reverse of L is given by

$$G^R = (V,T,P^R,S)$$

P^R can be obtained from P by reversing the right hand side of the production.

If $A \rightarrow \alpha^R$ is a production in P^R.

CHAPTER 6

PUSHDOWN AUTOMATA

6.1. Pushdown Automata

A finite automation with control of both input tape and a stack on which it can store a string of stack symbols. Simply PDA is a finite automaton with stack.

It can remember on infinite amount of information with help of a stack.

A finite state control reads i/p, one symbol at a time. The PDA is allowed to observe the symbol at the top of the stack and based its transition on its current state, the input symbol, and the symbol at the top of stack. In one transition of the PDA:

- The control head reads the input symbol, and then go to the new state.

- Replaces the symbol at the top of the stack by any string.

6.1.1. Formal Definition of PDA

A PDA consists of seven components. A PDA P can be written as,

$$P = (Q, \Sigma, \delta, q_0, z0, \Gamma, F)$$

where,

Q$\rightarrow$ A finite set of states

$\Sigma \rightarrow$ A finite set of input symbols

$\Gamma \rightarrow$ A finite stack symbols which is allowed to push on the stack

$\delta \rightarrow$ Transition function

It takes as arguments a triple $\delta(q,a,x)$ where,

q $\rightarrow$ q is a state in Q input

a $\rightarrow$ a is either a symbol in Σ or a $\in \in$

x$\rightarrow$ stack symbol.

q0$\rightarrow$ initial state of Q

z0 $\rightarrow$ Initial state of stack

F $\rightarrow$ Accept or Final states

6.1.2. Moves

The moves of the push down automata from current state to next state can be represented by the symbol.

Moves by reading an input symbol:

$$(q, aw, x) \mid\text{-------} (p, w, y)$$

This moves represents after reading the input symbol a in state q, moves to state p and replaces the top symbol of stack x to y.

6.1.3. Instantaneous Description of PDA

The execution status of the push down automata is represented by the instantaneous descriptions (ID) of PDA. It is used to show the processing of strings. It records the state, stack contents and the input symbols. It contains three tuples. There are,

1. q-state of PDA
2. a –input symbol
3. γ-stack contents

If a PDA P= (Q, Σ, δ,q_0, z0, Γ,F) has the transition $^\delta$(q,a,x)=(p,y) then for all the strings w in Σ^* and $^\beta$ in Γ, the ID is given by

(q,aw,x) $\mid\text{------}$(p,w,y) this means that by reading the input symbol 'a' at the state q with x as top stack symbol replaces y and reaches the state 'p'.

6.1.4. Languages of PDA

1. Accepting by final state
2. Accepted by empty stack

    1. Let M = (Q, Σ, δ,q_0, Γ,z0,F) be a PDA. Thus the language accepted by a final state is

    L(M) = { ω/(q_0, ω, z_0) (p,$\in$, α)} for *some p in f and δ in Σ accepted by empty stack.*

    2. Let M = (Q,Σ, δ,q_0 Γ,z_0,F) be a PDA. Thus the languages accepted by an empty state is

    L(M) = {ω/ (q_0,ω,z_0) (p,$\in$, $\in$) for some P in Q}

    1. Construct a PDA for a language L = {$\omega\omega^R$/ω in (0+1)*}

    $\omega = 010$

    $\omega^R = 010$

    $\delta(q_1, 0, z_0) = \delta(q_1, 0z_0)$

    $\delta(q_1, 1, 0) = \delta(q_1, 10z_0)$

    $\delta(q_1, 0, 1) = \delta(q_1, 010z_0)$

    Pop top symbol from stack, if it's same as next input symbol (ω^R)

$\delta(q_1, 0, 0) = \delta(q_2, \epsilon)$

$\delta(q_2, 1, 1) = \delta(q_2, \epsilon)$

$\delta(q_2, 0, 0) = \delta(q_2, \epsilon)$

$\delta(q_2, \epsilon, z_0) = \delta(q_F, \epsilon)$

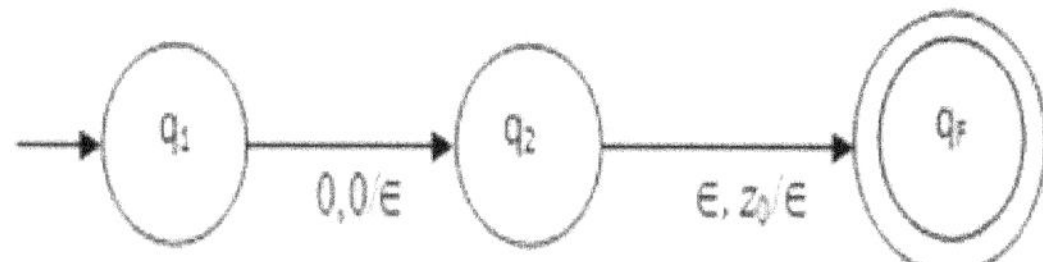

2. Construct the PDA for the language L= {aⁿbⁿ , n≥ 1}.

   W = aabb

1. Read each symbol of the input string of the 'a' and push on stack, until 'b' is encountered

$\delta(q_1, a, z_0) = \delta(q_1, az_0)$

$\delta(q_1, a, a) = \delta(q_1, aaz_0)$

2. Once 'b' is encountered , move to next state by performing pop operation

$\delta(q_1, b, a) = \delta(q_1, \epsilon)$

$\delta(q_1, b, a) = \delta(q_2, \epsilon)$

3. Once the stack is empty (0) input is epsilon, move to next state

$\delta(q_2, \epsilon, z_0) = \delta(q_F, \epsilon)$

The transition diagram is given by,

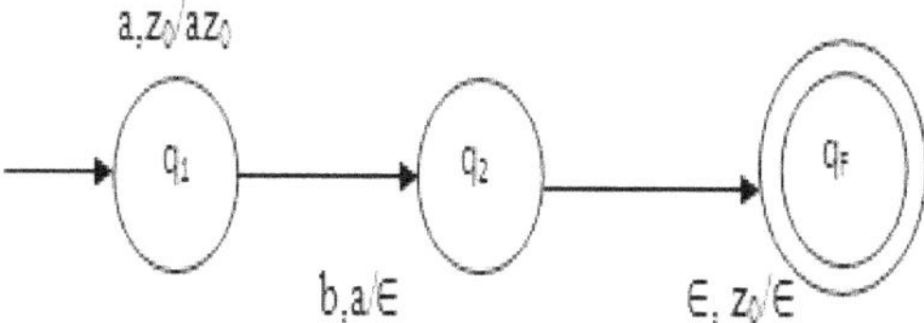

1. The PDA P i.e., given by,

   P = ((q₁,q₂,qF) , (a,b) , (a,b,z₀) , δ, q₁, z₀, qF)

3.Construct a PDA accepting $\{a^n\, b^m\, a^n /\ m, n \geq 1\}$ by empty stack.

Let P be a PDA,

$P = (Q, \Sigma, \delta, q_0, \Gamma, z0, F)$

n = 2, m = 2 (or) n = m = 2

w = aabbaa

1. The sequence of 'a' is should be pushed onto the top of the stack

$\delta(q_0, a, z_0) = (q_0, az_0)$

$\delta(q_0, a, a) = (q_0, aaz_0)$

2. On first b, the machine moves to next state and remains there for 'b' s, 'b' s will have no effect on the stack.

$\delta(q_0, b, a) = (q_1, a)$

$\delta(q_1, b, a) = (q_1, a)$

3. For every 'a' and 'a' i.e., popped from the stack

$\delta(q_1, a, a) = (q_2, \in)$

$\delta(q_2, a, a) = (q_2, \in)$

$\delta(q_2, \in, z_0) = (q_2, \in)$

The transition diagram is

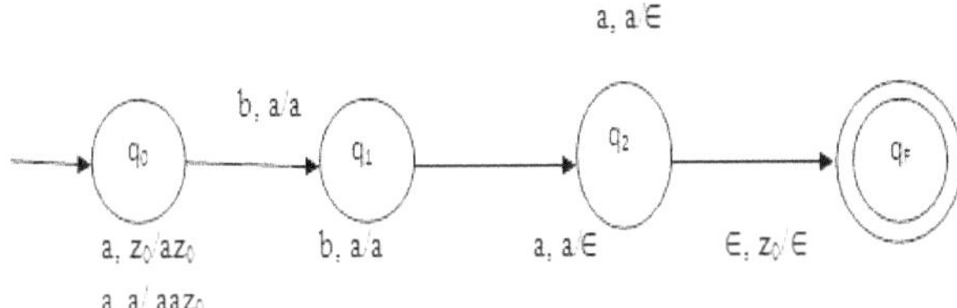

The PDA is given by,

$P = (\{q_0, q_1, q_2, q_F\}, \{a,b\}, \{a, z_0\}, \delta, q_0, z_0, q_F\}$

4. Construct a PDA for the language $\{a^n, b^{2n} /\ n \geq 0\}$

Let P be a PDA

$P = (Q, \Sigma, \delta, q_0, z_0, F)$

n = 2

w = aabbbb

1. The sequence of a's should be pushed onto top of the stack

$\delta(q_0, a, z_0) = \delta(q_0, a, z_0)$

$\delta(q_0, a, a) = \delta(q_0, aaz_0)$

2. For every pair of b's , one 'a' is popped from the stack

$\delta(q_0, b, a) = \delta(q_1, a)$

$\delta(q_1, b, a) = \delta(q_1, \in)$

$\delta(q_1, b, a) = \delta(q_1, a)$

$\delta(q_1, b, a) = \delta(q_1, \in)$

$\delta(q_1, \in, z_0) = \delta(q_F, \in)$

The transition diagram is given by,

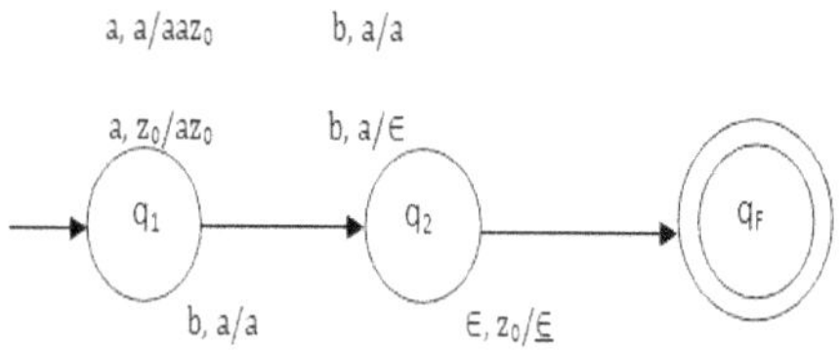

The PDA is given by,

$P = (\{q_0, q_1, q_f\}, \{a, b\}, \{a, z_0\}, \delta, q_0, z_0, q_F)$

5. Construct a PDA that accepts the Language
   $L = \{a^n b^m c^m d^n / m, n > 1\}$ by empty stack

   Let $M = \{Q, \Sigma, \Gamma, \delta, q_0, z_0, q_f\}$

   $W = abcd$

   1. a & b should be pushed

   $\delta(q_0, a, z_0) = (q_1, az_0)$

   $\delta(q_1, b, a) = (q_2, baz_0)$

   2. c & d should be popped from the stack

   $\delta(q_2, c, b) = (q_3, \varepsilon) | (q, az_0)$

   $\delta(q_3, d, a) = (q_4, \varepsilon) | (q_4, z_0)$

   $\delta(q_4, \varepsilon, z_0) = (q_F, \varepsilon)$

   Transaction diagram is given by,

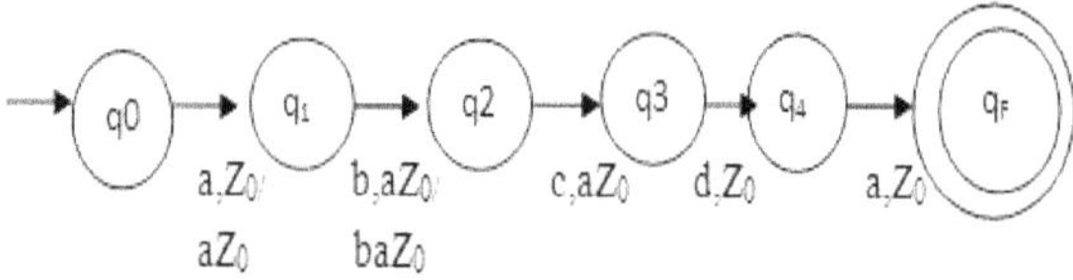

The PDA id given by,

$PDA = \{\{q_0, q_1, q_2, q_3, q_4, q_F\}, \{a, b, c, d\}, Z_0, q_0, q_F\}$

6. Construct a PDA accepting by empty stack the language $\{a^m b^m c^n \ / \ m,n \geq 1\}$

7. Design a PDA for recognizing the language $\{a^m b^n c^m \ / \ n,m \geq 1\}$

8. Construct a PDA to accept language $\{(ab)^n \ / \ n \geq 1\}$

9. Design a PDA for the deduction palindrome over $\{a,b\}$

6.2. Deterministic Pushdown Automata

There are two types of push down automata:

1. DPDA

2. NPDA

In a DPDA there is only one move in every situation. Whereas, in NDPA there could be multiple moves in every situation.

- DPDA is less powerful than NPDA.

- Every context free grammar cannot be recognized by a DPDA but it can be recognized by NPDA.

- The class of language a DPDA can accept lies between a regular language and CFL.

- In DPDA there is only one move in every situation. A DPDA is less powerful than NPDA. Every context free language cannot be accepted by a DPDA.

A DPDA is defined as:

$$M=\{ \ Q, \Sigma, \ \Gamma, \delta, q_0, z_0, F\}, \text{ where}$$

$\delta(q_0, a, x)$ has one move for any $q \in Q$, $x \in T$ and $a \in \Sigma$

6.3. Equivalence of PDA's and CFG's

The CFG G and Push down Automata P are said to be equivalent iff L (G) = L (P). The class of Language accepted by PDA is exactly the class of CFL. The following three classes of languages are same:

1. CFG

2. Language accepted by final state of PDA

3. Language accepted by empty stack of PDA

6.3.1. Conversion from CFG to PDA

Let G = (V, T, P, S) be a context free Grammar

Construct the PDA P that accepts L(G) by empty stack as follows

$$P = (\{q\}, T, V \cup T, \delta, q, \emptyset\}$$

where,

δ is defined by

1. For each variable A

    $\delta(q,\in,A) = \{(q, \beta) \ / \ A \rightarrow \beta$ is a production in G$\}$

2. For every terminal symbol a,

    $\delta(q,a, a) = \{(q,\in)\}$

1. Construct a grammar CFG to PDA

    E$\rightarrow$E+E

    E$\rightarrow$id

Solution:

The equivalent PDA is given by, s

$$P=(\{q\},\{id,+\},\{E,+,id\},\delta, q, \emptyset)$$

Where δ is defined by,

$\delta(q, \in, E) \qquad \rightarrow \{(q,E+E),\{q,id\}\}$

$\delta(q, id, id) \qquad \rightarrow \{(q,\in)\}$

$\delta(q, +, +) \qquad \rightarrow \{(q,\in)\}$

Test whether the input id+id+id is in N(P)

String w=id+id+id

$\delta(q, id + id + id, E) \rightarrow (q, id + id + id, E + E)$

$\rightarrow (q, id + id + id, id + E)$

$\rightarrow (q, +id + id, +E)$

$\rightarrow (q, id + id, E)$

$\rightarrow (q, id + id, E + E)$

$\rightarrow (q, id + id, id + E)$

$\rightarrow (q, +id, +E)$

$\rightarrow (q, id, E)$

$\rightarrow (q, id, id)$

$\rightarrow (q,\in, \in)$

id+id+ id $\in$ N(P)

2. Construct a PDA equivalent to CFG

$S \rightarrow 0BB$

$B \rightarrow 0S/1S/0$

Show that if L is generated by a CFG then there exist a PDA accepting L

Solution:

$S \rightarrow 0BB$

$B \rightarrow 0S/1S/0$

The equivalent PDA is given by,

$M=(\{q\},\{0,1\},\{0,1,S,B\},\delta,q, \emptyset)$

Where δ is defined by,

$\delta(q,\epsilon,S) \rightarrow \{(q,0BB)\}$ [S,B - Variables]

$\delta(q,\epsilon,B) \rightarrow \{(q,0S),(q,1S),(q,0)\}$

$\delta(q,0,0) \rightarrow \{(q,\in)\}$ [0,1 -Terminals]

$\delta(q,1,1) \rightarrow \{(q,\in)\}$

3. Construct a PDA equivalent of the grammar given below

$S \rightarrow aAA$

$A \rightarrow aS/bS/a$

Solution:

$S \rightarrow aAA$

$A \rightarrow aS/bS/a$

The equivalent PDA is given by,

$M=(\{q\},\{a,b\},\{a,b,S,A\},\delta,q, \emptyset)$

Where δ is defined by,

$\delta(q,\epsilon,S) \rightarrow \{(q,aAA)\}$ [A,S - Variables]

$\delta(q,\epsilon,A) \rightarrow \{(q,aS),(q,bS),(q,a)\}$

$\delta(q,a,a) \rightarrow \{(q,\in)\}$ [a,b - Terminals]

$\delta(q,b,b) \rightarrow \{(q,\in)\}$

4. Construct a PDA for the grammar

    S → aB/bA

    A → a/aS/bAA

    B → b/bS/aBB

Solution:

    S → aB/bA

    A → a/aS/bAA

    B → b/bS/aBB

The equivalent PDA is given by,

    $G = (\{q\}, \{a,b\}, \{a,b,S,A,B\}, \delta, q, \emptyset)$

Where δ is defined by,

    $\delta(q, \epsilon, S) \rightarrow \{(q,aB),(q,bA)\}$ [A,B,S -Variables]

    $\delta(q, \epsilon, A) \rightarrow \{(q,a),(q,aS),(q,bAA)\}$

    $\delta(q, \epsilon, B) \rightarrow \{(q,b),(q,bS),(q,aBB)\}$

    $\delta(q, a, a) \rightarrow \{(q,\epsilon)\}$ [a,b-Terminals]

    $\delta(q, b, b) \rightarrow \{(q,\epsilon)\}$

5. Construct a NPDA that accepts the language generated by a grammer

    S → aSbb/aab

Solution:

    S → aSbb/aab

The equivalent PDA is given by,

    $G = (\{q\}, \{a,b\}, \{a,b,S\}, \delta, q, \emptyset)$

Where δ is defined by,

    $\delta(q, \epsilon, S) \rightarrow \{(q,aSbb),(q,aab)\}$[S - Variable]

    $\delta(q, a, a) \rightarrow \{(q,\epsilon)\}$ [a,b -Terminals]

    $\delta(q, b, b) \rightarrow \{(q,\epsilon)\}$

6. Construct a pushdown automata that accepts the language generated by a grammar G=({S,A},{a,b},q,S) with the productions

   S → AA/a

   A → SA/b

   Solution:

   G =({S,A},{a,b},q, Ø)

   V = {S,A}

   T={a,b}

   Productions

   S → AA/a

   A → SA/b

   The equivalent PDA is given by,

   G=({q},{a,b},{a,b,S,A},δ,q,S)

   Where δ is defined by,

   $\delta(q, \epsilon, S)$ → {(q,AA),(q,a)} [S,A - Variables]

   $\delta(q, \epsilon, A)$ → {(q,SA),(q,b)}

   $\delta(q, a, a)$ → {(q,∈)}   [a,b - Terminals]

   $\delta(q, b, b)$ → {(q,∈)}

7. Convert the Grammar S→0S1/A, A→1A0/S/ε, into a PDA that accepts the same language by empty stack, Check whether 0101 belongs to N (P).

   The equivalent PDA is given by,

   M = {{q}, {0, 1}, {0, 1}, {0, 1, S, A}, q, Ø}

   Where δ is given by,

   δ (q, ε, S) → {(q,0S1), (q ,A)}

   δ (q, ε, A) → {(q,1A0), (q ,S), (q ,ε)}

   δ (q, 0, 0) → (q, ε)

   δ (q, 1, 1) → (q, ε)

w=0101

   (q, 0101, S) → (q, 0101, 0S1)

                → (q, 101, S1)

                → (q, 101, A1)

                → (q, 101, 1A01)

                → (q, 01, A01)

                → (q, 01, 01)

                → (q, 1, 1)

                → (q, ε, ε)

Therefore 0101 ε N (P)

6.3.2. *Construction of CFG from PDA*

We can find the Context Free Grammar G for any PDA, M such that

   L (G)=L(M)

We can construct an equivalent CFG for a PDA.

The variables of the CFG will be in the form of

   V={S, [pXq]} , where p,q ∈Q and X∈ Γ

Let the PDA is given by,

   M= {Q, Σ, Γ, $^\delta$, q0, z0, F}

Where, z0 is the initial stack symbol.

Then equivalent CFG is given by,

   G= {V, T, P, S}, where

   V={S,[pXq]} where p,q ∈ Q and X∈ Γ

Productions for the start symbol S is defined by,

   S→[$q_0 z_0 q_i$] for each q_i∈ Q,where z0 is the content of stack.

a.   The transition function $^\delta$ in the form of

   δ (q_0, 0, z0) =(q_0,XZ_0)

   q a A $q_1 B_1 B_2$

The equivalent productions are

$$[qAq_1] \rightarrow a[q_1B_1q]$$

b. The transition function δ in the form of

$$\delta (q_0 \ a \ A) = (q, \epsilon)$$

The equivalent production is

$$[q_0 \ Aq_1] \rightarrow a$$

c. The transition function δ in the form of

$$\delta (q_0, a, A) = (q, Z)$$

P a A   q B

The equivalent productions are

$$[PAq] \rightarrow a \ [qAq]$$

$$[PAP] \rightarrow a[qAp]$$

1. Convert the PDA $P = \{\{p, q\}, \{0, 1\} \{x, z_0\}, \delta, q, z_0\}$ to a CFG, if δ is given by

- $\delta (q, 1, z_0) = (q, xz_0)$
- $\delta (q, 1, x) = (q, xx)$
- $\delta (q, 0, x) = (p, x)$
- $\delta (q, \epsilon, z_0) = (q, \epsilon)$
- $\delta (p, 1, x) = (p, \epsilon)$
- $\delta (q, 0, z_0) = (q, z_0)$

Solution:

Variable $V = \{s, [qxq] \ [qxp] \ [pxp][pxq] \ [qz_0q] \ [qz_0p] \ [pz_0q] \ [pz_0p]\}$

The productions for start symbol S are,

$$S \rightarrow [qz_0q] \ / \ [qz0p]$$

(i) $\delta(q,1,z_0) = (q, xz_0)$

$$[qz_0q] \rightarrow 1 \ [qxq] \ [qz_0q]$$

$$[qz_0q] \rightarrow 1 \ [qxp] \ [pz_0q]$$

$$[q \ z_0 \ p] \rightarrow 1[qxq] \ [qz_0p]$$

$$[q \ z_0 \ p] \rightarrow 1[qxp] \ [pz_0p]$$

(ii) $\delta(q, 1, x) = (q, xx)$

$[qxq] \rightarrow 1[qxq][qxq]$

$[qxq] \rightarrow 1[qxp][pxq]$

$[qxp] \rightarrow 1[q\times q][qxp]$

$[qxp] \rightarrow 1[q\times p][pxp]$

(iii) $\delta(q,0,x) = (p,x)$

$[qxq] \rightarrow 0[pxq]$

$[qxp] \rightarrow 0[pxp]$

(iv) $\delta(q,\epsilon z_0) = (q,\epsilon)$

$[q z_0 q] \rightarrow \epsilon$

(v) $\delta(p,1,x)=(p,\epsilon)$

$[pxp] \rightarrow 1$

(vi) $\delta(p,0,z_0)=(q,z_0)$

$[pz_0q] \rightarrow 0[qz_0q]$

$[pz_0p] \rightarrow 0[qz_0p]$

After eliminating the unwanted variables, The CFG is given by

$S \rightarrow [qz_0q]$

$[qz_0q] \rightarrow \{1[qxp][pz_0q]\}$

$[qxp] \rightarrow \{1[qxp][pxp],0,[pxp]\}$

$[pxp] \rightarrow 1$

$[pz_0q] \rightarrow 0[qz_0q]$

2. Convert a given PDA to CFG.

PDA=$\{ (q_0,q_1), (0,1),(x,z_0), \delta, q0,z0, F \}$ δ is defined by

(i) $\delta(q_0,1,x) = (q_1,\epsilon)$

(ii) $\delta(q_0,0,x) = (q_1,xx)$

(iii) $\delta(q_1,\epsilon, x) = (q_1,\epsilon)$

(iv) $\delta(q_0,1,x) = (q_1,\epsilon)$

(v) $\delta(q_1,\varepsilon,x_0) = (q_1,\epsilon)$

(vi) $\delta\ (q_0,0,z_0) = (q_0,xz_0)$

Solution:

G= {V, T, P,S}

V={S, q_0 xq_1}, {S, q_0 **xz_0** q_1}

   ={S, q0xq1, q0z0q1, q1xq0, q1z0q0, q0xq0, q0z0q0, q1xq1, q1z0q1}

T={0,1}

S→[q0z0q1]/[q0z0q0]

Transition functions

(i) $\delta\ (q0,1,x) = (q1,\epsilon)$

   [q0 A q1]→a

   [q0 x q1]→ 1

(ii) $\delta\ (q0,0,x) = (q1,xx)$

   [q0xq1]→0[q0xq0][q0xq0]

   [q0xq1]→0[q0xq1][q1xq0]

   [q0xq0]→0[q0xq1][q0xq0]

   [q0xq0]→0[q0 xq1][q1xq0]

(iii) $\delta\ (q1,\epsilon, x) = (q1,\epsilon)$

   [q0Aq1]→a

   [q1xq1]→ ϵ

(iv) $\delta\ (q0,1,x) = (q1,\epsilon)$

   [q0Aq1]→a

   [q0xq1]→1

(v) $\delta\ (q1,\varepsilon,x0) = (q1,\epsilon)$

   [q0Aq1]→a

   [q1z0q1]→ ϵ

(vi) $\delta\ (q0,0,z0) = (q0,xz0)$

   [q0z0q0]→0[q0xq0][q0z0q0]

[q0z0q0]→0[q0xq1][q1z0q0]

[q0z0q1]→0[q0xq0][q0 z0q1]

[q0z0q1]→0[q0xq1][q1z0q1]

The productions are

[q0 x q1]→ 1

[q0 x q0]→0[q0xq0][q0xq0]/[q0xq1]→0[q0xq1][q1xq0]

[q0xq0]→0[q0xq1][q0xq0]/[q0xq0]→ 0[q0xq1][q1xq0]

[q1 x q1]→ ϵ

[q0 x q1]→1

[q1 z0 q1]→ ϵ

[q0z0q0]→0[q0xq0][q0z0q0]/ [q0z0q0] →0[q0xq1][q1z0q0]

[q0z0q1]→0[q0xq0][q0z0q1]/[q0z0q1]→ 0[q0xq1][q1z0q1]

3. Convert a given PDA to CFG

P = {{q0, q1},{a,b}, {z0,z} q0,z0,F} δ is

i) (q0, b,z0) = (q0zz0)

ii) (q0,ε,z0) = (q0,z)

iii) (q0,b,z) = (q0,zz)

iv) (q0,a,z) = (q1,z)

v) (q1,b,z) = (q1,ε)

vi) (q1,a,z0)=(q0,z0)

Solution:

V = {s, [q0Xq1]}

= {s, [q0 z0 z q1]}

= {s, [q0 z0 q1], [q0 z q1],[qz0q0] [q1zq0] [q0z0q0] [q0zq0][q1 z0q1][q1zq0]}

T = {a,b}

S → [q0 z0 q]

→ [q0 z0 q1] / [q0 z0 q0]

(i) δ (q0, b, z0) = (q0,zz0)

    q A q1   → a[qBq]

    [q0 z0 q0] → b[q0zq0] [q0z0q0]

    [q0 z0 q0] →b[q0zq1][q1z0q0]

    [q0 z0 q1]→ b[q0zq0] [q0z0q1]

    [q0 z0 q1]→ b[q0zq1] [q1z0q1]

(ii) δ (q0,ε,z0) = (q0,ε)

    [q0 A q1] → a

    [q0 z0 q0] → ε

(iii) δ (q0, b, z) = (q0,zz)

    q A q1   → a[q B1 q]

    [q0 z q0] → b[q0 z qo] [q0 z q0]

    [q0 z q0] →b[q0 z q1] [q1 z q0]

    [q0 zq1] → b[q0 z qo] [q0 z q1]

    [q0 zq1] → b[q0 z q1] [q1 z q1]

(iv)δ(q0,a,z) =(q1,z)

    P a A   q B1

    [PAq]   →a [qAq]

    [pAp]   →a[qAp]

    [q0zq1]   →a[q1zq1]

    [q0zq0]   →a[q0zq0]

(v). δ(q,b,z) =(q1, ε)

    [q0zq1]→b

vi). δ(q1, a, z0) = (q0, z0)

    P a A   q B1

    [PAq]→a [qAq]

    [pAp]→a[qAp]

[q1z0q0]→a[q0z0q0]

[q1z0q1]→a[q0z0q1]

The productions are,

[q0 z0 q0] → b[q0zq0] [q0z0q0] /[q0 z0 q0] →b[q0zq1][q1z0q0]

[q0 z0 q1]→ b[q0zq0] [q0z0q1] /[q0 z0 q1]→ b[q0zq1] [q1z0q1]

[q0 z0 q0]→ ε.

[q0 z q0] → b[q0 z qo] [q0 z q0] / [q0 z q0] →b[q0 z q1] [q1 z q0]

[q0 zq1] → b[q0 z qo] [q0 z q1] /[q0 zq1]→ b[q0 z q1] [q1 z q1]

[q0zq1] →a[q1zq1]

[q0zq0] →a[q0zq0]

[q0zq1] →b

[q1z0q0]→a[q0z0q0]

[q1z0q1]→a[q0z0q1]

6.4.   Pumping Lemma for CFG

Let G be a context free grammar. Then there exists a constant n such that any string w $\in$ L(G) with |w|>n can be written as w=uvxyz, subject to the following conditions:

1. |vxy|<= n, the middle portion is less than n.
2.   vy = ϵ, strings v and y will be pumped.
3.   For all i > 0, $uv^i xy^i z$ is in L. The two strings v and y can be pumped zero or more times.

Proof

Let us assume that the grammar

G is given by (V, T, P, S), 0(G) denotes that largest number of symbols on the right-hand side of a production in P.

In pumping lemma, it is a requirement that the constant n should satisfy the following condition:

$$n > 0(G)^{|V-T|}$$

Let us take a string w $\in$L(G), such that |w| > n. Let us construct a parse tree T with root as S. The parse tree T generates w with smallest number of leaves.

The tree T will have a path length of at least $|V - T| + 1$. This path will have $|V - T| + 2$ nodes with the last node labeled as terminal and remaining non-terminals.

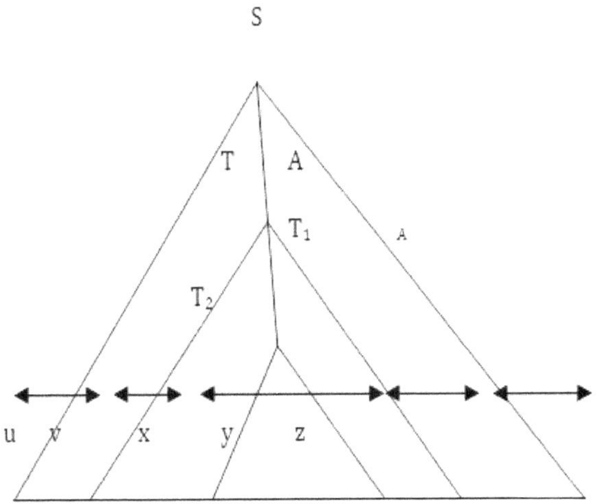

- x is generated by T_2.
- y is generated by T_1.
- u is generated by T.
- T_1 excluding T_2 can be replaced any number of items.

This will yield the string of the form uv^ixy^iz where $i > 0$.

1.   Prove that $L=\{a^ib^ic^i/i>1\}$ is not a CFL.

Solution

1.   Let us assume that L is CFL.

2.   Let us pick up a word $w=a^nb^nc^n$ where the constant n is given as per the pumping lemma.

3.   w is rewritten as uvxyz.

     Where $|vxy|< n$ and $vy \neq \epsilon$ i.e., both v and y are not null.

4.   From pumping lemma, if uvxyz $\in$ L then uv^ixy^iz is in L(G) for each i=0,1,2,………

     There are two cases:

     Case 1: vy contains all three symbols a,b and c.

     If vy contains all three symbols a,b and c then either v or y contains t two symbols. The exact ordering of a,b and c will be broken in uv^2xy^2z and hence $uv^2xy^2z \in$ L(G).

Case 2: If vy does not contain three symbols a,b and c then uv^2xy^2z will have unequal number of a's , b's and c's and hence $uv^2xy^2z \in L(G)$.Hence, it is proved by contradiction.

2. $A=\{\, a^{n2} \mid n \geq 1 \,\}$ is context free. If so, enumerate some members of the equivalent CFL.

Solution

$L=\{\, a^{n2} \mid n \geq 1 \,\}$ is not a context free language.

Proof that L is not a CFL

It can be proved using a contradiction. Let us assume that L is a context free language.

1. Let n be the constant as per the pumping lemma.
2. Let us choose a word $w=a^{n2}$.
3. w is rewritten as uvxyz.

Where $|vxy| \leq n$ and $v.y \neq \varepsilon$, both v and y are not null.

$|uvxyz|_= |a^{n2}|_= n^2$

$|uv^2xy^2z|_= |uvxyz| + |vy| > n^2$

And $|uv^2xy^2z| \leq n^2 + n$

$$\leq n^2 + 2n + 1$$

$$\leq (n+1)^2$$

$|uv^2ny^2z|$ is a square for every $i, uv^ixy^iz \in L$. But there is no square between n^2 and $(n+1)^2$. This is a contradiction. Therefore, L is not a CFL.

3. Prove that $L=\{\, 0^i\,1^i\,2^i\,3^j \mid i>=1 \text{ and } j>=1 \,\}$ is not context free.

Solution

1. Let us assume that L is CFL.
2. Let us pick up a word $\omega = 0^n\,1^n\,2^n\,3^n$, where the constant n is given as per the pumping lemma.
3. ω is rewritten as uvxyz where $|vxy| \leq n$ and $v.y \neq \varepsilon$ i.e., both v and y are not null.
4. From pumping lemma, if uvxyz ε L then uv^ixy^iz is in L(G) for each i=0,1,2,.........

There are two cases.

Case I: vy contains three symbols. These three symbols could be 0,1,2 or 1,2,3.The exact ordering 0,1,2,3 will be broken in uv^2xy^2z and hence uv^2xy^2z ε L(G)

Case II: If vy does not contain three symbols then uv^2xy^2z will have Either unequal number of 0's and 2's or unequal number of 1's And 3's.Hence, uv^2xy^2z ε L(G).

Thus, proved by contradiction.

CHAPTER 7

TURING MACHINES

7.1. Introduction

The machine consists of a finite control, which can be in any of a finite set of state.

There is a tape divided into squares or cells, each cell holds any one of a finite number of symbols.

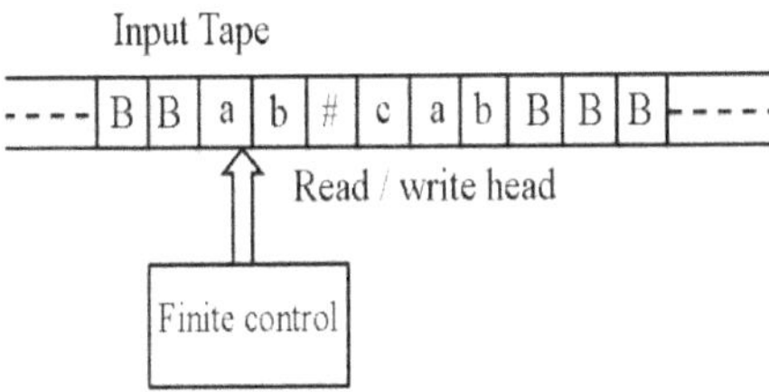

1. The input which is a finite length string of symbols chosen from the input alphabet, B placed on the tape.
2. The blank B is a tape symbol, but not an input symbol and there may be other tape symbols decide the input symbols and the blank.

The head is capable of performing three operations

1. Reading a symbol being scanned
2. Modifying a symbol being scanned
3. Shifting either to previous square (L) or next square (R)

Turing began by considering a human computer that is, a human who is solving some problem algorithmically using a pencil and paper. Turing decided that without any loss of generality, the computer could be assumed to operate under these three rules. It is used to define languages and to computer integer functions.

7.1.1. Components of a Turing Machine

A Turning machine is usually described as consisting of the following three components.

1. Tape
2. Head
3. Control unit

1. *Tape*

A tape is divided into a segment of numbered cells or squares. Each cell contains a symbol from some finite alphabet.

The alphabet contains a blank symbol (B) and one or more other symbol. The set of symbols of the tape is denoted by Γ.

2. *Head*

A tape head is always stationed at one of the tape cells and provides communication for the interaction between the tape and the control unit.

3. *Control Unit*

The reading from the tape or writing into the tape determined by the control unit. It contains a finite set of states Q.

Every computer algorithm can be implemented as a Turing machine, Therefore, C, C++, Prolog, Lisp, Small talk, and Java programs can be simulated in Turing machines.

Definition: A programming language is **Turing-complete** if it is equivalent to a Turing machine.

7.1.2. *Definition of Turing Machine*

A Turing Machine (TM) consists of 7 components or tuples

$$T = (Q, \Sigma, \Gamma, \delta, q_0, B, F)$$

where,

$Q \rightarrow$ Finite set of states

$\Sigma \rightarrow$ Finite set of input symbols

$\Gamma \rightarrow$ Finite set of tape symbols

$\delta \rightarrow$ Transition function mapping the state of finite automation and tape symbols

to states, tape symbols and movement of the head

i.e., $Q \times \Gamma \rightarrow Q \times \Gamma \times \{L, R\}$

$q_0 \rightarrow$ Initial state

$F \rightarrow$ Final state

$B \varepsilon \Gamma \rightarrow$ Blank symbol

Configuration

As Turing machine computes, it may halt with 'accept' or 'reject' or it may never halt. During computation, changes occur in:

1. The current state,
2. The current tape contents, and
3. The current head location.

The above three items form a "configuration" of the Turing machine.

7.1.3. Instantaneous Description for TM

A Turing machine changes its Configuration upon each move. We use instantaneous descriptions (IDs) for describing such configurations.

- Denoted by (α_1, q, α_2) where $q \in Q$, $\alpha_1, \alpha_2 \in \Gamma$ are strings and q is the current state.
- The move can be defined as: $(X_1, X2,.....X_{i-1}q\ X_i,X_{i+1},.....X_n)$ be an ID.

Church-Turing Thesis

Every function which would naturally be computed can be computed by a Turing machine. Every function that can be physically computed by a TM called as physically church-Turing thesis.

Types of Turing Machine

1. A random access Turing machine
2. Universal Turing machine
3. Alternating Turing machine
4. Oracle Turing machine
5. Probabilistic Turing machine

The language which is accepted by a Turing machine is called recursive enumerable language.

Comparison between TM and FA

S.No	TM	FA
1.	It is more powerful	Less power compare to TM.
2	It is both reading and writing machine.	It is a reading machine.
3.	It can modify its own input.	It can't modify its own input.
4.	TM can perform arithmetic operations.	It cannot be used for arithmetic operations.
5.	TM can handle CFL and context sensitive language.	The language accepted by FA is RL. It can't handle CFL.
6.	The read/write head moves to both left and right direction.	The read/write head moves only one direction (right)

7.2. Computable Languages and Functions

7.2.1. Computable Function

- A function 'f' defined from N→N (f : N→N) is a computable function with 'k' arguments, if there exists a TM M , that halts with the tape consisting of 0^m where f(i1,i2,......ik) = m
- Total recursive function : Computed by Turing machine that always halts
- Partial recursive function : Computed by Turing machine that may or may not halts

Examples

Design a Turing machine for

f(n) = n+1

f(x,y) = x

f(m,n) = m+n

The class of computable functions can be defined in many equivalent models of computation, including

- Turing machines.
- μ-recursive functions.
- Lambda calculus.
- Post machines (Post–Turing machines and tag machines).
- Register machines

Although those models use different representations for the functions, their inputs and their outputs, translations exist between any two models. Each computable function f takes a fixed, finite number of natural numbers as arguments.

Partial Recursive Functions

Note that the functions are partial in general, i.e. they may not be defined for every possible choice of input.

If a computable function is defined for a certain input, then it returns a single natural number as output (this output can be interpreted as a list of numbers using a pairing function). These functions are also called partial recursive functions.

In computability theory, the domain of a function is taken to be the set of all inputs for which the function is defined.

Total Recursive Function

A function which is defined for all possible arguments is called total. If a computable function is total, it is called a total computable function or total recursive function.

The notation $f(x_1, ..., x_k)\downarrow$ indicates that the partial function f is defined on arguments $x_1, ..., x_k$, and the notation $f(x_1, ..., x_k) = y$ indicates that f is defined on the arguments $x_1, ..., x_k$ and the value returned is y. The case that a function f is undefined for arguments $x_1, ... x_k$ is denoted by $f(x_1, ..., x_k)\uparrow$.

7.2.2. *Characteristics of Computable Functions*

The basic characteristic of a computable function is that there must be a finite procedure (an algorithm) telling how to compute the function. The models of computation listed above give different interpretations of what a procedure is and how it is used, but these interpretations share many properties. The fact that these models give equivalent classes of computable functions from the fact that each model is capable of reading and mimicking a procedure for any of the other models, such as a compiler is able to read instructions in one computer language and emit instructions in another language.

Enderton [1977] gives the following characteristics of a procedure for computing a computable function, similar characterizations have been given by Turing [1936], Rogers [1967], and others.

- "There must be exact instructions (i.e. a program), finite in length, for the procedure."
  Thus every computable function must have a finite program that completely describes how the function is to be computed. It is possible to compute the function by just following the instructions; no guessing or special insight is required.
- "If the procedure is given a k-tuple x in the domain of f, then after a finite number of discrete steps the procedure must terminate and produce f(x)."
  Intuitively, the procedure proceeds step by step, with a specific rule to cover what to do at each step of the calculation. Only finitely many steps can be carried out before the value of the function is returned.
- "If the procedure is given a k-tuple x which is not in the domain of f, then the procedure might go on forever, never halting.
- Thus if a value for f(x) is ever found, it must be the correct value. It is not necessary for the computing agent to distinguish correct outcomes from incorrect ones because the procedure is always correct when it produces an outcome.

Enderton goes on to list several clarifications of these 3 requirements of the procedure for a computable function:

1. The procedure must theoretically work for arbitrarily large arguments. It is not assumed that the arguments are smaller than the number of atoms in the Earth, for example.
2. The procedure is required to halt after finitely many steps in order to produce an output, but it may take arbitrarily many steps before halting. No time limitation is assumed.
3. Although the procedure may use only a finite amount of storage space during a successful computation, there is no bound on the amount of space that is used. It is assumed that additional storage space can be given to the procedure whenever the procedure asks for it.

The field of computational complexity studies functions with prescribed bounds on the time and/or space allowed in a successful computation.

7.2.3. Computable Sets and Relations

A set A of natural numbers is called computable (synonyms: recursive, decidable) if there is a computable, total function f such that for any natural number n, $f(n) = 1$ if n is in A and $f(n) = 0$ if n is not in A.

A set of natural numbers is called computably enumerable (synonyms: recursively enumerable, semi decidable) if there is a computable function f such that for each number n, $f(n)$ is defined if and only if n is in the set. Thus a set is computably enumerable if and only if it is the domain of some computable function. The word enumerable is used because the following are equivalent for a nonempty subset B of the natural numbers:

*   B is the domain of a computable function.
*   B is the range of a total computable function. If B is infinite then the function can be assumed to be injective.

If a set B is the range of a function f then the function can be viewed as an enumeration of B, because the list $f(0), f(1), \ldots$ will include every element of B.

Because each finitary relation on the natural numbers can be identified with a corresponding set of finite sequences of natural numbers, the notions of computable relation and computably enumerable relation can be defined from their analogues for sets.

In computability theory in computer science, it is common to consider formal languages. An alphabet is an arbitrary set. A word on an alphabet is a finite sequence of symbols from the alphabet; the same symbol may be used more than once. For example, binary strings are exactly the words on the alphabet {0, 1}. A language is a subset of the collection of all words on a fixed alphabet.

A language is called **computable** (synonyms: recursive, decidable) if there is a computable function f such that for each word w over the alphabet, $f(w) = 1$ if the word is in the language and $f(w) = 0$ if the word is not in the language. Thus a language is computable just in case there is a procedure that is able to correctly tell whether arbitrary words are in the language.

A language is **computably enumerable** (synonyms: recursively enumerable, semi decidable) if there is a computable function f such that $f(w)$ is defined if and only if the word w is in the language

7.2.4. Examples

The following functions are computable:

- Each function with a finite domain; e.g., any finite sequence of natural numbers.
- Each constant function $f: \mathbf{N}^k \to \mathbf{N}, f(n_1,...n_k) := n$.
- Addition $f: \mathbf{N}^2 \to \mathbf{N}, f(n_1,n_2) := n_1 + n_2$
- The function which gives the list of prime factors of a number.
- The greatest common divisor of two numbers is a computable function.

The following examples illustrate that a function may be computable though it is not known which algorithm computes it.

- The function f such that $f(n) = 1$ if there is a sequence of *at least* n consecutive fives in the decimal expansion of π, and $f(n) = 0$ otherwise, is computable. (The function f is either the constant 1 function, which is computable, or else there is a k such that $f(n) = 1$ if $n < k$ and $f(n) = 0$ if $n \geq k$. Every such function is computable.
- It is not known whether there are arbitrarily long runs of fives in the decimal expansion of π, so we don't know *which* of those functions is f. Nevertheless, we know that the function f must be computable.)
- Each finite segment of an uncomputable sequence of natural numbers (such as the Busy Beaver function Σ) is computable. E.g., for each natural number n, there exists an algorithm that computes the finite sequence $\Sigma(0), \Sigma(1), \Sigma(2), ..., \Sigma(n)$ — in contrast to the fact that there is no algorithm that computes the *entire* Σ-sequence, i.e. $\Sigma(n)$ for all n. Thus, "Print 0, 1, 4, 6, 13" is a trivial algorithm to compute $\Sigma(0), \Sigma(1), \Sigma(2), \Sigma(3), \Sigma(4)$; similarly, for any given value of n, such a trivial algorithm *exists* (even though it may never be *known* or produced by anyone) to compute $\Sigma(0), \Sigma(1), \Sigma(2), ..., \Sigma(n)$.

Incomputable Functions and Unsolvable Problems

Every computable function has a finite procedure giving explicit, unambiguous instructions on how to compute it. Furthermore, this procedure has to be encoded in the finite alphabet used by the computational model, so there are only countable many computable functions. For example, functions may be encoded using a string of bits (the alphabet $\Sigma = \{0, 1\}$).

Concrete examples of such functions are busy beaver, Kolmogorov complexity, or any function that outputs the digits of a non computable number, such as Chaitin's constant. Similarly, most subsets of the natural numbers are not computable. The Halting problem was the first such set to be constructed.

7.3. Techniques for Turing Machine Construction

A Turing machine is also as powerful as a conventional computer. The following are the different techniques of constructing a TM to meet high level needs.

1.   Storage in the finite control (or) state.
2.   Multiple tracks.
3.   Sub-routines
4.   Checking off symbols.

7.3.1. *Storage in the State (or) Storage in the Finite Control*

The finite control can also be used to hold finite amounts of information along with the task of representing a position in the program. The state is written as a pair of elements, one for control and the other storing a symbol.

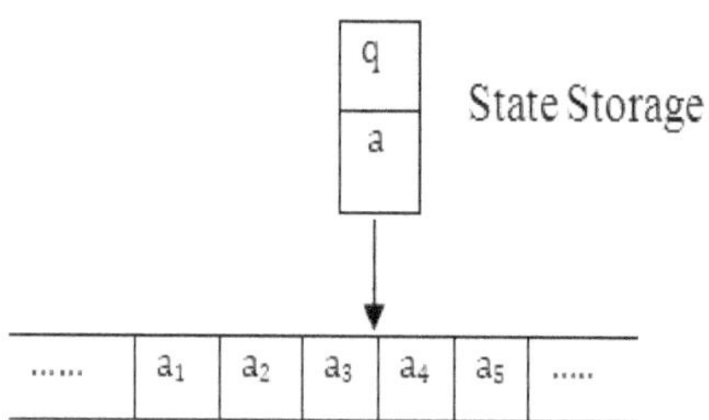

7.3.2. *Multiple Tracks*

It is also possible that a Turing machines input tape can be divided into several tracks. Each track can hold one symbols and the tape alphabet of the TM consists of tapes with one component for each track.

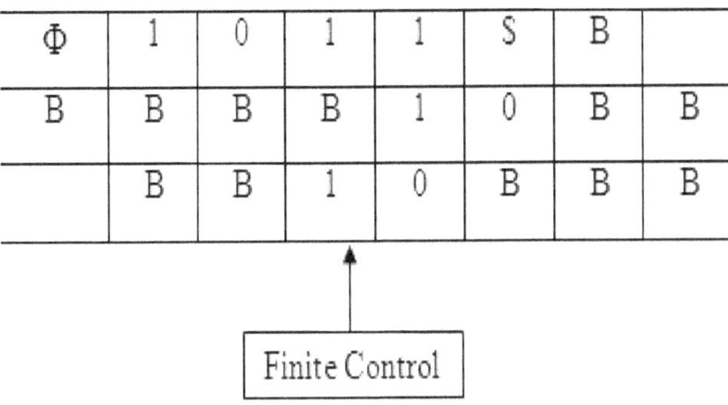

A three track Turing machine

7.3.3. Sub-routines

A problem with same tasks to be repeated for many number of times, can be programmed using sub-routines. A Turing machine with sub-routine is a set of states that perform some useful process.

The idea here is to write part of a TM programs to serve as a sub-routine which has its own initial state and a return state for returning to the calling routine. It improves the modular or top-down programming design.

Example

Design a Turing machine to check whether the given input is prime or not using multiple tracks.

Solution

The binary input greater than two is placed on the first track and also the same input is placed on the third track. Then TM writes the number two in binary form on the second track. Then divide the three tracks by the second as follows.

The number on the second track is subtracted from the third track as many times as possible, till getting the remainder. If the remainder is zero, then the number on the first track is not a prime.

If the remainder is non zero, then increase the number on the second track by one. If the second track equals the first, the number given is a prime because it should be divided by one and itself.

7.4. Multi-head and Multi-tape Turing Machine

7.4.1. *Multi-head Turing Machine*

A Turing machine with single tape can have multiple heads. Let us consider a Turing machine with two heads H_1 and H_2. Each head is capable of performing read or write or move operation independently.

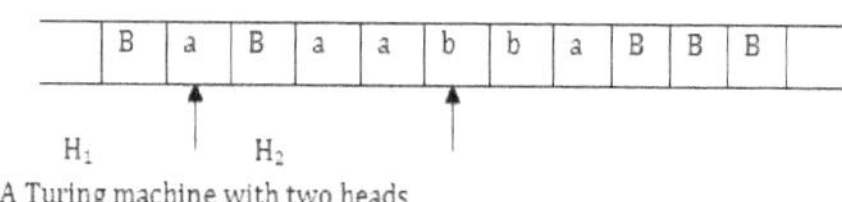

A Turing machine with two heads

The transition behavior of two head with one tape Turing machine can be defined as,

δ (state, symbol under H1, symbol under H2) = (New state), (S_1, M_1), (S_2, M_2))

Where,

S_1 = The symbol to be written in the cell under H_1

M_1 = The movement (L, R, N) of H_1

S_2 = The symbol to be written in the cell under H_2

M_2 = The movement (L, R, N) of H_2

7.4.2. *Multi-tape Turing Machine*

A Multi-tape Turing machine has a finite control with some finite no. of tapes. Each tape is an infinite in both directions. It has its own initial state and some acceptance states. Initially,

- The finite set on input symbols is placed on the first tape.
- All the other cells of all the tapes hold the blank.
- The control head of the first tape is at the left end of the input.

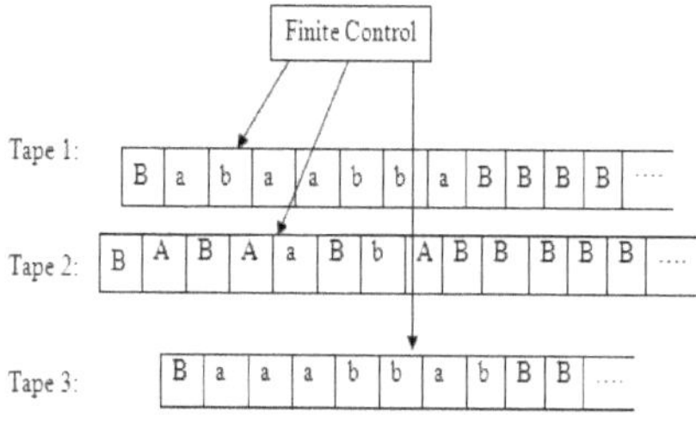

Multi-tape Turing machine

In one move, the multi-tape TM can

1. Change state.
2. Print a new symbol on each of the cells scanned by its tape heads.
3. Move each of its tape heads, independently, one cell to the left or right or keep it stationary.

7.5.   Turing Machine Variants

Turing machines can be extended in various ways, but so long as a new TM only reads and writes a finite number of symbols in each step, an old TM can still simulate it.

- Multitape TM
- Non-deterministic TM
- Enumerators
- Equivalence: All have same power
    1. Recognize the same class of languages
    2. Can be simulated by an ordinary TM

7.5.1. Multitape TM

A Turing machine with additional tapes where each tape is accessible individually, with the input on the first tape, and with the others blank at the beginning.

Theorem

Every Multitape Turing machine has an equivalent single-tape Turing machine.

Multitape TM

Put # in a single tape for separation of original k tapes.

Each movement of M is simulated by a series movement of S on each segment.

For a right move on the rightmost cell of i th tape in M, S write blank symbol in $(i+1)th$, and right-shift all symbols after that one cell.

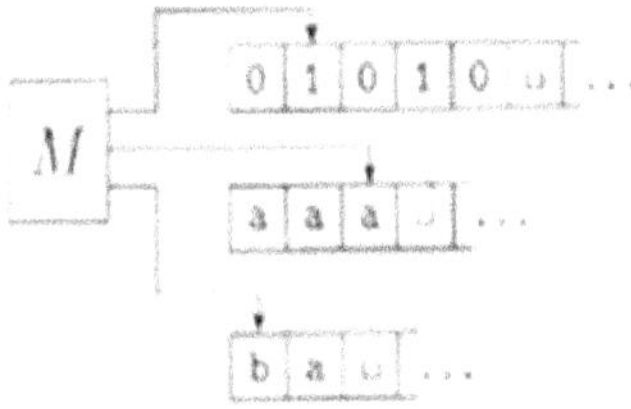

7.5.2. *Nondeterministic TMs*

- A nondeterministic Turing machine is one in which the transition is mapping to the power set of Q X Γ X {L,R}.It accepts an input if it enters an accepting state for some computation path.

- A non-deterministic TM is identical to an ordinary TM except: $\delta : Q \, X \, \Gamma \rightarrow P(Q \, X \, \Gamma X\{ L,R\})$

- At any point the head has several possibilities to read/write/move.

- In deterministic TM, a computation is a single path with sequence of configurations.

- In nondeterministic TM, a computation is a tree or a directed accepts an input string if there exists a path acyclic graph .A NTM leading to an accept state.

- If all paths lead to reject state, then this input is rejected.

    Theorem:

    Every NTM has an equivalent   DTM.

    For a computing tree of a NTM   N with an input w, simulated with a 3-tape DTM M:

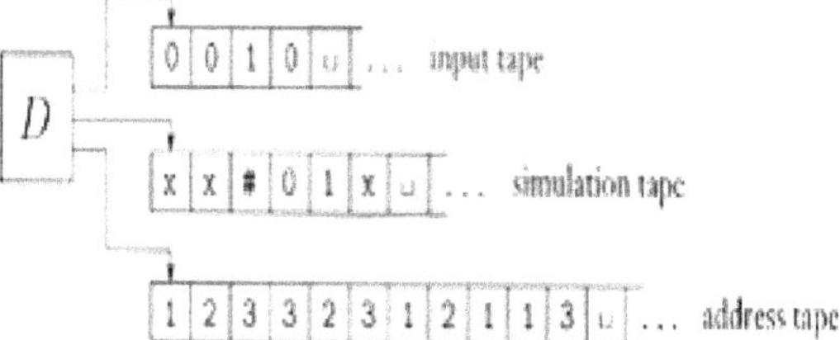

1st tape: input w

2nd tape: tape of a computing path with N

3rd tape: address tape (finite)

Non Deterministic TMs

1. Initially tape 1 contains the input w, and tapes 2 and 3 are empty.

2. Copy tape 1 to tape 2.

3. Use tape 2 to simulate N with input w on one branch of its non-deterministic computation. Before each step of N consult the next symbol on tape 3 to decide which branch to move. If no symbol remains or this choice is invalid goto step 4. If reject also goto 4.

4. Increase the count on tape 3 and go to step 2.

7.5.3. *Enumerator*

- Semantically, an enumerator is a TM with an attached printer
- Every time the TM wants to add a string to its output list, it sends the string to the printer.
- The language enumerated by an enumerator E is the collection of all the strings that E eventually prints out.

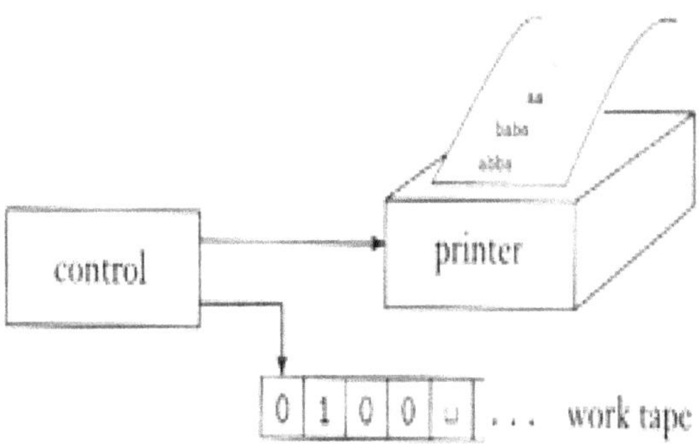

Enumerator

Theorem:

A language is Turing-recognizable iff some enumerator enumerates it.

- For a language, if E enumerates it, then construct a TM M works as:
    - Run E Every time that E outputs a string, compare it with input w.
    - If w appears in the output of E, *accept*.
- For a language recognized by a TM M, construct
    - Run M for i steps on each input, $s1, s2, ..., si$.
    - If any computations accept, print out the corresponding sj.
    - Repeat the above two steps with all possible inputs
- An enumerator can be regarded as a 2-tape TM.

7.6. Halting Problem

Alan Turing proved in 1936 that a general algorithm to solve the halting problem for all possible program-input pairs cannot exist. A key part of the proof was a mathematical definition of a computer and program, which became known as a Turing machine; the halting problem is undecidable over Turing machines.

Undecidable Languages

For an undecidable language, there is no Turing Machine which accepts the language and makes a decision for every input string **w** (TM can make decision for some input string though). A decision problem **P** is called "undecidable" if the language **L** of all yes instances to **P** is not decidable. Undecidable languages are not recursive languages, but sometimes, they may be recursively enumerable languages.

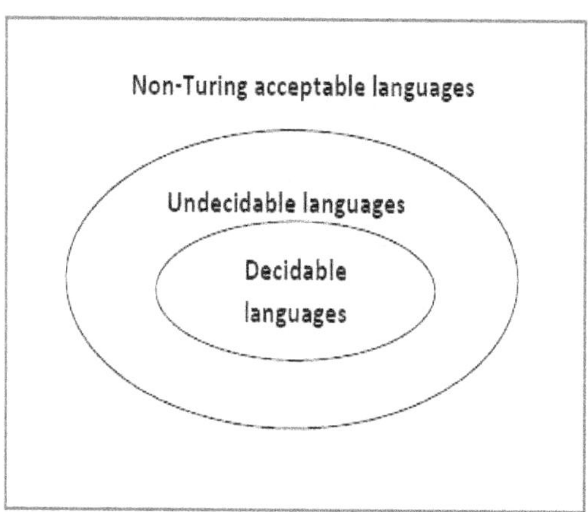

Example

- The halting problem of Turing machine
- The mortality problem
- The mortal matrix problem

The Post correspondence problem, etc.

One of well known unsolvable problems is the halting problem. It asks the following question: Given an arbitrary Turing machine M over alphabet Σ = {a ,b}, and an arbitrary string w over Σ, does M halt when it is given w as an input ?

It can be shown that the halting problem is not decidable, hence unsolvable.

Theorem 1: The halting problem is undecidable.

Proof (by M.L. Minsky): This is going to be proven by "proof by contradiction". Suppose that the halting problem is decidable. Then there is a Turing machine T that solves the halting problem. That is, given a description of a Turing machine M (over the alphabet Σ) and a string w, T writes "yes" if M halts on w and "no" if M does not halt on w, and then T halts.

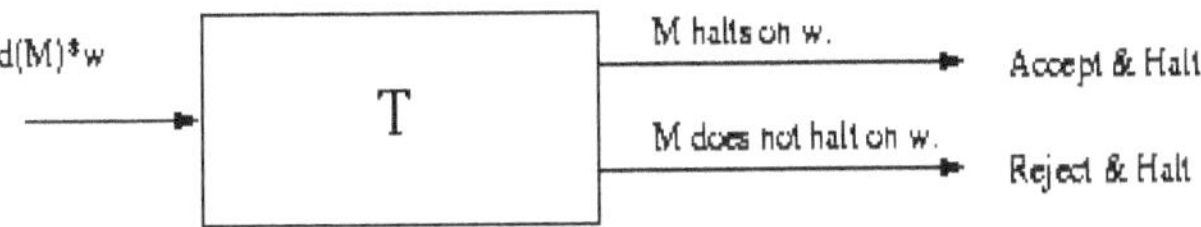

Turing machine T

We are now going to construct the following new Turing machine T_c. First we construct a Turing machine T_m by modifying T so that if T accepts a string and halts, then T_m goes into an infinite loop (T_m halts if the original T rejects a string and halts).

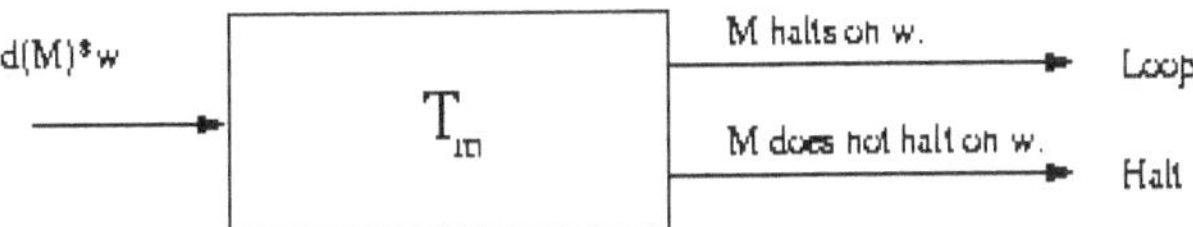

Turing machine T_m

Next using T_m we are going to construct another Turing machine T_c as follows: T_c takes as input a description of a Turing machine M, denoted by d(M), copies it to obtain the string d(M)*d(M), where * is a symbol that separates the two copies of d(M) and then supplies d(M)*d(M) to the Turing machine T_m

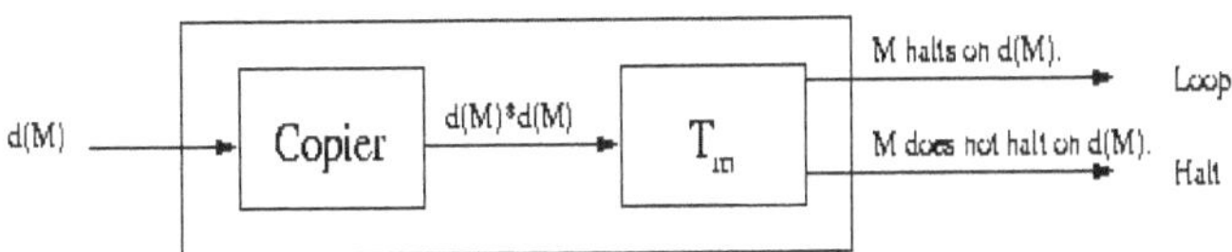

Turing machine T_c

Let us now see what T_c does when a string describing T_c itself is given to it. When T_c gets the input d(T_c) , it makes a copy, constructs the string d(T_c)*d(T_c) and gives it to the modified T. Thus the modified T is given a description of Turing machine T_c and the string d(T_c).

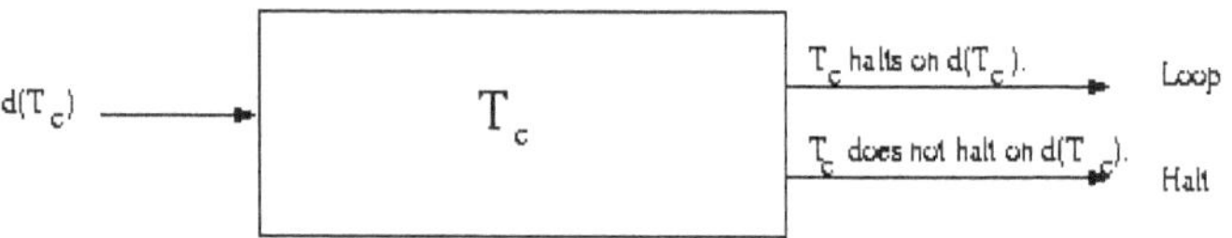

Turing machine T_c on input $d(T_c)$

The way T was modified the modified T is going to go into an infinite loop if T_c halts on $d(T_c)$ and halts if T_c does not halt on $d(T_c)$. Thus T_c goes into an infinite loop if T_c halts on $d(T_c)$ and it halts if T_c does not halt on $d(T_c)$. This is a contradiction. This contradiction has been deduced from our assumption that there is a Turing machine that solves the halting problem. Hence that assumption must be wrong. Hence there is no Turing machine that solves the halting problem.

7.6.1. Rice's Theorem

Any nontrivial property about the language recognized by a Turing machine is undecidable.

A property about Turing machines can be represented as the language of all Turing machines, encoded as strings, that satisfy that property. The property P is *about the language recognized by Turing machines* if whenever L(M)=L(N) then P contains (the encoding of) M iff it contains (the encoding of) N. The property is non-trivial if there is at least one Turing machine that has the property, and at least one that hasn't.

Proof: Without limitation of generality we may assume that a Turing machine that recognizes the empty language does not have the property P. For if it does, just take the complement of P. The undecidability of that complement would immediately imply the undecidability of P.

In order to arrive at a contradiction, suppose P is decidable, i.e. there is a halting Turning machine B that recognizes the descriptions of Turing machines that satisfy P. Using B we can construct a Turning machine A that accepts the language {(M,w)| M is the description of a Turing machine that accepts the string w}. As the latter problem is undecidable this will show that B cannot exists and P must be undecidable as well. Let MP be a Turing machine that satisfies P (as P is non-trivial there must be one). Now A operates as follows:

1. On input (M,w), create a (description of a) Turing machine C(M,w) as follows:
    1. On input x, let the Turing machine M run on the string w until it accepts (so if it doesn't accept C(M,w) will run forever).
    2. Next run MP on x. Accept iff MP does.

Note that C(M,w) accepts the same language as MP if M accepts w; C(M,w) accepts the empty language if M does not accept w.

Thus if M accepts w the Turing machine C(M,w) has the property P, and otherwise it doesn't.

2. Feed the description of C(M,w) to B. If B accepts, accept the input (M,w); if B rejects, reject.

7.7. Solvability

Solvable

- An algorithm to solve
- A TM decides it.

Unsolvable

- No algorithm to solve
- No TM can decide it.

Decidable Language

- Acceptance problem: Whether a particular DFA B accepts a given input string w.
- Regular language: R is a regular expression that generates w
- Finite Automata: M is a NFA that accepts string w

Recognizing vs. Deciding Language

- A language is Turing-recognizable if some Turing machine recognizes it is called as recursively enumerable language.
- Turing-recognizable: A language L is "Turing-recognizable" if there exists a TM M such that for all strings w:

  If $w \in L$ eventually M enters a_{ccept}

  If $w \notin L$ either M enters q_{reject} *or* M never terminates.

Solvable & Partially Solvable Problems

- A problem P is *decidable* (*solvable*) if there is a Turing machine T that solves P; such a T always halts, else P is *undecidable* (*unsolvable*).
- A problem P is *semidecidable* (*partially decidable, partially solvable*) if there is a Turing machine T that *partially solves* P; such a T solves all instances of P for which the right answer is "yes", but fails to halt for all instances of P for which the right answer is "no".

Examples

- The blank tape halting problem is semi decidable if there is a Turing machine M such that TM T, halts and says "yes" if T halts on blank tape, but M fails to halt if T fails to halt on blank tape

- The passing problem is semi decidable if there is a Turing machine M that, given an encoding of a student A, halts and says "yes" if A passes the course, but fails to halt if A fails the course.

- Any problem whose base set is finite, is decidable.

7.8.   Problems about Turing Machine

a.   Construct a Turing Machine for Language $L=\{a^n b^n, n>=1\}$

L={ab,aabb,aaabbb,................................}

Q= {q0, q1, q2, q3, q4}

Γ={a, b,B,X,Y}

q0=initial state

q4=final state or halting state

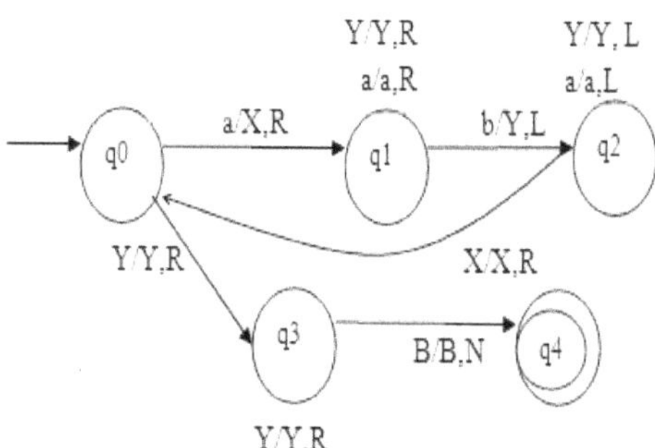

Input Γ States	a	b	X	Y	B
q0	(q1,X,R)	-	-	(q3,Y,R)	-
q1	(q1,a,R)	(q2,Y,L)	-	(q1,Y,R)	-
q2	(q2,a,L)	-	(q0,X,R)	(q2,Y,L)	-
q3	-	-	-	(q3,Y,R)	(q4,B,N)
q4	-	-	-	-	-

b. Construct a Turing Machine for the Language, L={ $0^n 1^n, n>=1$}

L= {01, 0011, 000111,.................................}

Q= {q0, q1, q2, q3, q4}

Γ= {0, 1, B, X, Y}

q0=initial state

q4=final state or halting state

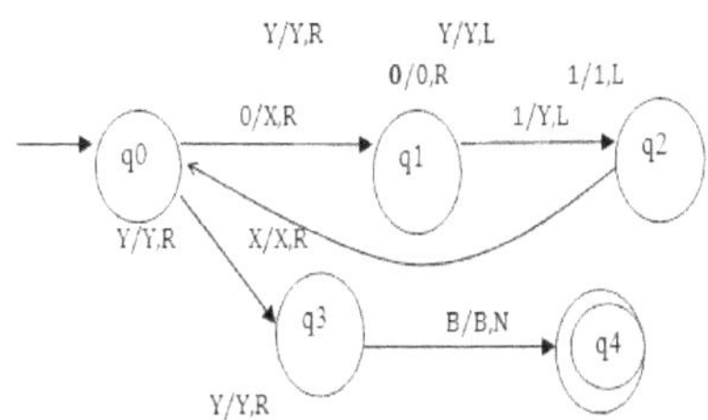

Input Γ States	0	1	X	Y	B
q0	(q1,X,R)	-	-	(q3,Y,R)	-
q1	(q1,0,R)	(q2,Y,L)	-	(q1,Y,R)	-
q2	(q2,0,L)	-	(q0,X,R)	(q2,Y,L)	-
q3	-	-	-	(q3,Y,R)	(q4,B,N)
q4	-	-	-	-	-

c. Construct a Turing Machine for the Language L={ $a^n b^n c^n, n>=1$}

L={abc,aabbcc,....................}

Q={q0,q1,q2,q3,q4,q5}

B-Blank symbol

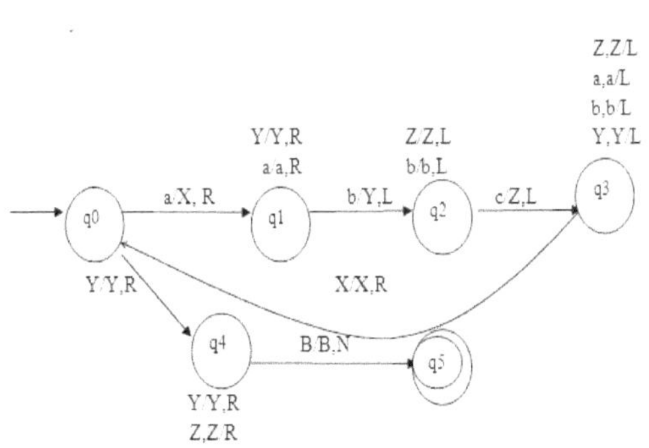

Input Γ / States	a	b	c	X	Y	Z	B
q0	(q1,X,R)	-	-	-	(q4,Y,R)	-	-
q1	(q1,a,R)	(q2,Y,R)		-	(q1,Y,R)	-	-
q2	-	(q2,b,R)	(q3,Z,L)	-	-	(q2,Z,R)	-
q3	(q3,a,L)	(q3,b,L)	-	(q0,X,R)	(q3,Y,L)	(q3,Z,L)	-
q4	-	-	-	-	(q4,Y,R)	(q4,Z,R)	(q5,B,N)
q5	-	-	-	-	-	-	-

d. Construct a Turing Machine Accept the String Over the Alphabet which Contains Even Number of 1's

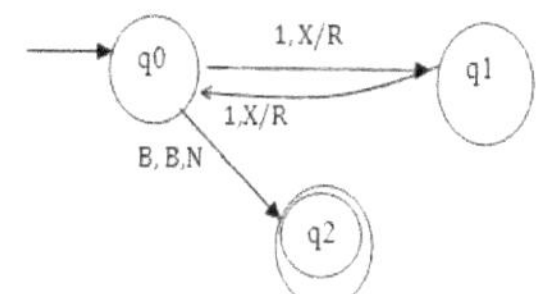

Input/States	1	X	B
q0	(q1,X,R)	-	(q2,B,N)
q1	(q0,X,R)	-	-
q2	-	-	-

e. Construct Turing Machine for Language, $L=\{a^n b^n c^n d^n, n \geq 1\}$

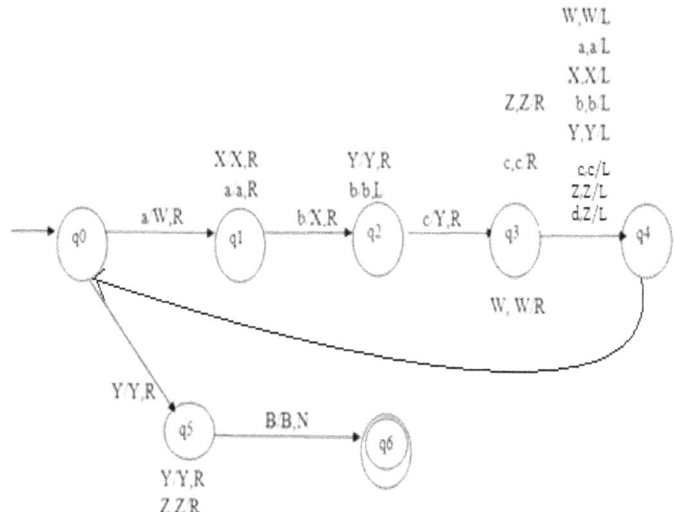

Input Γ \ States	a	b	c	d	W	X	Y	Z	B
q0	(q1,X,R)	-	-		-	(q4,Y,R)	-		-
q1	(q1,a,R)	(q2,Y,R)			-	(q1,Y,R)	-		-
q2	-	(q2,b,R)	(q3,Z,L)		-	-	(q2,Z,R)		-
q3	(q3,a,L)	(q3,b,L)	-		(q0,X,R)	(q3,Y,L)	(q3,Z,L)		-
q4	-	-	-		-	(q4,Y,R)	(q4,Z,R)		(q5,B,N)
q5	-	-	-		-	-	-		-

7.9. Chomskian Hierarchy of Languages

The Chomsky hierarchy is a containment hierarchy of classes of formal grammars. The Chomsky Hierarchy, in essence, allows the possibility for the understanding and use of a computer science model which enables a programmer to accomplish meaningful linguistic goals systematically.

A formal grammar of this type consists of a finite set of production or rules (left-hand side $\rightarrow$ right-hand side), where each side consists of a sequence of the following symbols:

- a finite set of non terminal symbols (indicating that some production can yet be applied).
- a finite set of terminal symbols (indicating that no production can be applied).
- a start symbol (a distinguished non terminal symbol).

A formal grammar defines (or generates) a formal language, which is a (usually infinite) set of finite-length sequences of symbols (i.e. strings) that may be constructed by applying productions to another sequence of symbols which initially contains just the start symbol.

A rule may be applied to a sequence of symbols by replacing an occurrence of the symbols on the left-hand side of the rule with those that appear on the right-hand side.

A sequence of rule applications is called a derivation. Such a grammar defines the formal language, all words consisting of terminal symbols which can be reached by a derivation from the start symbol.

The Hierarchy

The Chomsky hierarchy consists of the following levels:

- **Type-0 grammars** (unrestricted grammars) include all formal grammars. They generate exactly all languages that can be recognized by a Turing machine. These languages are also known as the recursively enumerable languages.
- **Type-1 grammars** (context-sensitive grammars) generate the context-sensitive languages. These grammars have rules of the form $\alpha A \beta \rightarrow \alpha \gamma \beta$ with A a non terminal and α, β

and γ strings of terminals and/or non terminals. The strings α and β may be empty, but γ must be non empty. The rule $S \rightarrow \varepsilon$ is allowed if S does not appear on the right side of any rule. The languages described by these grammars are exactly all languages that can be recognized by a linear bounded automaton .

- **Type-2 grammars** (context-free grammars) generate the context-free languages. These are defined by rules of the form $A \rightarrow \gamma$ with A a non terminal and γ a string of terminals and/or non terminals. These languages are exactly all languages that can be recognized by a non-deterministic pushdown automaton.

- **Type-3 grammars** (regular grammars) generate the regular languages. Such a grammar restricts its rules to a single non terminal on the left-hand side and a right-hand side consisting of a single terminal, possibly followed by a single non terminal (right regular).

Every regular language is context-free, every context-free language (not containing the empty string) is context-sensitive, every context-sensitive language is recursive and every recursive language is recursively enumerable. These are all proper inclusions, meaning that there exist recursively enumerable languages which are not context-sensitive, context-sensitive languages which are not context-free and context-free languages which are not regular.

The following table summarizes each of Chomsky's four types of grammars, the type of automaton that recognizes it, and the form its rules must have.

Grammar	Languages	Automaton	Production rules (constraints)
Type-0	Recursively enumerable	Turing machine	$\alpha \rightarrow \beta$ (no restrictions)
Type-1	Context-sensitive	Linear-bounded non-deterministic Turing machine	$\alpha A \beta \rightarrow \alpha \gamma \beta$
Type-2	Context-free	Non-deterministic pushdown automaton	$A \rightarrow \gamma$
Type-3	Regular	Finite state automaton	$A \rightarrow a$ and $A \rightarrow aB$

7.10. Post Correspondence Problem (PCP)

Post correspondence problem is an abstract problem which involves strings rather than Turing machines. Now we have to prove that this PCP problem about strings to be undecidable, and then use its undecidability to prove other problems undecidable by reading by reducing PCP. We shall prove PCP undecidable by reducing Lu to PCP. To prove this, we introduce Modified the modified PCP (MPCP) and reduce modified problem to the original PCP.

Then, we reduce Lu to the modified PCP, and it is shown below,

Reducing Lu to Modified PCP

Since the original Lu is known to be undecidable, we conclude that PCP is also undecidable.

Definition of PCP

PCP consists of two lists of strings over the alphabet Σ. The two lists must be of equal length. The lists are represented as A and B

$$A = w_1, w_2, \ldots, w_k$$

$$B = x_1, x_2, \ldots, x_k$$

For some integer "k". For each I, the pair (w_i, x_i) is said to be a "Corresponding Pair". The instance of the PCP has a solution, if there is a sequence of one or more integers $i_1, i_2 \ldots, i_m$ that when interpreted as indexes for strings in the A and B lists, yield the same string. That is,

$$w_1\, w_2 \ldots \ldots w_k = x_1\, x_2 \ldots \ldots x_k$$

Such that.

$$w_{i1}\, w_{i2} \ldots \ldots w_{ik} = x_{i1}\, x_{i2} \ldots \ldots x_{ik}$$

The sequence $i_1, i_2, \ldots \ldots i_m$ is a solution to this instance of PCP. The post correspondence problem is,

"Given an instance of PCP, tell whether this Instance has a solution"

Example Problems for PCP Instance

1. Let $\Sigma = \{0,1\}$ and let A and B be the lists defined as follows,

	LIST A	LIST B
i	w_i	x_i
1	1	111
2	10111	10
3	10	0

Find the instance of PCP.

Solution: From the above table,

    $W_1=1$ $x_1=111$

    $W_2=10111$ $x_2=10$

    $W_3=10$ $x_3=0$

Now to find the instance of PCP, we have to find the indexes for strings such that A and B yield the same string.

$$W_1\, W_2 \ldots\ldots\ldots\ldots\ W_k = X_1\, X_2 \ldots\ldots\ldots\ldots .X_k$$

Let us take m=4 and take the combination

2, 1, 1, 3

By concatenating the strings in the order for the two lists, we get,

$W_2\, W_1\, W_1\, W_3 = X_2\, X_1\, X_1\, X_3$

101111110=101111110

Instance of PCP = 2, 1, 1, 3.

2.   Let $\Sigma = \{0,1\}$ and A and B be the list as,

	LIST A	LIST B
i	w_i	x_i
1	1	101
2	011	11
3	101	011

Find the instance of PCP.

Solution: From the above table,

    $W_1=1$ $x_1=101$

    $W_2=011$ $x_2=11$

    $W_3=101$ $x_3=011$

Let us take m=4 and take the combination

1, 3

$W_1,\, W_3 = X_2\, X_3$

10101=101010

So this instance of PCP has no solution.

Modified PCP

An Intermediation (or) intermediate version of PCP is Modified PCP (MPCP). In MPCP, there is the additional requirement on solution that the first pair on the A and B lists must be the pair in the solution. An instance of MPCP is two lists.

$$A = w_1, w_2, \ldots, w_k$$

$$B = x_1, x_2, \ldots, x_k$$

And a solution is a list of '0' or more integers $i_1, i_2 \ldots, i_m$ such that

$$w_i \, w_{i1} \, w_{i2} \, \ldots \ldots \ldots \, w_{im} = x_i \, x_{i1} \, x_{i2} \, \ldots \ldots \ldots \ldots \, x_{im}$$

Notice that the pair (w_i, x_i) is forced at the beginning of the two strings, even the index 1 is not mentioned at the front of the list that is the solution .In PCP, the solution should have at least one integer on the instance solution list. But however in MPCP, the empty list could be a solution if $w_1 = x_1$

Example of MPCP

Consider the following list A and B and find the instance.

i	LIST A w_i	LIST B x_i
1	1	101
2	011	11
3	101	011

Solution

Now the sequence taken is 2,3

So,

$$w_1 \, w_2, \, w_3 = x_1 \, x_2 \, x_3$$

$$1011011 = 1011011$$

Instance of MPCP = 2, 3

Reducing MPCP to PCP (Construction of PCP from MPCP)

Given an instance of MPCP with alphabet Σ, we construct an instance of PCP as follows,

Let us have the instance of MPCP with the lists $A = w_1, w_2, \ldots, w_k$ and $B = x_1, x_2 \ldots, x_k$. we assume that * and \$ are symbols not present in the alphabet Σ of this MPCP instance .Let us construct PCP instance with list C and D as,

$$C = Y_0 Y_1 \ldots \ldots Y_{K+1}$$

$$D = Z_0 Z_1 \ldots \ldots Z_{K+1}$$

That is defined as follows

1. For i=1, 2……..k, let y_i be with w_i with a "*" after each symbol of $w_{i \text{ and}}$ let z_i be x_i with a "*" before each symbol of x_i

2. $Y_0 = {}^*Y_1$, and $Z_0 = Z_1$.

   That is, the 0th pair looks like pair 1, expect that there is an extra * at the beginning of the string from the first list. The 0th pair will be the only pair in the PCP instance will where both strings begin with the same symbol, so any solution to this PCP instance will have to begin with index "0"

3. $Y_{K+1}=\$$ and $Z_{K+1}=\$$

Example Problem for Reducing MPCP to PCP

1. Consider the following table is an MPCP instance and construct PCP.

	LIST A	LIST B
i	w_i	x_i
1	1	111
2	10111	10
3	10	0

	LIST A	LIST B
i	w_i	x_i
0	*1*	*1*1*1
1	*1*	*1*1*1
2	1*0*1*1*1*	*1*0
3	1*0*	*0
4	$	*$

Theorem 10.1

MPCP reduces to PCP

Proof: First, suppose $i_1, i_2, \ldots \ldots \ldots \ldots i_m$ is a solution to the given MPCP instance with lists A and B. Then, we know

$$w_i \, w_{i1} \, w_{i2} \ldots \ldots \ldots w_{im} = x_i \, x_{i1} \, x_{i2} \ldots \ldots \ldots \ldots x_{im}$$

If we were to replace the w's by y's and the x's by z's, we would have two strings that were almost the same

$$y_i \, y_{i1} \, y_{i2} \ldots \ldots \ldots y_{im} = z_1 \, z_{i1} \, z_{i2} \ldots \ldots \ldots \ldots z_{im}$$

The difference is that the first string would be missing a* at the beginning and the second string would be missing a* at the end. That is,

$$*y_i\, y_{i1}\, y_{i2} \ldots\ldots\ldots y_{im} = z_1\, z_{i1}\, z_{i2} \ldots\ldots\ldots\ldots z_{im}\, *$$

Put $Y_0 = *Y_1$, and $Z_0 = Z_1$.

So we can fix the initial * by replacing the first index by 0.so now we get

$$y_i\, y_{i1}\, y_{i2} \ldots\ldots\ldots y_{im}\, y_{k+1} = z_0\, z_{i1}\, z_{i2} \ldots\ldots\ldots\ldots z_{im}\, z_{k+1}$$

Here we append the index,

$$Y_{K+1} = \$ \text{ and } Z_{K+1} = \$$$

So $0, i_1, i_2 \ldots\ldots\ldots i_m, k+1$ is a solution to the instance of PCP

Thus, a solution to the PCP instance implies a solution to the MPCP instance. Thus, there is a reduction of MPCP to PCP, which confirms that if PCP were decidable, MPCP would also be decidable.

Completion of the Proof of PCP Undecidability

Here we are going to reduce Lu to MPCP. That with is, with the given a pair (M, w) we construct an instance (A, B) of MPCP such that TM M accepts input w if and only if (A,B) has a solution. MPCP instance (A, B) simulates in its partial solution, the computation of M on input w. Partial solutions has the strings that are prefixes of the sequence of ID's of Turing machine M.

(Instantaneous Description) ID's of M: - $\#\alpha_1\, \#\alpha_2\, \#\alpha_3\, \#\alpha_4\, \#...$

Where

$\alpha_1 \longrightarrow$ Initial ID of M with input w.

$\alpha_i \longrightarrow \alpha_{i+1}$ sub for all i

The string from B list will always be one Id ahead of the string from the A list, unless M enters an accepting state.

- To construct MPCP instance, we assurance that, out TM never prints a blank and never moves left from its initial head position.
- In that case, an ID of the Turing machine will always be a string of the form $\alpha q\beta$, where α and β are the strings of the nonblank tape symbols, and q is a state.
- We shall allow being empty if the head is at the blank immediately to the right of α, rather than placing a blank to the right of the state.

- Thus, the symbols α and β will correspond exactly to the contents of the cells that held the input, plus any cells to the right that the head has previously visited.

Let M = (Q, Σ, ʃ, q_0, B, F) be a TM and let w in Σ* be an input string. We construct an instance of MPCP as follows (i. e) the first list to be one ID behind the second list, unless M accepts.

Rules

1. The First pair is,

LIST A	LIST B
#	#q_0w#

This pair starts any solution according to the rules of MPCP, begin the simulation of *M* on input W. B list is a complete ID ahead of the A list.

2. Tape symbols and the separator # can be appended to both lists as,

LIST A	LIST B
X	X
#	#

The above pair allows symbols not involving the state to be copied.

3. To simulate a move of *M*, we have certain pairs. For each q in Q – F where q is an non accepting state, p in Q, X, Y and Z in We have,

LIST A	LIST B	Transition
qX	YP	if δ (q, X) = (P, Y, R)
ZqX	PZY	if δ (q, X) = (P, Y, L) Z is any tape symbol
q#	YP#	if δ (q, B) = (P, Y, R)
Zq#	PZY#	if δ (q, B) = (P, Y, L)

4. For each *q* in *F*, where *q* is an accepting state, then for all tape symbols X and Y , there are pairs,

LIST A	LIST B
XqY	q
Xq	q
qY	q

5. Finally, once the accepting state has consumed all the tape symbols, it stands alone as the last ID on the B string. Then we use the final pair to complete the solution

LIST A	LIST B
q ##	#

Example problem for PCP solution:

Let us convert the TM

$$M = (\{q_1, q_2, q_3\}, \{0,1\}, \{0,1,B\}, \text{del}, q_1, B, \{q_3\})$$

Where is given by,

q_i	$\delta(q_i, 0)$	$\delta(q_i, 1)$	$\delta(q_i, B)$
q_1	$(q_2, 1, R)$	$(q_1, 0, L)$	$(q_2, 1, L)$
q_2	$(q_3, 0, L)$	$(q_1, 0, R)$	$(q_2, 1, R)$
q_3	-	-	-

And the input string $w = 0.1$. Find the solution.

Solution:

First let us construct the MPCP instance as per the rules 1 to 5 and it is shown below,

Rule 1:

LIST A	LIST B	Source
#	#$q_1$01	w=01
		q_1= Initial State

Rule 2:

LIST A	LIST B	Source
0	0	
1	1	Tape symbols and the separator
#	#	# is applied

Rule 3:

LIST A	LIST B	Source
$q_1$0	1 q_2	$\delta(q_1, 0) = (q_2, 1, R)$
1 q_1 1	q_2 00	$\delta(q_1, 1) = (q_2, 0, L)$
1 q_1 1	q_2 10	$\delta(q_1, 1) = (q_2, 0, L)$
0 q_1 #	q_2 01#	$\delta(q_1, B) = (q_2, 1, L)$
1 q_1 #	q_2 11#	$\delta(q_1, B) = (q_2, 1, L)$
0 q_2 0	$q_3$00	$\delta(q_2, 0) = (q_3, 0, L)$
1 q_2 1	q_3 10	$\delta(q_2, 1) = (q_3, 0, L)$
q_2 1	0 q_1	$\delta(q_2, 1) = (q_1, 0, R)$
q_2 #	0 q_2	$\delta(q_2, B) = (q_2, 0, R)$

Rule 4:

LIST A	LIST B	Source
0 q_3 0	q_3	
0 q_3 1	q_3	
1 q_3 0	q_3	
1 q_3 1	q_3	q_3 is an Accepting state
0 q_3	q_3	
1 q_3	q_3	
q_3 0	q_3	
q_3 1	q_3	

Rule 5:

LIST A	LIST B	Source
q_3 # #	#	q_3 is an Accepting state

The input w = 01

The first pair is,

    A: #

    B: # q_1 01 #

The sequence of moves for the string 01 is,

$$q_1\ 01 \vdash 1\ q_2 1 \mid 10\ q_1 \mid 1q_2 01 \mid q_1\ 101$$

The first pair is,

    A: #

    B: # q_1 01 #

From Rule (3), use the pair (q_1, 0, q_2) from the table, we get the partial solution as,

    A: # q_1 0

    B: # q_1 01 # 1 q_2

Now from Rule (2) extend it to get second ID as,

A: # q_1 01 # 1

B: # q_1 01 # 1 q_2 1 # 1

#1 is inserted in A means it should also be inserted in B. Now use the rule 3 (q_2, 1, 0 q_1)

A: # q_1 01 # 1 q_2 1

B: # q_1 01 # 1 q_2 1 # 10 q_1

Now use Rule (2) to copy #1 as

A: # q_1 01 # 1 q_2 1 # 1

B: # q_1 01 # 1 q_2 1 # 10 q_1 # 1

Now use Rule (3) (0 q1 #, q201 #) as

A: # q_1 01 # 1 q_2 1 # 10 q_1 #

B: # q_1 01 # 1 q_2 1 # 10 q_1 # 1 q_2 01 #

Now use the pair (1q20, $q_3$10)

A: # q_1 01 # 1 q_2 1 # 10 q_1 # 1 q_2 0

B: # q_1 01 # 1 q_2 1 # 10 q_1 # 1 q_2 01 # q_3 10

Now we can use the pairs from Rule (4) to eliminate all but q_3 from Id (Instantaneous Description) as,

A: # q_1 01 # 1 q_2 1 # 10 q_1 # 1 q_2 01 # q_3 101 # q_3 01 # q_3 1 #

B: # q_1 01 # 1 q_2 1 # 10 q_1 # 1 q_2 01 # q_3 101 # q_3 01 # q_3 1 # q_3 #

Now we can use the Rule (5) as (q_3 # #, #) to finish the solution as,

A: # q_1 01 # 1 q_2 1 # 10 q_1 # 1 q_2 01 # q_3 101 # q_3 01 # q_3 1 # q_3 # #

B: # q_1 01 # 1 q_2 1 # 10 q_1 # 1 q_2 01 # q_3 101 # q_3 01 # q_3 1 # q_3 # #

CHAPTER 8

UNSOLVABLE PROBLEMS & COMPUTABLE FUNCTIONS

8.1. Unsolvable Problems and Computable Functions

8.1.1. Primitive Recursive Functions

This is a very interesting class of functions defined by Gödel as part of his proof of the incompleteness Theorem. We are interested in functions f from N^r to N, for $r = 0, 1, 2, \ldots$. Here r is called the arity of the function f, i.e., the number of arguments that it takes.

Gödel started with three very simple functions:

i.   The initial functions

ii.   Two natural closure operations

Composition and primitive recursion, each of which take some already defined functions and use them to define a new one. The important idea is that the primitive recursive functions comprise a very large and powerful class of computable functions, all generated in an extremely simple way.

We begin with the three *initial* primitive recursive functions:

- ζ, the zero function of arity 0, $\zeta(\ ) = 0$,

- η, the identity function of arity 1, $\eta(n) = n$; and,

- σ, the successor function of arity 1, $\sigma(n) = n + 1$.

Now consider the following two operations:

- **Composition**: if f is a primitive recursive function of arity a, and $g_1, \ldots, g_a$ are primitive recursive functions of arities $r_1, \ldots, r_a$, and $k \in \mathbf{N}$, then the following is a primitive recursive function of arity k:

  $h(x_1, \ldots, x_k) = f(g_1(w_1), \ldots, g_a(w_a))$,

  where each w_i is a list of r_i arguments, perhaps with repetition, from $x_1, \ldots, x_k$; and,

- **Primitive recursion**: if f and g are primitive recursive functions of arity k and $k+2$, respectively, then there is a primitive recursive function, h, of arity $k+1$ satisfying the following conditions:

  $h(0,x_1,\ldots,x_k) = f(x_1,\ldots,x_k)$; and,

  $h(n+1,x_1,\ldots,x_k) = g(h(n,x_1,\ldots,x_k), n,x_1,\ldots,x_k)$.

212

Here composition is the natural way to combine functions, and primitive recursion is a restricted kind of recursion in which h with first argument $n+1$ is defined in terms of h with first argument n, and all the other arguments unchanged.

The primitive recursive functions to be the smallest class of functions that contains the initial functions and is closed under composition and primitive recursion.

The primitive recursive functions have a very simple definition and yet they are extremely powerful. Gödel proved inductively that every primitive recursive function can be simply represented in first-order number theory. He then used the primitive recursive functions to encode formulas and even sequences of formulas by numbers. He finally used the primitive recursive functions to compute properties of the represented formulas including that a formula was well formed, a sequence of formulas was a proof, and that a formula was a theorem. The following are a few examples showing that addition, multiplication, and exponentiation are primitive recursive.

Define the addition function, $P(x,y)$, as follows:

- $P(0,y) = \eta(y)$
- $P(n+1,y) = \sigma(P(n,y))$

Next, define the multiplication function, $T(x,y)$, as follows:

- $T(0,y) = \zeta(\ )$
- $T(n+1,y) = P(T(n,y),y)$

Next, we define the exponential function, $E(x,y)$. (Usually 0^0 is considered undefined, but since primitive recursive functions must be total, we define $E(0,0)$ to be 1.) Since primitive recursion only allows us to recurse on the first argument, we use two steps to define the exponential function:

- $R(0,y) = \sigma(\zeta(\ ))$
- $R(n+1,y) = T(R(n,y),y)$

Finally we can define $E(x,y) = R(\eta(y),\eta(x))$ by composition. (Recall that η is the identity function so this could be more simply written as $E(x,y) = R(y,x)$.)

The exponential function, E, grows very rapidly, for example, $E(10,10)$ is ten billion, and $E(50,50)$ is over 10^{84} (and thus significantly more than the estimated number of atoms in the universe).

- $H(0,y) = y$
- $H(n+1,y) = E(2,H(n,y))$

Thus, $H(2,2) = 2^4 = 16$, $H(3,3) = 2^{256}$ is more than 10^{77} and comparable to the number of atoms in the universe. If that's not big enough for you then consider $H(4,4)$. To write this number in decimal notation we would need a one, followed by more zero's than the number of particles in the universe.

8.2.   Recursive Functions

The set of primitive recursive functions is a huge class of computable functions. In fact, they can be characterized as the set of functions computable in time that is some primitive recursive function of n, where n is the length of the input. For example, since $H(n,n)$ is a primitive recursive function, the primitive recursive functions include all of $\text{TIME}[H(n,n)$.

Thus, the primitive recursive functions include all functions that are feasibly computable by any possible measure of feasible, and much beyond that. However, the primitive recursive functions do not include all functions computable in principle. To see this, we can again use diagonalization. We can systematically encode all definitions of primitive recursive functions of arity 1, calling them p_1, p_2, p_3, and so on.

We can then build a Turing machine to compute the value of the following diagonal function, $D(n) = p_n(n) + 1$.

Notice that D is a total, computable function from $\mathbf{N}$ to $\mathbf{N}$, but it is not primitive recursive. Why? Suppose for the sake of a contradiction that D were primitive recursive. Then D would be equal to p_d for some $d \in \mathbf{N}$. But it would then follow that

$$p_d(\mathrm{d}) = p_d(\mathrm{d}) + 1,$$

which is a contradiction. Therefore, D is not primitive recursive.

Alas, the above diagonal argument works on any class of total functions that could be considered a candidate for the class of all computable functions. The only way around this, if we want all functions computable in principle, not just in practice, is to add some kind of unbounded search operation. This is what Gödel did to extend the primitive recursive functions to the recursive functions.

Define the unbounded minimization operator, μ, as follows. Let f be a perhaps partial function of arity k+1. Then $\mu[f]$ is defined as the following function of arity k. On input x_1, ..., x_k do the following:

For $i = 0$ to ∞ do {

if $f(i,x_1,...,x_k) = 1$, then output I }

Thus if $f(i,x_1,...,x_k) = 1$, and for all $j < i$, $f(j,x_1,...,x_k)$ is defined, but not equal to 1, then $\mu\,[f](x_1, ..., x_k) = i$. Otherwise $\mu[f](x_1, ..., x_k)$ is undefined.

Gödel defined the set of *Recursive functions* to be the closure of the initial primitive recursive functions under composition, primitive recursion, and μ. With this definition, the Recursive functions are exactly the same as the set of partial functions computable by the Lambda calculus, by Kleene Formal systems, by Markov algorithms, by Post machines, and by Turing machines.

8.2.1. Recursive and Recursively Enumerable Languages

Let $L \subseteq \Sigma^*$ be the language. A Turing machine M with input Σ is said accept L if L(M) = L. That is, M recognizes L if M halts in state for every string w in Σ.

A Language L is recursively enumerable if there is a TM that accepts L & recursive if there is a T that recognizes L. These languages are called Turing-acceptance language and Turing decidable respectively.

1. Every Turing decidable language is Turing acceptable.
2. Every Turing acceptable language need not be Turing decidable.

8.2.2. Turing Acceptable Language

A language $L \subseteq \Sigma^*$ is said to be a Turing acceptable language. If there is Turing machine M which halts on every $w \,\varepsilon\, L$ with an answer 'yes' however, if w L then M may not halt.

8.2.3. Turing Decidable Language

A language $L \subseteq \Sigma^*$ is said to be Turing machine if there is a Turing machine M which always halts on every $w \,\varepsilon\, \Sigma^*$. If $w \,\varepsilon\, L$ then M halts with answer "Yes" if w L then M halts, with answer "No". A problem P is said to be decidable/solvable if the problem (set of solution) is Turing decidable.

Two recursive language L_1 and L_2, each of the following is recursive.

i) $L_1 \cup L_2$

ii) $L_1 \cap L_2$

iii) $L_1{}'$

Solution: i) $L_1 \cup L_2$

Let the TM M_1, decides L_1 and M_2 decides L_2. If a word $w \,\varepsilon\, L_1$, the M_1 returns "Y" else it returns "N". Similarly if a word $w \,\varepsilon\, L_2$, the M_2 returns "Y" else it returns "N".

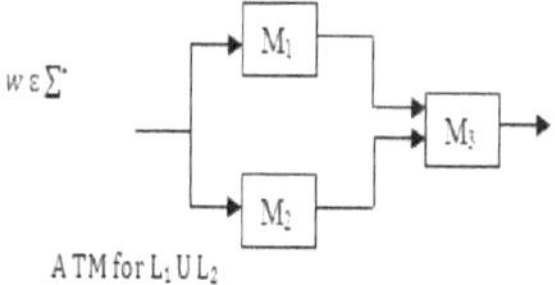

ATM for $L_1 \cup L_2$

- Output of machine M_1 is written on the tape of M_3.
- Output of machine M_2 is written on the tape of M_3.
- The machine M_3 is return "Y" as output, if at least one of the outputs of M_1 (or) of M_2 is "Y".
- That is M_3 decides $L_1 \cup L_2$ are Turing decidable after a finite time both M_1 and M_2 will halt with answer "Y" (or) "N".
- The machine M_3 halts with "Y" if $w \varepsilon L_1$ (or) $w \varepsilon L_2$, else M_3 halts with output N.

Solution: ii) $L_1 \cap L_2$ is Recursive

Let TM M, decides L_1 and L_2 decides L_2. If a word $w \varepsilon L$ then M_1 returns "Y" else it returns "N". Similarly, if a word $w \varepsilon L_2$ then M_2 returns "Y" else it returns "N".

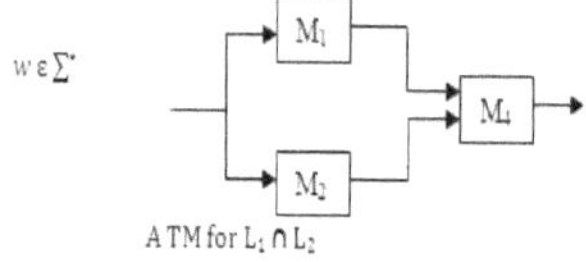

ATM for $L_1 \cap L_2$

- Output of machine M_1 is written on the tape of M_3.
- Output of machine M_2 is written on the tape of M_3.
- The machine M_3 is return "Y" as output, if both outputs of M_1 and M_2 are "Y" otherwise M_3 returns "N".
- The machine M_4 halts with answer "Y" if $w \varepsilon L_1$ and $w \varepsilon L_2$, else M_4 halts with answer "N".

Solution: ii) L_1' is Recursive

Let the TM M_1, decides L_1.

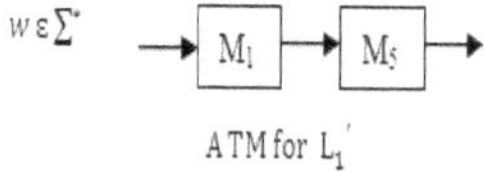

ATM for L_1'

- Output of machine M_1 is written on the tape of M_2.

- The machine M_2 returns "Y" as output, if the output of M_1 is "N" otherwise M_2 returns "N".

- The machine M_2 halts with answer "Y" if $w \, \varepsilon \, L_1$ else M_2 halts with answer "N".

8.3. Universal Turning Machine

- A general purpose computer can be programmed to solve different types of problems. A TM can also behave like a general purpose computer.

- A TM is known as universal Turing machine, can solve all sorts of solvable problems.

- That is UTM should be able to simulate every Turing machine.

- A Turing machine M is defined to solve a particular problem P, can be specified as,

    1. The initial state of the TM M.

    2. The transition function δ of M can be specified as,

        If the current state of M is a_i and the symbol under the lead is a_j then the machine mores to state q_j while changing a_i to a_j. The move of tape lead may be

        i) Left

        ii) Right

        iii) No move

        Such a move of TM can be represented by,

        $$\left\{ (qi, a_i, q_j, a_j, m_f) \; q_i, q_j \, \varepsilon \, Q; a_i, aj \, \varepsilon \, \Gamma \; ; m_f \, \varepsilon \, (L,R,N) \right\}$$

        UTM should be able to simulate every TM simulation of a TM will involve,

        i) Encoding behavior of a particular TM as a program.

        ii) Execution of the above program by UTM.

A move of the form $(q_i, a_i, q_j, a_j, m_f)$ can be represented as, $10^{i+1} \, 10^i \, 10^{j+1} \, 10^j \, 10^k$, where

k=1 if move is to the left

k=2 if move is to the right

k=3 if move is to no move

State q_0 is represented by 0,

State q_1 is represented by 00,

State q_n is represented by 0^{n+1}.

First symbol can be represented by 0,

Second symbol can be represented by 00 and so on.

Two moves are separated by 11.

Execution by UTM

We can assume the UTM as a 3-tape Turing machine.

1. Input is written on the first tape.
2. Moves of the Tm is encoded form is written on the second tape.
3. The current state of TM is written on the third tape.

The control unit of UTM by counting number of 0's between 1's can find out the current symbol under the lead. It can find the current state from the tape 3.

Now it can locate the appropriate move based in current input and current state form the tape 2. Now the control unit can extract the following form the tape 2:

1. Next state
2. Next symbol to be written
3. Move of the head.

Based on this information, the control unit can take the appropriate action.

8.4.   Classifying Complexity

For solving a decidable problem, there may be more than one algorithm. The algorithms may differ in time taken or memory required to execute and produce the result, for the same input.

This is known as computational complexity. It concerns with the question "which is the efficient algorithm for solving a decision problem.

Types of computational complexity:

 Mainly two types of complexities are measured for an algorithm.

There are,

1. Time complexity
2. Space complexity

1. Time Complexity

The time complexity of a program for a given input is the number of elementary instructions (number of basic steps required) that this program executes. This number is computed based on the length (n) of the input. if $A(n)$ is the time complexity for an algorithm X for a problem P then the number of steps required to produce the output t from an input of length n is less than or equal to n.

2. Space Complexity

The space complexity of a program for a given input is the number of elementary objects that this program needs to store (memory required) during its execution. This number is computed based on the length of the input. if $A(n)$ is the space complexity for an algorithm X for a problem P then the number of memory locations required to produce the output from an input of length n is less than or equal to n.

8.5. Tractable and Intractable Problems

Tractable languages are those languages are recognize within reasonable time and space constraints. Tractable problem is to be solvable in polynomial time. The sets P and Pspace include any language that can be recognized by a TM with time complexity (or) space complexity, respectively bounded by some polynomial. If a problem can be solved in polynomial time on some computer, then it is in P.

8.6. P and NP Completeness

A language L is decidable in polynomial time if there is a standard TM M that accepts L with tcM $\in O(nr)$. The family of languages decidable in polynomial time is denotes P. Any problem that is polynomially solvable on a standard TM is in P, and the choice of DTM models (e.g., multi-tape, multi-track) for the analysis is invariant.

A language L is accepted in nondeterministic polynomial time if there is a NTM M, that accepts L with tcM $\in O(nr)$. The family of languages accepted in non-deterministic polynomial time is denoted NP. Since every DTM is a NTM, P$\subseteq$NP.

The family NP is a subset of the recursive languages,, since the number of transitions ensure all computations terminates

P Completeness

The set of all problems that can be solved by deterministic algorithms in polynomial time.

The class of polynomially solvable problems contains all sets in which membership may be decided by an algorithm whose running time is bounded by a polynomial.

NP Completeness

The set of all problems that can be solved by nondeterministic algorithms in polynomial time. NP-Completeness problems are set of problems that have been proved to be in NP. That is, a non-deterministic solution is quite trivial, and yet no polynomial time algorithm has yet been developed.

Formal Definition of NP-completeness

A decision problem C is NP-complete if:

1. C is in NP, and
2. Every problem in NP is reducible to C in polynomial time.

C can be shown to be in NP by demonstrating that a candidate solution to C can be verified in polynomial time.

Note that a problem satisfying condition 2 is said to be NP-hard, whether or not it satisfies condition 1.

A consequence of this definition is that if we had a polynomial time algorithm (on a UTM, or any other Turing-equivalent abstract machine) for C, we could solve all problems in NP in polynomial time.

- This set of problems has an additional property which does seem to indicate that P = NP.

- If any of the problems can be solved in polynomial time on a deterministic machine, then all the problems can be solved in NP (Cook's Theorem).

- It turns out that many interesting practical problems have this characteristic.

8.6.1. Examples of NP-Complete

Travelling Salesman Problem

Given a set of cities and distances between all pairs, find a tour of all the cities of distance less than M.

Hamiltonian Cycle

Given a graph, find a simple cycle that includes all the vertices.

Partition

Given a set of integers, can they be divided into two sets whose sum is equal?

Integer Linear Programming

Given a linear program is there an integer solution?

Vertex Cover

Given a graph and an integer N, is there a set of fewer than N vertices which touches all the edges?

8.6.2. Polynomial Time Reductions

Reduction is a problem -solving technique employed to avoid "reinventing the wheel" when encountering a new problem transform the instances of the new problem into those of a problem that has been solved establish the decidability and tractability of problems Let L be a language over alphabet $\Sigma 1$ and Q be a language over $\Sigma 2$. L is many-to-one reducible to Q if there exists a Turing computable function r: $\Sigma 1^* \to \Sigma 2^*$ such that $w \in L$ if, and only if, r (w) $\in Q$. if a language L is reducible to a decidable language Q by a function r , then L is also decidable.

Example

Let R be the TM that computes the reduction, i.e., input (L) to input (Q), and M the TM that accepts language Q. The sequential execution of R and M on strings from $\Sigma 1^*$ accepts language L(by accepting inputs to Q) is R, the reduction TM, which does not determine membership in either L or Q, transforms strings from $\Sigma 1^*$ to $\Sigma 2^*$.Strings in Q are determined by M, and strings in Lare by the combination of R and M.

A function f is polynomial-time computable if there is a Turing machine M with $\tau_M = O(n^r)$ that computes f.

Let L_1, $L_2 \subseteq \Sigma^*$ be languages. L_1 is polynomial-time reducible to L_2 if there is a polynomial-time computable total function $f : \Sigma^* \to \Sigma^*$ such that for all $x \in \Sigma^*$, $x \in L_1$ if and only if $f(x) \in L_2$.

Theorem

Let L_1 be polynomial-time reducible to L_2. Then: $L_2 \in P$ implies $L_1 \in P$; $L_2 \in NP$ implies $L_1 \in$ NP.

Proof

Since $L_2 \in P$ there is a Turing machine M_2 with polynomial time complexity that decides L_2. Moreover, since L_1 is polynomial-time reducible to L_2, there is a Turing machine M with polynomial-time complexity such that $f_M : \Sigma^* \to \Sigma^*$ satisfies for all $x \in \Sigma^*$, $x \in L_1$ if and only if $f_M(x) \in L_2$.

Let M_1 be the composite Turing machine MM_2 which first runs M and then runs M_2 on the output of M, then $L(M_1) = L_1$.

Since $|f_M(x)|$ cannot exceed max $(\tau_M(|x|), |x|)$, the number of transitions of M_1 is bounded by the sum of the following estimates of the separate computations:

$$\tau_{M1}(n) \le \tau_M(n) + \tau_{M2}(\max(\tau_M(n), n))$$

Let $\tau_M = O(n^r)$, then there are constants c and n_0 with $\tau_M(n) \le c \cdot n^r \ \forall \ n \ge n_0$.

Let $\tau_{M2} = O(n^t)$, then there are constants c_2 and n_2 with $\tau_{M2}(n) \le c_2 \cdot n^t \ \forall \ n \ge n_2$.

Hence $\tau_{M2}(n) \le c_2.n^t + d_2, \ \forall \ n \ge 0$, where $d_2 = \{\tau_{M2}(k) \mid k < n_2\}$.

It follows $\tau_{M2}(\tau_M(n)) \le c_2 \cdot (\tau_M(n))^t + d_2$, for all $n \ge 0$, and hence $\tau_{M2}(\tau_M(n)) \le c_2 \cdot (c \cdot n^r)^t + d_2$, for all.

$n \ge 0$ So, $\tau_{M2}(\tau_M(n)) \le c_2 c^t \cdot n^{rt} + d_2 \ \forall \ n \ge 0$.

Thus, by formula (a) above, $\tau_{M1} = O(n^{rt})$, hence $L_1 \in P$ (r and t are constants, therefore $n^{rt} \in P$).

8.6.3. Hardness

If L_1 is polynomial-time reducible to L_2, then L_1 is no harder than L_2. Equivalently, L_2 is at least as hard as L_1.

A language L is NP-hard if every language in NP is polynomial-time reducible to L; A NP-hard language is at least as hard to decide as every language in NP. Equivalently, no language in NP is harder to decide than any NP-hard language.

A language L is NP-complete if it is NP-hard and belongs to NP; a NP-complete language is a "hardest" language in NP. Corollary, for every NP-complete language L, L$\in$ P if and only if P = NP.

8.7. The Satisfiability Problem

Establishes whether decision problems are (only) theoretically decidable, i.e., decides whether each solvable problem has a practical solution that can be solved efficiently. A theoretically solvable problem may not have a practical solution, i.e., there is no efficient algorithm to solve the problem in polynomial time–an intractable problem.

Solving intractable problems require extraordinary amount of time and memory.

Efficiently solvable problems are polynomial (P) problems. Intractable problems are non-polynomial (NP) problems.

Can any problem that is solvable in polynomial time by a non-deterministic algorithm also be solved deterministically in polynomial time, i.e., P= NP?

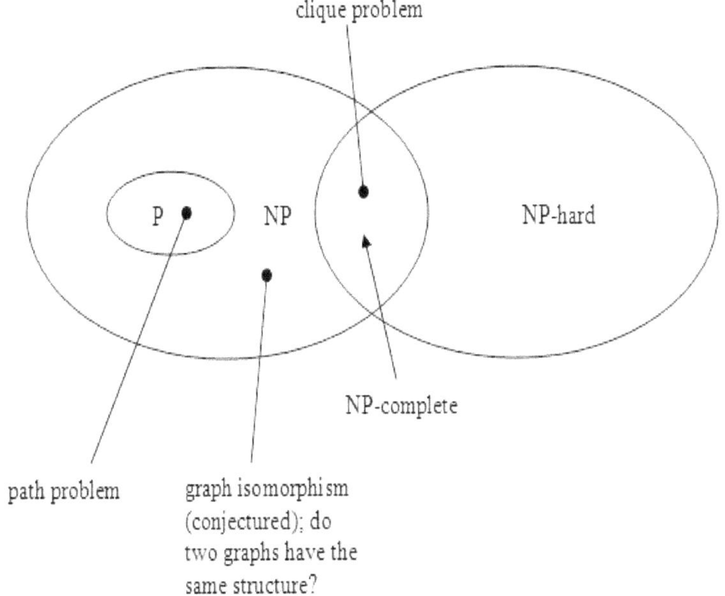

Consider Boolean expressions built from variables x_i and connectives $\wedge$, $\vee$ and $\neg$. A literal is either a variable x_i, or a negated variable $\neg x_i$. An expression $C_1 \wedge C_2 \wedge \ldots \wedge C_n$ is in conjunctive normal form (CNF) if $C_1,\ldots, C_n$ are disjunction of literals.

An expression C is satisfiable if there is an assignment of truth values to variables that make C true.

e.g., $C = (x_1 \vee x_3) \wedge (\neg x_1 \vee x_2 \vee x_4) \wedge \neg x_2 \wedge \neg x_4$. In this case, C is satisfiable by the assignment $\alpha = \{x_1, x_2, x_4 \rightarrow \text{false}, x_3 \rightarrow \text{true}\}$

The satisfiability problem takes input of a boolean expression C in CNF, and the question is "Is C satisfiable?"

Theorem: The satisfiability problem is NP-complete. This was proved by S. A. Cook in 1971 was was the first problem to be shown to be NP-complete.

To prove a problem is NP-complete, any NP-complete problem should be reducible to it. e.g., a polynomial-time reduction of the satisfiability problem to the clique problem. What we need is a function $f : x \rightarrow (G_x, k_x)$, where x if a CNF expression and (G_x, k_x) is a pair depending on x, such that x is satisfiable if and only if G_x has a clique with k_x vertices.

Let $x = \bigwedge^c_{i=1} \bigvee^d_{ij=1} a_{i,j}$, where $\wedge$ and $\vee$ are conjuncts and each $a_{i,j}$ is a literal.

Observation: Pick one literal from each conjunct and connect each pair of picked literals that is not complimentary (e.g., x and $\neg x$ are complimentary). If this yields a complete graph, then x is satisfiable. Vice versa, if x is satisfiable, then a complete subgraph can be constructed in this way.

Idea: Choose G_x as the graph consisting of all occurrences of literals and all connections between literals that are in different conjuncts and not complimentary.

Define $G_x = (V_x, E_x)$ by $V_x = \{(i, j) \mid 1 \le i \le c \wedge 1 \le j \le d_i\}$ and $E_x = \{((i, j), (l, m)) \mid i \ne l \wedge a_{i,j} \not\equiv \neg a_{l,m}\}$, and let $k_x = c$.

By construction of G_x: Two vertices are linked if and only if their literals are in different conjuncts and there is a truth assignment making both literals true. Next, we show that f is a reduction from the satisfiability problem to the clique problem.

"Only if": Let x be satisfiable. Then there is a truth assignment α such that for each i, there is some literal a_i, j_i with $\alpha(a_i, j_i) = $ true. Hence, by construction of E_x, the vertices $(1, j_1), (2, j_2), ...,$ (k_x, j_{kx}) forms a clique in G_x. Note that $a_{i,ji} \not\equiv \neg a_{i,ji}$, because $\alpha(a_i, j_i) = $ true $ = \alpha(a_{i,ji})$.

"If": Let G_x have a clique with k_x many vertices. Then, by definition of E_x, the literals of these vertices must be pairwise non-complimentary. Hence, there is a truth assignment making all of these literals true. Moreover, by the definition of E_x, these k_x literals are in k_x different conjuncts. So α makes each of the $k_x = c$ conjuncts true. Thus, x is satisfiable.

The complexity of computational problems can be discussed by choosing a specific abstract machine as a model of computation and considering how much time and/or space machines of that type requires for the solutions. In order to compare two problems it is necessary to look at instances of different sizes. Using the criterion of runtime example, the most common approach is to compare the growth rates of two runtimes, each viewed as a function of the instance size.

8.7.1. Notation for Comparing Growth Rates

Suppose $f, g : N \rightarrow N$ are partial functions, and each partial functions, and each is defined at all but a finite number of points. We write

$$f(n) = O(g(n))$$

Or simply $f = O(g)$, if there are constants C and n_0 so that for every $n \ge n_0$, $f(n)$ and $g(n)$ are defined and $f(n) \le Cg(n)$.

We write

$$f \ominus (g)$$

to mean that f=0(g) and g=0(f). finally,

$$f(n) = o(g(n))$$

or f = o(n) means that for every positive constant C, there is a constant n_0 so that for every n $\geq n_0, f(n) \leq Cg(n)$.

Theorem

The relation R_1 defined by

$$F \; R_1 g \text{ if and only if } f = 0(g)$$

Interpreted informally to mean the growth rate of f is no larger than that of g, is reflexive and transitive.

The relation R_2 defined by

$$f \; R_2 g \text{ if and only if } f = o(g)$$

Interpreted to mean the growth rate of f is less than that of g, is transitive and asymmetric (i.e., iff R_2g, then$\neg$, g R_2f).

the relation R_3 defined by

$$f \; R_3 g \text{ if and only if } f = \ominus(g) \text{ is an equivalence relation.}$$

Proof

We verify the statements involving R_1 and leave the others as excises. The relation R_1 is reflexive, because in the definition we can take the constants C and n_0 to be 1 and 0, respectively. Suppose that

$$f = 0(g) \text{ and } g = 0(h).$$

Then for some constants $C_1, n_1, C_2,$ and n_2

2 Marks Questions and Answers

1. Define TOC

TOC describes the basic ideas and models underlying computing. TOC suggests various abstract models of computation, represented mathematically.

2. What are the applications of TOC?

Compiler Design

Robotics

Artificial Intelligence

Knowledge Engineering.

3. Define Finite Automaton(FA)

FA consists of a finite set of states and a set of transitions from state to state that occur on input symbols chosen from an alphabet _. Finite Automaton is denoted by a 5- tuple(Q,Σ, δ,q0,F), where Q is the finite set of states , _ is a finite input alphabet, q0 in Q is the initial state, F is the set of final states and _ is the transition mapping function Q * _ to Q.

4. What is a : (a) String (b) Regular language

A string x is accepted by a Finite Automaton M=(Q, Σ, δ.q0,F) if δ (q0,x)=p, for some p in F.FA accepts a string x if the sequence of transitions corresponding to the symbols of x leads from the start state to accepting state.

The language accepted by M is L(M) is the set {x | _(q0,x) is in F}. A language is regular if it is accepted by some finite automaton.

5. Why are switching circuits called as finite state systems?

A switching circuit consists of a finite number of gates, each of which can be in any one of the two conditions 0 or 1.Although the voltages assume infinite set of values,the electronic circuitry is designed so that the voltages orresponding to 0 or 1 are stable and all others adjust to these value. Thus control unit of a computer is a finite statesystem.

6. What is Deductive proofs?

A deductive proof consists of a sequence of statements which starts from a hypothesis or a given statement to a conclusion. Each step is satisfying some logical principle.

7. Define proof by contrapositive

It is the other form of if then statement. The contrapositive of the statement " if H then C " is If not C then not H ".

8. Define the concatenation of two strings

Suppose x and y are two strings then the concatenation of x and y is xy.

Ex: if x = 0011 and y = 1100 then xy = 00111100.

9. What is the principle of mathematical induction. April/May 2008

Let $P(n)$ be a ststement about a non negative integer n. Then the principle of mathematical induction is that $P(n)$ follows from

(i) $P(1)$ and

(ii) $P(n-1)$ implies $P(n)$ for all n>1.

Condition(i) is called the basis step and condition (ii) is called the inductive step. $P(n-1)$ is called the induction hypothesis.

10. List any four ways of theorem proving

(i) Deductive

(ii) If and only if

(iii) Induction

(iv) Proof by contradiction.

11. Lists the operations on Strings.

1. Length of a string
2. Empty string
3. Concatenation of string
4. Reverse of a string
5. Power of an alphabet
6. Kleene closure
7. Substring
8. Palindrome

12. Lists the operations on Languages.

1. Product
2. Reversal
3. Power
4. Kleene star
5. Kleene plus

6. Union

7. Intersection

13. Define Language

A set of strings all of which are chosen from some Σ^*, where Σ is a particular alphabet is called a language.

14. Define String

A string is a collection of alphabet over an Σ^*, where Σ is a particular alphabet.

15. Define Substring

A string v appears within another string w(w=uv) is called "substring of w." IF w=uv, then substrings u & v are said to be prefix and suffix of w respectively

16. Define Graphs

A graph denoted by G=(V,E) consists of a finite set of vertices (or) nodes V and a set E, a pair of vertices called edges.

17. Define automaton

Automaton is a abstact computing device. It is a mathematical model of a system,with discrete inputs, outputs, states and set of transitions from state to state that occurs on input symbols from alphabet Σ.

18. What are the applications of automata theory?

- In compiler construction.
- In switching theory and design of digital circuits.
- To verify the correctness of a program.
- Design and analysis of complex software and hardware systems.
- To design finite state machines such as Moore and mealy machines.

Ex: The language L over {0,1} where set of strings with an equal number 0's and 1's.

L = { ε, 01, 10, 0011, 0101, 1001, 1100,......}

19. Define a Deterministic Finite Automaton.

A Determinstic finite automaton consists of :

- A finite set of states, often denoted by Q
- A finite set of input symbols, often denoted by Σ
- A transition function that takes as arguments a state and an input symbol   and returns a state.

- A start state, one of the states in Q
- A set of final or accepting states F.

20. Define a Non Deterministic Finite Automaton.

A Non Deterministic Finite Automaton consists of

- A finite set of states, often denoted by Q
- A finite set of input symbols, often denoted by Σ
- A transition function that takes as arguments a state and an input symbol in Σ, and returns a subset of Q.
- A start state, one of the states in Q
- A set of final or accepting states F.

21. What are the components of Finite automaton model?

The components of FA model are Input tape, Read control and finite control.

a. The input tape is divided into number of cells. Each cell can hold one i/p symbol
b. The read head reads one symbol at a time and moves ahead.
c. Finite control acts like a CPU. Depending on the current state and input symbol read from the input tape it changes state.

22. Define Transition diagram.

Transition diagram is a directed graph in which the vertices of the graph correspond to the states of FA. If there is a transition from state q to state p on input a, then there is an arc labeled ' a ' from q to p in the transition diagram.

23. Define Transition Diagram.

Transition Diagram associated with DFA is a directed graph whose vertices correspond to states of DFA, The edges are the transitions from one state to another.

24. Differentiate NFA and DFA

NFA or Non Deterministic Finite Automaton is the one in which there exists many paths for a specific input from current state to next state. NFA can be used in theory of computation because they are more flexible and easier to use than DFA.

Deterministic Finite Automaton is a FA in which there is only one path for a specific input from current state to next state. There is a unique transition on each input symbol.(Write examples with diagrams).

25. Give the examples/applications designed as finite state system.

Text editors and lexical analyzers are designed as finite state systems. A lexical analyzer scans the symbols of a program to locate strings corresponding to identifiers, constants etc, and it has to remember limited amount of information.

26. Define the language accepted by a NFA

We define the language of a NFA $A = (Q, \Sigma, \delta, q_0, F)$ by

$$L(A) = \{ w/\delta^\wedge(q_0, w) \cap F \neq \varphi\}.$$

27. Define the language accepted by a DFA

We define the language of a DFA $A = (Q, \Sigma, \delta, q_0, F)$ by

$$L(A) = \{ w/\delta^\wedge(q_0, w) \text{ is in } F\}.$$

28. What is ε-closure of a state q0?

ε-closure(q_0) denotes a set of all vertices p such that there is a path from q0 to p labeled ε. Example :closure(q0)={q0,q1}

REGULAR EXPRESSIONS AND LANGUAGES

1. What is a regular expression?

A regular expression is a string that describes the whole set of strings according to certain syntax rules. These expressions are used by many text editors and utilities to search bodies of text for certain patterns etc. Definition is: Let _ be an alphabet. The regular expression over _ and the sets they denote are:

1. _ is a r.e and denotes empty set.
2. _ is a r.e and denotes the set {_}
3. For each 'a' in _ , a+ is a r.e and denotes the set {a}.
4. If 'r' and 's' are r.e denoting the languages R and S respectively then (r+s), (rs) and (r*) are r.e that denote the sets RUS, RS and R* respectively.

2. Differentiate L* and L+

$\overline{L*}$ denotes Kleene closure and is given by L* =U Li i=0

example : 0* ={_ ,0,00,000,..................................}

Language includes empty words also.

$\overline{L+}$ denotes Positive closure and is given by L+= U Li i=1 q0 q1

3. What is Arden's Theorem?

Arden's theorem helps in checking the equivalence of two regular expressions. Let P and Q be the two regular expressions over the input alphabet _. The regular expression R is given as : R=Q+RP Which has a unique solution as R=QP*.

4. Write a r.e to denote a language L which accepts all the strings which begin or end with either 00 or 11.

The r.e consists of two parts:

L1=(00+11) (any no of 0's and 1's) =(00+11)(0+1)*

L2=(any no of 0's and 1's)(00+11) =(0+1)*(00+11)

Hence r.e R=L1+L2 =[(00+11)(0+1)*] + [(0+1)* (00+11)]

5. Construct a r.e for the language over the set _={a,b} in which total number of a's are divisible by 3

(b* a b* a b* a b*)*

6. What is: (i) (0+1)*   (ii)(01)*   (iii)(0+1)   (iv)(0+1)+

(0+1)*= { _ , 0 , 1 , 01 , 10 ,001 ,101 ,101001,.....................}

Any combinations of 0's and 1's.

(01)*={_ , 01 ,0101 ,010101 ,..}

All combinations with the pattern 01.

(0+1)= 0 or 1,No other possibilities.

(0+1)+= {0,1,01,10,1000,0101,.......................................}

7. Reg exp denoting a language over _ ={1} having (i) even length of string (ii) odd length of a string

1. Even length of string R=(11)*
2. Odd length of the string R=1(11)*

8. Reg exp for: (i) All strings over {0,1} with the substring '0101' (ii) All strings beginning with '11 ' and ending with 'ab' (iii) Set of all strings over {a,b}with 3 consecutive b's. (iv) Set of all strings that end with '1'and has no substring '00'

1. (0+1)* 0101(0+1)*
2. 11(1+a+b)* ab
3. (a+b)* bbb (a+b)*
4. (1+01)* (10+11)* 1

9. Construct a r.e for the language which accepts all strings with atleast two c's over the set Σ={c,b}

(b+c)* c (b+c)* c (b+c)*

10. What are the applications of Regular expressions and Finite automata Lexical analyzers and Text editors are two applications.

Lexical Analyzers

The tokens of the programming language can be expressed using regular expressions.

The lexical analyzer scans the input program and separates the tokens.For eg identifier can be expressed as a regular expression as: (letter)(letter+digit)*

If anything in the source language matches with this reg exp then it is recognized as an identifier.The letter is{A,B,C,............Z,a,b,c....z} and digit is {0,1,...9}.Thus reg exp identifies token in a language.

Text Editors

These are programs used for processing the text. For example UNIX text editors uses the reg exp for substituting the strings such as: S/bbb*/b/

Gives the substitute a single blank for the first string of two or more blanks in a given line. In UNIX text editors any reg exp is converted to an NFA with Єtransitions, this NFA can be then simulated directly.

11. Reg exp for the language that accepts all strings in which 'a' appears tripled overthe set Σ ={a}

reg exp=(aaa)*

12. What are the applications of pumping lemma?

Pumping lemma is used to check if a language is regular or not.

(i)   Assume that the language(L) is regular.

(ii) Select a constant 'n'.

(iii) Select a string(z) in L, such that $|z|>n$.

(iv) Split the word z into u,v and w such that $|uv|<=n$ and $|v|>=1$.

(v) You achieve a contradiction to pumping lemma that there exists an 'i' Such that uvi

w is not in L.Then L is not a regular language.

13. What is the closure property of regular sets?

The regular sets are closed under union, concatenation and Kleene closure.

r1Ur2= r1 +r2

r1.r2= r1r2

(r)*=r*

The class of regular sets are closed under complementation, substitution, homomorphism and inverse homomorphism.

14. Reg exp for the language such that every string will have atleast one 'a' followed by atleast one 'b'.

R=a⁺b⁺

15. Write the exp for the language starting with and has no consecutive b's .

reg exp=(a+ab)*

16. Construct a regular expression denoting odd numbers in their binary representation

{0/1}*1

17. Construct a regular expression denoting even numbers in their binary representation

{0/1}*0

18. Construct a regular expression denoting the set of all strings over {a,b} such that all starts with a and ends with b

a{a/b}*b

19. Construct a regular expression denoting the set of all strings over {a,b} such that all starts with a and ends with ab

a{a/b}*ab

20. Construct a regular expression denoting the set of all strings over {a,b} such that all ends with abb

{a/b}*abb

21. Construct a regular expression denoting the set of all strings over {a,b} such that all contains three a's.

b*ab*ab*ab*

22. What does the following regular expression denote 0*1*2*

The set of all words over {0,1} such that all starts with 0 number of 0's or 1 0's or more number of 0's followed by similar patterns of 1's and 2's.

23. Construct a regular expression for the set of strings that consist alternate 0's and 1's

$(01)^* + (10)^* + 0(10)^* + 1(01)^*$

24. State Pumping lemma? April/May 2008

Let L be a regular language. Then there exists a constant n (which depends on L) such that for every string w in L such that $|w| \geq n$ we can break w into three strings w = xyz, such that,

1. $v \neq \varepsilon$
2. $|xy| \leq n$
3. For all $k \geq 0$ the string $xy^k z$ is also in L.

25. When do you say two states p and q are equivalent?

We say that two states p and q are equivalent if for all input strings w, $\delta^{\wedge}(p, w)$ is an accepting state if and only if $\delta^{\wedge}(q, w)$ is an accepting state.

26. Lists on the closure properties of Regular sets.

1. Union
2. Concatenation
3. Closure
4. Complementation
5. Intersection
6. Transpose
7. Substitutions
8. Homomorphism

27. Let R be any set of regular languages. Is regular? Prove it.

Yes. Let P,Q be any two regular languages .As per theorem

$$L(R)=L(P \cup Q)$$

$$=L(P+Q)$$

Since '+' is a operator for regular expresstions L(R) is also regular.

28. Show that $(r^*)^*=r^*$ for a regular expression r,

$$(r^*)^*==\{\varepsilon,r,rr,\ldots\ldots\ldots\}= r^*$$

29. What are the three methods of conversion of DFA to RE?

1. Regular Expression equation method
2. Arden's Theorem.
3. State elimination technique.

CONTEXT-FREE GRAMMARS AND LANGUAGES

1. What are the applications of Context free languages

Context free languages are used in :

i. Defining programming languages.

ii. Formalizing the notion of parsing.

iii. Translation of programming languages.

iv. String processing applications.

2. What are the uses of Context free grammars?

- Construction of compilers.

- Simplified the definition of programming languages.

- Describes the arithmetic expressions with arbitrary nesting of balanced parenthesis $\{(,)\}$.

- Describes block structure in programming languages.

- Model neural nets.

3. Define a Context Free Grammar

A context free grammar (CFG) is denoted as G=(V,T,P,S) where V and T are finite set of variables and terminals respectively. V and T are disjoint. P is a finite set of productions each is of the form A$\rightarrow$B, where A is a variable and B is a string of symbols from (V U T)*.

4. What is the language generated by CFG or G?

The language generated by G (L(G)) is {w | w is in T* and S=>w. That is a G   string is in L(G) if:

1. The string consists solely of terminals.

2. The string can be derived from S.

5. What is : (a) CFL (b) Sentential form

L is a context free language (CFL) if it is L(G) for some CFG G.

A string of terminals and variables α is called a sentential form if:

S => α , where S is the start symbol of the grammar.

6. What is the language generated by the grammar G=(V,T,P,S) where P={S$\rightarrow$aSb, S$\rightarrow$ab}?

S=> aSb=>aaSbb=>...........................=>$a^n b^n$

Thus the language L(G)={ $a^n b^n$ | n>=1}.The language has strings with equal number of a's and b's.

7. **What is :(i) derivation (ii)derivation/parse tree.**

  i. **Derivation**: Derivation is a process, in which the input string will be drived by repeatedly applying the production. In each step of derivation either variable or terminal symbol will be replaced.

  ii. **Derivation tree**:is also called as parse tree.It s graphical or pictorial representation of a derivation.

Parse Tree Construction

  1. The label of the root is start symbol S.
  2. The Interior node represents Non-terminal symbols.
  3. The leaf nodes represents terminal symbol.
  4. The input string will be read from left to right.

8. **If S→aSb | aAb , A→bAa , A→ba .Find out the CFL**

  soln. S→aAb=>abab

  S→aSb=>a aAb b =>a a ba b b(sub S→aAb)

  S→aSb =>a aSb b =>a a aAb b b=>a a a ba b bb

  Thus $L=\{a^n b^m a^m b^n$, where n,m>=1\}

9. **What is a ambiguous grammar?**

  A grammar is said to be ambiguous if it has more than one derivation trees for a sentence or in other words if it has more than one leftmost derivation or more than one rightmost derivation.

10. **Find CFG with no useless symbols equivalent to :**

  S→AB | CA , B→BC | AB, A→a , C→aB | b.

  S→AB

  S→CA

  B→BC

  B→AB

  A→a

  C→aB

  C→b are the given productions.

  A symbol X is useful if S => $\alpha X \beta$ => w

  The variable B cannot generate terminals as B→BC and B→AB. Hence B is useless symbol and remove B from all productions. Hence useful productions are: S→CA , A→a , C→b .

11. **Construct CFG without Є production from : S →a | Ab | aBa , A → | Є , B →b | A.**

S→a

S→Ab

S→aBa

A→b

A→€

B→b

   B→A are the given set of production.

     A→€ is the only empty production. Remove the empty production

       S→ Ab , Put A→€ and hence S→b.

       If B→A and A→€ then B→€

Hence S→aBa becomes S→aa .

Thus S→a | Ab | b | aBa | aa

    A→b

    B→b

Finally the productions are: S→ a | Ab | b | aBa | aa

    A→b

    B→b

12. Construct a CFG for the language $L(G) = \{0^n 1^n : n \geq 1\}$.

$G = \{V = \{S\}, T = \{0, 1\}, P, S\}$

where

   P ={S→0S

     S →01}

13. Construct a CFG for the language $L(G) = \{0^n 1^n : n \geq 0\}$.

$G = \{V = \{S\}, T = \{0, 1\}, P, S\}$

where

   P ={S→0S1

      S→ε}

14. Find a LM derivation for *aaabbabbba* with the productions.

$P : S \rightarrow aB \mid bA, A \rightarrow a \mid aS \mid bAA, B \rightarrow b \mid bS \mid aBB$

Solution

S → aB

S → aaBB

S → aaaBBB

S → aaabBB

S → aaabbB

S → aaabbaBB

S → aaabbabB

S → aaabbabbS

S → aaabbabbbA

S → aaabbabbba

15. Find a L(G) S → aSb, S → ab

Solution

S → aSb

  → aaSbb

  .

  .

  .

  → $a^i S b^i$

  → $a^i a b b^i$

  → $a^n b^n$

L(G) = $\{a^n b^n, n \geq 1\}$

16. For the grammar $S \rightarrow aCa, C \rightarrow aCa \mid b$. Find L(G)

Solution

S → aCa

  → aaCaa

  .   .

  → $a^n C a^n$

  S → $a^n b a^n$

L(G) = $\{a^n b a^n, n > 0\}$

17. Construct a CFG for the language over {a,b} which contains palindrome strings.

G = {V = {S}, T = {a, b}, P, S}

where

    P ={S → aSa

       S→ bSb

       S → a

       S→ b

       S→ε}

18. Define the language of a Grammar.

If G = (V, T, P, S) is a CFG, the language of G denoted by L(G), is the set of terminal strings that have derivations from the start symbol i.e. L(G) = {w in T / S → *w}

19. What are the three ways to simplify a context free grammar?

(i) Removing the useless symbols from the set of productions.

(ii) By eliminating the empty productions.

(iii) By eliminating the unit productions.

20. What are the properties of the CFL generated by a CFG?

Each variable and each terminal of G appears in the derivation of some word in L .here are no productions of the form A→B where A and B are variables.

21. Find the grammar for the language L={a ^{2n} bc ,where n>1 }

let G=({S,A,B}, {a,b,c} ,P , {S}) where P:

    S→Abc

    A→aaA | Є

22. Find the language generated by :

S→0S1|0A|0|1B|1 A→0A|0, B→1B|1

The minimum string is S→ 0 | 1

    S→0S1=>001

    S→0S1=>011

    S→0S1=>00S11=>000S111=>0000A111=>00000111

Thus L={ $0^n 1^m$ | m not equal to n, and n,m >=1}

23. Construct the grammar for the language $L=\{a^n b a^n \mid n>=1\}$.

The grammar has the production P as:

S→aAa

A→aAa | b

The grammar is thus : G=({S,A} ,{a,b} ,P,S)

24. Construct a grammar for the language L which has all the strings which are all palindrome over Σ={a, b}.

G=({S}, {a,b} , P, S)

P:{ S → aSa ,

S→ b S b,

S→a,

S→b,

S→Є } which is in palindrome.

25. Differentiate sentences Vs sentential forms

A sentence is a string of terminal symbols.

A sentential form is a string   containing a   mix of variables and terminal symbols or all variables.This is an intermediate form in doing a derivation.

26. Define Pushdown Automata.

A pushdown Automata M is a system $(Q, \Sigma, \Gamma, \delta, q_0, Z_0, F)$, here Q is a finite set of states.

Σ is an alphabet called the input alphabet.

Γ is an alphabet called stack alphabet.

q_0 in Q is called initial state.

Zo in Γ is start symbol in stack.

F   is the set of final states.

Δ is a mapping from Q X (Σ U {Є}) X Γ to finite subsets of

Q X Γ*.

27. Specify the two types of moves in PDA.

The move dependent on the input symbol(a) scanned is:

$\delta(q,a,Z) = \{ (p1, \gamma1), (p2,\gamma2), \ldots\ldots(p^m,\gamma^m) \}$

where q qnd p are states , a is in Σ ,Z is a stack symbol and

γi is in Γ^*. PDA is in state q , with input symbol a and Z the top symbol on state enter state p iReplace symbol Z by string γi

The move independent on input symbol is ($\in$-move):

$\delta(q,\in,Z) = \{ (p1,\gamma1), (p2,\gamma2), \ldots\ldots\ldots(p^m,\gamma^m) \}$. Is that PDA is in state q , independent of input symbol being scanned and with Z the top symbol on the stack enter a state p i and replace Z by γi.

28. What are the different types of language acceptances by a PDA and define them.

For a PDA $M=(Q, \Sigma ,\Gamma ,\delta ,q0 ,Z0 ,F)$ we define:

1. **Language accepted by final state L(M) as:**

$* \{ w \mid (q0 , w , Z0) \mid\!-\!- (p, \in, \gamma) \text{ for some p in F and } \gamma \text{ in } \Gamma^* \}$.

2. **Language accepted by empty / null stack N(M) is:**

$\{ w \mid (q0,w ,Z0) \mid\!-\!-\!-\!-(p, \in, \in) \text{ for some p in Q} \}$.

29. Is it true that the language accepted by a PDA by empty stack and final states are different languages.

No, because the languages accepted by PDA 's by final state are exactly the languages accepted by PDA's by empty stack.

30. Define Deterministic PDA.

A PDA $M =(Q, \Sigma,\Gamma,\delta,q0,Z0,F)$ is deterministic if:

- For each q in Q and Z in Γ , whenever $\delta(q,\in,Z)$ is nonempty then $\delta(q,a,Z)$ is empty for all a in Σ.

- For no q in Q , Z in Γ , and a in $\Sigma \cup \{ \in \}$ does $\delta(q,a,Z)$ contains more than one element. (Eg): The PDA accepting $\{wcw \: R \mid w \text{ in } (0+1)^* \}$.

31. Define Instantaneous description(ID) in PDA.

ID describe the configuration of a PDA at a given instant.ID is a triple such as (q, w ,γ) , where q is a state , w is a string of input symbols and γ is a string of stack symbols.

If $M =(Q, \Sigma ,\Gamma ,\delta ,q0 ,Z0 ,F)$ is a PDA we say that

$(q,aw,Z\alpha) \mid\!-\!-\!-\!-(p,,\beta\alpha)$ if $\delta(q,a,Z)$ contains (p, β).

M 'a' may be Є or an input symbol. Example: (q1, BG) is in δ(q1, 0 ,) ells that (q1, 011, GGR)|---- (q1, 11,BGGR).

32. What is the significance of PDA?

Finite Automata is used to model regular expression and cannot be used to represent non regular languages. Thus to model a context free language, a Pushdown Automata is used.

33. When is a string accepted by a PDA?

The input string is accepted by the PDA if:

- The final state is reached.
- The stack is empty.

34. Give examples of languages handled by PDA.

(1) L={ a ^{n}b^n | n>=0 },here n is unbounded , hence counting cannot be done by finite memory. So we require a PDA ,a machine that can count without limit.

(2) L= { wwR | w Є {a,b}* } , to handle this language we need unlimited counting capability.

35. Is NPDA (Nondeterministic PDA) and DPDA (Deterministic PDA)equivalent?

The languages accepted by NPDA and DPDA are not equivalent.   For example: wwR is accepted by NPDA and not by any DPDA.

36. Construct a PDA that accepts the language generated by the grammar

$S \rightarrow aSbb$

$S \rightarrow aab$

The PDA A = ({q}, {a,b}, {S,a,b}, δ, q, S}

where δ :

1. $\delta(q,z_0,S)$ = {(q, aSbb), (q, aab)}
2. $\delta(q, a, a)$ = {(q, ε)}
3. $\delta(q, b, b)$ = {(q, ε)}

37. Construct a PDA that accepts the language generated by the grammar

$S \rightarrow aABB$

$A \rightarrow aB \mid a$

$B \rightarrow bA \mid b$

The PDA is given by

A = ({q}, {a,b}, {S, A, B, Z, a, b}, δ, q, S}

where δ :

$\delta(q, z, S) = \{(q, aABB)\}$

$\delta(q, z, A) = \{(q, aB), (q, a)\}$

$\delta(q, z, B) = \{(q, bA), (q, b)\}$

$\delta(q, a, a) = \{(q, \varepsilon)\}$

$\delta(q, b, b) = \{(q, \varepsilon)\}$

38. What is the main difference between pushdown automata and finite automata?

A pushdown automaton has additional stack facility and it can recognize non - regular languages. i.e. Context free languages.

39. What language does deterministic PDA's accept?

The DPDA's accept a class of languages that is between the regular languages and the CFL's.

40. Is it true that non-deterministic PDA is more powerful than that of deterministic PDA? Justify your answer.

No, NPDA is not more powerful than DPDA. Because, NPDA may produce ambiguous grammar by reaching its final state or by emptying its stack. But DPDA produces only unambiguous grammar.

41. What is the additional feature PDA has when compared with NFA? Is PDA superior over NFA in the sense of language acceptance? Justify your answer.

PDA is superior to NFA by having the following additional features.

i.   Stack which is used to store the necessary tape symbols and use the state to remember the conditions.

ii.   Two ways of language acceptances, one by reaching its final state and another by emptying its stack.

42. State the equivalence of acceptance by final state and empty stack.

- If $L = L(M2)$ for some PDA M2 , then $L = N(M1)$ for some PDA M1.
- If $L = N(M1)$ for some PDA M1 ,then $L = L(M2)$ for some PDA M2

where $L(M)$ = language accepted by PDA by reaching a final state.

$N(M)$ = language accepted by PDA by empty stack.

Properties of Context-Free Languages

1. **What are the two major normal forms for context-free grammar?**

   The two Normal forms are

   - Chomsky Normal Form
   - Greibach Normal Form

2. **What is a useless symbol? Nov/Dec 2007**

   A symbol x is useful if there is a derivation.

   $$S \overset{*}{\Longrightarrow} \alpha \, x \, \beta \overset{*}{\Longrightarrow} w \text{ for some } \alpha, \beta, w \in T^*$$

   or else, it is useless.

3. **What is ε-Production rule?**

   Any production rule of the form A $\rightarrow$ ε is known as ε - production.

4. **Define Unit Production.**

   Any production rule of the form A $\rightarrow$ B is known as unit production.

5. **When do you say a symbol is useful?**

   We say a symbol is useful either if it derives a string of terminals or it can be used in the middle of a derivation which yields a terminal or a string of terminals.

6. **Define Chomsky's Normal form.**

   A CFG whose production rules are of the form

   A $\rightarrow$ BC or A $\rightarrow$ a

   where A, B, and C are variables and a is terminal.

7. **Write the procedure to eliminate ε - productions.**

   - For all productions A $\rightarrow$ ε, put A into V_1
   - Repeat the following steps until no new variables are added.
     a. For all productions

        B $\rightarrow$ $A_1 A_2 A_3 \ldots A_n$

        where $A_1 A_2 A_3 \ldots A_n$ are in V_1
     b. Put B into V_1

8. **Write the procedure to eliminate the unit productions.**

- Find all variables B, for each A such that

  A ==> B

- The new grammar G' is obtained by letting into P' all non – unit productions of P.

- For all A and B satisfying A ==>, add to P'

  $A \rightarrow y_1 \mid y_2 \mid \ldots \mid y_n$

  where $B \rightarrow y_1 \mid y_2 \mid \ldots \mid y_n$ is the set of productions in P'

9. **Eliminate the useless symbol from the following**

   $S \rightarrow AB \mid a$

   $A \rightarrow b$

   B is an useless symbol since it doesn't derive a terminal. Eliminating it we get

   $S \rightarrow a$

   $A \rightarrow b$

10. **Define Greibach Normal form. Nov/Dec 2009**

    A CFG whose production rules are of the form $A \rightarrow \alpha$ where a is a terminal and α is either empty or a string of non – terminals.

11. **State pumping lemma for Context free language. April/May 2008**

    Let L be a CFL. Then there exists a constant n such that if z is any string in L such that $|z| \leq n$ then we can write z = uvwxy subject to the following conditions.

    a) $|vwx| \leq n$

    b) $vx \neq \varepsilon$

    c) for all $i \geq 0$ $uv^i wx^i y$ is in L.

12. **What is the use of pumping lemma for CFG.**

    It is used to check whether a given language is context free language or not.

13. **What operations that preserve CFL's.**

    1. Substitution
    2. Union
    3. Concatenation
    4. Closure (star)
    5. Reversal

14. **Let G= ({S,C} ,{a,b},P,S) where P consists of S→aCa , C→aCa |b. FindL(G).**

S→ aCa => aba

S→aCa=> a aCa a=>aabaa

S→aCa=> a aCa a=> a a aCa a a =>aaabaaa

Thus L(G)= { $a^n b a^n$,where n>=1 }

15. **Find L(G) where G= ({S} ,{0,1}, {S→0S1 ,S→ϵ },S) , is in L(G)**

S→0S1 =>0ϵ1=>01

S→0S1=>0 0S11=>0011

Thus L(G)= { $0^n 1^n$ | n>=0}

16. **What is a parser?**

A parser for grammar G is a program that takes as input a string w and produces as output either a parse tree for w ,if w is a sentence of G or an error message indicating that w is not a sentence of G.

17. **What are the closure properties of CFL?**

CFL are closed under union, concatenation and Kleene closure.

CFL are closed under substitution , homomorphism. CFL are not closed under intersection , complementation. Closure properties of CFL's are used to prove that certain languages are not context free.

18. **State the pumping lemma for CFLs.**

Let L be any CFL. Then there is a constant n, depending only on L, such that if z is in L and |z| >=n, then z=uvwxy such that :

i. |vx| >=1

ii. |vwx| <=n and

iii.   for all i>=0 uviwxiy is in L.

19. **What is the main application of pumping lemma in CFLs?**

The pumping lemma can be used to prove a variety of languages are not context free . Some examples are:

L1 ={ aibici | i>=1} is not a CFL.

L2= { aibjcidj | i>=1 and J>=1 } is not a CFL.

20. Give an example of Deterministic CFL.

The language L={anbn : n>=0} is a deterministic CFL

21. What are the properties of CFL?

Let G=(V,T,P,S) be a CFG

- The fanout of G ,(G) is largest number of symbols on the RHS of any rule in R.
- The height of the parse tree is the length of the longest path from the root to some leaf.

22. What is a turing machine? April/May 2008

Turing machine is a simple mathematical model of a computer. TM has unlimited and unrestricted memory and is a much more accurate model of a general purpose computer. The turing machine is a FA with a R/W Head. It has an infinite tape divided into cells, each cell holding one symbol.

23. What are the special features of TM?

In one move, TM depending upon the symbol scanned by the tape head and state of the finite control:

- Changes state.
- Prints a symbol on the tape cell scanned, replacing what was written there.

Moves the R/w head left or right one cell.

24. Define Turing machine.

A Turing machine is denoted as M=(Q,Σ,Γ,δ ,q0, B,F)

Q is a finite set of states.

Σ is set of i/p symbols ,not including B.

Γ is the finite set of tape symbols.

q0 in Q is called start state.

B in Γ is blank symbol.

F   is the set of final states.

δ -is a transition function mapping from Q X Γ to Q X Γ X {L,R}.

25. Define Instantaneous description of TM.

The ID of a TM M is denoted as α1q α2 . Here q is the current state of M s in Q; α1 α2 is the string in Γ * that is the contents of the tape up to the rightmost nonblank symbol or the symbol to the left of the head, whichever is the rightmost.

26. What are the applications of TM?

TM can be used as:

- Recognizers of languages.
- Computers of functions on non negative integers.
- Generating devices.

27. What is the basic difference between 2-way FA and TM?

Turing machine can change symbols on its tape , whereas the FA cannot change symbols on tape. Also TM has a tape head that moves both left and right side ,whereas the FA doesn't have such a tape head.

28. What is (a)total recursive function and (b)partial recursive function

If f(i1,i2,.........ik) is defined for all i1,.....ik then we say f is a total recursive function. They are similar to recursive languages as they are computed by TM that always halt.

A function f(i1,...ik) computed by a Turing machine is called a partial recursive function. They are similar to r.e languages as they are computed by TM that may or may not halt on a given input.

29. Give examples of total recursive functions.

All common arithmetic functions on integers such as multiplication , n!, [log2n] and 22n are total recursive functions.

1. What are(a) recursively enumerable languages (b) recursive sets?

The languages that is accepted by TM is said to be recursively enumerable (r. e) languages. Enumerable means that the strings in the language can be enumerated by the TM.

The recursive sets include languages accepted by at least one TM that halts on all inputs.

2. What are the various representation of TM?

We can describe TM using:

- Instantaneous description.
- Transition table.
- Transition diagram.

3. What is P-type problem?

The problems which can be solved in polynomial time are known as P – type problem.

4. What do you mean by NP type problems?

The problems which can be accepted by a non deterministic TM are known as NP type problems.

5. What are the possibilities of a TM when processing an input string?

- TM can accept the string by entering accepting state.
- It can reject the string by entering non-accepting state.
- It can enter an infinite loop so that it never halts.

6. What are the techniques for Turing machine construction?

- Storage in finite control.
- Multiple tracks.
- Checking off symbols.
- Shifting over
- Subroutines.

7. Define Modified Post's correspondence problem.

Given lists A and B of K strings each from Σ^*, say

$$A = w_1, w_2, \ldots w_k$$

$$B = x_1, x_2, \ldots x_k$$

does there exist a sequence of integers $i_1, i_2, \ldots i_r$ such that

$$w_1\, w_{i1}\, w_{i2} \ldots w_{ir} = x_1\, x_{i1}\, x_{i2} \ldots x_{ir}$$

The sequence of $i_1, i_2, \ldots i_m$ is a solution to this instance of PCP.

8. Define the classes P and NP.

P consists of all those languages or problems accepted by some Turing Machine that runs in some polynomial amount of time, as a function of its input length.

NP is the class of languages or problems that are accepted by nondeterministic TM's with a polynomial bound on the time taken along any sequence of non – deterministic choices.

9. What is the storage in FC?

The finite control(FC) stores a limited amount of information. The state of the Finite control represents the state and the second element represent a symbol scanned.

10. When is checking off symbols used in TM?

Checking off symbols is useful method when a TM recognizes a language with repeated strings and also to compare the length of substrings.

(eg) : { ww | w _ _ * } or {$a^i b^i$ | i>=1}. This is implemented by using an extra track on the tape with symbols Blank or $\sqrt{}$.

11. When is shifting over Used ?

A Turing machine can make space on its tape by shifting all nonblank symbols a finite number of cells to the right. The tape head moves to the right , repeatedly storing the symbols in the FC and replacing the symbols read from the cells to the left. The TM can then return to the vacated cells and prints symbols.

12. What is a multihead TM?

A k-head TM has some k heads. The heads are numbered 1 through k, and move of the TM depends on the state and on the symbol scanned by each head. In one move, the heads may each move independently left or right or remain stationary.

13. What is a 2-way infinite tape TM?

In 2-way infinite tape TM, the tape is infinite in both directions. The leftmost square is not distinguished. Any computation that can be done by 2-way infinite tape can also be done by standard TM.

14. How can a TM used as a transducer?

A TM can be used as a transducer. The most obvious way to do this is to treat the entire nonblank portion of the initial tape as input , and to treat the entire blank portion of the tape when the machine halts as output. Or a TM defines a function y=f(x) for strings x ,y _ _* if: q0X | --- qfY, where qf is the final state.

15. What is a multi-tape Turing machine?

A multi-tape Turing machine consists of a finite control with k-tape heads and ktapes ; each tape is infinite in both directions. On a single move depending on the state of finite control and symbol scanned by each of tape heads ,the machine can change state print a new symbol on each cells scanned by tape head, move each of its tape head independently one cell to the left or right or remain stationary.

16. What is a multidimensional TM?

The device has a finite control , but the tape consists of a k-dimensional array of cells infinite in all 2k directions, for some fixed k. Depending on the state and symbol scanned , the device changes state , prints a new symbol and moves its tapehead in one of the 2k directions, either positively or negatively, along one of the k-axes.

17. When a recursively enumerable language is said to be recursive ? Is it true that the language accepted by a non-deterministic Turing machine is different from recursively enumerable language?

A language L is recursively enumerable if there is a TM that accepts L and recursive if there is a TM that recognizes L. Thus r.e language is Turing acceptable and recursive language is Turing decidable languages. No , the language accepted by non-deterministic Turing machine is same as recursively enumerable language.

18. What is Church's Hypothesis?

The notion of computable function can be identified with the class of partial recursive functions is known as Church-hypothesis or Church-Turing thesis. The Turing machine is equivalent in computing power to the digital computer.

19. When we say a problem is decidable? Give an example of undecidable problem?

A problem whose language is recursive is said to be decidable. Otherwise the problem is said to be undecidable. Decidable problems have an algorithm that takes as input an instance of the problem and determines whether the answer to that instance is "yes" or "no".(eg) of undecidable problems are 1. Halting problem of the TM.

20. Give examples of decidable problems.

1. Given a DFSM M and string w, does M accept w?
2. Given a DFSM M is L(M) = _ ?
3. Given two DFSMs M1 and M2 is L(M1)= L(M2) ?
4. Given a regular expression _ and a string w ,does _ generate w?
5. Given a NFSM M and string w ,does M accept w?

21. Give examples of recursive languages?

    i.   The language L defined as L= { "M" ,"w" : M is a DFSM that accepts w} is recursive.

    ii.   L defined as { "M1" U "M2" : DFSMs M1 and M2 and L(M1)=L(M2) } is recursive.

22. What are UTMs or Universal Turing machines?

Universal TMs are TMs that can be programmed to solve any problem, that can be solved by any Turing machine. A specific Universal Turing machine U is:

Input to U: The encoding "M " of a Tm M and encoding "w" of a string w.

Behavior : U halts on input "M" "w" if and only if M halts on input w.

23. What is the crucial assumptions for encoding a TM?

There are no transitions from any of the halt states of any given TM .Apart from the halt state , a given TM is total.

24. What properties of recursive enumerable seta are not decidable?

- Emptiness
- Finiteness
- Regularity
- Context-freedom.

25. Define L .When is a trivial property?

L is defined as the set { <M> | L(M) is in M } is a trivial property if is empty or it consists of all regular languages.

26. What is a universal language Lu?

The universal language consists of a set of binary strings in the form of pairs (M,w) where M is TM encoded in binary and w is the binary input string.Lu = { < M,w> | M accepts w }.

27. What is a Diagonalization language Ld?

The diagonalization language consists of all strings w such that the TM M whose code is w doesnot accept when w is given as input.

28. What properties of r.e sets are recursively enumerable?

- $L \neq \Phi$
- L contains at least 10 members.
- w is in L for some fixed w.
- $L \cap Lu \neq \Phi$

29. What properties of r.e sets are not r.e?

- $L = \Phi$
- $L = \Sigma^*$.
- L is recursive
- L is not recursive.
- L is singleton.
- L is a regular set.

30. How can a TM acts as a generating device?

In a multi-tape TM ,one tape acts as an output tape, on which a symbol, once written can never be changed and whose tape head never moves left. On that output tape , M writes strings over some alphabet _ , separated by a marker symbol # , G(M) (where G(M) is the set w in Σ^{**} such that w is finally printed between a pair of #'s on the output device).

31. What are the different types of grammars/languages?

- Unrestricted or Phase structure grammar.(Type 0 grammar). (for TMs)
- Context sensitive grammar or context dependent grammar (Type1) (for Linear Bounded Automata)
- Context free grammar (Type 2) (for PDA)
- Regular grammar (Type 3) (for Finite Automata).

This hierarchy is called as Chomsky Hierarchy.

32. Show that AMBIGUITY problem is un-decidable.

Consider the ambiguity problem for CFGs. Use the "yes-no" version of AMB. An algorithm for FIND is used to solve AMB. FIND requires producing a word with two or more parses if one exists and answers "no" otherwise. By the reduction of AMB to FIND we conclude there is no algorithm for FIND and hence no algorithm for AMB.

33. State the halting problem of TMs.

The halting problem for TMs is: Given any TM M and an input string w, does M halt on w? This problem is undecidable as there is no algorithm to solve this problem.

34. Define PCP or Post Correspondence Problem.

An instance of PCP consists of two lists , A = w1,w2,....wk and B = x1,......xk of strings over some alphabet.This instance of PCP has a solution if there is any sequence of integers i1,i2,..im with m >=1 such that wi1, wi2,...wim = xi1,xi2 ,...xim The sequence i1 ,i2 ,....im is a solution to this instance of PCP.

35. Define MPCP or Modified PCP.

The MPCP is : Given lists A and B of K strings from * ,say A = w1 ,w2, ...wk and B= x1, x2,......xk does there exists a sequence of integers i1,i2,...ir such that w1wi1wi2......wir = x1xi1xi2...xir?

36. What is the difference between PCP and MPCP?

The difference between MPCP and PCP is that in the MPCP ,a solution is required to start with the first string on each list.

37. What are the concepts used in UTMs?

- Stored program computers.
- Interpretive Implementation of Programming languages.
- Computability.

38. What is NP- Complete problem?

Let L be a language (problem) in NP. We say that L is NP–complete if the following statements are true.

- L is in NP.
- For every language L' in NP there is a polynomial–time reduction of L' to L.

16 Marks Questions

1. Prove that, if L is accepted by an NFA with ε -transitions, then L is accepted by an NFA without ε -transitions.

2. Prove that for every regular expression there exist an NFA with ε -transitions.

3. Construct the NFA with ε -transitions from the given regular expression.

4. Conversion of NFA to DFA

   Draw the NFA's transition table

   Take the initial state of NFA be the initial state of DFA.

   Transit the initial state for all the input symbols.

   If new state appears transit it again and again to make all state as old state.

   All the new states are the states of the required DFA

   Draw the transition table for DFA

   Draw the DFA from the transition table.

5. Prove the equivalence of NFA and DFA. (8)

6. Construct a NFA for regular expression (a/b)*abb and draw its equivalent DFA. April/May2008

REGULAR EXPRESSIONS AND LANGUAGES

1. Consider the following ε-NFA. Compute the ε–closure of each state and find its equivalent DFA. (8) Nov/Dec 2006

	ε	A	B	c
p	{q}	{p}	φ	φ
q	{r}	φ	(q)	φ
r	φ	φ	φ	{r}

2. Convert the following NFA to its equivalent DFA.

	0	1
->p	{p,q}	{p}
q	{r}	{r}
r	{s}	{φ}
*s	{s}	{s}

3. Explain the construction with transition from any regular expression (8)

4. Find the regular expression for the set of all strings denoted by R132 from the deterministic fininte automata given below. (8)

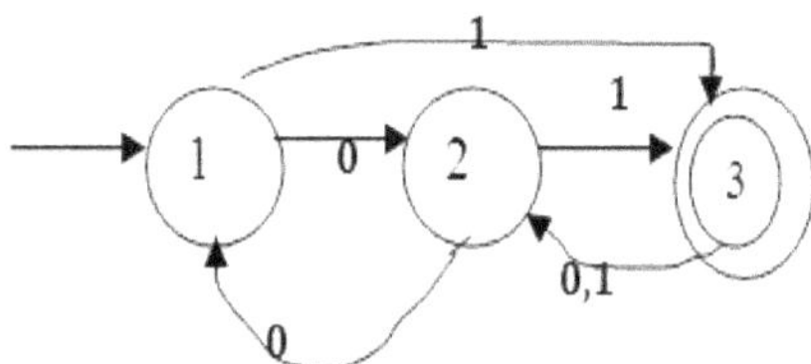

5. Construct the regular expression to the transition diagram. April/may 2008

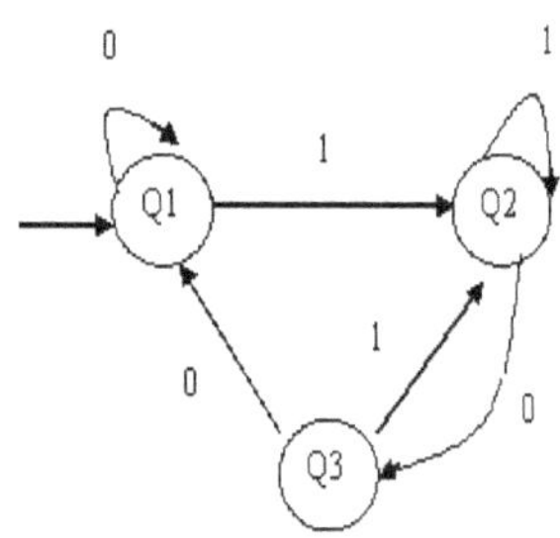

6. Show that the language p is a prime is not regular. Nov-Dec2007

7. Conversion of DFA into regular expression.

Arden's theorem is used to find regular expression from the DFA. using this theorem if the equation is of the form R=Q+RP, we can write this as R=QP*.

- Write the equations for all the states.
- Apply Ardens theorem and eliminate all the states.
- Find the equation of the final state with only the input symbols.
- Made the simplifications if possible
- The equation obtained is the required regular expression.

CONTEXT-FREE GRAMMARS AND LANGUAGES

1. Construction of reduced grammar.

Elimination of null productions

In a CFG,productions of the form A→∈ can be eliminated, where A is a variable.

Elimination of unit productions

In a CFG,productions of the form A→B can be eliminated, where A and B are variables.

Elimination of Useless symbols

These are the variables in CFG which does not derive any terminal or not reachable from the start symbols. These can also eliminate.

2. Chomsky normal form(CNF)

If the CFG is in CNF if it satisfies the following conditions

All the production must contain only one terminal or only two variables in the right hand side.

Example: Consider G with the production of S→aAB , A→ bC , B→b, C→c.

G in CNF is S→EB , E→DA , D→ a , A→FC , F→ b , B→b , C→ c.

3. Conversion of CFL in GNF.

4. Design a PDA that accepts the language {wwR | w in (0+1)*}.

5. Prove that if L is L(M2) for some PDA M2,then L is N(M1) for some PDA M1.

6. If L is a context-free language, then prove that there exists a PDA M such that L=N(M).

7. Construct a context free grammar for the given language Nov Dec 2006

   L={$a^n b^n$ |/n>=1}U{amb2m/m>=1} and hence a PDA accepting L by empty stack

8. Explain Leftmost and rightmost derivations.

If we apply a production only to the leftmost variable at every step to derive the required string then it is called as leftmost derivation.

If we apply a production only to the rightmost variable at every step to derive the required string then it is called as rightmost derivation.

Example:

Consider G whose productions are S→aAS|a , A→SbA|SS|ba. For the string

w=aabbaa find the leftmost and rightmost derivation.

LMD: S=>aAS

=>aSbAS

=>aabAS

=>aabbaS

=>aabbaa

RMD: S=>aAS

=>aAa

=>aSbAa

=>aSbbaa

=>aabbaa

9. Prove that for every derivations there exist a derivation tree.

10. Show that L = {an : n>=0} is not regular (8)

11. Convert the grammar S→ABb|a, A→aaA|B, B→bAb into greibach normal form .

12. Construct a context free grammar for the languages L(G1)={a^i b ^{2i} /I>0} and L(G2)= {anban/n>0}

PROPERTIES OF CONTEXT-FREE LANGUAGES

1. Conversion of PDA into CFL.

2. State and prove the pumping lemma for CFL

3. Explain the various techniques for Turing machine construction.

   storage in finite control

   multiple tracks

   checking off symbols

   shifting over

   subroutines.

4. Briefly explain the different types of Turing machines.

   - two way finite tape TM
   - multi tape TM
   - nondeterministic TM
   - multi dimensional TM
   - multihead TM

5. Design a TM to perform proper subtraction.

6. Design a TM to accept the language $L=\{0^n1^n \mid n>=1\}$

7. Explain how a TM can be used to determine the given number is prime or not?

It takes a binary input greater than 2,written on the first track, and determines whether it is a prime. The input is surrounded by the symbol $ on the first track.

To test if the input is a prime, the TM first writes the number 2 in binary on the second track and copies the first track on to the third. Then the second track is subtracted as many times as possible, from the third track effectively dividing the third track by the second and leaving the remainder.

If the remainder is zero, the number on the first track is not a prime.If the remainder is non zero,the number on the second track is increased by one.If the second track equals the first,the number on the first track is the prime.If the second is less thanfirst,the whole operation is repeated for the new number on the second track.

8. Construct a Turning machine to perform multiplication.

9. Design a Turing Machine to recognize each of the following languages.

    i. $\{0^n 1^n \mid n = 1\}$ (8)

    ii. $\{ww^R \mid w ? (0 + 1)^*\}$ (8)

10. (a)Prove that the function fadd $(x,y)=x+y$ is a primitive recursive

    (b)Show there exists aTM for which the halting problem is solvable

11. Design Turing Machine M for $f(x,y)=x*y$ where x,y are stored in the tape in the form $0^x 1 0^y 1$

UNDECIDABALITY

1. State and explain RICE theorem.

2. Define Lu and prove that Lu is recursive enumerable.

3. Define Ld and prove that Ld is undecidable.

4. Prove that if a language L and its complement are both recursively enumerable, then L is recursive.

5. Prove that the halting problem is undecidable.

6. Prove that there exists an recursively enumerable language whose complement is not recursively enumerable

7. Find whether the following languages are recursive or reclusively enumerable.

    (i)   Union of two recursive languages

    (ii) Union of two recursively enumerable languages

    (iii) Lif L and complement of L are recursively enumerable

    (iv) L_u

8. Consider the turing machine M and w=01,

    where M=({q1,q2,q3},{0,1}, δ ,q1, B, {q3}) and δ is given by

q	$\delta(q_i,0)$	$\delta(q_i,1)$	$\delta(q_i,B)$
q1	(q2,1,R)	(q2,0,L)	(q2,1,L)
q2	(q3,0,L)	(q1,0,R)	(q2,0,R)
q3	-	-	-

    Reduce the above problem to Post correspondence problem and find whether that PCP has a solution or not. (12)

9. Find the language obtained from the following operations

    a. Union of two recursive languages. (6)

    b. Union of two recursively enumerable language. (6)

    c. L if L and complement of L are recursively enumerable (4)

GATE QUESTIONS-THEORY OF COMPUTATION

GATE 1992

1. Which of the following problems is not NP-hard?

   (a) Hamiltonian circuit problem

   (b) The 0/1 Knapsack problem

   (c) Finding bi-connected components of a graph

   (d) The graph coloring problem

2. Which of the following regular expression identifies is true?

   (a) $r(*) = r*$ (b) $(r*s*) = (r + s)*$

   (c) $(r + s)* = r* + s*$ (d) $r * s* = r* + s*$

3. If G is a context-free grammar and w is a string of length I in L(G), how long is a derivation
   of w in G, if G is Chomsky normal form?

   (a) 2l   (b) 2l + 1

   (C) 2l - 1   (d) 1

4. Context-free languages are

   (a) closed under union   (b) closed under complementation

   (c) closed under intersection   (d) closed under Kleene closure

5. In which of the cases stated below is the following statement true?

   "For every non-deterministic machine M_1 there exists an equivalent deterministic machine
   M_2 recognizing the same language".

   (a) M_1 is non-deterministic finite automaton

   (b) M_1 is a non-deterministic PDA

   (c) M_1 is a non-deterministic Turing machine

   (d) For no machine M_1 use the above statement true

6. Which of the following three statements are true? Prove your answer.

   (i) The union of two recursive languages is recursive.

   (ii) The language $\{0^n \mid n$ is a prime$\}$ is not regular.

   (iii) Regular languages are closed under infinite union.

GATE 1993

1. Draw the state transition of a deterministic finite state automaton which accepts all strings
   from the alphabet {a,b}, such that no string has 3 consecutive occurrences of the letter b.

GATE 1994

1. Which of the following conversions is not possible (algorithmically)?

    (a) Regular grammar to context free grammar

    (b) Non-deterministic FSA to deterministic FSA

    (c) Non-deterministic PDA to deterministic PDA

    (d) Non-deterministic Turing machine to deterministic Turing machine

2. Which of the following features cannot be captured by context-free grammars?

    (a) Syntax of if-then-else statements

    (b) Syntax of recursive procedures

    (c) whether a variable has been declared before its use

    (d) Variable names of arbitrary length

3. The regular expression for the language recognized by the finite state automaton of figure
    is _________

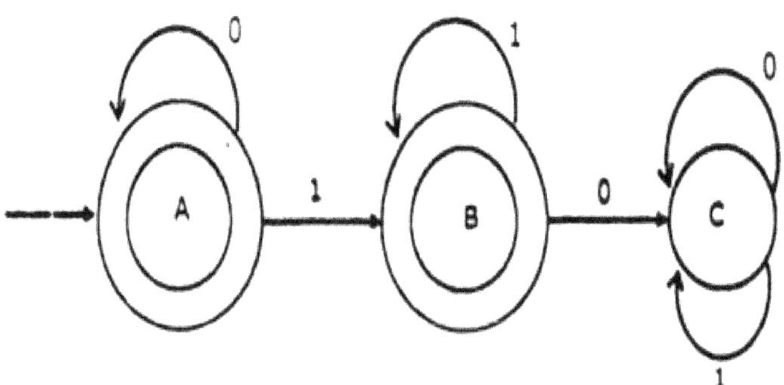

4. State True or False with one line explanation

    A FSM (Finite State Machine) can be designed to add two integers of any arbitrary length
    (arbitrary number of digits).

5. Match the following items

(i) Backus – Naur form	(a) Regular expressions
(ii) Lexical analysis	(b) LALR(I) grammars
(iii) YACC	(c) LL(I) grammars
(iv) Recursive descent parsing	(d) General context-free grammars

6. A grammar G is in Chomsky-Normal Form (CNF) if all its productions are of the form
    A→BC or A → A, where A, B and C, are non-terminals and a is a terminal. Suppose G is a
    CFG in CNF and w is a string in L(G) of length, then how long is a derivation of w in G?

GATE 1995

1. In some programming languages, an identifier is permitted to be a letter following by any number of letters or digits. If L and D denote the sets of letters and digits respectively, which of the following expressions defines an identifier? (a)

   (a) $(L \cup D)$ (b) $L (L \cup D)^*$ (c) $(L.D)^*$ (d) $L.(L.D)^*$

2. Consider a grammar with the following productions

   $S \rightarrow a \propto b| \, b \propto c| \, aB$

   $S \rightarrow \propto \, S| \, b$

   $S \rightarrow \propto b \, b| \, ab$

   $S \propto \, \rightarrow bd \, b| \, b$

   The above grammar is:

   (a) Context free   (b) Regular

   (c) Context sensitive   (d) LR(k)

3. Which of the following definitions below generates the same language as L, where $L = \{x^n y^n$ such that $n >= 1\}$?

   I. $E \rightarrow xE \, y| \, xy$ II. $x \, y| \, (x^+ xyy^+)$ III. $x^+ y^+$

   (a) I only   (b) I and II   (C) II and III   (d) II only

4. A finite state machine with the following state table has a single input x and a single out z.

present state	next state, z	
	x = 1	x = 0
A	D, 0	B, 0
B	B, 1	C, 1
C	B, 0	D, 1
D	B, 1	C, 0

   If the initial state is unknown, then the shortest input sequence to reach the final state C is:

   (a) 01   (b) 10   (c) 101   (d)110

5. Let $\Sigma = \{0,1\}$, $L = \Sigma^*$ and $R = \{0^n 1^n$ such that $n > 0\}$ then the languages $L \cup R$ and R are respectively

   (a) regular, regular   (b) not regular, regular

   (c) regular, not regular   (d) not regular, no regular

6. Let L be a language over Σ i.e., $L \leq \Sigma^*$. Suppose L satisfies the two conditions given below

   (i) L is in NP and

   (ii) For every n, there is exactly one string of length n that belongs to L.

       Let L^c be the complement of L over Σ^*. Show that L^c is also in NP

GATE 1996

1. Which two of the following four regular expressions are equivalent? (ε is the empty string)

   (i) $(00)^* (\varepsilon + 0)$ (ii) $(00)^*$ (iii) 0^* (iv) $0(00)^*$

   (a) (i) and (ii)   (b) (ii) and (iii)   (c) (i) and (iii)   (d) (iii) and (iv)

2. Which of the following statements is false?

   (a) The Halting problem of Turing machines is undecidable.

   (b) Determining whether a context-free grammar is ambiguous is undecidable.

   (c) Given two arbitrary context-free grammars G_1 and G_2 it is undecidable whether $L(G_1) = L(G_2)$.

   (d) Given two regular grammars G_1 and G_2 it is undecidable whether $L(G_1) = L(G_2)$.

3. Let $L \subseteq \Sigma^*$ where $\Sigma = \{a, b\}$. Which of the following is true?

   (a) $L = \{x | x$ has an equal number of a's and b's $\}$ is regular

   (b) $L = \{a^n b^n | n \geq 1\}$ is regular

   (c) $L = \{x | x$ has more a's than b's $\}$ is regular

   (d) $L = \{a^m b^n | m \geq, n \geq 1\}$ is regular

4. If L_1 and L_2 are context free languages and R a regular set, one of the languages below is not necessarily a context free language. Which one?

   (a) $L_1 L_2$ (b) $L_1 \cap L_2$ (c) $L_1 \cap R$ (d) $L_1 \cup L_2$

5. Define a context free languages $L \leq \{0, 1\}$ init $(L) = \{u/uv \in L$ for some v in $\{\{0, 1\}\}$ (in other words, init(L) is the set of prefixes of L)

   Let L $\{w/w$ is nonempty and has on equal number of 0's and 1's

   Then init (L) is

   (a) The set of all binary strings with unequal number of 0's and 1's

   (b) The set of all binary strings including the null string

   (c) The set of all binary strings with exactly one more 0's than the number of 1's, or one more 1than the number of 0's.

   (d) None of these

6. The grammar whose productions are

   $\rightarrow$ if id then <stmt>

   $\rightarrow$ if id then <stmt> else <stmt>

   $\rightarrow$ id:=id

   is ambiguous because

   (a) the sentence

   if a then if b then c: = d

(b) the left most and right most derivations of the sentence

if a then if b then c: = d

give rise two different parse trees

(c) the sentence

if a then if b then c: = d else c: = f

has more than two parse trees

(d) the sentence

if a then if then c: = d else c: = f

has two parse trees

7. Let G be a context-free grammar where G = ({S, A, B, C}, {a, b, d}, P, S) with the productions in P given below.

S → ABAC

A → aA| ε

B → bB| ε

C → d

(ε denotes the null string). Transform the grammar G to an equivalent context- free grammar G that has no ε productions and no unit productions. (A unit production is of the form x → y, and y are non terminals).

8. Given below are the transition diagrams for two finite state machines M_1 and M_2 recognizing languages L_1 and L_2 respectively.

(a) Display the transition diagram for a machine that recognizes L_1 L_2, obtained from transition diagrams for M_1 and M2 by adding only and transitions and no new states.

(b) Modify the transition diagram obtained in part (a) to obtain a transition diagram for a machine that recognizes (L_1 L_2) by adding only ε transitions and no new states.

(Final states are enclosed in double circles).

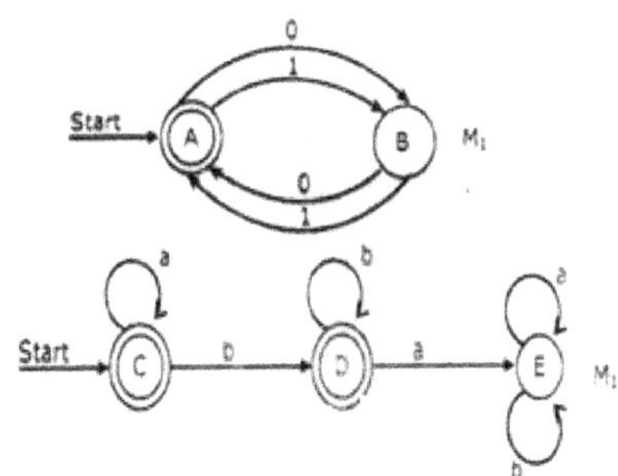

9. Let $Q = (q_1, q_2)$ (a, b), (a, b, Z) δ, qi, Z, $\emptyset$) be a pushdown automaton accepting by empty stack for the language which is the set of all nonempty even palindromes over the set {a, b}. Below is an incomplete specification of the transition d. complete the specification. The top of stack is assumed to be at the right end of the string representing stack contents.

(1) $\delta(q_1, a, Z) = \{(a_1, aZ)\}$

(2) $\delta(q_1, b, Z) = \{(q_1, bZ)\}$

(3) $\delta(q_1, a, a) = \{\ldots\ldots,\ldots\}$

(4) $\delta(q_1, b, b) = \{\ldots\ldots,\ldots\}$

(5) $\delta(q_2, a, a) = \{(q_2, \varepsilon)\}$

(6) $\delta(q_2, b, b) = \{(q_2, \varepsilon)\}$

(7) $\delta(q_2, \varepsilon, Z) = \{(q_2, \varepsilon)\}$

GATE 1997

1. In the following grammar

$X ::= X \oplus \dfrac{Y}{Y}$

$Y ::= Z .* \dfrac{Y}{Z}$

$Z ::= \text{id}$

Which of the following is true?

(a) '$\oplus$' is left associative while '*' is right associative

(b) Both '$\oplus$' and '*' is left associative

(c) '$\oplus$' is right associative while '*' is left associative

(d) None of these

2. Given $\Sigma = \{a, b\}$, which one of the following sets is not countable?

(a) Set of all strings over Σ

(b) Set of all languages over Σ

(c) Set of all regular languages over Σ

(d) Set of all languages over Σ accepted by Turing machines

3. Which one of the following is not decidable?

(a) Given a Turing machine M, a stings s and an integer k, M accepts s within k steps

(b) Equivalence of two given Turing machines

(c) Language accepted by a given finite state machine is not empty

(d) Language generated by a context free grammar is non empty

4. Which of the following language over {a, b, C} is accepted by a deterministic pushdown automata?

(a) $\{wcw^R \mid w \in \{a, b\}^*\}$

(b) $\{ww^R \mid w \in \{a,b,c\}^*\}$

(c) $\{a^n b^n c^n \mid n \geq 0\}$

(d) $\{w \mid w$ is a palindrome over $\{a,b,c\}\}$

Note: w^R is the string obtained by reversing 'w'.

5. Consider the grammar

$S \rightarrow bSe$

$S \rightarrow PQR$

$P \rightarrow bPc$

$P \rightarrow \varepsilon$

$Q \rightarrow cQd$

$Q \rightarrow \varepsilon$

$R \rightarrow dRe$

$R \rightarrow \varepsilon$

Where S, P, Q, R are non-terminal symbols with S being the start symbol; b, c, d, e are terminal symbols and 'ε' is the empty string. This grammar generates strings of the form $b^i c^j d^k e^m$ for some i, j, k, m $\le$ 0.

(a) What is the condition on the values of i,j,k,m?

(b) Find the smallest string that has two parse trees.

6. Construct a finite state machine with minimum number of states, accepting all strings over (a, b) such that the number of a's is divisible by two and the number of b's is divisible by three.

7. Given that L is a language accepted by a finite state machine, show that L^P and L^R are also accepted by some finite state machines, where

$L^P = \{s | ss' \in L$ some string. s'$\}$.

$L^P = \{s | s$ obtainable by reversing some string in L$\}$.

GATE 1998

1. Which of the following set can be recognized by a Deterministic Finite state Automaton?

(a) The numbers 1, 2, 4, 8, ... 2^n , ...written in binary

(b) The numbers 1, 2, 4, ..., 2^n, ...written in unary

(c) The set of binary string in which the number of zeros is the same as the number of ones.

(d) The set $\{1, 101, 11011, 1110111, ...\}$

2. Regarding the power of recognition of languages, which of the following statements is false?

(a) The non-deterministic finite-state automata are equivalent to deterministic finite-state automata.

(b) Non-deterministic Push-down automata are equivalent to deterministic Pushdown automata.

(c) Non-deterministic Turing machines are equivalent to deterministic Push-down automata.

(d) Non-deterministic Turing machines are equivalent to deterministic Turing machines.

(e) Multi-tape Turing machines are equivalent to Single-tape Turing machines.

3. The String 1101 does not belong to the set represented by

(a) $110^*(0 + 1)$

(b) $1 (0 + 1)^* 101$

(c) $(10)^* (01)^* (00 + 11)^*$

(d) $(00 + (11)^*0)^*$

4. Let L be the set of all binary strings whose last two symbols are the same. The number of states in the minimum state deterministic finite 0 state automaton accepting L is

(a) 2   (b) 5

(c) 8   (d) 3

5. Give a regular expression for the set of binary strings where every 0 is immediately followed by exactly k 1's and preceded by at least k 1's (k is a fixed integer)

6. Design a deterministic finite state automaton (using minimum number of states) that recognizes the following language:

$L = \{w \in \{0, 1\}^* | w$ interpreted as binary number (ignoring the leading zeros) is divisible by five.

7. Consider the grammar

$S \rightarrow Aa|b$

$A \rightarrow Ac|Sd|\epsilon$

Construct an equivalent grammar with no left recursion and with minimum number of production sales.

8. Let $M = (\{q_0, q_1\},\{0,1\},\{z_0, X\},\delta,q_0,z_0, \emptyset)$ be a Pushdown automation where is given by

$\delta (q_0, 1, z_0) = \{(q_0, xz_0)\}$

$\delta (q_0, \epsilon, z_0) = \{(q_0, \epsilon)\}$

$\delta (q_0, 1, X) = \{(q_0, XX)\}$

$\delta (q_1, 1, X) = \{(q_1, \epsilon)\}$

$\delta (q_0, 0, X) = \{(q_1, X)\}$

$\delta (q_1, \epsilon, z_0) = \{(q_1, \epsilon)\}$

(a) What is the language accepted by this PDA by empty store?

(b) Describe informally the working of the PDA.

9. (a) Let $G_1 = (N, T, P, S_1)$ be a CFG where,

$N = \{S_1, A, B\}$ $T = \{a, b\}$ and

P is given by

$S_1 \rightarrow a, S_1\, b$ $S_1 \rightarrow a\, B\, b$

$S_1 \rightarrow a\, A\, b$ $B \rightarrow Bb$

$A \rightarrow a\, A$ $B \rightarrow b$

$A \rightarrow a$

what is $L(G_1)$?

(b) Use the grammar in Part (a) to give a CFG for $L_2 = (a^i b^i a^k b^1 \,|i, j, k.1 \geq 1, i = j$ or $k = 1)$ by adding not more than 5 production rules.

(c) Is L_2 inherently ambiguous?

GATE 1999

1. Consider the regular expression $(0 + 1) (0 + 1)$.... N times. The minimum state finite automation that recognizes the language represented by this regular expression contains.

    (a) n states   (b) n + 1states   (c) n + 2 states   (d) None of these

2. Context-free languages are closed under:

    (a) Union, intersection   (b) Union, Kleene closure

    (c) Intersection, complement   (d) Complement, Kleene closure

3. Let L_D be the set of all languages accepted by a PDA by final state and L_E the set of all languages accepted by empty stack. Which of the following is true?

    (a) $L_D = L_E$ (b) $L_D \supset L_E$

    (c) $L_E = L_D$ (d) None of these

4. If L is context free language and L2 is a regular language which of the following is/are false?

    (a) L1 - L2 is not context free   (b) L1 $\cap$ L2 is context free

    (c) ~LI is context free   (d) ~L2 is regular

5. A grammar that is both left and right recursive for a non-terminal, is

    (a) Ambiguous   (b) Unambiguous

    (c) Information is not sufficient to decide whether it is ambiguous or unambiguous

    (d) None of these

6. (a) Given that A is regular and (A$\cup$B) is regular, does it follow that B is necessarily regular? Justify your answer.

    (b) Given two finite automata M1, M2, outline an algorithm to decide if $L(M1) \subseteq L(M2)$.

       (note: strict subset)

7. Show that the language L{xcx | x ∈ {0,1}* and c is a terminal symbol} is not context free. c is not 0 or 1.

GATE 2000

1. Let S and T be language over Σ = {a, b} represented by the regular expressions (a+b*)* and (a+b)*, respectively. Which of the following is true?

   (a) $S \subset t$ (b) $T \subset S$

   (c) $S = T$ (d) $S \cap T = \emptyset$

2. Let L denotes the language generated by the grammar $S \rightarrow 0S0/00$.
   Which of the following is true?

   (a) $L = 0^+$ (b) L is regular but not 0^+

   (c) L is context free but not regular   (d) L is not context free

3. What can be said about a regular language L over {a} whose minimal finite state automation has two states?

   (a) L must be {a^n|n is odd}   (b) L must be {a^n|n is even}

   (c) L must be {a^n|≥ 0}   (d) Either L must be {a^n|n is odd}, or L must be {a^n| n is even}

4. Consider the following decision problems:

   (P1) Does a given finite state machine accept a given string

   (P2) Does a given context free grammar generate an infinite number of stings Which of the following statements is true?

   (a) Both (P1) and (P2) are decidable   (b) Neither (P1) nor (P2) are decidable

   (c) Only (P1) is decidable   (d) Only (P2) is decidable

5. (a) Construct as minimal finite state machine that accepts the language, over {0,1}, of all strings that contain neither the substring 00 nor the substring 11.

   (b) Consider the grammar

   $S \rightarrow aS\ Ab$

   $S \rightarrow \quad \epsilon$

   $A \rightarrow \quad bA$

   $A \rightarrow \quad \epsilon$

   Where S, A are non-terminal symbols with S being the start symbol; a,b are terminal symbols and ϵ is the empty string. This grammar generates strings of the form $a^i\ b^j$ for some i, j $\geq$ 0, where i and j satisfy some condition. What is the condition on the values of i and j?

6. A pushdown automaton (pda) is given in the following extended notation of finite state diagrams:

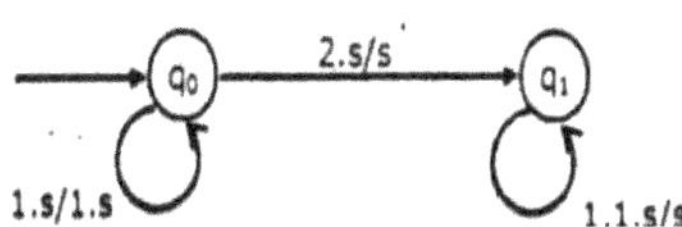

The nodes denote the states while the edges denote the moves of the pda. The edge labels are of the form d, s/s' where d is the input symbol read and s, s' are the stack contents before and after the move. For example the edge labeled 1, s/1.s denotes the move from state q_0 to q_0 in which the input symbol 1 is read and pushed to the stack.

(a) Introduce two edges with appropriate labels in the above diagram so that the resulting pda accepts the language

$\{x2x^R \mid x \in \{0,1\}^*, x^R$ denotes revese of $x\}$, by empty stack.

(b) Describe a non-deterministic pda with three states in the above notation that accept the language $\{0^n1^m \mid n \le m \le 2n\}$ by empty stack.

GATE 2001

1. Consider the following two statements:

S1: $\{0^{2n} \mid n \ge 1\}$ is a regular language

S2: $\{0^m\,1^n\,0^{m+n} \mid m \ge 1$ and $n \ge 1\}$ is a regular language

Which of the following statements is correct? ·

(a) Only S1 is correct   (b) Only S2 is correct

(c) Both S1 and S2 are correct   (d) None of S1 and S2 is correct

2. Which of the following statements s true?

(a) If a language is context free it can always be accepted by a deterministic push-down automaton

(b) The union of two context free languages is context free

(c) The intersection of two context free languages is context free

(d) The complement of a context free language is context free

3. Given an arbitrary non-deterministic finite automaton (NFA) with N states, the maximum number of states in an equivalent minimized DFA is at least

(a) N^2 (b) 2^N

(C) 2N   (d) N1

4. Consider a DFA over $\Sigma = \{a, b\}$ accepting all strings which have number of a's divisible by 6 and number of b's divisible by 8. What is the minimum number of states that the DFA will have?

(a) 8   (b) 14   (c) 15   (d) 48

5. Consider the following languages:

$Ll = \{ww | w \in \{a, b\} *\}$

$L2 = \{ww^R | w \in \{a, b\}, w^R$ is the reverse of $w\}$

$L3 = \{0^{2i} | i$ is an integer$\}$

$L3 = \{0^{i^2} | i$ is an integer$\}$ Which of the languages are regular?

(a) Only L1 and L2   (b) Only L2, L3 and L4

(c) Only L3 and L4   (d) Only L3

6. Consider the following problem X.

Given a Turing machine M over the input alphabet Σ, any state q of M

And a word $w \in \Sigma^*$, does the computation of M on w visit the state q?

Which of the following statements about X is correct?

(a) X is decidable

(b) X is undecidable but partially decidable

(c) X is undecidable and not even partially decidable

(d) X is not a decision problem

7. Construct DFA'S for the following languages:

(a) $L = \{w | w \in \{a, b\}^*$, w has baab as a subsring$\}$

(b) $L = \{w | w \in \{a, b\}^*$, w has an odd number of a's and an odd nuber of b's$\}$

8. Give a deterministic PDA for the language $L = \{a^n cb^{2n} | n \geq 1\}$ over the alphabet $= \Sigma = \{a, b, c\}$. Specify the acceptance state.

9. Let a decision problem X be defined as follows:

X: Given a Turing machine M over Σ and nay word $w \in \Sigma$, does M loop forever on w?

You may assume that the halting problem of Turing machine is undecidable but partially decidable.

(a) Show that X is undecidable.

(b) Show that X is not even partially decidable.

10. (a) Remove left-recursion from the following grammar:

$S \to Sa | Sb | a | b$

(b) Consider the following grammar: $S \to aSbS | bSaS | \varepsilon$

Construct all possible parse trees for the string abab. Is the grammar ambiguous?

GATE 2002

1. The language accepted by a Pushdown Automaton in which the stack is limited to 10 items is best described as

   (a) Context free   (b) Regular   (c) Deterministic Context free   (d) Recursive

2. The finite state machine described by the following state diagram with A as starting state, where an arc label is $\frac{X}{Y}$ and x stands for 1-bit input and y stands for 2-bit output

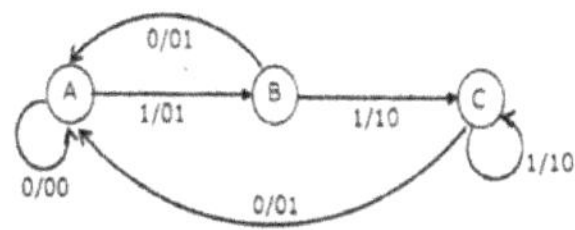

   (a) Outputs the sum of the present and the previous bits of the input

   (b) Outputs 01 whenever the input sequence contains 11

   (c) Outputs 00 whenever the input sequence contains 10

   (d) None of these

3. The smallest finite automaton which accepts the language {x |length of x is divisible by 3} has

   (a) 2 states   (b) 3 states   (c) 4 states   (d) 5 states

4. Which of the following is true?

   (a) The complement of a recursive language is recursive.

   (b) The complement of a recursively enumerable language is recursively enumerable.

   (c) The complement of a recursive language is either recursive or recursively enumerable.

   (d) The complement of a context-free language is context-free

5. The aim of the following question is to prove that the language {M | M is the code of a Turing Machine which, irrespective of the input, halts and outputs a 1}, is undecidable. This is to be done by reducing form the language
   {M',x|M' halts on x},which is known to be undecidable. In parts (a) and (b) describe the 2 main steps in the construction of M. in part (c) describe the key property which relates the behaviour of M on its input w to the behaviour of M' on x.

   (a) on input w, what is the first step that M must make?

   (b) On input w, based on the outcome of the first step, what is the second step that M must make?

   (c) What key property relates the behaviour of M on w to the behaviour of M' on x?

6. We require a four state automaton to recognize the, regular expression (a/b) * abb.

   (a) Give an NFA for this purpose.   (b) Give a DFA for this purpose.

GATE 2003

1. Ram and Shyam have been asked to show that a certain problem II is NP- complete. Ram shows a polynomial time reduction from the 3-SAT problem to II, and Shyam shows a polynomial time reduction from II to 3-SAT. Which of the following can be inferred from these reductions?

   (A) II is NP-hard but not NP-complete   (B) II is in NP, but is not NP-complete

   (C) II is NP-complete   (D) II is neither NP-hard, nor in NP

2. Nobody knows yet if P = NP. Consider the language L defined as follows.

$$L = \begin{cases} (0 + 1)^* & \text{if } P = NP \\ \emptyset & \text{otherwise} \end{cases}$$

   Which of the following statements is true?

   (A) L is recursive

   (B) L is recursively enumerable but not recursive

   (C) L is not recursively enumerable

   (D) Whether L is recursive or not will be known after we find out if P = NP

3. The regular expression $0^*(10^*)^*$ denotes the same set as

   (A) $(1^*0)^*1^*$ (B) $0+(0+10)^*$

   (C) $(0+1)^*10(0+1)^*$ (D) None of the above

4. If the strings of a language L can be effectively enumerated in lexicographic (i.e., alphabetic) order, which of the following statements is true?

   (A) L is necessarily finite

   (B) L is regular but not necessarily finite

   (C) L is context free but not necessarily regular

   (D) L is recursive but not necessarily context free

5. Consider the NFA M shown below.

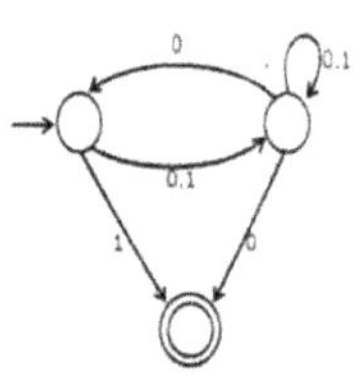

   Let the language accepted by M be L. Let L_1 be the language accepted by the NFA M_1 obtained by changing the accepting state of M to a non-accepting state and by changing the non-accepting states of M to accepting states. Which of the following statements is true?

   (A) $L_1 = \{0,1\}^* - L$ (B) $L_1 = \{0,1\}^*$ (C) $L_1 \subseteq L$ (D) $L_1 = L$

6. Consider the following deterministic finite state automaton M

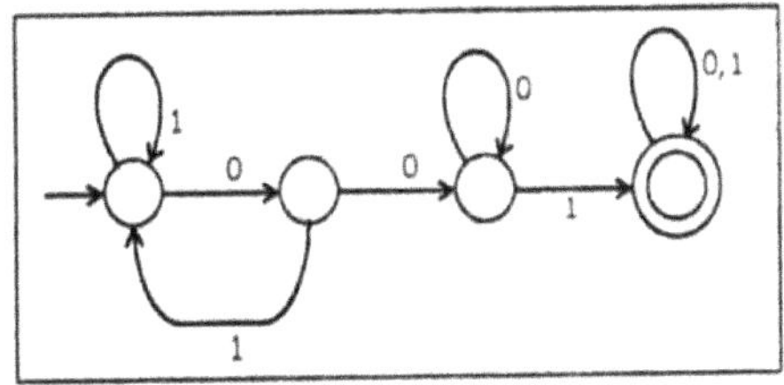

Let S denote the set of seven bit binary strings in which the first, the fourth, and the last bits are 1. The number of strings in S that are accepted by M is

(A) 1   (B) 5   (C) 7   (D) 8

7. Let G = ({S},{a, b},R, S) be a context free grammar where the rule set R is S → a S b |SS|U ε

Which of the following statements is true?

(A) G is not ambiguous

(B) There exist x,y ⊆ L(G) such that x,y ⇔ L(G)

(C) There is a deterministic pushdown automaton that accepts L.(G)

(D) We can find a deterministic Mite state automaton that accepts L(G)

8. A single tape Turing Machine M has two states q0 and q1, of which q0 is the starting state. The tape alphabet of M is {0, 1, B} and its input alphabet is {0,1}. The symbol B is the blank symbol used to indicate end of an input string. The transition function of M is described in the following table.

	0	1	B

	0	1	B
q_0	$q_{1,1,R}$	$q_{1,1,R}$	Halt
q_1	$q_{1.1.R}$	$q_{0,1,L}$	$q_{0,B,L}$

The table is interpreted as illustrated below. The entry (q1, 1, R) in row q0 and column1 signifies that if M is in state q0 and reads 1 on the current tape square, then it writes 1 on the same tape square, moves its tape head one position to the right and transitions to state q1.

Which of the following statements is true about M?

(A) M does not halt on any string in (0+1)*

(B) M does not halt on any string in (00+1)*

(C) M halts on all strings ending in a 0

(D) M halts on all strings ending in a 1

9. Define languages L0 andL1 as follows: L0 ={<M,w,0> |M halts on w} L1 ={<M,w,1>|M does
    not halt on w} Here <M, w, i>is a taplet whose first component, M, is an encoding of a
    Turing Machine, second component, w, is a string, and third component, i, is a bit. Let L =
    L0 ∀ L1. Which of the following is true?

    (A) L is recursively enumerable, but L is not

    (B) L is recursively enumerable, but L is not

    (C) Both L and L are recursive

    (D) Neither L nor L is recursively enumerable

GATE 2004

1. Which of the following grammar rules violate the requirements of an operator grammar?
    P, Q, R are nonterminals, and r, s, t are terminals.

    (i) P → QR   (ii) P → Q s R   (iii) P → ε   (iv)P → Q t R r

    (a) (i) only   (b) (i) and (iii) only

    (c) (ii) and (iii) only   (d) (iii) and (iv) only

2. The problem 3-SAT and 2-SAT are

    (a) Both in P

    (b) Both NP complete

    (c) NP-complete and in P respectively

    (d) Undicidable and NP-complete respectively

3. The following finite state machine accepts all those binary strings in which the number of
    1's and 0's are respectively

    (a) divisible by 3 and 2

    (b) odd and even

    (c) even and odd

    (d) divisible by 2 and 3

4. The language $\{a^m b^n c^{m+n} \mid m, n \geq 1\}$ is

    (a) regular   (b) context-free but not regular

    (c) context sensitive but not context free   (d) type-0 but not context sensitive

5. Consider the following grammar G:

    $S \rightarrow bS|aA|b$

    $A \rightarrow bA|aB$

    $B \rightarrow bB|aS|a$

    Let $N_a(\omega)$ and $N_b(\omega)$ denote the number of a's and b's in a string ω respectively.
    The language $L(G) \subseteq \{a, b\}^+$ generated by G is

(a) $\{\,\omega\,|\,N_a(\omega) > 3N_b(\omega)\}$

(b) $\{\,\omega\,|\,N_b(\omega) > 3N_a(\omega)\}$

(c) $\{\,\omega\,|\,N_a(\omega) = 3k,\ k \in \{0,1,2,...\}\}$

(d) $\{\,\omega\,|\,N_b(\omega) = 3k,\ k \in \{0,1,2,...\}\}$

6. L_1 is a recursively enumerable language over Σ. An algorithm A effectively enumerates its words as $\omega_1, \omega_2, \omega_3, \ldots$ define another language L_2 over $\Sigma \cup \{\#\}$ as $\{\,\omega_i, \#\,\omega_j : \omega_j \in L_1,\ i < j\}$. Here # is a new symbol. Consider the following assertions.

S_1: L_1 is recursive implies L_2 is recursive

S_2: L_2 is recursive implies L_1 is recursive

Which of the following statements is true?

(a) Both S_1 and S_2 are true

(b) S_1 is true but S_2 is not necessarily true

(c) S_2 is true but S_1 is not necessarily true

(d) Neither is necessarily true

GATE 2005

1. Consider three decision problems P_1, P_2 and P_3. It is known that P_1 is decidable and P_2 is undecidable. Which one of the following is TRUE?

(a) P_3 is decidable if P_1 is reducible to P_3

(b) P_3 is undecidable if P_3 is reducible to P_2

(C) P_3 is undecidable if P_2 is reducible to P_3

(d) P_3 is decidable if P_3 is reducible to P_2's complement

2. Consider the machine M:

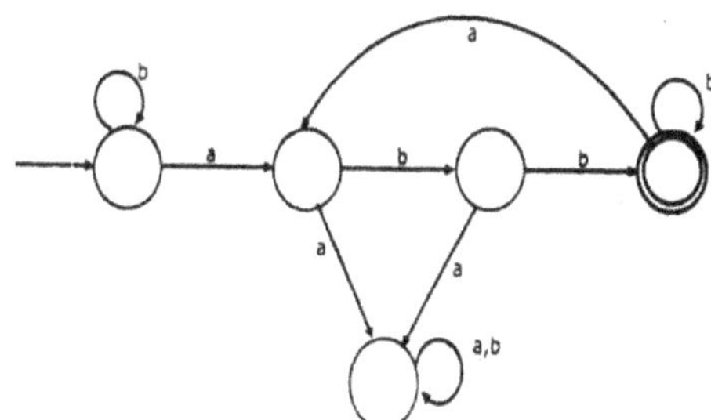

The language recognized by M is:

(a) $\{w \in \{a, b\}^* \mid$ every a in w is followed by exactly two b's$\}$

(b) $\{w \in \{a, b\}^* \mid$ every a in w is followed by at least two b's$\}$

(c) $\{w \in \{a,b\}^* \mid$ w contains the substring 'abb'$\}$

(d) $\{w \in \{a, b\}^* \mid$ w does not contain 'aa' as a substring)

3. Let N_f and N_p denote the classes of languages accepted by non-deterministic finite automata and non-deterministic push-down automata, respectively. Let D_f and D_p denote the classes of languages accepted by deterministic finite automata and deterministic push-down automata respectively. Which one of the following is TRUE?

(a) $D_f \subset N_f$ and $D_p \subset N_p$

(b) $D_f \subset N_f$ and $D_p = N_p$

(c) $D_f = N_f$ and $D_p = N_p$

(d) $D_f = N_f$ and $D_p \subset N_p$

4. Consider the languages: ·

$L_1 = \{a^n b^n c^m \mid n,m > 0\}$ and $L_2 = \{a^n b^m c^m \mid n,m > 0\}$

Which one of the following Statements is FALSE?

(a) $L_1 \cap L_2$ is a context-free language

(b) $L_1 \cup L_2$ is a context-free language

(c) L_1 and L_2 are context-free languages

(d) $L_1 \cap L_2$ is a context sensitive language

5. Let L_1 be a recursive language, and let L_2 be a recursively enumerable but not a recursive language. Which one of the following is TRUE?

(a) $\overline{L_1}$ is recursive and $\overline{L_2}$ is recursively enumerable

(b) $\overline{L_1}$ is recursive and $\overline{L_2}$ is not recursively enumerable

(c) $\overline{L_1}$ and $\overline{L_2}$ are recursively enumerable

(d) $\overline{L_1}$ is recursively enumerable and $\overline{L_2}$ is recursive

6. Consider the languages:

$L_1 = \{ww^R \mid w \in \{0,1\}^*\}$

$L_2 = \{w \# w^R \mid w \in \{0,1\}^*\}$, where # is a special symbol

$L_3 = \{ww \mid w \in \{0,1\}^*\}$

Which one of the following is TRUE?

(a) L_1 is a deterministic CFL

(b) L_2 is a deterministic CFL

(c) L_3 is a CFL, but not a deterministic CFL

(d) L_3 is a deterministic CFL

7. Consider the following two problems on undirected graphs:

$\propto$: Given G(V,E), does G have an independent set of size $|V|-4$?

β: Given G(V,E), does G have an independent set of size 5?

Which one of the following is TRUE?

(a) $\propto$ is in P and β is NP-complete

(b) $\propto$ a is NP-complete and β is in p

(c) Both $\propto$ and β are NP-complete

(d) Both $\propto$ and β are in P

8. The following diagram represents a finite state machine which takes as input a binary number from the least significant bit.

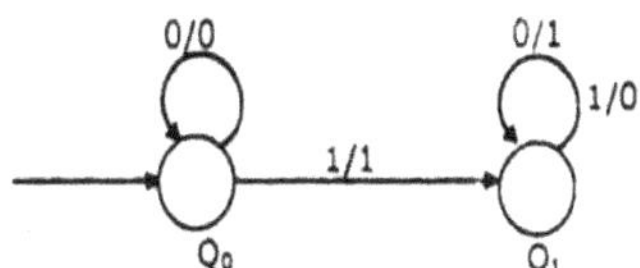

Which one of the following is TRUE?

(a) It computes l's complement of the input number

(b) It computes 2's complement of the input number

(c) It increments the input number

(d) It decrements the input number

GATE 2006

1. Let S be an NP-complete problem are Q and R be two other problems not known to be in NP. Q is polynomial time reducible to S and S is polynomial-time reducible to R. Which one of the following statements is true?

(a) R is NP-complete   (b) R is NP-hard

(c) Q is NP-complete   (d) Q is NP-hard

2. Let $L_1 = \{0^{n+m} 1^n 0^m \mid n, m \geq 0\}$, $L_2 = \{0^{n+m} 1^{n+m} 0^m \mid n, m \geq 0\}$, and $L_3 = \{0^{n-m} 1^{n+m} 0^{n+m} \mid n, m \geq 0\}$. Which of these languages are NOT context free?

(a) L_1 only   (b) L_3 only   (c) L_1 and L_2 (d) L_2 and L_3

3. If s is a string over $(0+1)^*$ then let n (s) denote the number of 0's in s and n_1 (s)the number of l's in s. Which one of the following languages is not regular?

(a) $L = \{s \in (0 + 1)^* \mid n_0 (s) \text{ is a 3-digit prime}\}$

(b) $L = \{s \in (0 + 1)^* \mid \text{ for every prefix s' of s}, |n_0 (s') - n. (s')| \leq 2\}$

(c) $L = \{s \in (0 + 1)^* \mid n_0 (s) - n_1 (s)| \leq 4\}$

(d) $L = \{s \in (0 + 1)^* \mid n_0 (s) \bmod 7 = n_1 (s) \bmod 5 = 0\}$

4. For $S \in (0 + 1)^*$ let d(s) denote the decimal value of (e.g.$d(101) = 5$)·

Let $L = \{s \in (0 + 1)^* \mid d(s) \bmod 5 = 2 \text{ and } d(s) \bmod 7 \neq 4\}$

Which one of the following statements is true?

(a) L is recursively enumerable, but not recursive

(b) L is recursive; but not context-free

(c) L 19 context-free, but not regular

(d) L is regular

5. Let SHAM$_3$ be the problem of finding a Hamiltonian cycle in a graph G =(V;E) with |V| divisible by 3 and DHAM$_3$ be the problem of determining if a Hamiltonian cycle exists in such graphs. Which one of the following is true?

(a) Both DHAM$_3$ and SHAM$_3$ are NP-hard

(b) SHAM$_3$ is NP-hard, but DHAM$_3$ is not

(c) DHAM$_3$ is NP-hard, but SHAM$_3$ is not

(d) Neither DHAM$_3$ nor SHAM$_3$ is NP-hard

6. Consider the following statements about the context free grammar

$G = \{S \to SS, S \to ab, S \to ba, S \to \epsilon\}$

I. G is ambiguous

II. G produces all strings with equal number of a's and b's

III. G Can be accepted by a deterministic PDA.

Which Combination below expresses all the true statements about G?

(a) I only   (b) I and III only   (c) II and III only   (d) I, II and III

7. Let L_1 be a regular language, L_2 be a deterministic context-free language and L_2 a recursively enumerable, but not recursive, language. Which one of the following statements is false?

(a) $L_1 \cap L_2$ is a deterministic CFL   (b) $L_3 \cap L_1$ is recursive

(c) $L_1 \cup L_2$ is context free   (d) $L_1 \cap L_2 \cap L_3$ is recursively enumerable

8. Consider the regular language L = (111+11111)*. The minimum number of states in any DFA accepting this languages is:

(a) 3   (b) 5   (c) 8   (d) 9

9. Which one of the following grammars generates the language $L = \{a^i b^j | i \neq j\}$?

(A) $S \to AC|CB$ (b) $S \to aS|Sb|a|b$

$\quad C \to aC b| a|b$

$\quad A \to a A| \epsilon$

$\quad B \to B b| \epsilon$

(C) $S \to A C| CB$ (d) $S \to A C| CB$

$\quad C \to aC b| \epsilon$ $\quad C \to aC b| \epsilon$

$\quad A \to a A| \epsilon$ $\quad A \to a A| a$

$\quad B \to B b| \epsilon$ $\quad B \to B b| b$

10. In the correct grammar above, what is the length of the derivation (number of steps starring from S) to generate the string $a^l b^m$ with l # m?

(a) max(l, m) + 2   (b) l + m + 2   (c) l + m + 3   (d) max (l, m) + 3

GATE 2007

1. Which of the following problems is un decidable?

   (a) Membership problem for CFGS.

   (b) Ambiguity problem for CFGs.

   (c) Finiteness problem for FSAs.

   (d) Equivalence problem for FSAs.

2. Which of the following is TRUE?

   (a) Every subset of a regular set is regular.

   (b) Every finite subset of a non-regular set is regular.

   (c) The union of two non-regular sets is not regular.

   (d) Infinite union of finite sets is regular.

3. A minimum state deterministic Mite automaton accepting the language $L = \{w|w \in \{0,1\}^*,$ number of 0s and 1s in w are divisible by 3 and 5, respectively$\}$ has

   (a) 15 states

   (b) 11 states

   (c) 10 states

   (d) 9 states

4. The language $L = \{0^i 2 1^i | i \geq 0\}$ over the alphabet $\{0,1,2\}$ is:

   (a) Not recursive

   (b) Is recursive and is a deterministic CFL.

   (c) Is a regular language.

   (d) Is not a deterministic CFL but a CFL.

5. Which of the following languages is regular?

   (a) $\{ww^R | w \in \{0,1\}^+\}$

   (b) $\{ww^R x | x, w \in \{0,1\}^+\}$

   (c) $\{wxw^R | x, w \in \{0,1\}^+\}$

   (d) $\{xww^R | x, w \in \{0,1\}^+\}$

Common Data Questions: 6 & 7

Consider the following Finite State Automaton:

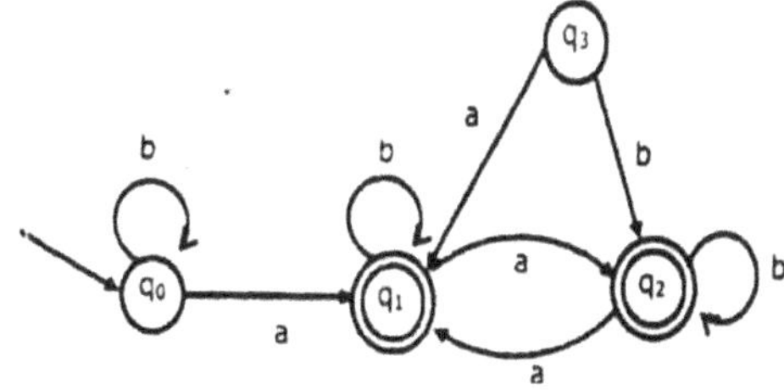

6. The language accepted by this automaton is given by the regular expression

   (a) b* ab* ab* ab*

   (b) (a + b)*

   (c) b*a(a + b)*

   (d) b*ab*ab*

7. The minimum state automaton equivalent to the above FSA has the following number of states

(a) 1   (b) 2   (c) 3   (d) 4

Statement for Linked Answer Questions: 8 & 9

Consider the CFG with {S,A,B} as the non-terminal alphabet, {a;b}as the terminal alphabet, S as the start symbol and the following set of production rules:

$$S \to aB \qquad S \to bA$$
$$B \to b \qquad A \to a$$
$$B \to bS \qquad A \to aS$$
$$B \to aBB \qquad S \to bAA$$

8. Which of the following strings is generated by the grammar?

(a) aaaabb   (b) aabbbb

(c) aabbab   (d) abbbba

9. For the correct answer strings to Q. 8, how many derivation trees are there?

(a) 1   (b) 2   (c) 3   (d) 4

GATE 2008

1. Which of the following is true for the language {a^p |p is a prime}?

   (a) It is not accepted by a Turing Machine

   (b) It is regular but not context-free

   (c) It is context-free but not regular

   (d) It is neither regular nor context-free, but accepted by a Turing machine

2. Which of the following are decidable?

   I. Whether the intersection of two regular languages is infinite

   II. Whether a given context-free language is regular

   III. Whether two push-down automata accept the same language

   IV. Whether a given grammar is context-free

   (a) I and II   (b) I and IV

   (c) II and III   (d) II and IV

3. If L and L are recursively enumerable then L is

   (a) Regular   (b) Context-free

   (c) Context-Sensitive   (d) Recursive

4. Which of the following statements is false?

   (a) Every NFA can be converted to an equivalent DFA

(b) Every non-deterministic Turing machine can be converted tj an equivalent deterministic Turing machine

(c) Every regular language is also a context-free language

(d) Every subset of a recursively enumerable set is recursive

5. Given below are two finite state automata ($\rightarrow$ indicates the start state and F indicates a final state)

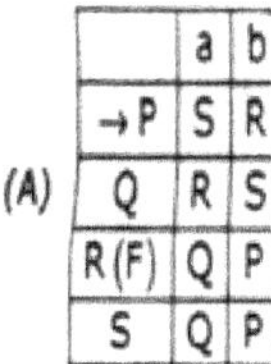

Y:

	a	b
$\rightarrow$1	1	2
2(F)	2	1

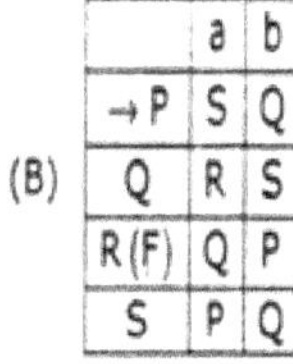

Z:

	a	b
$\rightarrow$1	2	2
2(F)	1	1

Which of the following represents the product automaton Z×Y?

(A)

	a	b
$\rightarrow$P	S	R
Q	R	S
R(F)	Q	P
S	Q	P

(B)

	a	b
$\rightarrow$P	S	Q
Q	R	S
R(F)	Q	P
S	P	Q

(C)

	a	b
$\rightarrow$P	Q	S
Q	R	S
R(F)	Q	P
S	Q	P

(D)

	a	b
$\rightarrow$P	S	Q
Q	S	R
R(F)	Q	P
S	Q	P

6. Which of the following statements are true?

I. Every left-recursive grammar can be converted to a right-recursive grammar and vice-versa

II. All ε-productions can be removed from any context-free grammar by Suitable transformations

III. The language generated by a context-free grammar all of whose productions are of the form X → w or X → wY (where, w is a string of terminals and Y is a non-terminal), is always regular

IV. The derivation trees of strings generated by a context-free- grammar in Chomsky Normal Form are always binary trees

(a) I,II,III and IV

(b) II, III and IV only

(c) I, III and IV only

(d) I, II and IV only

7. Match the following:

E. Checking that identifiers are declared before their use   P. $L = \{a^n b^m c^n d^m \mid n \geq 1, m \geq 1\}$

F. Number of formal parameters in the declaration of a   Q. $X \rightarrow XbX \mid XcX \mid dXf \mid g$
function agrees with the number of actual parameters
in use of that function

G. Arithmetic expressions with matched pairs of
parentheses

H. Palindromes

R. L = {wcw | w ∈ (a|b)*}

S. X → bXb | cXc | ε

(A) E - P, F - R, G – Q, H – S

(B) E - R, F - P, G – S, H – Q

(C) E - R, F - P, G – Q, H – S

(D) E - P, F - R, G – S, H - Q

8. Match the following NFAs with the regular expressions they correspond to

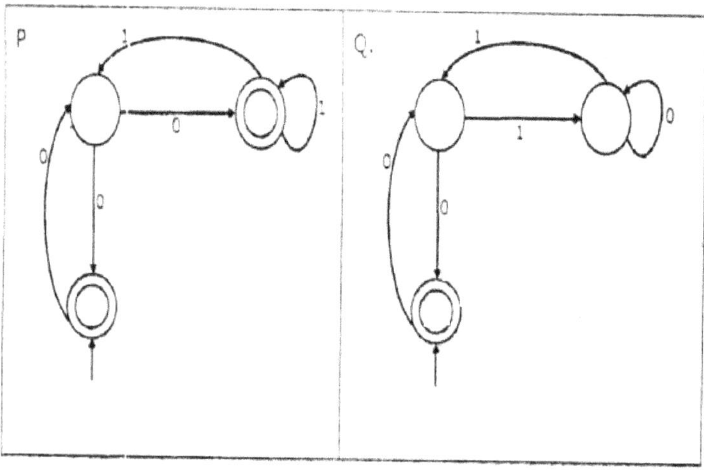

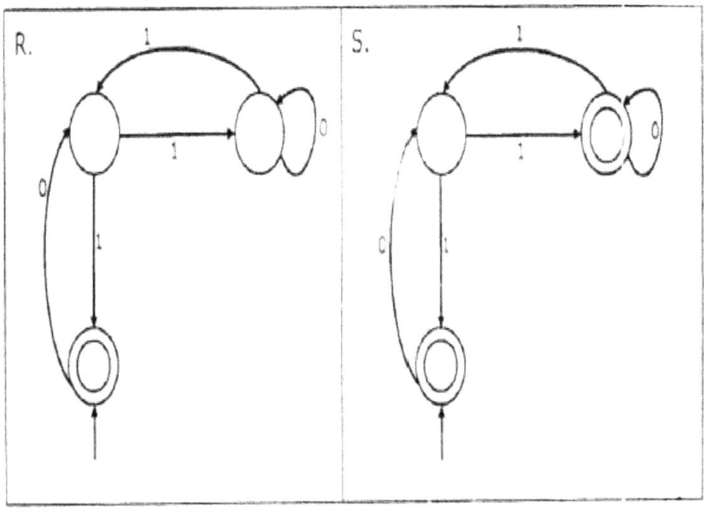

1. $\varepsilon + 0\ (01*1 + 00)*01*$

2. $\varepsilon + 0(10*1 + 00)*0$.

3. $\varepsilon + 0(10*1 + 10)*1$

4. $\varepsilon + 0(10*1 + 10)*10*$

(a) P-2, Q-1, R-3, S-4

(b) P-1, Q-3, R-2, S-4

(c) P-1, Q-2, R-3, S-4

(d) P-3, Q-2, R-1, S-4

9. Which of the following are regular sets?

I. $\{a^n b^{2m} \mid n \geq 0, m \geq 0\}$

II. $\{a^n b^m \mid n = 2m\}$

III. $\{a^n b^m \mid n \neq m\}$

IV. $\{xcy \mid x, y, \in \{a, b\}\ *\}$

(a) I and IV only

(b) I and III only

(c) I only

(d) IV only

GATE 2009

1. $S \rightarrow aSa|bSb|\ a|b$;The language generated by the above grammar over the alphabet $\{a,b\}$ is the set of

    (a) All palindromes

    (b) All odd length palindromes

    (c) Strings that begin and end with the same symbol

    (d) All even length palindromes

2. Let π_A be a problem that belongs to the class NP. Then which one of the following is TRUE?

    (a) There is no polynomial time algorithm for π_A

    (b) If π_A can be solved deterministically in polynomial time, then P = NP

    (c) If π_A is NP-hard, then it is NP-complete

    (d) π_A may be un decidable

3. Which one of the following languages over the alphabet $\{0,1\}$ is described by the regular expression: $(0+1)*0(0+1)*0(0+1)*?$

    (a) The set of all strings containing the substring 00

    (b) The set of all strings containing at most two 0's

    (c) The set of all strings containing at least two 0's

    (d) The set of all strings that begin and end with either 0 or 1

4. Which one of the following is FALSE?

    (a) There is unique minimal DFA for every regular language

    (b) Every NFA can be converted to an equivalent PDA

    (c) Complement of every context-free language is recursive

    (d) Every nondeterministic PDA can be converted to an equivalent deterministic PDA

5. Given the following state table of an FSM with two states A and-B, one input and one output:

Present state A	Present state B	Input	Next state A	Next state B	Output
0	0	0	0	0	1
0	1	0	1	0	0
1	0	0	0	1	0
1	1	0	1	0	0
0	0	1	0	1	0
0	1	1	0	0	1
1	0	1	0	1	1
1	1	1	0	0	1

If the initial state is A = 0, B=0, what is the minimum length of an input string which will take the machine to the state A=0, B=1 with Output=1?

(A) 3   (B) 4

(C) 5   (D) 6

6. Let $L = L_1 \cap L_2$, where L_1 and L_2 are languages as defined below:

$L_1 = \{a^m b^m c\, a^n b^m \mid m, n \geq 0\}$

$L_2 = \{a^i b^j c^j \mid i, j, k \geq 0\}$

Then L is

(a) Not recursive

(b) Regular

(c) Context free but not regular

(d) Recursively enumerable but not context free

7. The above DFA accepts the set of all strings over {0,1} that

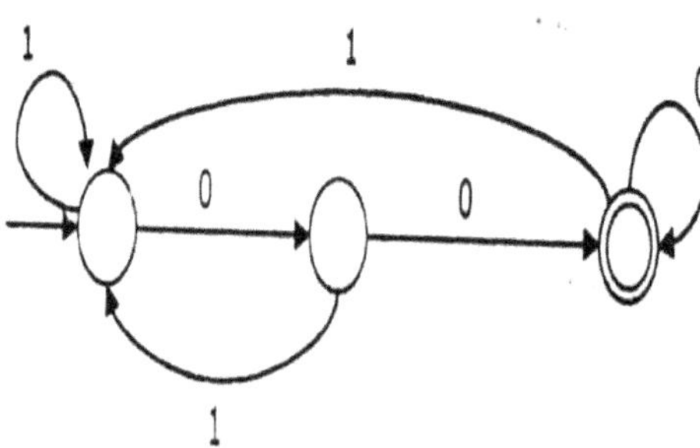

(a) begin either with 0 or 1   (b) end with 0

(c) end with 00   (d) contain the substring 00

GATE 2010

1. Let L1 be a recursive language.Let L2 and L3 be languages that are recursively enumerable but not-recursive. Which of the following statements is not necessarily true?

   (a) L2 - L1 is recursively enumerable

   (b) L1 - L3 is recursively enumerable

   (c) L2 ∩ L1 is recursively enumerable

   (d) L2 ∪ L1 is recursively enumerable

2. Let L = {w ∈ (0 + 1)* | w has even number of 1s}, i.e. L is the set of all bit strings with even number of 1s. Which one of the regular expressions below represents L?

   (a) (0 * 10 * 1)*

   (b) 0 * (10 * 10 *)*

   (c) 0 * (10 * 1 *) * 0 *

   (d) 0 * 1 (10 * 1) * 10 *

3. Consider the languages L1 = {0^i1^j | i ≠ j}. L2 = {0^i1^j | i = j}. L3 = {0^i1^j | i = 2j + 1}· L4 = {0^i1^j | i≠2j}). Which one of the following statements is true?

   (a) Only L2 is context free

   (b) Only L2 and L3 are context free

   (c) Only L1 and L2 are context free

   (d) All are context free

4. Let w be any string of length n in {0, 1}*. Let L be the set of all substrings of w. What is the minimum number of states in a non-deterministic finite automaton that accepts L?

   (a) n-l   (b) n   (c) n+1   (d) 2^{n-1}

GATE 2011

1. The lexical analysis for a modern computer language such as java needs the power of which one of the following machine models in a necessary and sufficient sense?

   (a) Finite state automata

   (b) Deterministic pushdown automata

   (c) Non-Deterministic pushdown automata

   (d)Turing machine

2. Let P be a regular language and Q be a context free language such that Q ⊆ P. (For example, let P be the language represented by the regular expression p*q* and Q be {p^nq^n | n ∈ N}). Then which of the following is ALWAYS regular?

   (a) P ∩ Q   (b) P - Q   (c) Σ * - P   (d) Σ * - Q

3. Which of the following pairs have DIFFERENT expressive power?

   (a)Deterministic finite automata (DFA) and Non-deterministic finite automata (NFA)

   (b)Deterministic push down automata (DPDA) and Non-deterministic push down automata (NPDA) (c)Deterministic single-tape Turing machine and Non-deterministic single tape Turing machine

(d)Single-tape Turing machine and multi-tape Turing machine

4. Definition of a language L with alphabet {a} is given as following $L = \{a^{nk} \mid k > 0,$ and n is a positive integer constant}

   What is the minimum number of states needed in a DFA to recognize L?

   (a) k+1 (b) n+1 (c) 2^{n+1} (d) 2^{k+1}

5. A deterministic finite automation (DFA)D with alphabet $\Sigma = \{a,b\}$ is given below

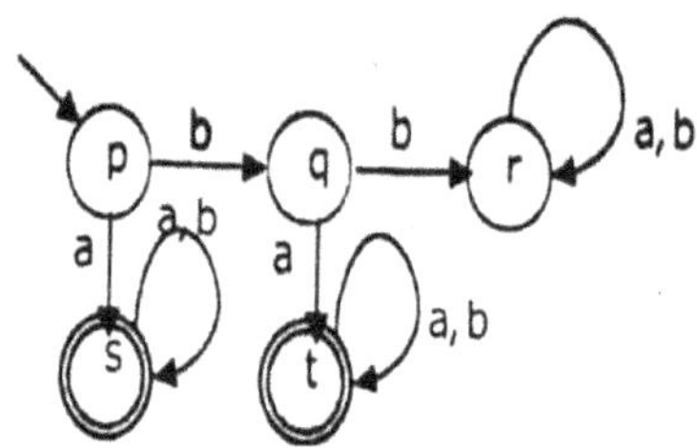

   Which of the following finite state machines is a valid minimal DFA which accepts the same language as D?

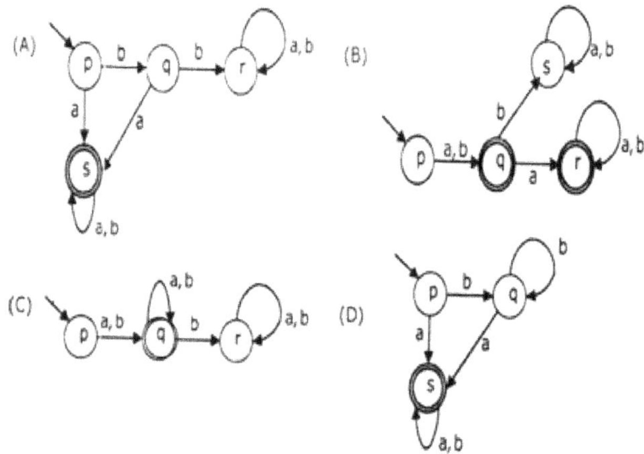

6. Consider the languages L1, L2 and L3 as given below

   $L1 = \{0^p1^q \mid p, q \in N\}$

   $L2 = \{0^p1^q \mid p, q \in N$ and $p = q\}$ and

   $L3 = \{0^p1^q0^r \mid p, q, r \in N$ and $p = q = r\}$

Which of the following statements is NOT TRUE?

(a) Push Down Automata(PDA) can be used to recognize L1 and L2

(b) L1 is a regular language

(c) All the three languages are context free

(d)Turing machines can be used to recognize all the languages

GATE 2004 (IT)

1. Which one of the following regular expressions is NOT equivalent to the regular expression $(a + b + C)$ *?

    (a) $(a^* + b^* + c^*)^*$ (b) $(a^* b^* c^*)^*$

    (c) $((ab)^* + c^*)^*$ (d) $(a^* b^* + c^*)^*$

2. Which one of the following statement Is FALSE?

    (a) There exist context free languages such that all the context free grammas generating them are ambiguous

    (b) An unambiguous context free grammar always has a unique parse tree for each string of the language generated by it

    (c) Both deterministic and non-deterministic pushdown automata always accept the same set of languages

    (d) A finite set of string from one alphabet is always a regular language

3. Let $M = (K, \Sigma, r, \Delta, s, F)$ be a pushdown automaton, where $K = \{s, f\}$, $F = \{f\}$, $\Sigma = \{a,b\}$, $f = \{a\}$ and

    $\Delta = \{((s, a, \varepsilon),(s, a)),((s, b, \varepsilon),(s\ a)),\ ((s, a, \varepsilon),\ (f, e))\ ,((f, a, a),(f, \varepsilon))\ ,((f, b, a),(f, \varepsilon))\}$

    Which one of the following strings is not a member of L(M)?

    (a) aaa   (b) aabab   (c) baaba   (d) bab

4. Let $M = (K, \Sigma, \delta, s, F)$ be a finite state automaton, where

    $K = \{A,B\}$, $\Sigma = \{a, b\}$, $s = A$, $F = \{B\}$,

    $\delta (A, a) = A$, $\delta(A, b) = B$, $\delta (B, a) = B$ and $\delta (B,b) = A$

    A grammar to generate the language accepted by M can be specified as $G = (V, \Sigma, R, S)$, where $V = K \cup \Sigma$, L and $S = A$.

    Which one of the following set of rules will make L(G) = L(M)?

    (a) $\{A \rightarrow a3, A \rightarrow bA, B \rightarrow bA, B \rightarrow aA, B \rightarrow \varepsilon\}$

    (b) $\{A \rightarrow aA, A \rightarrow bB, B \rightarrow B, B \rightarrow bA, B \rightarrow \varepsilon\}$

    (c) $\{A \rightarrow bB, A \rightarrow aB, B \rightarrow aA, B \rightarrow bA, B \rightarrow \varepsilon\}$

    (d) $\{A \rightarrow aA, A \rightarrow bA, B \rightarrow aB, B \rightarrow bA, A \rightarrow \varepsilon)$

GATE 2005 (IT)

1. Let L be a regular language and M be a context free language, both over the alphabet E. Let L^c and M^c denote the complements of L and M respectively. Which of the following statements about the language $L^c \cup M^c$ is TRUE?

   (a) It is necessarily regular but not necessarily context free

   (b) It is necessarily context free

   (c) It is necessarily non-regular

   (d) None of the above

2. Which of the following statements is TRUE about the regular expression 01*0?

   (a) It represents a finite set of finite strings.

   (b) It represents an infinite set of Mite strings.

   (c) It represents a finite set of infinite strings.

   (d) It represents an infinite set of infinite strings.

3. The language $\{0^n 1^n 2^n \mid 1 \le n \le 10^6\}$ is:

   (a) Regular

   (b) Context free but not regular

   (c) Context free but its complement is not context free

   (d) Not context free

4. Consider the non-deterministic finite automation (NFA) shown in the figure. State X is the starting state of the automaton. Let the language accepted by the NFA with Y as th02 only accepting state be L1. Similarly, let the language accepted by the NFA with Z as the only accepting state be L2. Which of the following statements about L1 and L2 is TRUE?

   (a) L1 = L2   (b) L1 ⊂ L2

   (c) L2 ⊂ LI   (d) None of the above

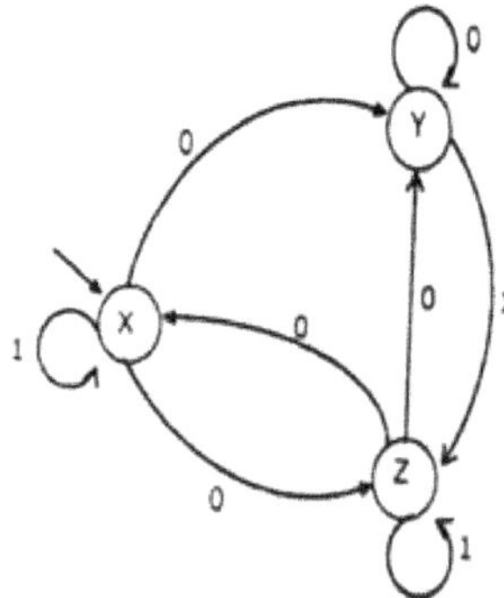

5. Let P be a non-deterministic pushdown automaton (NPDA) with exactly one state, q, and exactly one symbol, Z, in its stack alphabet. State q is both the starting as well as the accepting state of the PDA. The stack is initialized with one Z before the start of the operation of the PDA. Let the input alphabet of the PDA be Σ. Let L(P) be the language accepted by the PDA by reading a string and reaching its accepting state. Let N(P) be the language accepted by the PDA by reading a string and emptying its stack.

Which of the following statements is TRUE?

(a) L(P) is necessarily Σ^* but N(P) is not necessarily Σ^*

(b) N(P) is necessarily Σ^* but L(P) is not necessarily Σ^*

(c) Both L(P) and N(P) is necessarily Σ^*

(d) Neither L(P) nor N(P) are necessarily Σ^*

6. Consider the regular grammar:

$$S \rightarrow X\,a \mid Y a$$

$$X \rightarrow Z a$$

$$Z \rightarrow S\,a \mid B$$

$$Y \rightarrow W a$$

$$W \rightarrow S a$$

Where S is the starting symbol, the set of terminals is {a} and the set of non-terminals is {S,W,X,Y,Z}.

We wish to construct a deterministic finite automaton (DFA) to recognize the same language. What is the minimum number of states required for the DFA?

(a) 2   (b) 3   (c) 4   (d) 5

7. A language L satisfies the Pumping Lemma for regular languages, and also the Pumping Lemma for context free languages. Which of the following statements about L is TRUE?

(A) L is necessarily a regular language

(B) L is necessarily a context free language, but not necessarily a regular language

(C) L is necessarily a non-regular language (D) None of the above

Consider the context-free grammar

$$E \rightarrow E+E$$

$$E \rightarrow (E * E)$$

$$E \rightarrow id$$

Where E is the starting symbol, the set of terminals is {id,(, +,), *) and the set of non-terminals is {E}.

8. A. Which of the following terminal strings has more than one parse tree when parsed according to the above grammar?

(a) id + id + id + id

(b) id + (id* (id * id))

(c) (id * (id*id)) + id

(d) ((id * id + id) * id)

8 B. For the terminal string with more than one parse tree obtained as solution to Question 8A, how many parse trees are possible?

(a) 5

(b) 4

(c) 3

(d) 2

GATE 2006 (IT)

1. In the automaton below, s is the start state and t is the only final state.

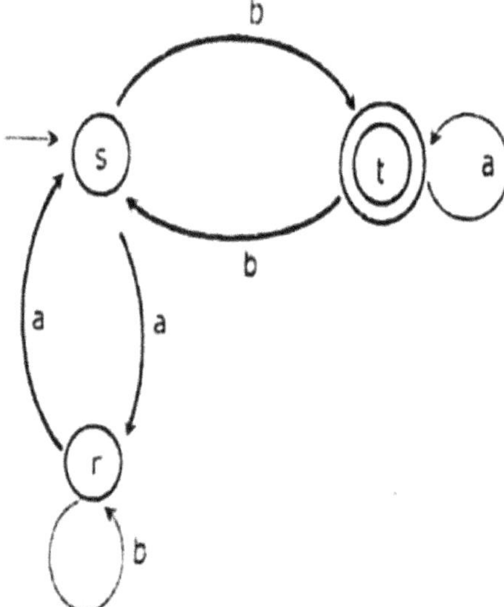

Consider the strings u = abbaba, v = bab, and w = aabb. Which of the following statements is true?

(a) The automaton accepts u and v but not w

(b) Thee automaton accepts each of u, v, and w

(c) The automaton rejects each of u, v, and w .

(d) The automaton accepts u but rejects v and w

2. In the context-free grammar below, S is the start symbol, a and b are terminals, and ε denotes the empty string

S → aSa |bSb |a|b|ε

Which of the following strings is NOT generated by the grammar?

(a) aaaa   (b) baba   (c) abba   (d) babaaabab

3. Which regular expression best describes the language accepted by the non-deterministic automation below?

(a) $(a + b)^* a(a + b)b$ (b) $(abb)^*$

(c) $(a + b)^* a(a + b)^* b(a + b)^*$ (d) $(a + b)^*$

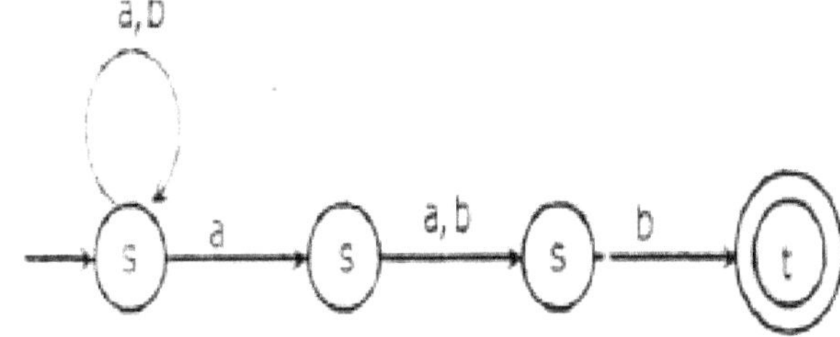

4. Consider the regular grammar below

S → bS |aA| ε

A → a S| b A|

The Myhill-Nerode equivalence classes for the language generated by the grammar are,

(a) $\{\{w\varepsilon\ (a+b)^* \ |\#_a\ (w)$ is even$\}$ and $\{w\varepsilon\ (a + b)^* \ |\#_a\ (w)$ is odd$\}\}$

(b) $\{\{w\varepsilon\ (a+b)^* \ |\#_b\ (w)$ is even$\}$ and $\{w\varepsilon\ (a + b)^* \ |\#_b\ (w)$ is odd$\}\}$

(c) $\{\{w\ \varepsilon\ (a + b)^* \ |\#_a\ (w) = \#_b\ (w)\}$ and $\{w\ \varepsilon\ (a + b)^* \ |\#_a\ (w) \neq \#_b\ (w)\}\}$

(d) $\{\varepsilon\}, \{wa\ |w\ \varepsilon\ (a + b)^*$ and $wb|\ w\ \varepsilon\ (a + b)^*\}$

5. Which of the following statements about regular languages is NOT true?

(a) Every language has a regular superset

(b) Every language has a regular subset

(c) Every subset of a regular language is regular

(d) Every subset of a finite language is regular

6. Which of the following languages is accepted by a non-deterministic pushdown automaton (PDA) but NOT by a deterministic PDA?

(a) $\{a^n b^n c^n \ |n \geq 0\}$

(b) $\{a^l b^m c^n \ |l \neq m$ or $m \neq n\}$

(c) $\{a^n b^n \mid n \geq 0\}$

(d) $\{a^m b^n \mid m, n \geq 0\}$

7. Let L be a context-free language and M a regular language. Then the language $L \cap M$ is

(a) Always regular

(b) Never regular

(c) Always a deterministic context-free language

(d) Always a context-free language

8. Consider the pushdown automaton (PDA) below which runs over the input alphabet (a, b, c). It has the stack alphabet $\{Z_0, X\}$ where Z_0 is the bottom-of-stack marker. The set of states of the PDA is $\{s, t, u, f\}$ where s is the start state and f is the final state. The PDA accepts by final state. The transitions of the PDA given below are depicted in a standard manner. For example, the transition $(s, b, X) \rightarrow (t, XZ_0)$ means that if the PDA is in state s and the symbol on the top of the stack is X, then it can read b from the input and move to state t after popping the top of stack and pushing the symbols Z_0 and X (in that order) on the stack.

$(s, a, Z_0) \rightarrow (s, XXZ_0)$

$(s, \varepsilon, Z_0) \rightarrow (f, \varepsilon)$

$(s, a, X) \rightarrow (s, XXX)$

$(s, b, X) \rightarrow (t, \varepsilon)$

$(t, b, X) \rightarrow (t, \varepsilon)$

$(t, c, X) \rightarrow (u, \varepsilon)$

$(u, c, X) \rightarrow (u, \varepsilon)$

$(u, \varepsilon, Z_0) \rightarrow (f, \varepsilon)$

The language accepted by the PDA is

(a) $\{a^l b^m c^n \mid l = m = n\}$

(b) $\{a^l b^m c^n \mid l = m\}$

(c) $\{a^l b^m c^n \mid 2l = m + n\}$

(d) $\{a^l b^m c^n \mid m = n\}$

9. In the context-free grammar below, S is the start symbol, a and b are terminals, and ε denotes the empty string.

$S \rightarrow aSAb \mid \varepsilon$

$A \rightarrow bA \mid \varepsilon$

The grammar generates the language

(a) $((a + b)^* b)^*$

(b) $\{a^m b^n \mid m \leq n\}$

(c) $\{a^m b^n \mid m = n\}$

(d) $a^* b^*$

GATE 2007 (IT)

1. Consider an ambiguous grammar G and its disambiguated version D. Let the language recognized by the two grammars be denoted by L(G) and L(D) respectively.

   Which one of the following is true?

   (a) $L(D) \subset L(G)$

   (b) $L(D) \supset L(G)$

   (c) $L(D) = L(G)$

   (d) $L(D)$ is empty

2. The two grammars given below generate a language over the alphabet $\{x, y, z\}$

   G1: $S \rightarrow x|z|xS|zS|yB$

   $\quad B \rightarrow y|z|yB|zb$

   G2: $S \rightarrow y|z|yS|zS|xB$

   $\quad B \rightarrow y|yS$

   Which of the following choices describes the properties satisfied by the strings in these languages?

   (a) G1: No y appears before any x

   G2: Every x is followed by at least one y

   (b) G1: No y appears before any x

   G2: No x appears before any y

   (c) G1: No y appears after any x

   G2: Every x is followed by at least one y

   (d) G1: No y appears after any x

   G2: Every y is followed by at least one x

3. Consider the following DFA in which s_0 is the start state and s_1, s_3 are the final states

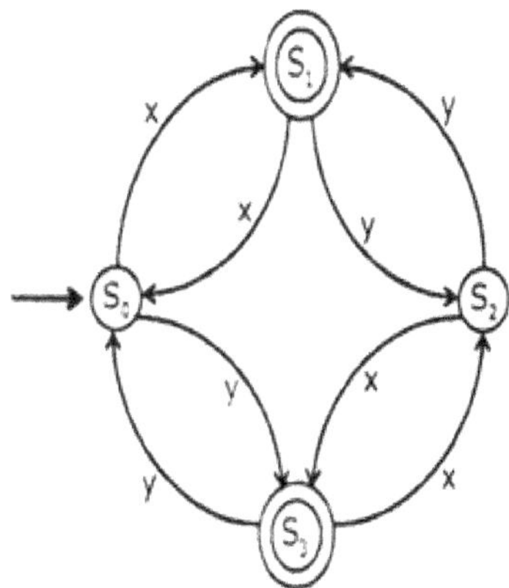

What language does this DFA recognize?

(a) All strings of x and y

(b) All strings of x and y which have either even number of x and even number of y or odd
number or x and odd number of y

(c) All strings of x and y which have equal number of x and y

(d) All strings of x and y with either even number of x and odd number of y or odd number
of x and even number of y

4. Consider the grammar given below

$S \rightarrow xB|yA$

$A \rightarrow x|xS|yAA$

$B \rightarrow y|yS|yBB$

Consider the following strings.

(i) xxyyx

(ii) xxyyxy

(iii) xyxy

(iv) yxxy

(vi) yxx

(vi) xyx

Which of the following strings are in L(G)

(a) (i),(ii) and (iii)

(b) (ii), (v) and (vi)

(c) (ii), (iii), and (iv)

(D) (i),(iii), and (iv)

5. Consider the following grammars: Names representing terminals have been specified in
capital letters

G_1 : stmnt → WHILE(expr) stmnt

    stmnt → OTHER

    expr ID → ID

G_2 : stmnt → WHILE(exp r) stmnt

    stmnt → OTHER

    expr → expr + expr

    expr → expr * expr

    expr → ID

Which one of the following statements is true?

(a) G_1 is context-free but not regular and G_2 is regular

(b) G_2 is context-free but not regular and G_1 is regular

(c) Both G_1 and G_2 are regular

(d) Both G_1 and G_2 are context-free but neither of them is regular

6. Consider the following Mite automata P and Q over the alphabet {a, b, C}. The start states are indicated by a double arrow and final states are indicated by a double circle. Let the languages recognized by them be denoted by L(P) and L(Q) respectively.

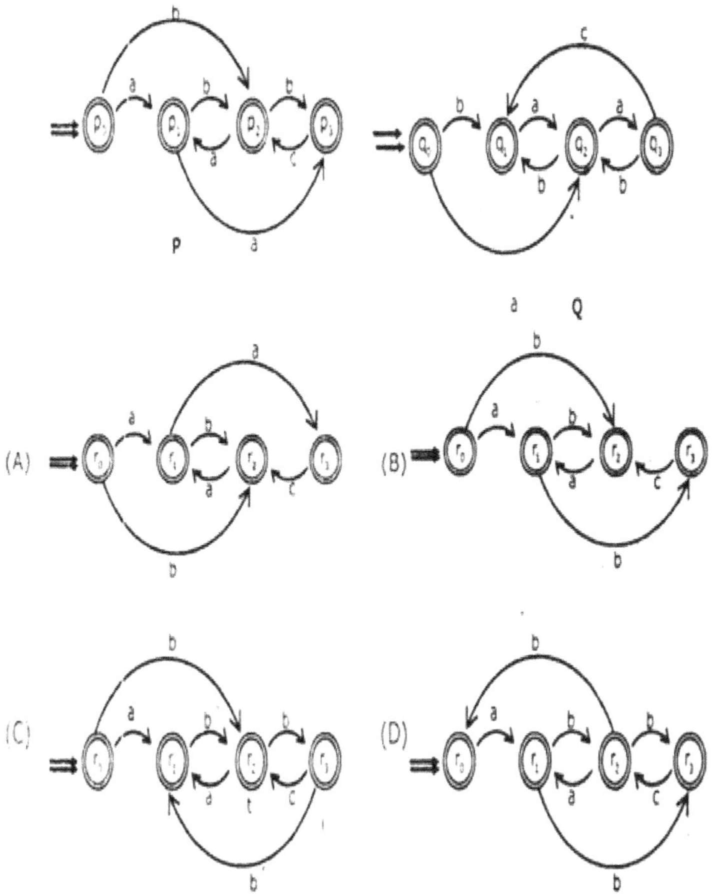

Common Data Questions: 7, 8 & 9

Consider the regular expression R = (a + b) * (aa + bb) (a + b) *

7. Which of the following non-deterministic finite automata recognizes the language defined by the regular expression R? Edges labeled λ denote transitions on the empty string.

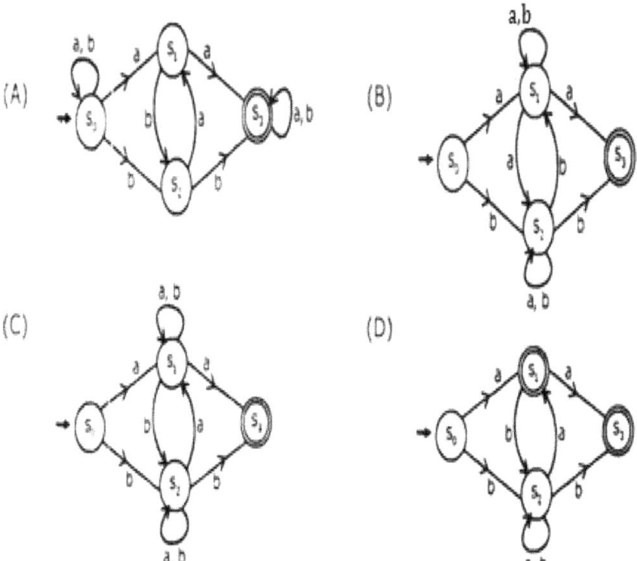

8. Which deterministic finite automaton accepts the language represented by the regular expression R?

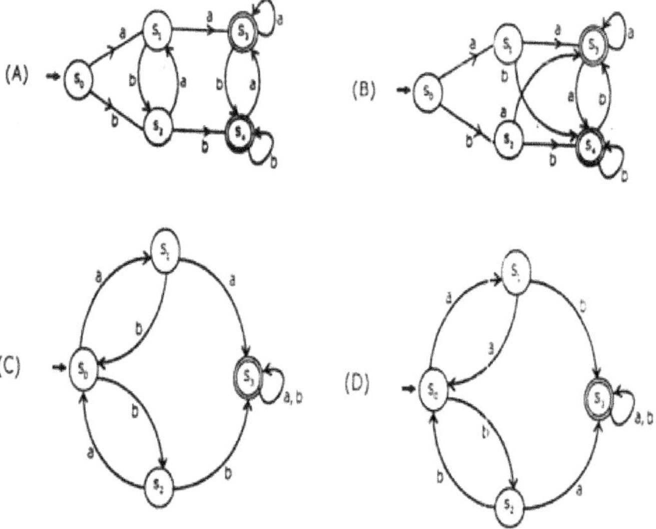

9. Which one of the regular expressions given below defines the same language as defined by the regular expression R?

(a) (a(ba)* + b(ab)*)* (a + b)*

(b) (a(ba)* + b(ab)*)* (a + b)*

(c) (a(ba)* (a + bb) + b (ab)* (b + aa)) (a + b)*

(d) (a(ba)* (a + bb) + b(ab)* (b + aa)) (a + b)

GATE 2008 (IT)

1. Which of the following regular expressions describes the language over $\{0,1\}$ consisting of strings that contain exactly two 1's?

(a) (0 +1)*11(0 +1)*

(b) 0*110*

(c) 0*10*10*

(d) (0 + 1)*1(0+1)*1(0+1)*

2. Let N be an NFA with n states and let M be the minimized DFA with m states recognizing the same language. Which of the following is NECESSARILY true?

(a) $m \leq 2^n$

(b) $n \leq m$

(c) M has one accept state

(d) $m = 2^n$

3. For problems X and Y, Y is NP-complete and X reduces to Y in polynomial time. Which of the following is true?

(a) If X can be solved in polynomial time, then so can Y

(b) X is NP-complete

(c) X is NP-hard

(d) X is in NP, but not necessarily NP-complete

4. If the final states and non-final states in the DFA below are interchanged, then which of the following languages over the alphabet {a, b} will be accepted by the new DFA?

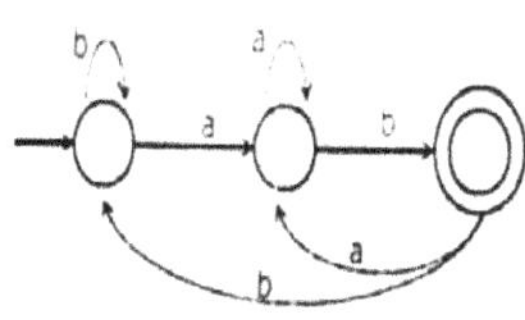

(a) Set of all strings that do not end with ab

(b) Set of all strings that begin with either an a or a b

(c) Set of all strings that do not contain the substring ab

(d) The set described by the regular expression b*aa*(ba)*b*

5. Consider the following languages.

$L_1 = \{a^i b^j c^k \mid i = j, k \geq 1\}$

$L_2 = \{a^i b^j \mid j = 2i, i \geq 0\}$

Which of the following is true?

(a) L_1 is not a CFL but L_2 is

(b) $L_1 \cap L_2 = \emptyset$ and L_1 is non-regular

(c) $L_1 \cup L_2$ is not a CFL but L_2 is

(d) There is a 4-state PDA that accepts L_1, but there is no DPDA that accepts L_2

6. Consider a CFG with the following productions.

$S \rightarrow AA \mid B$

$A \rightarrow 0A \mid A0 \mid 1$

$B \rightarrow 0B00 \mid 1$

S is the start symbol, A and B are non-terminals and 0 and 1 are the terminals.

The language generated by this grammar is

(a) $\{0^n 1 0^{2n} \mid n \geq 1\}$

(b) $\{0^i 1 0^j 1 0^k \mid i, j, k \geq 0\} \cup \{0^n 1 0^{2n} \mid n \geq 1\}$

(c) $\{0^i 1 0^j \mid i, j \geq 0\} \cup \{0^n 1 0^{2n} \mid n \geq 1\}$

(d) The set of all strings over $\{0, 1\}$ containing at least two 0's

7. Which of the following languages is (are) non-regular?

$L_1 = \{0^m 1^n \mid 0 \leq m \leq n \leq 10000\}$

$L_2 = \{w \mid w \text{ reads the same forward and backward}\}$

$L_3 = \{w \in \{0,1\}^* \mid w \text{ contains an even number of 0's and an even number of 1's}\}$

(a) L_2 and L_3 only

(b) L_1 and L_2 only

(c) L_3 only

(d) L_2 only

8. Consider the following two finite automata. M_1 accepts L_1 and M_2 accepts L_2 Which one of the following is true?

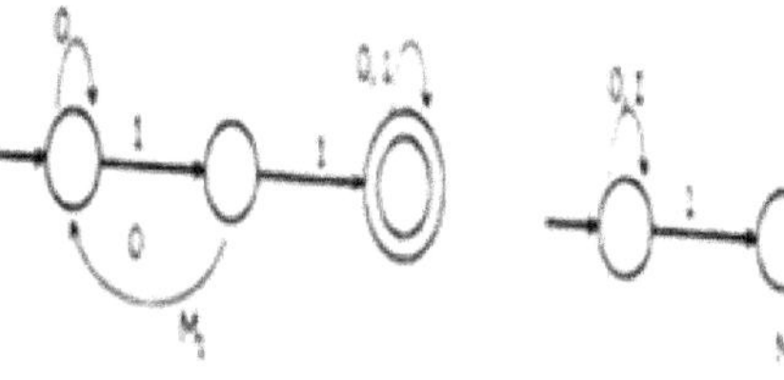

(a) $L_1 = L_2$

(b) $L_1 \subset L_2$

(c) $L_1 \cap \overline{L_2} = \emptyset$

(d) $L_1 \cup L_2 \neq L_1$

GATE 2012

1. Which of the following problems are decidable?

    1. Does a given program ever produce an output?
    2. If L is context free language, then, is $\bar{L}$ also context-free?
    3. If L is regular language, then, is $\bar{L}$ also regular?
    4. If L is recursive language, then, is L also recursive?

    (A) 1,2,3,4   (B) 1,2

    (C) 2,3,4   (D) 3,4

2. Given the language L-{ab, aa, baa}, which of the following strings are in L*?

    1. abaabaaabaa
    2. aaaabaaaa
    3. baaaaabaaaab
    4. baaaaabaa

    (A) 1,2 and 3   (B) 2,3 and 4

    (C) 1,2 and 4   (D) 1,3 and 4

3. What is the complement of the language accepted by the NFA show below?
    Assume $\Sigma = \{a\}$ and ε is the empty string.

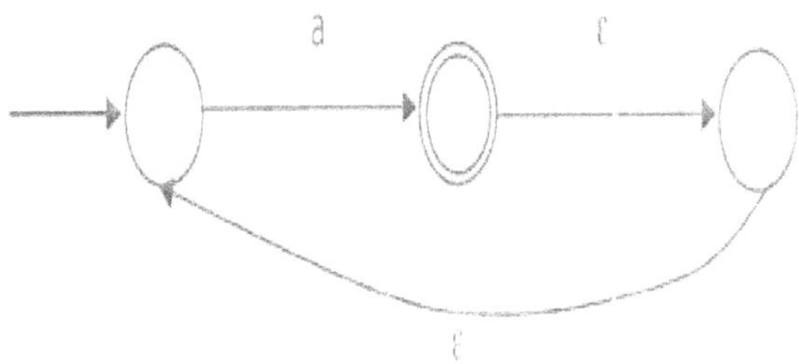

    (A) ∅   (B) {ε}

    (C) a*   (D) {a, ε}

4. Consider the set of strings on {0,1} in which, *every substring of 3 symbols* has at most two zeros. For example, 001110 and 011001 are in the language, but 100010 is not. All strings of length less than 3 are also in the language. A partially completed DFA that accepts this language is shown below.

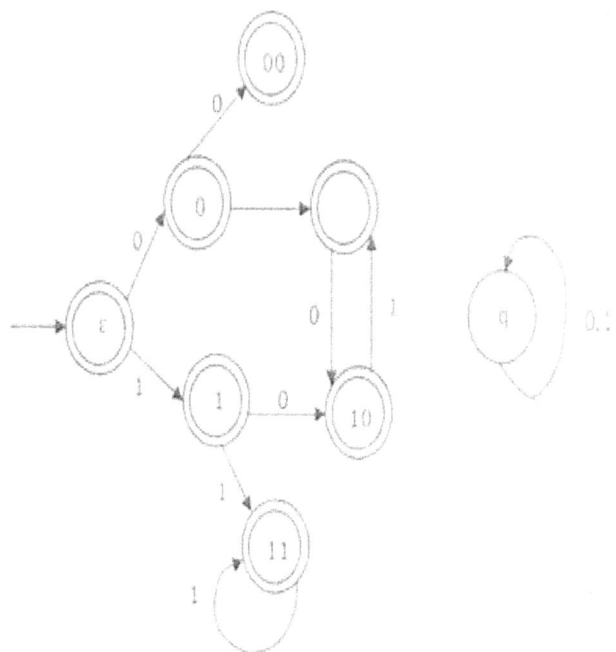

The missing arcs in the DFA are

(A)

	00	01	10	11	q
00	1	0			
01			1		
10	0				
11		0			

(B)

	00	01	10	11	q
00		0			1
01		1			
10				0	
11		0			

(C)

	00	01	10	11	q
00		1			0
01	1				
10		0			
11	0				

(D)

	00	01	10	11	q
00		1			0
01			1		
10	0				
11		0			

GATE 2013

1. Which of the following statements is/are FALSE?

   1. For every non-deterministic Turing machine, there exists an equivalent deterministic Turing machine.
   2. Turing recognizable languages are closed under union and complementation.
   3. Turing decidable languages are closed under intersection and complementation.
   4. Turing recognizable languages are closed under union and intersection.

   (A) 1 and 4 only (B) 1 and 3 only (C) 2 only (D) 3 only

2. What is the maximum number of reduce moves that can be taken by a bottom-up parser for a grammar with no epsilon and unit-production (i.e., of type $A \to \epsilon$ and $A \to a$) to parse a string with n tokens?

   (A) n/2 (B) n-1 (C) 2n-1 (D) 2^n

3. Consider the language $L_1 = \emptyset$ and $L_2 = \{a\}$. Which one of the following represents $L_1 L_2^* \cup L_1^*$?

   (A) $\{\epsilon\}$ (B) $\emptyset$ (C) a^* (D) $\{\epsilon, a\}$

4. Which of the following is/are undecidable?

   1. G is a CFG. Is $L(G) = \phi$?
   2. G is a CFG. IS $L(G) = \Sigma^*$?
   3. M is a Turning machine. Is L(M) regular?
   4. A is a DFA and N is a NFA. Is $L(A) = L(N)$?

   (A) 3 only (B) 3 and 4 only (C) 1,2 and 3 only (D) 2 and 3 only

5. Consider the DFA given below.

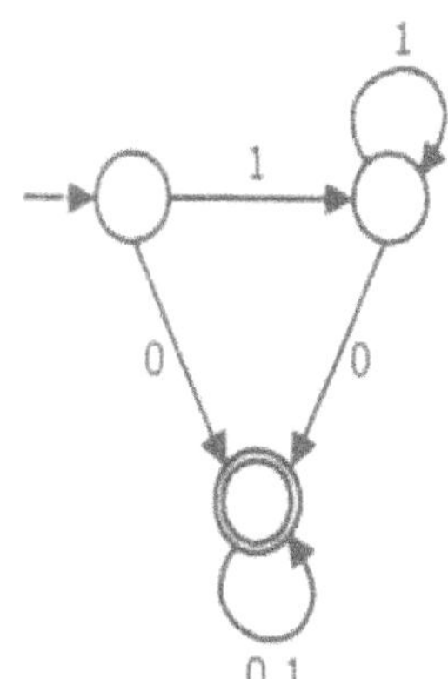

Which of the following are FALSE?

1. Complement of L(A) is context-free
2. L(A) = L (11*0+0) (0+1)*0*1*)
3. For the language accepted by A,A is the minimal DFA
4. A accepts all strings over {0, 1} of length at least 2

(A) 1 and 3 only   (B) 2 and 4 only   (C) 2 and 3 only   (D) 3 and 4 only

6. Consider the following languages

$L_1 = \{0^p 1^q 0^r \mid p, q, r \geq 0\}$

$L_2 = \{0^p 1^q 0^r \mid p, q, r \geq 0, p \neq r\}$

Which one of the following statements is FALSE?

(A) L_2 is context-free

(B) $L_1 \cap L_2$ is context-free

(C) Complement of L_2 is recursive

(D) Complement of L_1 is context-free but not regular

GATE 2014

1. The length of the shortest string NOT in the language (over $\Sigma = \{a, b\}$) of the following regular expression is ___________. a*b*(ba)* a*

2. Let Σ be a finite non-empty alphabet and let 2^{Σ^*} be the power set of Σ^*. Which one of the following is TRUE?

(A) Both 2^{Σ^*} and Σ^* are countable

(B) 2^{Σ^*} is countable Σ^* is uncountable

(C) 2^{Σ^*} is uncountable and Σ^* is countable

(D) Both 2^{Σ^*} and Σ^* are uncountable

3. Which one of the following problems is undecidable?

(A) Deciding if a given context-free grammar is ambiguous.

(B) Deciding if a given string is generated by a given context-free grammar.

(C) Deciding if the language generated by a given context-free grammar is empty.

(D) Deciding if the language generated by a given context-free grammar is finite.

4. Consider the following languages over the alphabet $\Sigma = \{0,1,c\}$

$L_1 = \{0^n 1^n \mid n \geq 0\}$

$L_2 = \{wcw^r \mid w \in \{0,1\}^*\}$

$L_3 = \{ww^r \mid w \in \{0,1\}^*\}$

Here w^r is the reverse of the string w. Which of these languages are deterministic Context-free languages?

(A) None of the languages

(B) only L_1

(C) Only L_1 and L_2

(D) All the three languages

GATE 2015

1. For any two languages L_1 and L_2 such that L_1 is context-free and L_2 recursively enumerable but not recursive, which of the following is/are necessarily true?

   I. $\bar{L}_1$ (complement of L_1) is recursive

   II. $\bar{L}_2$ (complement of L_2) is recursive

   III. $\bar{L}_1$ is context-free

   IV. $\bar{L}_1 \cup L_2$ is recursively enumerable

   (A) I only

   (B) III only

   (C) III and IV only

   (D) I and IV only

2.

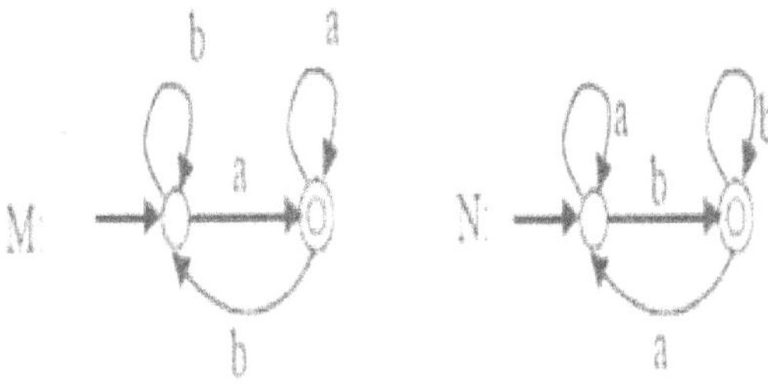

   Consider the DFAs M and N given above. The number of states in a minimal DFA that accepts the language $L(M) \cap L(N)$ is ____________

3. Consider the NPDA $\langle Q = \{q_0, q_1, q_2\}, \Sigma = \{0,1\}, \Gamma = \{0,1, \perp\}, \delta, q_0, \perp, F = \{q_2\}\rangle$, where (as per usual convention) Q is the set of states, Σ is the input alphabet, Γ is the stack alphabet, δ is the state transition function, q_0 is the initial state, $\perp$ is the initial stack symbol, and F is the set of accepting states.

The state transition is as follows:

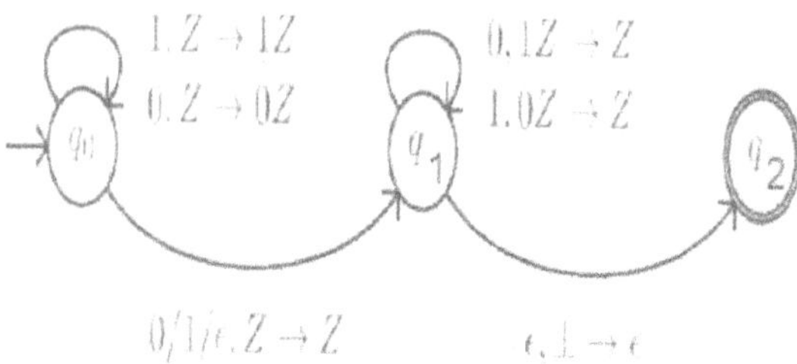

Which one of the following sequences must follow the string 101100 so that the overall string accepted by the automaton?

(A) 10110 (B) 10010

(C) 01010 (D) 01001

4. Consider the following statements.

I. The complement of every Turing decidable language is Turing decidable

II. There exists some language which is in NP but is not Turing decidable

III. If L is a language in NP, L is Turing decidable

Which of the above statements is/are true?

(A) Only II (B) Only III

(C) Only I and II (D) Only I and III

5. Language L_1 is polynomial time reducible to language L_2 Language L_3 is polynomial time reducible to L_2, which in turn is polynomial time reducible to language L_4. Which of the following is/are true?

I. if $L_4 \in P$, then $L_2 \in P$

II. if $L_1 \in P$ or $L_3 \in P$, then $L_2 \in P$

III. $L_1 \in P$, if and only if $L_3 \in P$

IV. if $L_4 \in P$, then $L_1 \in P$ and $L_3 \in P$

(A) II only (B) III only

(C) I and IV only (D) I only

6. Which of the following languages are context-free?

$L_1 = \{a^m\, b^n\, a^n\, b^m \mid m, n \geq 1\}$

$L_2 = \{a^m\, b^n\, a^m\, b^n \mid m, n \geq 1\}$

$L_3 = \{a^m\, b^n \mid m = 2n + 1\}$

(A) L_1 and L_2 only (B) L_1 and L_3 only

(C) L_2 and L_3 only (D) L_3 only

GATE 2016

1. Consider the following context-free grammars:

   $G_1 : S \rightarrow aS \mid, B \rightarrow b \mid bB$

   $G_2 : S \rightarrow aA \mid bB, A \rightarrow aA \mid B \mid \varepsilon, B \rightarrow bB \mid \varepsilon$

   Which one of the following pairs of languages is generated by G_1 and G_2 respectively?

   (a) $\{a^m b^n \mid m > 0 \text{ or } n > 0\}$ and $\{a^m b^n \mid m > 0 \text{ and } n > 0\}$

   (b) $\{a^m b^n \mid m > 0 \text{ and } n > 0\}$ and $\{a^m b^n \mid m > 0 \text{ or } n \geq 0\}$

   (c) $\{a^m b^n \mid m \geq 0 \text{ or } n > 0\}$ and $\{a^m b^n \mid m > 0 \text{ and } n > 0\}$

   (d) $\{a^m b^n \mid m \geq 0 \text{ and } n > 0\}$ and $\{a^m b^n \mid m > 0 \text{ or } n > 0\}$

2. Consider the transition diagram of a PDA given below with input alphabet $\Sigma = \{a, b\}$ and stack alphabet $\Gamma = \{X, Z\}$. Z is the initial stack symbol. Let L denote the language accepted by the PDA.

   Which one of the following is TRUE?

   (a) $L = \{a^n b^n \mid n \geq 0\}$ and is not accepted by any finite automata

   (b) $L = \{a^n \mid n \geq 0\} \cup \{a^n b^n \mid n \geq 0\}$ and is not accepted by any deterministic PDA

   (c) L is not accepted by any Turing machine that halts on every input

   (d) $L = \{a^n \mid n \geq 0\} \cup \{a^n b^n \mid n \geq 0\}$ and is deterministic context-free

3. Let X be a recursive language and Y be a recursively enumerable but not recursive language. Let W and Z be two languages such that $\bar{Y}$ reduces to W, and Z reduces to $\bar{X}$ (reduction means the standard many-one reduction). Which one of the following statements is TRUE?

   (a) W can be recursively enumerable and Z is recursive

   (b) W can be recursive and Z is recursively enumerable.

   (c) W is not recursively enumerable and Z is recursive.

   (d) W is not recursively enumerable and Z is not recursive.

4. Which of the following language is generated by the given grammar?

$S \rightarrow aS \mid bS \mid \varepsilon$

(a) $\{a^n b^m \mid n, m \geq 0\}$

(b) $\{ w \in \{a, b\}^* \mid w \text{ has equal number of a's and b's}\}$

(c) $\{a^n \mid n \geq 0\} \cup \{b^n \mid n \geq 0\} \cup \{a^n b^n \mid n \geq 0\}$

(d) $\{a, b\}^*$

5. Which of the following decision problems are undecidable?

I. Given NFAs N_1 and N_2, is $L(N_1) \cap L(N_2) = \Phi$?

II. Given a CFG $G = (N, \Sigma, P, S)$ and a string $x \in \Sigma^*$, does $x \in L(G)$?

III. Given CFGs G_1 and G_2, is $L(G_1) = L(G_2)$?

IV. Given a TM M, is $L(M) = \Phi$?

(a) I and IV only   (b) II and III only

(c) III and IV only   (d) II and IV only

6. Which one of the following regular expressions represents the language: *the set of all binary strings having two consecutive 0s and two consecutive 1s?*

(a) $(0 + 1) *0011 (0 + 1)* + (0 + 1) *1100 (0 + 1)*$

(b) $(0 + 1)* (00 (0 + 1)* 11 + 11(0 + 1)*00) (0 + 1)*$

(c) $(0 + 1)*00 (0 + 1)* + (0 + 1)* 11 (0 + 1) *$

(d) $00(0 + 1)* 11 + 11(0 + 1)*00$

GATE EXPLANATIONS–THEORY OF COMPUTATION

GATE 1992

1. (B)

    0/1 Knapsack problem is not NP-hard. A solution based on dynamic programming is possible for the problem.

    (C) Finding bi-connected components of a graph is not NP - hard.

2. Since $(r + s)^* = (r^* + s^*)^* = (r^* + s^*)^*$ none of (b), (c), (d) are true.

    Strictly speaking r(*) is not a regular expression by definition because parenthesis can be only put around a proper regular expression to get another legal regular expression. But if the parentheses are considered to be redundant of course it is true.

3. (C)

    $2l - 1$. A simple proof by induction can be offered.

4. (A), (D)

5. (A), (C)

6. (i) True.

    Construct a TM M from two other TMs M_1 & M_2 that accept two recursive languages.

    On input ω, M runs as follows :

    (i) Run ω on M_1 : Accept, if M_1 accepts ω

    (ii) Run ω on M_2 : Accept, if M_2 accepts ω

(iii) Reject, otherwise

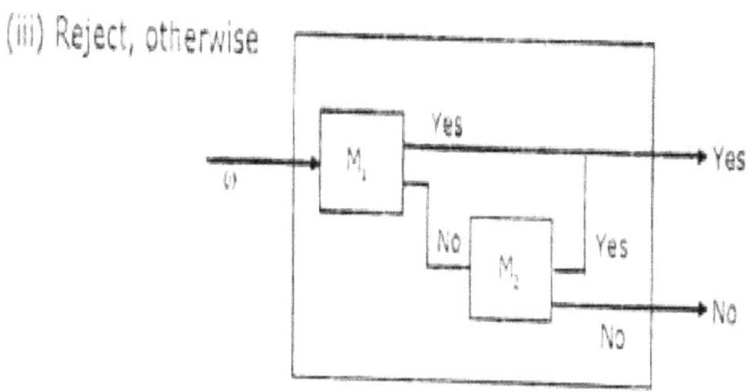

Clearly, $L(M) = L(M_1) \cup L(M_2)$ is recursive

(ii) True.

$\{0^n \mid n$ is a prime$\}$ is not regular. This can be proved by pumping lemma. Refer to Ulmann Hoperoft for a detailed proof.

(iii) False.

The sets {01}, {0011}, {000111}.... are a;; regular. But their infinite union is $\{0^n1^n \mid n \geq 1\}$ which is known to be not regular.

Hence, closure under infinite union fails.

GATE 1993

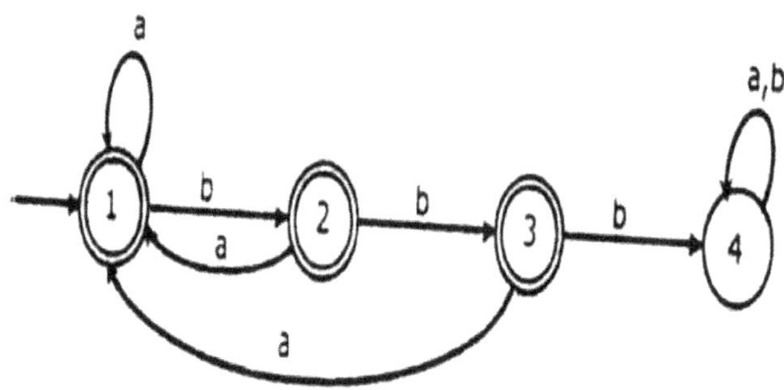

GATE 1994

1. (C)

2. (B)

3. 0*1*

4. False. To and from motion of the head to scan input a result is not possible in FSMs

5. (i) (d)   (ii) (a)

    (iii) (b)   (iv) (c)

6. If ω is of length l the derivation involves $2l - 1$ steps.

    For Length = 1, no of step required   = 1 (A → used)

    $$= 2(1)-1$$

    For Length = 2 , no of step required   = 3 = 2(2) - 1

    (Productions used of the form: A → BC, B → b, C → c)

    Let, the no. of steps required to derive a string of length l be $2l - 1$.

    Now, if another terminal t is added to the string, i.e., length becomes l+1, two more productions are to be used during derivation (of the form A → BT, T → t). Thus, total no. of steps = $2l + 1$, for a string of length l + 1.

    Hence, the proposition is proved by induction.

GATE 1995

1. (B) L (L ∪ D)*

2. (C) Context sensitive.

3. (A)

4. (B) 10. Try out the options one by one. Starting in A, 01takes the FSM to B. But, 10 take the FSM to C whether it starts from A, B, C, or D. The other two options are longer than 01 thus need not be checked.

5. (C)

6. Since there is only one string in L, and it is verifiable in polynomial time whether the string belongs to L, it is also verifiable in polynomial time whether the string belongs to L. Hence L. Hence L is NP.

GATE 1996

1. (C)

    (i) and (iii)

    From (i), all odd length strings of 0's can be derived as $(00)^* 0$ and all even length strings can be derived as $(00)^*$. Thus $(00)^* (\epsilon + 0) \equiv 0^*$

    In (ii), odd length strings are missing.

    In (iv), even length strings are missing.

2. (D)

    Regular grammars represent regular languages. Whether $L(G_1) = L(G_2)$ can be decided as follows construct the two DFAS corresponding to the two regular grammars, M_1 & M_2. Let the languages accepted by M_1 & M_2 be L_1 & L_2 respectively. Construct M to accept.

    $(\overline{L_1} \cap L_2) \cup (L_1 \cap \overline{L_2})$. If M accepts a string, $L_1 = L_2$, and $L(G_1) = L(G_2)$, otherwise $L(G_1) \neq L(G_2)$.

3. (D)

    $L = \{a^m b^n \mid m \geq 1, n \geq 1)$ is equivalent to the regular expression aa*bb*.

4. C, $L_1 \cap R$ is not necessarily be CFL since

$L = \{0^n 1^n / n \geq 0\}$		$L = \{0^n 1^n\}$	
(1) $R = \{0^* 1^*\}$	(2)	$R = \{1\}$	
$L \cap R = \{0^n 1^n\}$		$L \cap R = \{1\}$	
		Regular	

5. (B):

6. (D):

The two parse trees are:

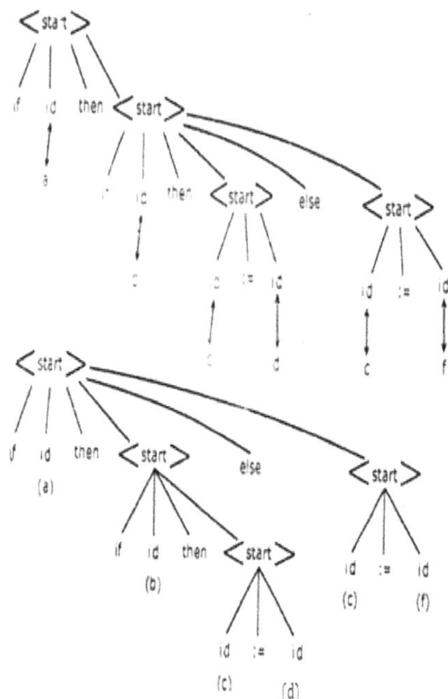

7. After removing null productions

    S → ABAC | ABC | AAC | AC | C | BC | BAC

    A → aA| a

    B → bB| b

    C → d

    After removing null productions:

    S → ABAC | ABC | AAC | AC | BC | BAC | d

    A → aA| a

    B → bB| b

    C → d

8. b)

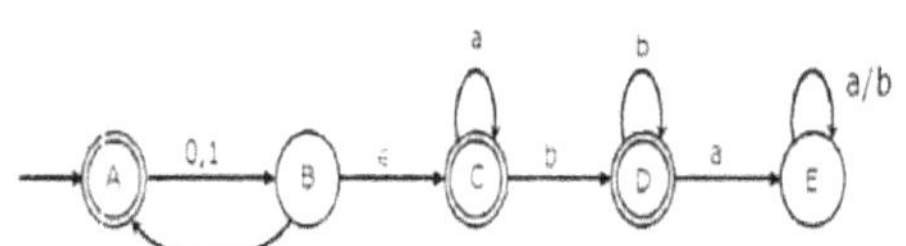

9. $\{(\xi_1, aa), (\xi_2 \in)\}$

   $\{(\xi_1, bb), (\xi_2 \in)\}$

GATE 1997

1. (A)

2. (B)

   Set of all strings over Σ^* can be enumerated by considering each letter as a digit is a number system. Strong can then be systematically generated as increasing numbers in the number system.

   Regular language has a finite description and hence can be enumerated.

   TMs can be enumerated, Refer to the section, Turing Machines Codes (Section 8.3, chapter on Undesirability in Ullmann Hop croft) to know exactly how TMs are numbered.

3. (B)

   One has to try an infinite number of strings before deciding whether two TMs are equivalent. The No. answer however can be given as soon as one string is accepted by one TM and not accepted by another. Off course, if the TM represents a non-recursive language, even the No, answer is not possible.

4. (A) Since a string and its reverse is separated by 'c'.

5. (A)

   Condition satisfied: $I + k = j + m$ and $u, j, k, m \geq 0$

6. (B)

   Smallest string to have two parse trees: be

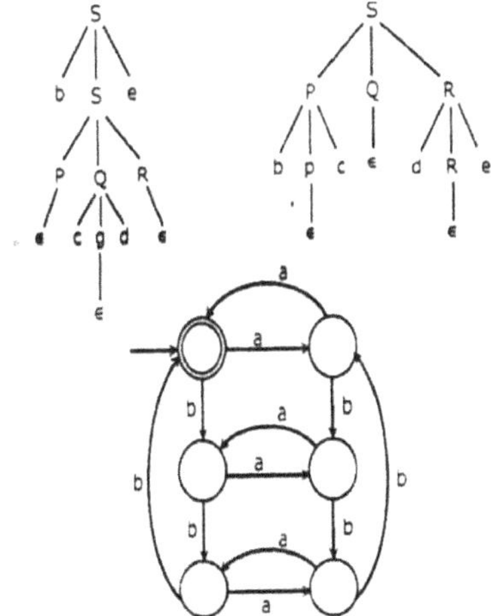

7. L^P is accepted by a DFA,M', constructed from the DFA,M, to accept L in the following fashion. Mark the start and all states, P, of the DFA as final in M', such that there is a path from the start state to the final state through P in M.

It can be obtained through NFA, step (1) Reverse all the arcs (2) Make the start state only the final state (3) Introduce a new start state and define the ε transmissions from P to all the final states of the machine.

GATE 1998

1. (a) DFA to accept {1,2, 4,....2⁴....} in binary

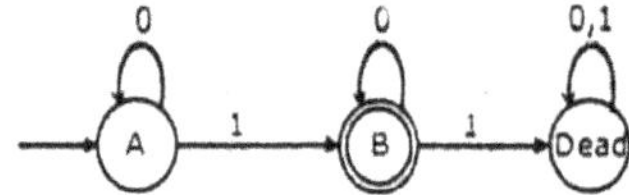

2. (b), (c)
3. (c), (d)
4. (b)

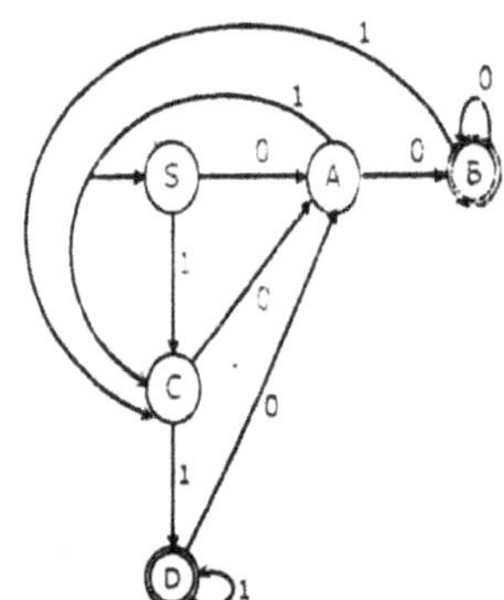

5. $1^k1^* (01^k)^*$

6.

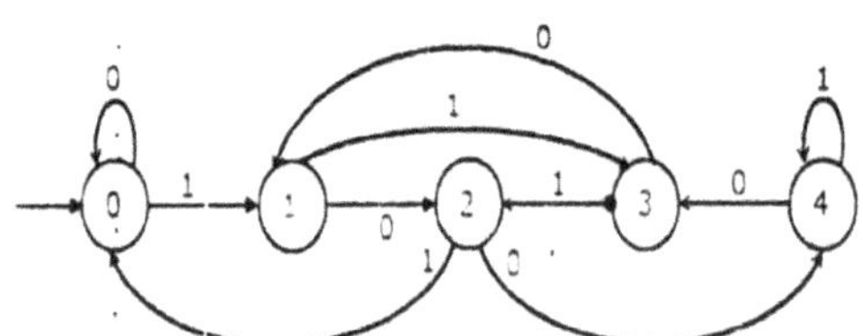

7. Removing indirect left recursion we get:

$S \to Aa \mid b$

$A \to Ac \mid AAd \mid \epsilon \mid bd$

Further remove left recursion in A-productions.

$S \to Aa \mid b$

$A \to A' \mid bd\, A'$

$A' \to cA' \mid Ad\, A' \mid \epsilon$

Again, there is indirect recursion in A'

$S \to Aa \mid b$

$A \to bd\, A' \mid A'$

$A' \to bd\, A'\, d\, A'A'' \mid cA'\, A'' \mid A''$

$A'' \to d\, A'\, A'' \mid \epsilon$

8. (a) $\{1^n\, 01^n \mid n \geq 1\} \cup \{e\}$ is the language accepted by the PDA.

   (b) For each 1 scanned in state q_0, a X is placed on the stack. Now, on getting a 0 as input state change to q_1. In q_1, one X is removed from the stack, every time 1 is input.

9. a). $L(G_1) = \{a^i\, b^j \mid i \neq j, i,j \geq 1\}$

   b). Productions to be added to get L_2

   $S \to S_1E \mid ES_1 \mid EE$

   $E \to aEb \mid ab$

   (c)

   No, L_2 is not inherently ambiguous.

GATE 1999

1. (B)

2. (B)

3. (A)

4. (C)

   Note : $L_1 - L_2 = L_1 \cap L_2^c$. Now intersection of a regular set & a CFL is context free.

5. (C)

   For example, $E \to E + E \mid id$ is not ambiguous; But, $E \to E + E \mid E*E \mid id$ is ambiguous.

6. a. No, B is not necessarily regular.

   For example, $L_1 \Sigma^*$, $L_2 \{0^n\, 1^n \mid n \geq 1\}$; $L_1 \cup L_2 = \Sigma^*$, hence regular.

   L_1 is regular but L_2 is not.

   b. Construct a DFA M_3 to accept $L(M_2) - L(M_1)$ i.e., $L(M_2) \cap L(M_1)^c$.

   Again, construct M_4 to accept $L(M_3) \cap L(M_2)^c$;

Now, $L(M_1) \subseteq L(M_2)$ (proper subset) if:

1) $L(M_3)$ is empty

2) $L(M_4)$ is empty.

7. Proof by pumping lemma.

GATE 2000

1. (C)

2. (B)

L is regular $L = (00)^{*}$

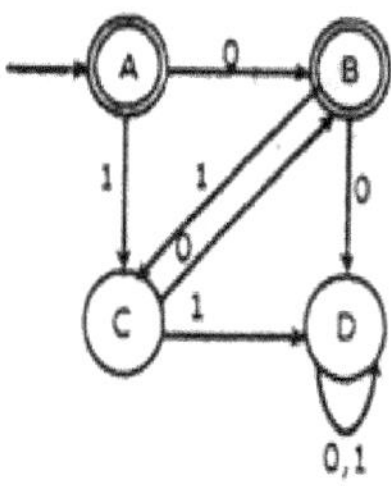

3. (D)   4. (A)

5.a)

(b) Condition: $j \geq i$

6.a)

6.b) $S \rightarrow 0s1 \mid 1$

$\delta (q_0, \lambda, z) \rightarrow \{(q_1, sz)\}$

$\delta (q_1, 0, s) \rightarrow \{(q_1, s1)\}$

$\delta (q_1, 1, s) \rightarrow \{(q_1, \lambda)\}$

$\delta (q_1, \lambda, z) \rightarrow \{(q_f, z\}$

1. (A) S1: 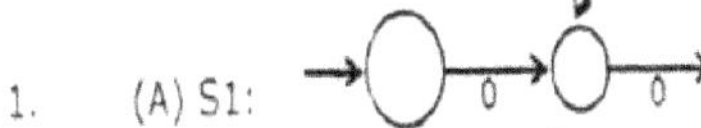

2. (B)   3. (B)   4. (D)   5. (D)   6. (B)

7.a)

$(a+b)^* baab(a+b)^*$

7.b)

	a	b
q_a	q_a	q_b
q_a	q_{aa}	q_{ab}
q_b	q_{ab}	q_{bb}
q_{aa}	q_a	q_{aab}
q_{ab}	q_{aab}	q_{abb}
q_{bb}	q_{abb}	q_b
q_{aab}	q_{ab}	q_s
q_{abb}	q_s	q_{ab}

q_s : Starting state

From the transition table draw the corresponding DFA.

8. $M = (\{q_0, q_1, q2\}, \{a, b, c\}, \{x, z_0\}, \{q_0, z_0\}, \{q_2\})$

Alternate

$\delta (q_0, a, z_0) = (q_0, xxz_0)$ (1) $\delta (\xi_0, a, z_0) \rightarrow (\xi_0, xz_0)$

$\delta (q_0, a, x) = (q_0, xxx)$ (2) $\delta (\xi_0, a, x) \rightarrow (\xi_0, xx)$

$\delta (q_0, c, x) = (q_1, x)$ (3) $\delta (\xi_0, c, x) \rightarrow (\xi_0, x)$

$\delta (q_1, b, x) = (q_1, \epsilon)$ (4) $\delta (\xi_1, b, x) \rightarrow (\xi_2, x)$

$\delta (q_1, \epsilon, z_0) = (q_2, \epsilon)$ (5) $\delta (\xi_2, b, x) \rightarrow (\xi_1, \epsilon)$

                                  (6) $\delta (\xi_1, \epsilon, z_0) \rightarrow (\xi_f, \epsilon)$

10.a)

$S \rightarrow aS'|bS'$

$S' \rightarrow aS'|bS'|\epsilon$

b)

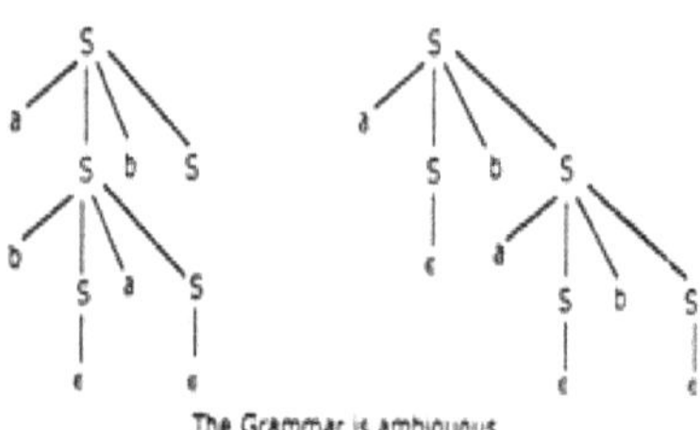

GATE 2002

1. (B)

2. (A)

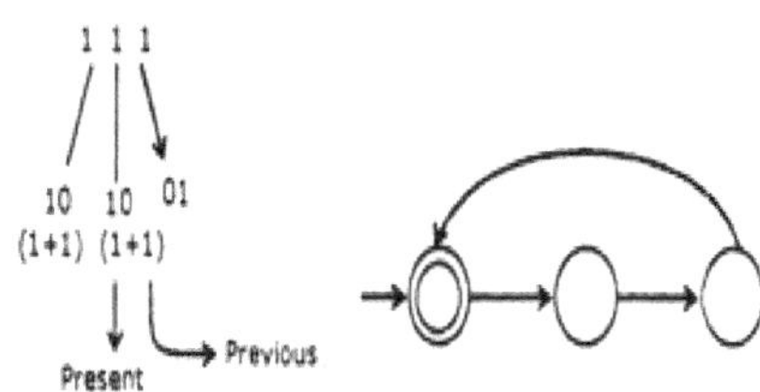

3. (B)   4. (A)

5.a)It gives the input to M′

b)If M′ halts then M outputs 1 otherwise M goes to infinite loop.

c)If an m-decidable problem is reducible to another problem, then the other problem is also un-decidable.

6.a) NFA to recognize (a/b)* abb.

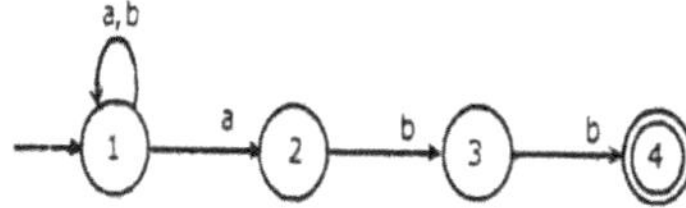

b) DFA to accept (a/b)* abb.

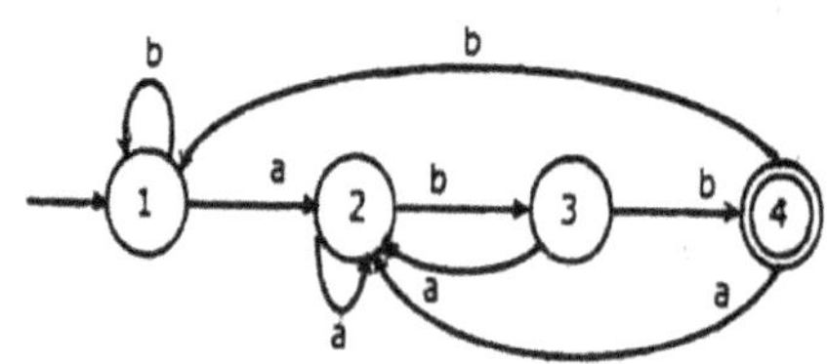

GATE 2003

1. (C)

2. (B)

3. (A) Both equivalent to (0 + 1)*

4. (D)

5. (B)

    M_1

    L is accepting 1 and L_1 is also accepting

    1. So, (A) is not true.

    L is not accepting 0 but L_1 is accepting 0

    So (C) and (D) are not true.

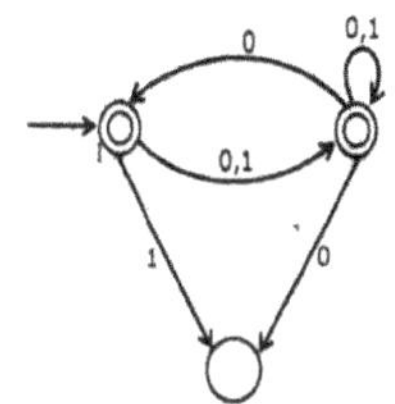

6. (C)

    The given DFA accepts the expression (0+1)* 001 (01+1)*

    The strings are

    1001001

    1001011

    1001101

    1001111

    1111001

    1011001

    1101001

    Total = 7 strings

7. (C)

    Given grammar is ambiguous, it is not regular,

    If x,y, $\in$ L(G) then xy also belongs to L(G)

    Since S $\rightarrow$ SS Production is there

8. (A)

9. (A)

GATE 2004

1. (B) An operator grammar is a CFG with no ε-productions such that no consecutive symbols on the right sides of productions are variables.

2. (C)

3. (A)

4. (B)

5. (C) Above Regular grammar is equivalent to FA as follows

   abaa is accepted, hence (a) and (b) are contradictory

   bb is accepted, so, (d) is contradictory

6. (B)

GATE 2005

1. (B) To show that problem A is undecidable, we show that any known. Undecidable problem B can be reduced to A.

2. (B)

   Given DFA accepts 'abbb' which contradicts option A

   It does not accept 'aabb' which contradicts Option C

   It does not accept abab which contradicts option D

   Language accepted by given machine contains all the strings in which every a is followed by at least 2b's which is option B

3. (D)

   Non determinism doesn't give any power to FA. DCFL is a subset of CFL

4. (A)

   CFL's are not closed under intersection

5. (B) Complement of recursive language is recursive

6. (B)

7. (D)

8. (B)

   Take example mm say

   100

   ↓↓↓ o/p

   1 0 0 → which is 2's complement of 100

GATE 2006

1. (A)

   If P_1 is NP complete and it is reduced to P_2 in a polynomial time, then P_2 is also NP complete.

2. (D)

   L_2 is not context free since m and (m+n) are related i.e. m is not independent.

   $a^n b^n c^n$ is not context free, hence L_3 is not context free.

3. (A)

4. (B)

5. (C)

   $SHAM_3$: Instance of a problem

   $DHAM_3$: Generalization of a problem

6. (A)

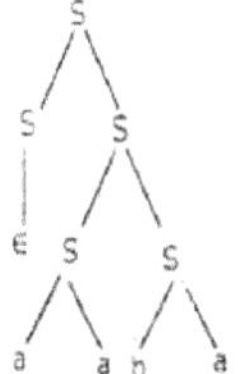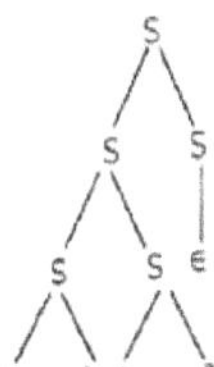

   G is ambiguous

   G doesn't produce aaabbb.

7. (C)

   $L_1 : \Sigma^*$ over$\{a, b\}$ which is regular

   $L_2 : \{a^n b^n, n \geq 1)$ is DCFL

   but $L_1 \cup L_2$ is L_1 which is regular not CFL.

8. (D)

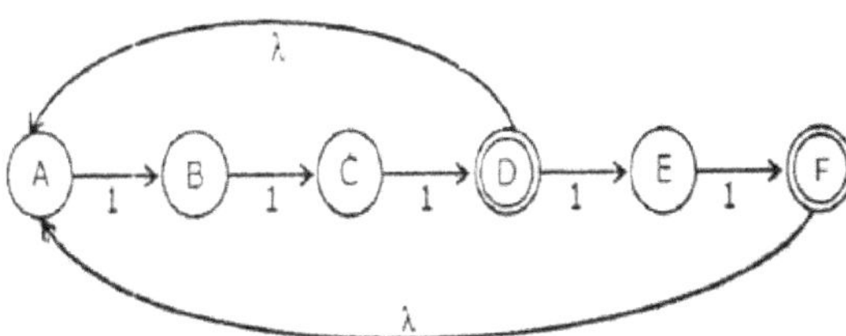

Step 1: convert this NFA – λ to NFA

Step 2: convert NFA to DFA

Step 3: minimize the resulting DFA.

9. (D) (A)S → AC → aAC → aC → ab   (B)S → aS → ab   (C)S→ AC →C →aCb → ab

10. (D)

GATE 2007

1. (B) There is no algorithm to determine the ambiguity of the grammar, hence it is undecidable.

2. (B)

3. (A) A minimum state finite Automata accepting the strings in which number of 0's and 1's divisible by 3 & 5 respectively will have 3*5 = 15 states

4. (B) $0^i 2 1^i$ is deterministic push down automata, every CFL is recursive

5. (C)

6. (C)

7. (B)

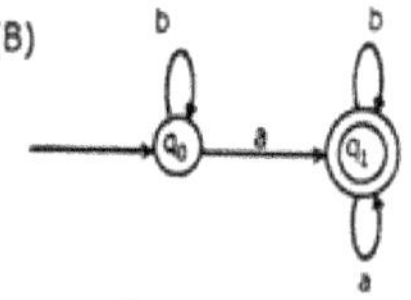

8. (C)

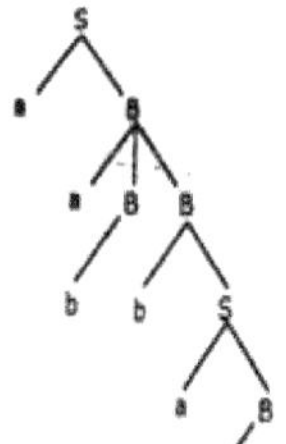

9. (B)

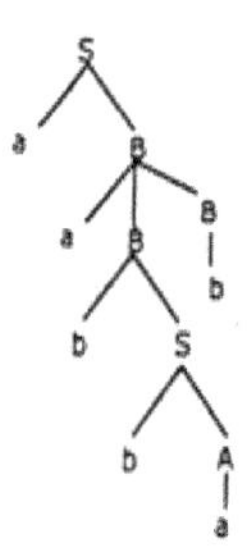

GATE 2008

1. (D)
2. (B)
3. (D) If L and L are recursive enumerable, then L should be recursive
4. (D)
5. (A)
6. (A)
7. (C)
8. (C)
9. (A)

GATE 2009

1. (B) It generates all odd length Palindromes.
2. (C)
3. (C)
4. (D)
5. (A)

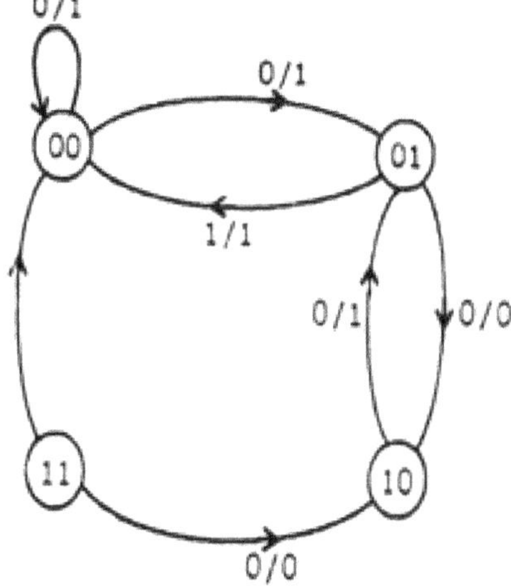

6. (C) [$L_1 \cap L_2 = \{a^n b^n c / n \geq 0\}$, Which is context free but not regular]
7. (C)

GATE 2010

1. (B)

    Union of two recursive enumerable is not R.E and also the Intersection, L_2-L_1 is r.E is True
    but L_1 - L_3 need not to be recursive enumerable

2. (B)

    Every string should contain even number of '1' s. min string are ε, 0, 11, 101, 1010 …….. we
    get those string from the expression 0* (10* 10*)*

    In option C and D Min. string is not ε. In option A we don't get, 0,00,000....

3. (D)

    (C) All the given languages can be recognized by the push-Down Automation

4. (C)

    Ex: Let w = 01

    substring are 0, 1, 01

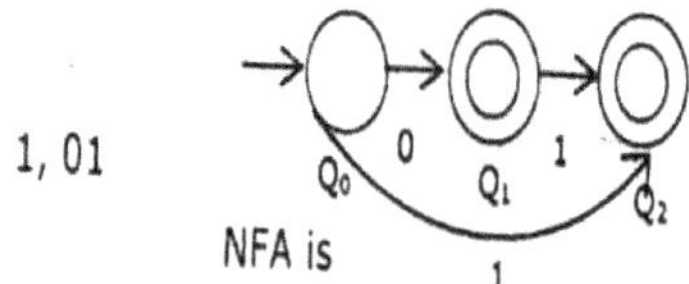

    If requires Min 3,

    So, If string length is 'n' It required n + 1 states.

GATE 2011

1. (A) Lexical Analysis is implemented by finite automata

2. (C) Σ* - P is the complement of P so it is always regular,

    Since regular languages are closed under complementation

3. (B) NPDA is more powerful than DPDA.

    Hence answer is (B)

4. (B)

    Let n = 3 and k=1

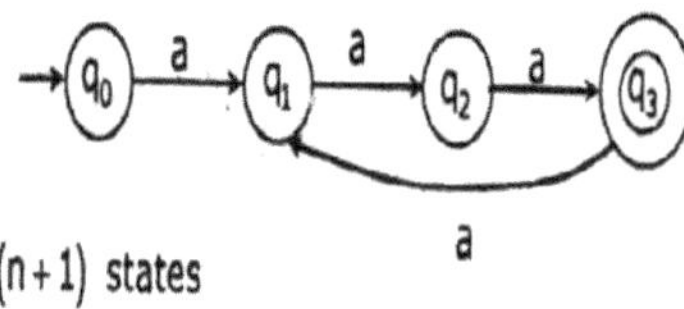

5. (A)

Options B and C will accept the string b

Option D will accept the string "bba"

Both are invalid strings.

So the minimized DFA is option A 6. (C)

6. (C)

LI: regular language

L2: context free language

L3: context sensitive language

GATE 2004 (IT)

1. (C)

Option A and B will generate all string of (a + b + C)* but option C will not generate string bc.

2. (C)

If every CFG generated by L is Ambiguous then the language L is inherently Ambiguous

3. (B)

4. (B)

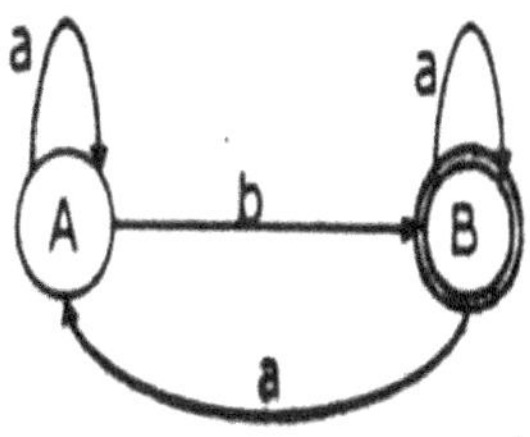

A → aA; A → bB/b; B aB/a; B → aA

GATE 2005 (IT)

1. (D)

2. (D) Since total strings infinite, string length also can be infinite.

3. (A) Since it is finite set.

4. (B)

5. (A)

6   (B)

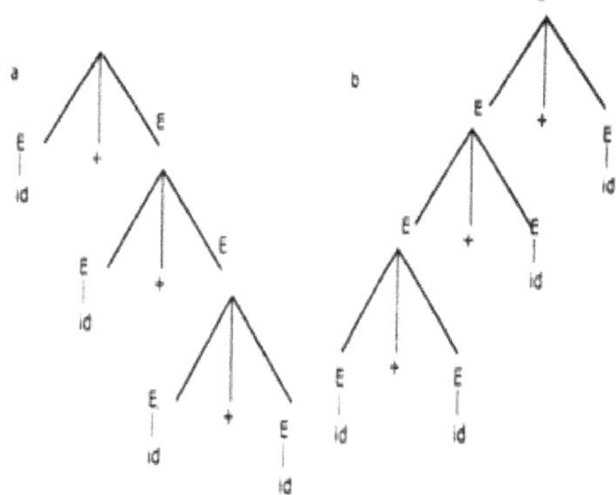

	a
S	x, y
x	z
z	S
y	w
w	S

After minimization

7.   (B)

8.   (A)

id + id + id + id

8.B) (D)

GATE 2006 (IT)

1.   (D)

2.   (B) Given CFG generates set of all palindromes

3.   (A)

4.   (A) Given grammer can be converted into DFA

Classes (s) = even as

Class (A) = odd as

5.   (C)

Let $L_1 = 0^*1^*$

$L_2 = 0^n1^n$

$L_2 \subset L_1$

But L_2 is not regular

6. (B)
7. (D)
9. (B)

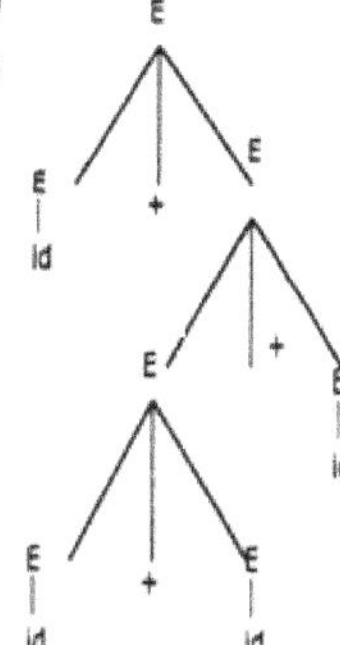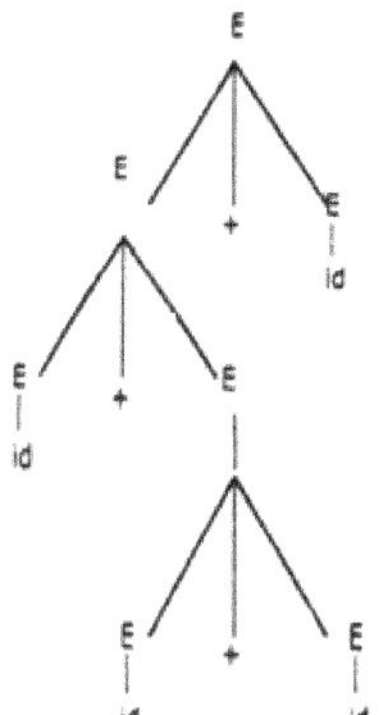

GATE 2007 (IT)

1. (A)
2. (A)
3. (D)
4. (C) equal instances of x and y
5. (8)
6. (B)
7. (A)
8. (C)
9. (C)

GATE 2008 (IT)

1. (C)

   (B) and (C) but in case of (B) it denotes regular expression containing two consecutive 1's, hence RE represented by B is a subset of RE represented by C

2. (A)

   If the NFA has n states, the resulting DFA can have up to 2^n states

3. (D)

4. (A) Given DFA accepts all strings ending with 'ab'.

5. (B)

   L_1, L_2 are both CFL and CFL'S are closed under union.

   Here $L_1 \cap L_2 = \emptyset$ since L_2 doesn't contain c but L_1 contains at least one c

6. (C) None of the languages are giving the string '1'

7. (D) Since L_1 is finite set, L_3 can be accepted by DFA

8. (A)

$L_1 = 0^*1\ (00^*1)^*\ 1(0+1)^*$

$L_2 = (0 + 1)^*\ 11\ (0+1)^*$

GATE 2012

1. Answer: (D)

   Exp: CFL's are not closed under complementation, Regular and recursive languages are closed under complementation.

2. Answer: (C)

   Exp: L = {ab, aa, baa}

   Let S1 = ab, S2 = aa and S3 = baa

   abaabaaabaa can be written as S1S2S3S1S2

   aaaabaaaa can be written as S1S1S3S1

   baaaaabaa can be written as S3S2S1S2

3. Answer: (B)

   Exp: Language accepted by NFA is a*, so complement of this language is {ε}

4. Answer: (D)

   Exp: The complete DFA is

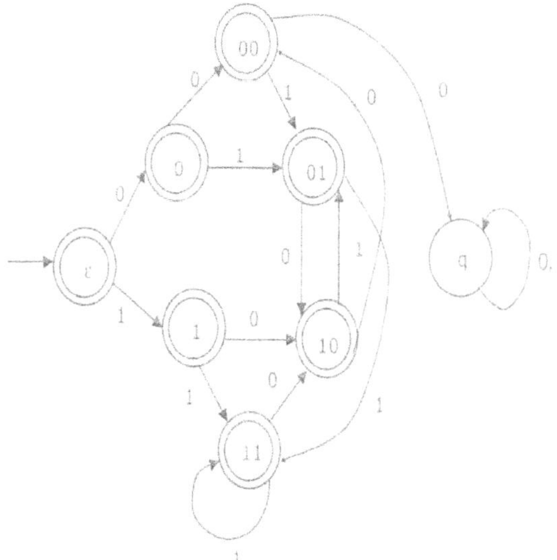

GATE 2013

1. Answer: (C)

   Exp: (1) NTM ≅ DTM

   (2) RELs are closed under union & but not complementation

   (3) Turing decidable languages are recursive and recursive languages are closed under intersection and complementation

   (4) RELs are closed under union & intersection but not under complementation

2. Answer: (B)

   Exp: To have maximum number of reduce moves, all the productions will be of the type A → $\alpha\beta$ (where α and β could be terminals or non-terminals). Consider the following illustration then:

3. Answer: (A)

   Exp: Concatenation of empty language with any language will give the empty language and $L_1{}^* = \emptyset^* = \epsilon$. Hence L1 $L_2{}^*$ U$L_1{}^*$= {ϵ}

4. Answer: (D)

   Exp: There is an algorithm to check whether the given CFG is empty, finite or infinite and also to convert NFA to DFA hence 1 and 4 are decidable

5. Answer: (D)

   Exp:

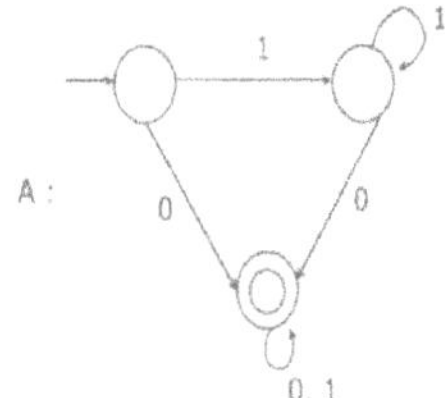

   (1) L(A) is regular, its complement is also regular and if it is regular it is also context free.

(2) L(A) = (11*0+0) (0+1)*0*1*=1*0(0+1)*

Language has all strings where each string contains '0'

(3) A is not minimal, it can be constructed with 2 states

(4) Language has all strings, where each string contains '0'. (at least length one)

6. Answer: (D)

Exp: $L_1 = \{0^p\,1^q\,0^r \mid p, q, r \geq 0\}$ is regular

$L_2 = \{0^p\,1^q\,0^r \mid p, q, r \geq 0, p \neq r\}$ is CFL

(A) L_2 is CFL (True)

(B) $L_1 \cap L_2$ = CFL (True)

(C) L_2 complement is recursive (True)

(D) L1 complement is CFL but not regular (False) as L_1 is regular $\bar{L}_1$ regular

GATE 2014

1. Answer: (3)

Exp: R.E=a*b*(ba)*a*

Length 0 is present as it accepts ϵ all length 1 strings are present (a,b) also aa, ab, ba, bb are present, but 'bab' is not present. So it is 3

2. Answer: (C)

Exp: 2^{ε^*} is the power set of ε^*

ε^* is countabily infinite

The power set of countabily infinite set is uncountable.

So 2^{ε^*} is uncountable and ε^* is countable.

3. Answer: (A)

Exp: There were algorithms to find the membership of CFG (using CYK algorithm) and finiteness of CFG (using CNF graph) and emptiness. But there is no algorithm for ambiguity of CFG. So it is undecidable.

4. Answer: (C)

Exp: For the languages L_1 and L_2 we can have deterministic push down automata, so they are DCFL's, but for L_3 only non-deterministic PDA possible. So the language L_3 is not a deterministic CFL.

GATE 2015

1. Answer: D

2. Correct Answer: 1

3.   Answer: B

4.   Answer: D

5.   Answer: C

6.   Answer: B

GATE 2016

1.   Answer:

 a can be 0.

 b can't be 0.

2.   Answer: String will be of form $a^n b^n$

4.   Answer:

 $S \to aS \mid bS \mid \varepsilon$

 $S \to \varepsilon, S \to a, S \to b, S \to aa$

 $S \to ab, S \to ba, S \to bb$ ....

 Hence $\{a, b\}^*$.

5. Answer:

 $L[N_1] \cap L[N_2] \neq \Phi$ – undecidable

 $x \in L(G)$ – decidable

 $L(G_1) = L(G_2)$ – decidable

 $L[M] = \Phi$ is also undecidable.

6. Answer: $(0 + 1)^* (00(0 + 1)^* 11 + 11(0 + 1)^*00) (0 + 1)^*$